T0094701

Prosecution for
TREASON

Epidemics, Weather War,
Mind Control, and
the Surrender of Sovereignty

Mary Maxwell, Ph.D.

Copyright © 2011 by Mary Maxwell

PROSECUTION FOR TREASON

by Mary Maxwell.
pp. 367, includes index
Set in Garamond ITC 11.5

EPUB (ISBN-13) 978-1-936296-22-4
MOBI (ISBN-13) 978-1-936296-23-1
Print (ISBN-13) 978-1-936296-21-7

1. Martial Law   2. AIDS Genocide   3. Mind Control
4. Citizen's Arrest   5. North American Union   6. Treason

Published by:
Trine Day LCC
PO Box 577
Walterville, OR 97489
www.TrineDay.com
publisher@TrineDay.net

Library of Congress Control number: 2010943177

First Edition
10 9 8 7 6 5 4 3 21

Printed in the USA
Distributed to the Trade by
Independent Publishers Group (IPG)
814 North Franklin Sreet
Chicago, Illinois 60610
312-337-0747
www.ipigbook.com

Publisher's Foreword

The conscious and intelligent manipulation of the organized habits and opinions of the masses is an important element in democratic society. Those who manipulate this unseen mechanism of society constitute an invisible government which is the true ruling power of our country.

— Edward Bernays, *Propaganda*, 1928

Credibility is a condition of persuasion. Before you can make a man do what you say, you must make him believe what you say. A necessary condition for gaining his credence is that you do not permit him to catch you in lies.

— Daniel Lerner, *Sykewar*, 1949

Without a doubt, psychological warfare has proven its right to a place of dignity in our military arsenal.

— Dwight Eisenhower, 1951

We need a program of psycho-surgery and political control of our society. The purpose is physical control of the mind. Everyone who deviates from the given norm can be surgically mutilated. The individual may think that the most important reality is his own existence, but this is only his personal point of view. This lacks historical perspective. Man does not have the right to develop his own mind. This kind of liberal orientation has great appeal. We must electrically control the brain. Some day armies and generals will be controlled by electrical stimulation of the brain.

— Dr. Jose Delgado, c1955

We live in a world not completely of our own making. As we get overwhelmed by the incessant sensory mediascape that transforms us into somnambulating zombies plodding through a tired script, there is something not right, something sticking in our craw. According to national-security maven Zbigniew Brzezinski, a "global political awakening" is underway: "The worldwide yearning for human dignity ... is socially massive and politically radicalizing ... the Internet is creating a community of shared perceptions.... These energies transcend sovereign borders and pose a challenge both to existing states as well as to the existing global hierarchy."

Brzezinski proposes "a world that is defined less by the fiction of state sovereignty and more by the reality of expanding and politically regulated interdependence." Thus our common inheritance is to be thrown away in favor of transnational technocratic governance.

Mary Maxwell's *Prosecution for Treason* gives us a handbook for understanding our political heritage and responsibilities, including blueprints of how to regain our republic, restore our legacy and renew our society. No shrinking violet, Maxwell informs of us of many schemes being foisted upon us, — to tear us apart, get us to fight each other — even daring to discuss many of the unmentionable undercurrents of the modern age including mind-control, weather modification, and provoked pestilence.

Prosecution for Treason is the first of a new TrineDay imprint, Credos Books, giving authors a wider platform than investigative works, allowing authors to give their views and beliefs about controversial topics of the day and possibly on how to start turning our situation around.

This book is a product of the Internet. I get calls all the time from all kinds of folks, truck drivers, housewives and PhDs, and they almost all start off the same: "I had no idea until I stumbled across something on the Internet." And thus grows the global political awakening that Mr. Brzezinski is so worried about.

I am very hopeful. Gutenberg's press helped to spark mankind's forward progress, and I feel that the Internet's explosive power has just begun. We don't need violent revolutions, we don't need a new form of government. As Maxwell tells us, all we have to do to take back our country is to vote enough good people into office: local, state and national. We can prosecute the traitors, preserve our Republic and protect our children's futures.

Will we simply stand by, allowing faceless rule through regulations, or will we stand up to meet our day's pressing civic challenge? It is a common struggle that merits our common courage.

Onwards to the Utmost of Futures,

Peace,
Kris Millegan
Publisher
TrineDay
December 08, 2010

To our prodigal sons,

Come home! Come home!

TABLE OF CONTENTS

TABLE OF LISTS: 3 LISTS AT THE END OF EACH CHAPTER

TABLE OF 39 GOVERNMENT DOCUMENTS IN US, BY TYPE

AUTHOR'S PREFACE

I once heard Dr. Earle Hackett make an interesting point about 'the elephant man' (a man with a cauliflower-like head whom no one could bear to look at). Dr Hackett said that the rare deformity is bound to come up in every billionth human or so, and therefore this particular elephant man happens to be carrying the burden for us all.

Since hearing it put that way I have also thought of great poets, musicians, etc. as being 'all of us.' Some of the character deformities described in this book are also all of us. Thus, regarding any particular traitor, I may as well say "There but for the grace of God go I."

This book, however, does *not* recommend patience with our ever-increasing number of traitors – far less does it say "Grant a blanket amnesty." Hell, no. It is a call to recognize the problem: a lot of our own folks, including ones who hold **positions of trust** are daily harming us, to the point where almost everyone's life is in danger.

I imagine some of them regret having been painted into a corner and would like to turn things around. For those who don't, let's threaten them with the law. We need urgently to protect our society, and for that we can use that bedrock of security, the Constitution.

Let's also revive the powers of the states, including their legislatures' ability to investigate any issue that affects their residents. For reasons of simple human biology I think we need to return to membership in smaller groups. **If any of the 50 states hold hearings on 9/11,** or the flu vaccine scandal, or 'funny hurricanes,' it will set an example of real community, while also being of legal benefit to the other 49 states. Please don't think solutions must be national or 100% complete. That is a fallacious idea and needs correcting *now.*

May I please introduce myself? I grew up in Boston in the baby boom. I was drilled in matters constitutional at an impressionable age. If ever a girl walked around thinking she was lucky to live in a country where no political-type harm would come to her, 'twas I.

I also had a sufficient mathematical talent (sent by my high school to M.I.T. one summer to learn computer programming when it was called FORTRAN!) to recognize that the Constitution is a mathematical wonder of the world. Sort of like hydraulics with power flowing all around and being stopped where necessary.

So when I found out – in February, 2005 – that Bin Laden was not the culprit, and that we were therefore in big danger, I knew where to look:

<u>We the people of the…[etc] do ordain and establish this [fabulous] Constitution.</u> Dear reader, if you do not now believe me that the parchment has got the goods, I challenge you to get through this book without changing your mind. By the way, if you want to read the Constitution first, just hop to Appendix Q.

That said, there is a certain odd factor in my red-white-and-blue background. Namely, I left the US just before Reagan was elected in 1980 and have only returned for a couple of years since then. I have been president of the South Australian branch of the Australian Institute for International Affairs, and I managed to pick up a Ph.D. in Politics. I am rather ashamed that I 'earned' the degree without ever realizing that the Cold War was a hoax. Anyway, I was married to a British Australian, the late George Maxwell, M.D., who taught me enough to make up for that lack. He never stopped re-reading Collier's *Decision in Philadelphia*, about the 1787 constitutional convention, and always referred to the US as "the Great Republic."

In 2006 I ran for a Congressional seat from New Hampshire, and as of late 2010 I expect to be home in Marblehead, near Boston. My next career, if God spares me, will be to work on the United States Truth and Reconciliation Coalition. (See unitedstatestrc.com), and to be an editor for Trine Day. That's my payback to Kris Millegan for his only-man-in-America willingness to publish my work.

A Word to Teachers

Greetings, O Teachers. A lot of hemming and hawing went on as I tried to figure out how much you could get away with, for this book to be used as a classroom text. In case it's a wipeout, I shall upload to the Web all 26 appendices, 12 frontispieces, and 36 lists, in hope that you might thusly be able to share them with students. Nary a one is under copyright. Being a trifle didactic ("I Was a Teenage Didact"), I went to town on the bibliography too.

My assumption is that your school will not welcome this book, because it says, for example, "Go hard on judges." But remember when we were in high school (if you are pre-Generation X), our teachers would all have said without hesitation that if the US government should go rogue, the right thing for schools to teach would be the facts in the case. Have I got facts-in-the-case for you!

Another approach could be that you posit my text as example of junk and invite the students to present a rebuttal. I'd love that!

A Word to Students

Hi, Students. I care about you. (Seriously.) Since everybody is into brainwashing you I thought I'd join in. Hence the book is full of doodads, the aim of which is to make you aware of some great quotes from the past. I hear you have been cheated. But my generation was not cheated. We were given many clues from the past to think about the present and future. Merely doing that as an intellectual exercise triggers an endorphin in the old noodle (the grey matter, the cerebrum, whatever you call it).

Might you do me a favor, please? I want you to read something. It's an excerpt from Cicero's oration in the Roman senate (which compares nicely with the Maori war chant on YouTube). Marcus Tullius Cicero, nick-named Tully, was trying here to arouse the Republic against naughty boy Catiline. I think Tully's real message was "Know your strength."

It has to be read out loud, *loud*. If you are on a bus, don't worry, the other passengers will think you are talking on the cell phone. If you are in a library, definitely don't worry: the librarian wants you to know about history. Use your oratory muscles. If you didn't know that you possess such muscles you can discover them now:

Array now, O Romans, against these splendid troops of Catiline, your guards and your armies, and, first of all, oppose to that worn-out and wounded gladiator your consuls and generals.
*Then, **against that banished and enfeebled troop of ruined men,** lead out the flower and strength of all Italy!*
Instantly the cities of the colonies and municipalities will match the rustic mounds of Catiline; and I will not condescend to compare the rest of your troops and equipments and guards with the want and destitution of that highwayman.
But if,
omitting all these things in which we are rich and of which he is destitute —the senate, the Roman knights, the people, the city, the treasury, the revenues, all Italy, all the provinces, foreign nations,
*— if, I say, omitting all these things, we choose to compare the causes themselves which are opposed to one another, **we may understand from that alone how thoroughly prostrate they are.***

You just never know when you're going to need to use this speech!

FOREWORD BY KATHLEEN A. SULLIVAN

When I was a victim of governmental human experimentation and slavery, I was brainwashed to believe that any person who dared to speak out about such covert abuses would be killed, compromised, or worse. This is why, when I first met Mary Maxwell at a conference in August 2005, I was confused by her willingness to boldly speak truth to power. How was she able to do it and still live?

Years later, I realized that my own history of enslavement and disempowerment had contributed to my belief that I had *no* rights as a US citizen. This realization occurred when I studied the US Bill of Rights and learned – for the first time – that modern slavery was illegal.

Until then, I truly did not understand that what had been done to me by US government officials, employees, and contractors was not only immoral and unethical, but was also illegal and unconstitutional. I had been a slave; they had been covert slave-owners, pimps, and handlers. They had severely violated my human, legal, and constitutional rights.

That new realization gave me strength and a sense of empowerment and helped me to understand where Mary had probably gained much of her own strength, boldness and empowerment…from her *own* studies of the US Constitution. I also realized that if we remain silent about abuses of power that we *know* are being performed by our government officials and representatives, we are in effect covertly sanctioning those abuses.

No longer comfortable about remaining silent, I chose to work with other governmental abuse survivors and concerned citizens towards the development of a United States Truth and Reconciliation Coalition (US TRC) that's modeled after the South Africa Truth and Reconciliation Commission. I posted this idea on my Survivor website, naffoundation.org, where Maxwell happened to read it in mid- 2010.

She then contacted me and asked me to read the manuscript for this book. As I reviewed it, I worried that, because Mary's focus was on prosecuting government perpetrators, she might be offended by my near-opposite goal of developing a full-fledged US Truth and Reconciliation Commission in the future that would offer legal amnesty to the same perpetrators. I even worried that she might believe that I had sold-out.

Eventually, I concluded that both of our goals were valid. The United States needs a US Truth and Reconciliation Commission *and* it needs full investigations into abuses of power committed by US government officials, employees, and contractors – particularly those who continue to deny and/or cover-up the existence of the abuses.

To date we have set up a 'coalition,' not an official commission (and Mary Maxwell has become a founding member!). The title of our group is United States Truth and Reconciliation Coalition. You can see our ongoing work at our website: unitedstatestrc.com. Its PO Box is 25287 Chattanooga TN 37422.

We will still need a Congressionally authorized US Truth and Reconciliation Commission (or similar entity in any of the states) because survivors of governmental abuses need to know that they will be safe and protected when they start naming names and providing details of the atrocities they've suffered.

Further, former perpetrators need to know that they will not be retaliated against for telling the truth about the abuses they've committed. Although some citizens will be understandably frustrated with us for not seeking to punish the perpetrators, we are the ones (there are thousands of us – shocking but true) who are most likely to be harmed and retaliated against if we do not receive adequate protection before providing public testimonies about our traumatic abuse histories.

When governmental perpetrators believe they are at risk of going to prison and suffering other serious losses, they may become more fear-based and primal in their behaviors and responses towards their former victims. Further, because many of them are still in power-over positions, our collective decision to use a reconciliatory approach towards them would be beneficial for us.

At the same time, I realize that if we *only* take the route of offering amnesty – especially to governmental perpetrators who have committed abuses and human rights violations equal to the atrocities that led to indictments during the Nuremberg Trials - such offers of amnesty would severely minimize and dishonor the terrible wounds that are still suffered by many of the survivors.

Perhaps our greatest challenge will be to determine how to hold the worst of the governmental perpetrators accountable for their crimes without minimizing the extensiveness of their atrocities. Further, we will need to determine how we can work together to ensure that similar abuses and human rights violations cannot be legally committed by our American government in the future.

Nearly twenty years ago, I read a quote from a US president, Harry Truman, that changed my life: "The buck stops here." I realized that if I want the world to change for the better, the change must begin with me. And now I know that if we genuinely desire an end to the kinds of governmental abuses of power detailed in *Prosecution for Treason*, we must first be willing to examine our own individual behaviors and actions, past and present, that have influenced us to enable such abuses to continue for nearly a half-century, if not more.

If we do not boldly speak truth to power, and if we do not join together to ensure that such atrocities cannot be allowed to continue; we will – through our silence and inaction – send a strong signal to our political leaders and representatives that we condone and sanction the abuses.

And if we continue to look to others to do our work for us, if we continue to avoid taking responsibility to act, to move, to speak out, or to, as a former first lady advised, "Just say no"; the abuses will certainly continue.

We are at a serious moral and ethical crossroads. Our future is up to each of us. I sincerely hope and pray that you will take courage and join us in choosing the correct moral and ethical path for our future generations.

Kathleen A. Sullivan, MSW
September 12, 2010

Welcome to Part One:

Traitors, Come Out with Your Hands Up!

Chapters: 1 Law
2 Fear
3 Tribe

from E. O. Wilson, *Naturalist*, 1994:

My father told me never to back down, and the Gulf Coast Military Academy ethos forbade it. It was unmanly to refuse a fight. I did decline twice, however, because the boys were too big to beat, and from different schools anyway and I knew I would not see them again. I retreated before their taunts, to my everlasting shame.

It is ridiculous, of course, but **I still burn a little when I think about my cowardice....**I never picked a fight, but once started I never quit....My face was sometimes a bloody mess; I still carry old lip and brow split scars. Even my father, proud that I was acting "like a little man," seemed taken aback. But later I savored the memories of my combat, and especially the victories. There is no finer sight on green Earth than a defeated bully.   [emphasis added]

Chapter 1   President Thomas Jefferson's Inaugural Address, 1801

Friends and Fellow-Citizens...
I humble myself before the magnitude of the undertaking...
Let us restore... that harmony and affection without which liberty
and even life itself are but dreary things...
We are all Republicans, we are all Federalists. If there be any
among us who would wish to dissolve this Union or to change its
republican form, let them stand undisturbed as monuments of the
safety with which error of opinion may be tolerated where reason
is left free to combat it. ....

I believe this the strongest Government on earth... the only one
where every man... would fly to the standard of the law, and
would meet invasions of the public order as his own personal
concern.   [I should state] what I deem the essential principles
of our Government ... Equal and exact justice to all men... peace,
commerce, and honest friendship with all
nations, entangling alliances with none; the support of the
State governments in all their rights, ...the preservation of
the General Government in its whole constitutional vigor,
as the sheet anchor of our peace at home and safety abroad;
a jealous care of the right of election by the people;...
the supremacy of the civil over the military authority;
economy in the public expense, that labor may be lightly
burthened;...freedom of the press,
and freedom of person under the protection of the habeas corpus,
and trial by juries impartially selected.

These principles form the bright constellation ... and should
we wander from them in moments of error or of alarm, let us
hasten to retrace our steps and to regain the road ...
I repair, then, fellow-citizens, to the post you have assigned me.
I shall often go wrong through defect of judgment ...
Relying, then, on the patronage of your good will, I advance with
obedience to the work, ready to retire from it whenever you
become sensible how much better choice it is
within your power to make.

1 Law

Fool me once, shame on you.
Fool me twice, shame on me.
— an old saying

And gentlemen in England now a-bed
Shall think themselves accursed they were not here,
And hold their manhoods cheap while any speaks
That fought with us upon Saint Crispin's Day.
— Wm Shakespeare, *Henry V, Act IV, scene iii*

1.1 TREASON

Article III, Section 3 of the Constitution says:

Treason against the United States, shall consist only in levying War against them, or in adhering to Enemies, giving them Aid and Comfort. No Person shall be convicted of Treason unless on the Testimony of two Witnesses to the same overt Act, or on Confession in open Court.

Many Americans holding government office have committed treason against the United States, and **are doing so today**, both in terms of the first definition, "levying war against the United States," and the second, "adhering to their enemies." (Note: the pronouns 'their' and 'them' were used by the Framers of the Constitution in 1787 because they thought of the 'United States' as plural, that is, the 13 states 'united' to form the federal entity.)

To levy war against the US could entail such out-and-out violence as detonating bombs or poisoning the water supply and, as we shall see, it includes more subtle activities. As for adhering to the enemies of the US, we would have to be clear as to who is our enemy. Would it need to be a foreign state, or could it be just an international organization or even a domestic 'fifth column'? It need not be a foreign state – **an enemy is an enemy**.

In 1868, President Andrew Johnson, who had succeeded to the presidency when Abe Lincoln was assassinated by John Wilkes

Booth, gave an amnesty to most persons in the Confederacy, that is, the Southern states that had levied open war against the US. No court ever decided that the South had in fact committed treason. (In the case of *Texas v White*, 1869, SCOTUS ruled the Texas act of secession null despite a vote by Texans 34,794 to 11, 235 to ratify it.)

What of John Wilkes Booth? If he had been caught could he have been tried for treason? Yes. Assassinating the nation's leader is a form of levying war against the nation. According to some revisionist historians such as Eustace Mullins (1985), Booth's motive was to prevent Lincoln from taking a firm hand against the bankers. The persons who conspired to kill President Kennedy in 1963 are traitors. Several of them are still alive **and should now be arrested**. There is no reason whatsoever to avoid dealing with this matter.

LAWS OF NEW HAVEN COLONY, 1656 *HURST* 69-70

If any person shall conspire, and attempt any invasion, insurrection, or publick Rebillion against this Jurisdiction, or shall endeavour to surprize, or seize any Plantation, or Town, any Fortification, Platform, or any great Guns provided for the defence of the Jurisdiction, ... or shall treacherously and perfidiously attempt the alteration and subversion of the frame of policy, or fundamentall Government laid, and setled for this Jurisdiction, he or they shall be put to death.

Or if any person shall consent unto any such mischievous practice, **or by the space of foure and twenty houres conceale it**, not giving notice thereof to some Magistrate, ...**he shall be put to death,** or severely punished.... [emphasis added]

Has anyone ever been convicted of treason? Yes. During the administration of President George Washington some liquor merchants in Pennsylvania forcibly resisted the collection of taxes on that product (the Whiskey Rebellion). They shot at the tax officers. After conviction they were pardoned. Only a handful of others have been tried for treason. During World War II, an American woman who took part in propaganda for an enemy nation was convicted and served 12 years in prison.

In the 1950s when the Cold War against the Soviet Union was revving up, Julius and Ethel Rosenberg were sent to the electric chair for having divulged secrets about atomic weapons. However, their death sentence was for espionage, not treason.

Prosecutions by the federal government are discretionary. To me it is obvious that our leaders do not want to bring alleged traitors to trial as it could open a can of worms. Later in this book it will be argued that Congress committed treason in 1913 by allowing a non-governmental entity, The Federal Reserve Bank, to take control of the nation's money supply. Wait – can a legislature be tried for treason? No, but individual legislators can. They have 'parliamentary immunity' against being sued by any persons who feel damaged by legislative decisions. But that means immunity from civil suits, not criminal prosecution. In the US, **no one is ever above the law.**

1.2 GUIDE TO THIS CHAPTER – *LAW*

It is difficult to indict politicians for crimes of office, rather than for personal venality. But it is not impossible, and this book presents many ways to get around the barriers – including merely psychological ways, such as refusing to accept a bizarre status quo as normal!

One way for citizens to present a case against officials is by using the institution known as the grand jury; that will be discussed in 1.3 below. A reasonable way to think about the misdeeds of officials is by considering their oaths of office; a look at that will follow in 1.4. Perhaps the most effective barrier to 'doing justice' in the US today is, ironically, the Department of Justice, the 'DoJ,' as will be claimed in 1.5, backed up by a substantive example, in 1.6, concerning the Oklahoma City bombing. American rule of law, the great treasure of our nation, will be celebrated in 1.7.

1.8 introduces the subject of *mind control*. Our opinions and even our brain physiology can be cleverly manipulated. (The CIA's work in this was revealed to Congress decades ago; UK-based Tavistock plays a part too.) I believe this affects our ability to perceive treason and thus to prosecute it. In 1.9 the scene switches to our alleged 'loss' of habeas corpus. At the end of each chapter there is a 'What to Do?' section. Here in 1.10 it will cover citizen's arrest.

Note: In this book any quote that is underlined is from the Constitution. If you go now to Appendix Q, you'll see how much of the parchment this book covers.

1.3 GRAND JURIES

Have you ever noticed that the Bill of Rights makes an important statement about the grand jury? If you are not familiar with the Bill, please go now to Appendix S and read it. You will love it. See how the 5th Amendment says we cannot try any person for a major crime unless his guilt has already been looked into by a grand jury?

Prior to the 20th century, grand juries were creatures of the community. Historically, the community precedes the state. Every society has a mechanism for charging someone with wrongdoing even if that mechanism consists only of gossip or of wreaking vengeance on him privately. By ancient times there were already formal, court-like mechanisms such that a righteous onlooker, rather than the aggrieved party, could ask the 'court' to try an accused.

The American colonists brought from Mother England the system of grand juries — 'grand' in the sense of large — they have up to 23 members. Grand juries do not try an accused. They only determine if there is enough evidence to bring an indictment. The 23 persons are typically empanelled for two years and during that time they can bring any crime to the attention of the state. In colonial days these persons also looked for problems such as a bridge that needed repair. They acted as inspectors of prisons — after all, prisoners are at the mercy of sadists if no one is taking a look.

In our day, government is trying to strip the grand juries of their independence. The prosecutor pushes them around. In *Bonfire of the Vanities* (1987), Tom Wolfe quoted Judge Sol Wachtler's remark that a prosecutor could get a grand jury "to indict a ham sandwich."

There's also the issue of secrecy in grand juries. Grand jurors may talk to the accused and to witnesses, but not to us. The rationale for secrecy is protection of a suspect's reputation, in the event that no case is made out — but secrecy is a famous hazard.

Suggestion: Now and again this book will make casual suggestions. Here is one: **you can start your own grand jury.** Without making any claim to be official, you can set about doing what the colonial grand juries used to do. Why not? Just gather some folks together and list the wrongs being committed publicly by officials. That is surely your protected right, if not duty. (Just don't offer immunity in exchange for testimony — but a real grand jury *is* able do that.)

It may be wise to create a name other than 'grand jury' so people won't worry that you are usurping a state function. In medieval England an entity of this type was called the "Clarendon Assize." If you take that name you will automatically gain a bit of authority! Grounding one's idea in an actual prototype like that helps people accept it more readily. Or you could modestly call it a Lay Inquest.

1.4 OATHS OF OFFICE

What is an oath? It is a calling down of God to be a party to one's undertaking. In the case of an evidentiary oath, one is swearing that the testimony presented is "the truth, the whole truth, and nothing but the truth." In an oath of office, which is a type of promissory oath, a person volunteers to incur God's wrath if she fails to uphold the duties of office.

In the four-yearly inauguration of US presidents, the taking of the oath is the centerpiece of the ceremony. Art. II, Sec 6: Before [the President] enter on the Execution of his Office, he shall take the following Oath or Affirmation – "I do solemnly swear that I will faithfully execute the Office..., and will to the best of my Ability preserve, protect and defend the Constitution of the United States."

All other title-bearers in government, including commissioned military officers, must take an oath. Per Art. VI, Sec 3: The Senators and Representatives..., and the members of the several State legislatures, and all executive and judicial Officers..., shall be bound by Oath or Affirmation, to support this Constitution.

An 'affirmation' is used when the person objects to referring to God. The affirmation is of equal import and the person must say "I solemnly affirm." Solemnity seems to be a natural psychological phenomenon that is experienced when one is personally involved in a public social event. So, at the time of the taking of the oath or affirmation, we assume that the taker is serious and honest about accepting the duty to support the Constitution.

Then why do we say things like "Oh, you know how politicians are..." or "That was very Machiavellian of him," when an elected official does something in his or her personal interest that violates the Constitution? It must be, in part, because so many of us have lost connection to a God, and don't think of the oath-taking or affirmation-taking as any big deal. But it is a big deal; it is actually a huge deal, and even though breaking one's oath of office is not a crime it can be punished informally. (Note: The crime of perjury has only to do with giving false testimony. Perjury is a felony, i.e., a crime greater than a misdemeanor.)

Judith Shklar, author of *Ordinary Vices* (1980: 183) reminds us why the oath of office means so much in the US. "A Lockean liberal society requires more trust from more people than any other. Consent and promises were the sole ties of Locke's constitutional vision. And if Americans resort to oaths constantly...they are again only following Locke and attempting to establish those relations of trust which they require politically."

See the following complaint about betrayal of trust. It shows a kind of banding together by intellectuals that used to be routine:

Law Professors' Full-page Ad in *New York Times*, 13 Jan. 2001:

We are professors of law at 137 American law schools, from every part of our country, of different political beliefs. But we all agree that when a bare majority of the U.S. Supreme Court halted the recount of ballots under Florida law, the five Justices were acting as political proponents for candidate Bush, not as judges. It is not the job of a federal court to stop votes from being counted.

By stopping the recount in the middle, **the five Justices acted to suppress the facts.** Justice Scalia argued that the Justices had to interfere even before [listening to] the Bush team's arguments…. By taking power from voters, the Supreme Court has tarnished its own legitimacy. **As teachers whose lives have been dedicated to the rule of law, we protest."**… [emphasis added]

1.5 THE PROBLEM OF OUR US DEPARTMENT OF JUSTICE

You may have heard that towards the end of his two-term presidency, George W. Bush fired eight US Attorneys, including Carol Lam – apparently because they were prosecuting persons whom Bush wanted to protect. There is an odd problem regarding the separation of powers that casts its shadow throughout this book. It is the fact that **it is the executive branch, not the judiciary**, that is constitutionally responsible for 'faithfully executing the laws.'

In short, the president, via his Department of Justice, is the law enforcer (of federal, not state, law). This has the effect of making it easy for members of the executive branch to commit crimes with impunity: they can prevent prosecution of themselves!

Additionally there is the problem of the mysterious FBI. It was never a statutory body (that is, an office brought into being by legislation). Rather, one day in 1908, Congress allocated funds for the Justice Department to establish a 'bureau of investigation' with 34 employees – one percent of the number of its employees today. In 1924 J. Edgar Hoover became head of the FBI; he soon performed the unusual (Tavistock-like) mission of investing in a big public relations campaign to enshrine the image of 'the G-man.' He also was known to hang around with organized crime figures!

George Washington, our first president, appointed Edmund Randolph to the position of Attorney General in 1789. He was to be a lawyer for the government, not a law enforcer. Today's Attorney General, Eric Holder, like all the 'AG's' since 1880, heads a Department of Justice. A glance at List 1a shows a mixed bag of duties – some police-like, some that purport to help the disadvantaged citizen, and some that portray the DoJ as lawyer for the nation.

The Civil Rights Office is entrusted with bringing civil actions against persons or organizations that deprive a person of his, her, or its rights. *Its* rights? Can an 'it' have a legal right? Yes. Since the case of *Santa Clara Co. v. Southern Pacific* in 1886, it has been possible for corporations to say they are entitled to the rights given to all Americans in the 14th Amendment. No joke. Well, actually it is a joke, as will be aired later. No judge ruled that way, but a 'typo' assisted the corporations. (Note: the Civil Rights Division does much of its work on behalf of corporations, not individuals.)

See the Antitrust Division [on my List 1a]? Its existence implies that the government will undertake to question mergers of large corporations. It seldom does so, but it did so in *U.S. v Microsoft,* in 2007. See the BATFE? The 'F' and 'E' – firearms and explosives – were added recently. The BAT 'Bureau of Alcohol and Tobacco' used to belong to the Treasury Department, for collecting tax on alcohol and tobacco – now worth billions of dollars per year.

What about police power? President Washington appointed 13 men as US Marshals for tasks such as guarding the courthouse and serving court summonses. When the DoJ was formed in 1870, the Marshals were absorbed into it. Constitutionally, however, **there is no federal police power.** That was confirmed by the Supreme Court in the 1995 case *US v Morrison* (see Ch 5.6 below).

A Pause for a Chat about Footnotes. You may be wondering where my footnotes are. I took the information in the above paragraph from pages 19 and 91 of *FBI and Law Enforcement Agencies* by Michael Kronenwetter, published in 1997. I could have used the Harvard system of citation: (Kronenwetter 1997: 91, 97), as I do occasionally in this book. However I have chosen not to cite him, as those public facts about the Customs Service, etc., were not original with him. (I did list Knonenwetter's book in the bibliography to show that it helped me.) The important quotes in this book are displayed in boxes; they include full citation.

Do you feel that you are being 'blitzed' with information? Good, that is the plan. Each chapter contains a lot of facts. The main theme, prosecution for treason, has to be pursued along several tracks. Shockingly bad behavior by the US government is presented in each chapter from 1 – 9. "The way the law works" is presented here and in the next chapter, plus Chs 7, 8, and 9 on the Constitution. Analysis of why we are so slow to arrest government criminals is another track of this book, mainly seen in Chs 4 – 6, and 11. You may skip around as you like, of course, but it is generally best to pursue the text in order. There is a reason for the structure.

1.6 THE OKLAHOMA CITY BOMBING

You may recall Longfellow's poem, *Paul Revere's Ride*, which begins "On the eighteenth of April in Seventy-five." Well, on the nineteenth of April in Ninety-five someone blew up the Murrah Federal Building in Oklahoma City, killing 168 people. Two years later Timothy McVeigh was convicted, and in 2001 he was executed.

It is not at all clear who did the bombing, but the shenanigans of the FBI – particularly in **destroying evidence**, and of the prosecutor – particularly in **refusing to call dozens of eager witnesses,** lead one to believe that the case against McVeigh was nonsense. As demonstration of that, consider four hushed-up deaths that occurred subsequent to the April 19th event:

Oklahoma City police Officer Terrance Yeakey found evidence of explosives planted in the structure of the building (incompatible with the idea that McVeigh's truck parked outside did the job alone). Yeakey ran into the absolutely standard response when he tried to get the material looked at. He must have been hard to bribe, intimidate, or discredit, however, judging from the fact that 'they' finally **had to terminate him**. His body was found in the woods and the death was ruled a suicide. Explanation? He was feeling bad about his recent divorce – something his ex-wife says is not true.

As for Glenn Wilburn, his two grandsons died in the Day Care Center of the Murrah Building. Soon after the bombing his daughter went on TV with the complaint that **all staff from the office of the BATF were out of the building,** and asked for an explanation of why they had that 'option' when her children did not. Mr. Wilburn soon became a spokesperson for the many people dissatisfied with the investigation of the bombing. A year later, at age 46, he developed pancreatic cancer and died.

Dr Don Chumley worked at a clinic near the bombing scene and showed up right away. According to a local journalist, as reported by David Hoffman in *The Oklahoma City Bombing* (1998), "Chumley was asked to bandage two federal agents who falsely claimed to have been trapped in the [Murrah that morning]. Since the pair was obviously not hurt, Chumley refused. When the agents petitioned another doctor at the scene, Chumley intervened, threatening to report them" (p. 297). Five months later, he was killed when his small plane, a Cessna 210, crashed into a field.

Why Evidence from the FBI Crime Lab May Be Tainted

William Thompson, a professor of criminalistics at the University of California, Irvine, agrees: "The culture of such places, run by police or agents, for police or agents, is often just inimical to good scientific practice. The reward system, promotion, incentives... in the end your pay check is based on successful prosecutions, not good science."

Nowhere is this truer than at the FBI laboratory in Washington, ...The FBI lab works for the prosecution and no one else....Generally, evidence submitted to the FBI laboratory cannot be taken elsewhere, or vice versa, even though that might be considered the peer review deemed essential by scientists.

~ John F. Kelly and Phillip K. Wearne, *Tainting Evidence* (1998) p. 15

The most amazing death connected to OKC is that of 44-year-old Kenneth Trentadue who was arrested in June 10, 1995, in San Diego for a minor parole violation. That led to his arriving at the Oklahoma City Federal Transfer Facility on Aug 18, the week after McVeigh, Nichols, and 'others unknown' were indicted for the April tragedy. While there, Kenneth Trentadue, a happily married man with a new baby, was beaten to death in prison.

Unluckily, he resembled a man the FBI was looking for named Richard Lee Guthrie, with reference to the Murrah Building bombs. Kenneth Trentadue even had the same dragon tattoo as Guthrie on his left forearm! (Note: the real Guthrie died the following year **by being beaten** in prison. Both deaths were called 'suicides.' A third prisoner, who wrote a deposition for the court about Kenneth's last hours, was also later found hanged in a federal prison, in California.)

Thus we have Officer Yeakey's suicide by gunshot, Dr Chumley's plane crash, Kenneth Trentadue's death by beating in prison, and Glenn Wilburn's cancer. These types of fatalities seem to happen whenever local people refuse to accept the government's version of events. (Single car crashes often figure in terminations, too, as do heart attacks.) Granted we cannot be sure that Wilburn's cancer was a covert job. It may have been the *digitum dei*. But for decades scientists have killed rats while testing the carcinogenicity of drugs and obviously it is possible to kill a human by cancer, via those drugs.

Let's make a rule of thumb, and call it the Yeakey rule, to wit: "When the authorities quickly determine a death to be suicide, in the face of plain evidence to the contrary, **guilt on the part of the authorities** will be tentatively presumed." Laws sometimes establish 'rebuttable presumptions' like that, in order to switch the onus of proof from the plaintiff to the defendant. Even if the 'Yeakey rule' does not get adopted by courts, it can be used by laypersons. Common sense tells us when officials are trying to hide something.

Luckily, in the OKC case, there are many tenacious citizens who are determined to keep up the pressure. One is an OKC journalist, Jayna Davis (2004), who reported in detail the fact that Iraqi immigrants in Oklahoma were very involved in the planning of the truck bomb. She also found that a German neo-Nazi, Andreas Strassmeier, was involved with the White Supremacists and was working **with the CIA's permission**. Davis collected witness statements from people who saw the Iraqis, but of course someone may have recruited the Iraqis in order that, once the building was bombed, Iraq could be blamed. Quite possibly the destruction of the Murrah was scheduled to be a *false flag* event – an earlier version of 9/11, that would justify a US military action in the Middle East.

If that be so, what were the White Supremacists, including Timothy McVeigh, doing in the picture? Implicating McVeigh may have been 'Plan B' if a last-minute decision was made to abandon blaming the Middle East. **All of Jayna Davis' efforts** to present her investigation of those Iraqi men **were rejected** by the government.

Instead, the government chose to say that McVeigh was a disillusioned soldier, a militia type, or whatever could cause people to think that their own countrymen are nuts and are dangerous.

Another tenacious citizen is Jesse Trentadue, brother of Kenneth, who practices law in Salt Lake City. He succeeded in having a million dollars in damages paid to the Trentadue family for the harm the FBI did to them. (Why should the taxpayers have to pay that million dollars?) He also got McVeigh's cellmate on Death Row to depose (i.e., to answer questions under oath) that McVeigh confided he was a government-run undercover operative and that he did the bomb work *as a member of the Aryan Resistance Army.*

1.7 RULE OF LAW

The marvelous thing about being an American is that we can count on rule of law for protection. The natural state for the human species is to have rule-by-bosses. Not until recent centuries did it become possible for persons on the lower rungs of the ladder to overturn that normal state of affairs. The US Founding Fathers, specifically the Framers of the Constitution, came up with a very comprehensive scheme so that **we could be ruled by the law itself.** This is intrinsically better than being ruled by law-free bosses.

Now let us apply rule-of-law sensibilities to the OKC bombing case. Although Timothy McVeigh has already gone to his grave (and accomplice Terry Nichols is in prison for life), the persons responsible for the 168 deaths needs to be tracked down. First let's note that allegations of involvement by 'White Supremacists' is a veritable give-away that a federal agency is behind the whole thing.

McVeigh hung around a religious group in Elohim City, OK. Also at that sight were Andreas Strassmeier, allegedly a neo-Nazi, but in fact an agent for Germany's covert agency [and] Sean Kenny, at the time **a private in the US Army**.... FBI and DoJ officers used up to 19 provocateurs... to encourage and help McVeigh finance, build, and strategically locate his truck bomb.... An FBI 302 report obtained by Jesse Trentadue shows that McVeigh attended a meeting with FBI informants and provocateurs at Elohim City in 1994. [So there!] Kenny was involved in Midwest bank robberies with McVeigh.... Strassmeier gave him advice on explosives....**Holloway was a CIA pilot** that...helped Strassmeier escape the INS to Germany after the OKC bombing.... **FBI teletypes show that [FBI Director Louis] Freeh knowingly allowed David Holloway to help Strassmeier escape.** A formal DoJ report later confessed the FBI crime lab officers **gave misleading** if not false testimony in the courts... about forensic analysis of the truck bomb. [emphasis added]

~ Patrick Briley, "FBI, SPLC, ATF behind OKC Bombing" (www.newswithviews.com) 3-27-07

In the above, Patrick Briley (a US veteran and interested citizen) has thus catalogued six items that are often used by covert agencies:

1. collusion with foreign covert agencies;
2. mingling with (perhaps actually creating?) groups of eccentrics whose possible fanaticism suggests to the public a mental disturbance or a desire to overthrow our traditional institutions;
3. training in terrorism by the infiltrating member of federal agency;
4. misleading testimony from an FBI crime lab person (confessed);
5. apparent mixing of US covert agencies and US military; and
6. FBI positively assisting wrongdoer to escape law enforcers.

Should we add another: "possible use of ordinary theft to obtain 'funding' for the project"? Briley says McVeigh participated in many bank robberies as part of the ARA. Could this mean that those robberies, and maybe other 'unsolved' bank robberies, **were carried out by government?** Wow, what a clever scheme that would be!

Whoa there! How could it be allowed? Have we all become certifiable mental cases? Of course not. This is America! We have law. This is no tin-pot dictatorship, this is the Great Republic. They cannot get away with it! Listen to this nonsense about a coroner:

In 1995 Kenneth Trentadue was murdered by federal agents in a federal prison in Oklahoma City... When the Trentadue family received Kenneth's body and heavy makeup was scraped away, the evidence [available in photos on the Internet] clearly shows a person who had been tortured and beaten. His throat was slashed… There are bruises, burns and cuts from the soles of Trentadue's feet to his head, wounds that **obviously** were not self-inflicted. As the state coroner noted at the time, every investigative rule was broken by the federal prison. **The coroner was not allowed into the cell**, and the cell was scrubbed down prior to investigation. [emphasis added]
~ Paul Craig Roberts, May 27, 2005, at Lewrockwell.com

Despite the fact that the alternative media states its revelations in that matter-of-fact way, it is essential for us to say, in the old-fashioned way, "Lawbreakers will get the punishment due to them."

Law constraints or it is a travesty to call it law…. Law transcends the power of the powerful and transforms the situation of the weak or it is a travesty to call it law. A legal system which does its best to make sense of murder, theft, exploitation, oppression, abuse of power, and injustice, perpetrated by public authorities in the public interest, is a perversion of a legal system. ~ Philip Allott, *Eunomia* (1990) p. 109

By the way, **the world is hoping America will come to its senses!**

14

1.8 MIND CONTROL (PROPAGANDA, PSY-OPS, CONDITIONING)

We must now look at the subject of mind control. It explains why it is so easy for traitors to trick us and get away with it.

At least one person in the OKC story, Timothy McVeigh, is suspected of being mind-controlled. All the photos of him in the media showed a young man with a stern face, walking like a robot. Pictures taken earlier, however, show a relaxed, smiling, regular guy. (That is not to say that mind-controlled people always walk like robots. Many are 'robots' in the sense of having been instructed to do such-and-such, yet their body language is normal.) Probably McVeigh was a 'Manchurian candidate' (that phrase is the title of R. Condon's novel about brainwashing) as will be outlined in Ch 5.7

The subject of mind control is key to this book. We will not go into high-tech stuff, such as ELF waves or RFID chips, because those things are not the main game. The main game is very simple. Certain people have studied social psychology carefully and know how to influence human behavior. Their success is staggering. For example, the mass media like to use 'block and flood.' In the OKC case, we were blocked from finding out interesting parts of the case. No mainstream press or TV network ever mentions the Trentadues or Officer Yeakey, much less our German visitor, Strassmeier. Having that data omitted from our brains certainly **deprives our brains of the ability to make a realistic evaluation of things.**

TV flooded us with the official story while magazines shared 'background material' to help us judge Timothy McVeigh's guilt. *The New Yorker*, which frequently dispenses disinformation in thoughtful guise, told us on May 8, 1995 about the dull life McVeigh led in a backwoodsy town. Hence, of course, his 'resentments.'

Did you know that physiologists believe that our brain stops questioning a problem once we hear an explanation? Almost any explanation will do. For a serial killer, the media likes to say that he was rejected by his classmates in school. And the reason government announces "a full investigation will take place" is that such a remark shuts down our blame-searching. Government knows this!

It's essential to realize that our brains are by no means all-rational. Much takes place subconsciously. When you come to a puddle, your brain automatically calculates how much you should stretch your leg muscles to jump over the puddle, right? No one insists that the calculation is done consciously. It is the same with **most of our social decisions.** They occur without our awareness.

Social psychologists know well that the easiest individuals to flood with information – because their neuronal pathways are forming at a rapid rate – are the young. (See Daniel Amen's *How To Make a Good Brain Great* (2009). Hence, a major part of mind control/manipulation is directed at children:

Quotes from Juliet Schor, *Born To Buy* (2001):
- Evidence of the marketers' success is everywhere – Kids bond to brands [and] have adopted cool as a paramount value.
- **Cool is associated with an anti-adult sensibility,** as ads portray kids with attitude, outwitting their teachers and tricking their parents.
- Online games are created around food products to keep kids interacting with brand logos for extended periods of time.
- [A marketer] noted that "if it grosses out Mom, if it empowers me the kid, **by setting me apart from my parents, then it's good.**" [emphasis added]   (pp. 189, 48, 121, 58)

One late afternoon, when I was checking in at an airport, I said to the airline lady "Have you had a long day?" The reply was "No, I just got here. I start at four o'clock so as not to be home when my kids get in from school, God forgive me." Perhaps if she read economist Juliet Schor's book, quoted above, she would know that the problem did not start with her, or her kids, but with some marketer's clever way of turning the young against grown-ups.

This is not to deny that there is major *governmental* involvement in psy-ops (psychological operations). As List 1c shows, for over a half century the CIA has tried to find chemicals that render the individual more pliable, more forgetful, etc. That document appears on the Internet along with many similar declassified documents that people have obtained through the Freedom Of Information Act.

These 'FOIA's" are handy to have when you get called a 'moonbat' for believing, say, that government uses hypnosis. A CIA memo, signed by Sidney Gottlieb on May 11, 1953, calls for study of "Recall of hypnotically acquired information by very specific signal."

For now, it's enough to say that government personnel themselves can be subjected to this insidious manipulation. Certainly if you try to have a more than one-minute conversation with a Congressman you can get the impression that his thinking may be **oddly constrained.** (I find this with parliamentarians in Australia, too.)

1.9 ETHNIC (AND RELIGIOUS) PERSECUTION

HELP! MATERIAL WITNESS IN SOLITARY

According to a report by Human Rights Watch and the American Civil Liberties Union, Tarek Albasti said this about his October 2001 experience of being held in solitary confinement – as a material witness: "After I got in the cell I went kind of crazy. I was calling the guards to find out exactly what was my crime. Where's my lawyer if I have a lawyer. Because nobody told us anything. What's going to happen or what's going on. Nobody answered me so I kept banging on the door. Of course I started crying... The guard came. He starts yelling at me. I yelled back and I said I need to know why I am here. I need to talk to somebody. He said we don't know, once we know, we will let you know. I felt he didn't know why we were being held. I had nothing to do but sit and cry. That's technically all we did. Sit and pray and cry." (6-27-05) alipac.us

---

Remember when the US didn't go in for this sort of thing? In 2001, after it had been 'established' that Osama Bin Laden magically knocked down some skyscrapers, there was open season on members of one religion, Islam. Attorney General John Ashcroft in effect shelved the right of habeas corpus, the right not to be detained without charges (guaranteed in Art. I, Sec 9). Ashcroft did it legally by using a 'technicality.' Namely the US has had a material-witness law since 1789, which permits us to hold someone who can give essential evidence in a case and who might disappear ('might be a flight risk'). Thousands of Muslims were rounded up and many were detained that way, without charges. Admittedly, many Muslims were not 'rounded up' strictly speaking; they were 'invited to register' at a government office. At the interview it might be discovered, say, that the person had at one time told a lie related to a credit card; then he could be arrested for fraud (Cole: 2003).

Presumably we Americans were deterred from reacting to the outrageous persecutions of fellow Americans – just as we failed to support the Japanese-Americans who were rounded up in 1942 – because we were mesmerized by 'security.' It is simply a fact that any national group can be stirred into fear of a 'foreign' group. That psychological trait, xenophobia, should be analyzed in high school civics classes. Our fears come not so much from the foreigners as from our automatic, inherited tendency to fear what is unfamiliar..

For now, it is important that we call a persecution a persecution. Confucian philosophy says that **calling things by their right names is the beginning of wisdom.** Confucius' 'rectification of names' works neurobiologically: a person must invoke the correct concept ('persecution') in order to fetch from the brain's storage area the appropriate learned principles (here: due process).

1.10 WHAT TO DO? PERFORM A CITIZENS' ARREST!

The law is not an ass. We wouldn't have the wonderful law that *we do have*, yet lack all means to enforce it. As shown above, many of the roads are blocked at present, but that only provokes creativity. As far as 'citizen's arrest' is concerned, one does not even need creativity. Each of the 50 states' codified law or common law allows it.

The common law has jurisprudence (case law) on this because it was an everyday occurrence in colonial times. There were no police forces; Boston got the first police in 1820. States are **unlikely to repeal** the law that allows citizen's arrest, as it is needed by security guards — they have no other power of arrest. It is also used routinely by the FBI — as Congress never legislated for them to make arrests!

Most states have, by statute, given a merchant's agent *extra* scope when detaining a shoplifter. For example, under West Virginia's code of law "One who has reasonable ground to believe that a person has committed shoplifting may detain such person [for up to] 30 minutes." Hence, if the person proves to be innocent she cannot expect to win damages from the agent who detained her.

On YouTube you can see a man in Monroe County TN trying to citizen-arrest the foreman of a grand jury because that person had been foreman for 20 years despite a state limit of 2 years. After challenging this irregularity through channels — without any luck — the citizen tried valiantly to set things right. However, it seems that his quarry hadn't committed any crime. If the law doesn't call it an "offense" or prescribe a penalty there is usually no crime.

If you are the arrestor you take risks. Two criteria that usually apply (unless you catch the criminal *in flagrante delicto*) are: You must be sure that a felony has in fact been committed, and you must have reasonable cause to think your arrestee is the felon. (A felony, as compared to a misdemeanor, is a crime that is punishable by a jail term not less than one year.) If your case does not meet the criteria the arrestee could sue you, and the state may prosecute you. Even where your attempt is lawful, let's face it, you risk governmental ire.

Be sure to check the particulars of your state's law. When making a citizen's arrest, you may use reasonable force. However, if the suspect thinks the arrest is unlawful, she may lawfully use force against you. Usually you are required to take the arrestee to the nearest police station immediately. (State laws are on the Internet.)

Lucklily, obstruction of justice is itself felonious (18 USC 1501). You might, conceivably, see a judge commit that crime *in flagrante delicto.* Consider Judge Wilfred Paquet, who obstructed justice by preventing members of a grand jury from doing their job. His purpose, apparently, was to protect Senator Ted Kennedy, who had claimed that he had driven off a bridge, with passenger Mary Jo Kopechne, at Chappaquiddick, Cape Cod, on July 19, 1969 (the day before the moon landing). She died by drowning.

Many people demanded an inquest into her death, as they did not believe his story that he escaped from the car at the bottom of the pond, and swam across to the mainland. The next morning her body was sent to her home state, on a Kennedy-chartered plane, thus avoiding Massachusetts' autopsy jurisdiction. A deputy sheriff, Christopher Look, had said he saw the car on dry ground an hour after it supposedly tumbled, **but he was not called to testify**.

> ~ from *Teddy Bare*, by Zad Rust (1971) p. 165-167:
> No court of inquiry is armed with greater powers of investigation than a grand jury. The ten men and ten women… could have conducted a complete investigation of their own…, could have subpoenaed any witness that they wished. The Dukes County Grand Jury met on April 6 to decide whether or not Mary Jo Kopechne's death involved a criminal act by Kennedy or others. It was dispersed…on April 7. It had heard only four unimportant local witnesses…who seemed to have been brought there only to obscure the fact that the grand jury had been forbidden any significant activity…. [In his opening charge] Judge Paquet [said that the grand jury could indict] if it found evidence of perjury. The course of events showed the irony of those remarks. No relevant witness was allowed to be heard. Judge Paquet sternly reminded the jury that it could not …seek judicial review of his ruling if he refused to permit the jurors to see the transcript of last January's inquest….
> He brought with him and invited to his bench the Rev Donald Cousa [who] offered a short prayer for "prejudice to be set aside and replaced by charity."

Suggestion: Try bluff. **Puffing up one's power** is an important part of human relations. Some pacing of the street by angry residents of Chappaquiddick Island may have altered the judge's confidence **as to what he could get away with.** You can call a meeting in your home, to which the local police chief, and anyone he or she wishes to bring, will be invited. Your purpose, along with a band of neighbors, will be to offer your services as helpers on some vague future occasion when the police may need citizen help.

There! You've done it; you've established your credentials! You have gone from being scared that such a thing is illegal (it isn't; see Appendix S for the First Amendment), to feeling powerful.

Then tell everybody about it. Media may not rush to assist you, but you can put a notice on the community bulletin boards at the supermarket and the library. You can hand out flyers after church. (Find out local rules: some towns forbid you to leave ads under the windshield wipers of cars; some have a 'litter law' against leafleting.)

As a very bold next step, you could designate your basement as a last-resort holding pen for arrestees. Or you could reserve outdoor space. For example, handcuffs could be attached to lamp-posts. Imagine Washington Mall entirely lined with Gitmo-type cages.

A Pause To Ask: Who Can Be Prosecuted for Treason? We saw that Dr. Chumley (whose Cessna later crashed) complained that two federal agents asked to be bandaged up so they could feign injury. Did they commit treason? If yes, what can be done about it? To ask a doctor to put a bandage on a non-existent wound is not a crime. You can't ask local police to arrest the bandagees for that. If you want to citizen-arrest the two as accessories-after-the-fact to treason, there must be a case that treason was committed.

In Part Three I give every legal lead I can think of for bringing governmental criminals to justice. Thus, Ch 9.9 recommends the prosecution of Congresspersons for treason, while Ch 8.10 shows how to deal with 'impostors' in the executive branch. Ch 7.10 urges the booking of anyone bookable for the crime of *menticide*, i.e., mind-killing — a term coined in 1951 by Dutch psychiatrist Joost Merloo.

There will not be a discussion of police brutality. This book does not attempt to inventory all our tribulations (or any international matters). Our concern is mainly with the decision-making class of people in government, and ones who seem *above* government. I shall refer to the latter as 'World Government' or 'the cabal.'

List 1a.   Chart of the US Department of Justice

Headed by Attorney General

Deputy General

>   Federal Bureau of Investigation
>   Drug Enforcement Administration
>   Executive Office for United States Attorneys
>   United States Attorneys
>   Bureau of Alcohol/Tobacco/Firearms/Explosives
>   Criminal Division   Bureau of Prisons
>   United States Marshals Service
>   U.S. National Central Bureau – Interpo
>   Office of the Federal Detention Trustee
>   Office of the Inspector General
>   Office of Intelligence Policy and Review
> Justice Management Division
> Executive Office for Immigration Review
> Professional Responsibility Advisory Office
>   Office of Professional Responsibility [legal ethics!]
>   Office of the Pardon Attorney
>   United States Parole Commission

Solicitor General

>   Office of the Solicitor General

Associate Attorney General

Executive Office for United States Trustees

>   Office on Violence against Women
>   Community Oriented Policing Services
>   Office of Information and Privacy
>   Foreign Claims Settlement Commission
>   Environment and Natural Resources Division
>   Office of Intergovernmental and Public Liaison
>   Office of Legal Policy   Office of Legislative Affairs
>   Office of Legal Counsel   Office of Dispute Resolution
>   Office of Public Affairs   Office of Justice Programs
>   Civil Rights Division   Tax Division
>   Antitrust Division   Civil Division
>   Community Relations Service

Note: INS (immigration) and Customs moved from DoJ to Homeland Security; it's now called ICE: Immigration and Customs Enforcement

SOURCE: DOJ.GOV

List 1b.   Ten Modes of Legal Redress

------ Ways To Set Things Right -----
(Corrective or Preventive; Federal or State)

1. PROSECUTION
Government enforces the law against wrong-doer: arrests him, charges him, takes him to court for arraignment; later, for trial.
2. LAWSUIT (Known as 'a civil action')
Individual or group seeks 'damages' for injuries and/or losses.

3. INJUNCTION (for example, an order to freeze assets)
One asks court to prevent a likely action from happening.

4. JURY 'NULLIFICATION'
Jury can lawfully refuse to convict if they think conviction would be unjust.

5. GRAND JURY (Some states no longer have grand juries)
Citizens decide whether somebody will be indicted for a crime.

6. RICO Racketeer Influenced and Corrupt Organization Act:
Here, *a pattern* of activity can constitute evidence of crime.

7. CONGRESSIONAL INVESTIGATION (hearings)
Congress can subpoena any individual to give sworn testimony.

8. COURT-INITIATED ACTION
Judge can issue a 'bench warrant' for arrest of any suspect.

9. INSPECTOR GENERAL
Many federal agencies have an I.G.. She watches for corruption.

10. STATE LICENSING BOARDS (their disciplinary arm)
Doctors, lawyers, accountants can lose their right to practice.

Note: You can search for Federal Law on the Internet by entering the original title of the law, such as Patriot Act, or by adding 'USC' to the name of the subject, such as 'treason, USC.' For state law, enter the state name, the word *law,* and subject. 'Iowa, law, larceny.'

List 1c.   Many Ways for the 'CIA' To Change the Brain

(research as described in a declassified memo from the *Technical Services Section* of the Chemical Division May 5, 1995):

1.   Substances, which will promote illogical thinking and impulsiveness **to the point where the recipient will be discredited in public.**
2.   Substances which increase the efficiency of mentation and perception.
3.   Materials, which will prevent or counteract the intoxicating effect of alcohol.
4.   Materials, which will promote the intoxicating effect of alcohol.
5.   Materials, which will produce the signs and symptoms of, recognized diseases in a reversible way so that they may be used for malingering, etc.
6.   Materials, which will render the indication of hypnosis easier or otherwise, **enhance its usefulness.**
7.   Substances, which will enhance the ability of individualsto withstand privation, torture and coercion during interrogation and so-called "brainwashing."
8.   Materials and physical methods, **which produce amnesia for events preceding or during their use.**
9.   Physical methods of producing **shock and confusion** over extended periods of time and capable of surreptitious use.
10. Substances, which produce physical disablement such as paralysis of legs, **acute anemia**, etc.
11. Substances, which will produce "pure" euphoria with no subsequent letdown.
12. Substances, which **alter personality structure** in such a way that **the tendency of the recipient to become dependent upon another person** is enhanced....
[emphasis added]

[Note that most of the above items are substances or materials, but #8 and #9 are called *physical methods*. Two of the 'methods' used on MK-Ultra children were electroshock and dislocation of the shoulder (which leaves no mark).]

Chapter 2 Nicolo Machiavelli, *The Prince*
Dedicated to Lorenzo di Medici in 1505

[A] prince may rise from a private station ...by some wicked or nefarious ways. ... I consider these two examples will suffice... *Agathocles*, the Sicilian, became King of Syracuse ...from a low and abject position. This man, the son of a potter, ... accompanied his infamies with so much ability of mind and body that, having devoted himself to the military profession, he rose to be Praetor.... **One morning he assembled the people and senate of Syracuse, as if he had to discuss with them things relating to the Republic, and at a given signal the soldiers killed all the senators and the richest of the people; these dead, he seized and held the princedom...**

In our times, ...Oliverotto da Fermo, having been left an orphan ...was brought up by his maternal uncle, Giovanni Fogliani.... But it appearing to him a paltry thing to serve under others, he resolved, with the aid of some citizens of Fermo, to whom the slavery of their country was dearer than its liberty, to seize Fermo. Oliverotto gave a solemn banquet to which he invited Giovanni and the chiefs of Fermo.
...Oliverotto artfully began certain grave discourses, speaking of the greatness of Pope Alexander and his son Cesare.... but he rose at once, saying that such matters ought to be discussed in a more private place, and he betook himself to a chamber, whither Giovanni and the rest of the citizens went in after him. No sooner were they seated than soldiers issued from secret places and slaughtered Giovanni and the rest.

After these murders Oliverotto, mounted on horseback, rode up and down the town and besieged the chief magistrate in the palace, so that in fear the people were forced to obey him....He ...strengthened himself with new ...civil ordinances.

[emphasis added] Trans. W. K. Marriot. See Constitution.org

2 Fear

The LAPD intelligence unit – despite public denial – was established wholly for purposes of political sabotage.... [F]ormer Green Beret and FBI provocateur William Lemmer [stated under oath] that he'd been instrumental in a homicidal strategy to disrupt the 1972 Republican convention by organizing "fire teams" armed with automatic weapons and incendiary devices!
– Alex Constantine, *Blood, Carnage, and the Agent Provocateur*

When the president talks of homeland security, I can truly say it's Greek to me.
– Rep Cynthia McKinney, January 31, 2003, public speech

2.1 AN IMF AUSTERITY PACKAGE - FOR NICE PEOPLE LIKE US?

Everyone can sense the insecurity of our nation today, especially economic insecurity. "What if the dollar collapses?" is asked by news columnists. More to the point, what if the food supply runs out? Very few Americans grow their own food. In cities, food arrives by truck and it is not unthinkable that roads could be blocked. There are also fears of storms and martial law; these will be tackled below.

In 1944 at Bretton Woods, New Hampshire, a group of international bankers (vaguely connected to the UN) set up two systems that would make it easy for them to control governments, namely the International Monetary Fund, IMF, and the Bank of International Settlements – the World Bank. They then made sure every nation got into debt – our debt is 13 trillion dollars at the moment, which effectively allows them to issue commands to nations.

Famous victims of the IMF's austerity packages have been Brazil, Argentina, and South Korea, while lesser-known ones include Germany, Australia, and Japan. The Bretton Woods conference also proposed a GATT Treaty: General Agreement on Tariffs and Trade.

We ratified it in 1949. Later, a private body called WTO, The World Trade Organization, sprang from GATT. Congress allowed the US to join WTO in 1995 without the formality of a treaty, which would have required a hard-to-get two-thirds majority in the Senate. Thus, the US **has joined a private club**, unconstitutionally at that.

25

The IMF bankers can, and do, make decisions as to which industries will exist in certain locations and *they decided, decades ago, to reduce American strength in manufacturing.* Therefore, an apparently free enterprise such as Ford Motors is actually not free to determine its own fate in Detroit, Michigan. Nor is there any respect for a nation's natural resources. People in Thailand had no say over, and gained no profit by, the destruction of their forests by the timber industry; Nigerian people get virtually no royalties on their oil.

If you don't hear complaints from the head of Ford Motors or the president of Nigeria, it may be because all higher-ups have been seduced into, or coerced into, the World Government. A discussion of the cabal (clique) of men that tries to govern the world will be postponed until Ch. 3. Familiar names include Henry Kissinger, Bill Clinton, some European royals, and corporate executives who meet each year 'in private' See Daniel Etsulin (2009) on the Bilderbergers.

I think the globalist cabal is caught in a power trap. They embarked on a too-grandiose plan to control the human race and now they're skidding. (We used to have a phrase, 'on the skids,' for a rather different set of men!) There will be a hint in Ch 12.5 about Truth Commissions in case they wish to surrender.

2.2 GUIDE TO THIS CHAPTER – *FEAR*

Section 2.3 is about Hurricane Katrina. 2.4 sketches laws on emergency. 2.5 'outs' Executive Orders. 2.6 is on weather warfare 2.7 proposes that we ask "What really is an emergency?" 2.8 inspects COG, REX-84, State Partnership Programs (of NATO) and FEMA. 2.9 looks at AIDS, autism, and vaccinations. 2.10, the What to Do? section, coins the term *nullable*, meaning if a federal law offends the Constitution it is null. Relevant Appendices are B, F, O, and Z.

A Pause for a Definition of 'Conspiracy.' The verb *to conspire*, from Latin *conspirare* (to breathe with) means "to plan in secret." The noun *conspiracy* refers to the plot itself; it's also the name of a crime in which one plots an illegal act This book accepts a theory that there is a cabal trying to harm us. I admit it is hard to explain how it secretly plans tasks that involve huge numbers of people. Anyway, that secrecy is slipping away today: the 'baddies' are being exposed.

In this chapter I make two claims. One is that some of the natural disasters we see are not natural. **They are attacks.** The second is that legislation produced by Congress to be used 'in case of natural disaster' is really a cover for federalizing the states' power.

26

2.3 WHAT WAS KATRINA ALL ABOUT?

In late August and early September 2005, over 1600 people were killed on the southern coast of the US and tens of thousands were made homeless. There were two causes: Hurricane Katrina, and a related event, the breach of the levees that caused the flooding of New Orleans, particularly its poor districts. Most of those who died were trying to escape the water, such as by climbing onto rooftops.

I think it likely that this catastrophe was man-made. In the 1920s, the US Army Corp of Engineers conducted an underwater explosion of the levees in New Orleans for beneficial purposes (*National Geographic*, Oct., 2004). Immediately after Katrina hit, residents reported that explosions were heard just before the flooding started. "The Video Congress Doesn't Want You To See," at youtube.com, shows the levee breaking – it was filmed from a high-rise building.

Later, Congress conducted hearings at which ordinary citizens told of the explosions, but every one of our 535 elected officials chose not to take them seriously. Do you recall the lady wearing an odd purple hat who was a witness at those hearings? The fact that mainstream TV allowed her to tell her story to the whole nation must mean that she was deemed a sufficiently odd individual that **she and her testimony could be ridiculed** – and they were.

Let us not dismiss her. A neighbor who hears a noise and reports it immediately has nothing to gain. So the correct behavior for Congress would be to follow up. Generally speaking, when a newsworthy event is described within minutes of its happening, by locals, they are the people to believe. If they get snubbed, that is all the more reason to suspect they have good information, isn't it?

But why would anyone explode the levees? And why would anyone steer a hurricane against the Gulf coast? Political scientists speculate on motive by asking *Cui bono?* To whose gain? Katrina's scattering of poor people away from the high-value real estate area may be of financial gain to some. But let us consider other motives.

This so-called natural disaster provided an occasion to bring in heavily-armed Blackwater mercenaries (now called Xe Services), to push people around. Maybe someone wanted a try-out of using force against citizens, including confiscating guns from registered gun owners. Presidential advisor Karl Rove (according to *Washington Post*, 5/12/06), asked Louisiana's Gov Kathleen Blanco to explore legal options to impose martial law "or as close as we can get." Who is Rove to make that request, and why did he want martial law?

2.4 HISTORY OF US LEGISLATION FOR EMERGENCY

The states, not the feds, have always had responsibility for the people's health and welfare, hence Congress did not get involved in legislating for emergencies. A rare exception was the Flood Control Act of 1944 that assigned work to the US Army Corp of Engineers.

Then, after WWII ended, the Cold War began. Americans were trained to recognize an air-raid siren and they heard their radio shows frequently interrupted by "This is a test...." Citizens were pleased that Congress passed a Civil Defense Act in 1950. In 1953, because of the Korean War, the International Economic Emergency Act added the idea that the 'emergency' need not be a domestic one.

In the 1960s there was exciting press coverage of the sudden loss of electricity in all the Northeast states, as well as several hurricanes, so no one objected to the 1974 Stafford Disaster Relief Act. It offered a mechanism by which a gubernatorial **declaration** of emergency in any of the states would **trigger federal funds**. (Previously, Congress had voted to assist on a case-by-case basis). Then in 1973 a Senate committee 'discovered' that wartime emergencies had never been cancelled, so a new bill was called for.

That was passed as the National Emergency Act of 1976. The give-away to the fact that Congress was not really interested in preventing a dictatorial Executive branch, lies in that Act's providing that a president all by himself can determine that an emergency exists and that **Congress will not rebut that** for at least six months!

Natural disasters having been catered for (as nuclear disasters were, earlier), the law started to treat crime, especially crime related to drugs and guns, as a factor that should prompt the government to protect people pre-emptively. Thus the Brady Bill of 1996 limited the sale of handguns, and the 1994 Violent Crimes Control Act allowed the military to participate in enforcing the law against drugs.

Meanwhile, airline hijackings that had occurred overseas caused the US to promote internationally harmonized laws — hence the identical security screening at all airports. As for 'Middle Eastern' terrorism, we got: Defense against Weapons of Mass Destruction Act of 1994, the Homeland Security Act of 2002 (Fathom it: 'homeland' 'security'!), and the Military Commissions Act of 2006.

In sum, I am unapologetically putting forth two theories: that our government sometimes **makes disasters happen** and that Congress enacts laws whose purpose is to justify a federal police force. If I hear anyone label these 'conspiracy theories, I shall be delighted.

2.5 EXECUTIVE ORDERS, OUT!

More than one half of the Constitution is occupied by its first Article, the article that invests Congress with authority. Authority to do what? To make laws. Neither of the other two branches is given that authority. A US president can never make law. Actually there is one exception. In *Hampton v US* (1928), SCOTUS (that is, the US Supreme Court) said Congress could, in minor matters, leave part of a law open, specifically asking the executive to "fill up the details."

In 1979, President Carter signed an EO that illegally delegated 'presidential' powers to an organization called FEMA that Congress had never authorized in the first place! FEMA was part of a secret operation run by Gen Alexander Haig and Col Oliver North from the White House basement during the Iran-Contra affair of 1986.

FEMA – Empowered by Pres Carter's Executive Order 12148
By the authority vested in me as President by the Constitution and laws of the United States of America, including the Federal Civil Defense Act of 1950, as amended (50 U.S.C. App. 2251 et seq.)... the Disaster Relief Act of 1974 (88 Stat. 143; 42 U.S.C 5121 et seq.), the Earthquake Hazards Reduction Act of 1977 (42 U.S.C. 7701 et seq.),... the National Security Act of 1947... the Defense Production Act of 1950, as amended... Reorganization Plan No. 1 of 1973, [etc.]... it is hereby ordered as follow: ... **All functions vested in the President by [the above Acts] are delegated, transferred or reassigned to the Director of the Federal Emergency Management Agency.** Signed July 20, 1979 [emphasis added]

Congress should have put paid to this caper right away. Then, if the president did not cooperate, **he should have been impeached.**

Note that presidents may handle ceremonial responsibilities, such as changing the date of a federal holiday, or awarding a medal, by signing an EO. These are then published in the Federal Register. Originally these were unnumbered; later, numbers were assigned, starting with those written by President Abe Lincoln. (Mayer, 2001)

The most famous EO amongst folks who worry about the long arm of the White House is EO 12,333. It gives investigatory powers of the government to unnamed organizations. (See Ch 8.6.) Citizens have wondered how it is that the Anti-Defamation League of B'nai B'rith seems to play a role in law enforcement. That EO is how. Still, EO's can't make what is unconstitutional, constitutional.

2.6 NOBODY TALKS ABOUT THE WEATHER (WARFARE)

Hurricanes can be man-made. (My guess is that Hurricane Betsy was an early success.) Control of weather as a weapon was acknowledged during the Vietnam conflict, but then got quickly hushed up.

> Technology would make available, to the leaders of major nations, techniques for conducting secret warfare, of which only a bare minimum of the security forces will be apprised.... [!!!] Techniques of weather modification could be employed to produce prolonged periods of drought or storm. ~ Z Brzezinski, *Between Two Ages* (1970)

In 2006 the Air Force couldn't suppress its enthusiasm any longer and wrote (in "Owning the Weather") *"Weather modification gives the warriors in the cockpit an operating environment literally crafted to their needs."*

The HAARP facility in Alaska deals with the ionosphere, a layer higher than Earth's atmosphere that is full of ions. **An 'ionospheric heater' was patented in 1905**. Yes, we can heat the ionosphere! Three names related to this are: Nikola Tesla, a great physicist of Croatia who came to the US in 1884, James Van Allen whose name was given (in 1958) to the Van Allen radiation belt that extends from 400 hundred to 40 thousand miles above Earth, and Bernard Eastlund, erstwhile patent-holder for the heater.

The HAARP (High Frequency Active Auroral Research Program) has been jointly managed by the Air Force and Navy since 1990. It can perform tomography, sending waves straight through the Earth, like ultrasound, to discover minerals there. HAARP, and other facilities, can send out extremely low frequency waves (ELF's) of 8 herz. (Human brainwaves happen to be 8 herz too. People who suspect that ELF's are being transmitted to affect the brain may wear a tinfoil hat for protection. Naturally this gives rise to ridicule.)

HAARP can also start **a fire** via lightning as Tesla himself could. The 2009 Australian bushfire was unusual in its jumping from place to place. Firefighters said they had never seen anything like it. On YouTube a soldier has said it reminds him of the military weapon 'Rolling Thunder.' Note: if the fires started by lightning, the source could be a HAARP-like installation in Armidale, New South Wales. Information I have personally collected suggests that the 1983 bushfire in South Australia was similarly an attack by the cabal. (The AF's research paper quoted above says that putting microscopic computer particles in a cloud "could achieve precision and trigger lightning strikes" and "the potential for psy-ops could be fantastic.")

The timing of some weather catastrophes suggests 'planning.' A Christmas Eve earthquake in Nicaragua's capital city Managua in 1979 was preceded a few weeks by the ouster of Somoza. He was a strong national leader, and that is a no-no for World Government. One reason to interpret the Managua quake as man-made is that the US, in 1991, 'softened up' the people of Baghdad preparatory to the ouster of Saddam Hussein — by using shock-and-awe. Losing your home via earthquake is equally shocking. And note the date: Dec. 24. Such events take place in the Christmas season more often than probability would dictate! The great tsunami of '04 occurred in late December. On Christmas Day in 1974, as an Aussie song says, "Santa never made it into Darwin" — thanks to Cyclone Tracy. The Bam earthquake in Iran was the day after Christmas, 2003.

The website of DHS, Kids' Page, has a display of tsunamis of the 20th century. In 1964 there was one in the Alaskan Sound, equidistant between the US and USSR -- a joint venture, perhaps?

Ten years ago, a newspaper in the Antipodes published this:

"New Zealand's Devastating War Secret"

Top-secret wartime experiments were conducted off the coast of Auckland to perfect a tidal wave bomb, declassified files reveal....

Professor Thomas Leech's work was considered so significant that United States defence chiefs said that if the project had been completed before the end of the war it could have played a role as effective as that of the atom bomb.... [may I repeat that: played a role as effective as...] News of his being awarded a CBE in 1947 for research on a weapon led to speculation in newspapers around the world about what was being developed [but] no details of it were released because the work was on-going. A former colleague of Professor Leech, Neil Kirton, told the Weekend Herald that **the experiments involved laying a pattern of explosives underwater to create a tsunami.** Small-scale explosions were carried out in the Pacific and off Whangaparaoa, which at the time was controlled by the Army. [emphasis added]

~ Eugene Bingham (Sept 25, 1999) nzherald.co.nz

Prof Leech was dean of Engineering. No doubt many scientists are well aware of the reality of manmade hurricanes, tsunamis, droughts. They may wish to glance at Appendix O, on punishment for genocide (under American law the penalty includes death).

Speaking of scientists, why don't they see to it that high school textbooks carry a reasonable amount of data about 'lob and lift,' two of the simple physical principles involved in weather control. Why keep such knowledge away from us? I don't mean the latest techniques, but enough for us to tell if a drought is from God or man.

I wasted money sending for a big book by Congressional Research Service on weather tampering (a.k.a. EN-MOD: environmental modification). It showed Congresspersons assigning funds for basic research on cloud-seeeding – recently! It has long been admitted that we did EN-MOD in Vietnam. Melvin Laird who was Defense Secretary at the time denied under oath that we did it:

[Reported at **sunshine-project**.org]: Benjamin Forman, a senior Dept of Defense lawyer, reiterated Laird's denial later that year: "We have not, as Secretary Laird has previously said, ever engaged in weather modification activities in Northern Vietnam." At the same hearing, the Deputy Director of the US Arms Control and Disarmament Agency had similar difficulties. Asked by Senator Pell if rainmaking projects had been approved by Laos and Thailand, Philip Farley replied: "I don't wish even to admit, sir, that there were such projects." — Senate Subcommittee on Oceans and International Environment, 26 July 1972 hearings

---

Suggestion: Breathe some new life into the old legal concept *hostis humani generis*. I propose that anyone who causes flood, forest fire, earthquake, drought, volcanic eruption, or tsunami be labeled, as pirates were once labeled, *hostis humani generis* – the enemy of all mankind. This used to mean that anyone is free to kill such persons, at least in theory, because no nation's law dealt with the problem.

So far we citizens have lacked ample fury to say the perpetrators of Katrina must be sent to the gallows. Mustn't they? What kind of nation are we if we don't act? How can we call ourselves a nation if we don't stand with Alabama, Louisiana, and Mississippi?

Although the word *Treason* is in the title of this book, and Katrina could have involved treason, the need is for prosecution, more so than for prosecution-for-treason. **We must punish the perpetrators of Katrina,** and if that means naming a different list of crimes, such as assault or simply the damaging of levees, that will do. It's a lot better than nothing!

In mentioning *hostis humani generis* I am not referring to 'universal jurisdiction.' Some countries (e.g., Belgium and Spain) have said that they can and will prosecute (even *in absentia*) persons who have committed genocide or torture: this is known as universal jurisdiction.

During the Bush administration in 2004, New York's Center for Constitutional Rights went to court in Karlsruhe, Germany to file a case there against Donald Rumsfeld, for war crimes committed in Iraq. As could have been predicted, the German government quietly dismissed that case. I think CCR should have filed in a US court.

This book is married for life to our institutions of law, and will lay out here every possible means for using the state and federal judiciary to apply law. Yet I raise the concept of 'enemies of all mankind' as we need to augment our legal thinking with attention to principle. The US Supreme Court once said **"The Constitution... is not a suicide pact."** That is a brilliant principle! (The case was about draft-dodging: see *Kennedy v Mendoza-Martinez*. Congress's power to call men up to defend the nation was not vitiated by the protections in the Bill of Rights). Here I am suggesting that we cogitate about *hostis humani generis*, and think of ways to use this idea.

Just as I was finishing this chapter, the Gulf oil leak happened. I assume it was a genuine accident. But say it had been 'planned.' What should Americans do if they came to a realization that it was malicious? Clearly we should not just stare at each other and sigh.

2.7 WHAT, REALLY, IS AN EMERGENCY?

Shortly after 9/11, Canada changed three excellent laws that had been on its books concerning what to do in emergency. Those three had quite separately covered health emergency, natural disasters, and emergency stemming from foreign attack. Then suddenly Canada imitated the American style of emergency legislation. That re-write by Canada tells me that such laws are written **in order to confuse citizens** about government authority – in the lead-up to a takeover.

Let's now look more critically at the concept of *emergency*. Your grandfather eats something he is allergic to and has to be rushed to the hospital. That is a normal emergency. Finding that you have run out of gasoline on the highway is another, so you call for assistance. Such emergencies are urgent – we have to attend to them.

As for 'acts of God,' such as wind and fire, one tries to think ahead, for instance by building with sensible architecture, or organizing a 'telephone tree,' or enacting a town plan that includes First Responders. If there is infestation of vermin, such as locusts, experts can be urgently contacted to advise on eradication.

Many human traits came about in evolutionary time to help us meet tricky situations. One is the *rush of adrenalin* that gives you extra energy. If your daughter phones to say she has run out of gasoline on the highway you will instantly feel the adrenalin – your heart rate will go up; you will sweat. Another trait is our **willingness to obey.** If your holiday camp is suddenly flooded, you will do what the leader says – such as "Don't go back in to get your belongings."

However, there is also the evolved trait of *panic.* A panicked animal is one that cannot figure out what to do. The brain perceives no options and no escape. It is significant that the word *panic* comes from the name of a mythological creature, Pan, who made people in lonely places terrified. (But we shouldn't feel 'lonely' in the US!)

Before we get panicked about a financial crisis that IMF may be planning (which would consist of a run on the banks, a depletion of food stocks, etc.), we should play with a bit of decoding. The word *emergency* has got to be emphatically shot down. Quite simply there are human emotions that get triggered by the very word 'emergency;' people who draft legislation have used that factor to manipulate us.

Here is a decoding rule ✓▣. Let's call it the Pretend Emergency rule. When Congress proposes a bill with the word 'terrorist' or 'emergency' in the title (or in its general theme), we immediately decode it, calling it the **Act To Reduce Citizen Power** – followed by the year of that Act, to distinguish it from many others. Thus the Patriot Act will be called the Act To Reduce Citizen Power, 2001; The National Emergencies Act will be called the Act To Reduce Citizen Power, 1976; etc. (Think of Confucius's *rectification of names.*)

As will be explained in Ch 9, strange things happen in Congress: legislation often has a hidden agenda. I mentioned that the recent efforts by the Canadian parliament, to come up with emergency law were obviously **not made in good faith**. Canada had fine law in place and must have wanted to replace it with stuff that would obfuscate the issues. Our own history of emergency law is not as clear-cut as Canada's; nevertheless, it is possible to discern bad faith.

For example, the 1974 Stafford Relief Act, which gave the feds a way to fund the states, is typical of a secret agenda in Congress to reduce the Constitutionally-grounded power of the states. (The same is seen in education and health.) This makes our government more 'national' than 'federal' (*federal* comes from the Latin *foedus,* a covenant. Our Constitution was a covenant among states).

Bad faith was again shown in the 1976 National Emergencies Act. Here Congress unconstitutionally handed power to the executive branch, by promising not to question decisions – for 6 months!

34

> **US Supreme Court's Reasoning on 'Emergency':**
> Emergency does not create power. Emergency does not increase granted power or remove or diminish the restrictions imposed upon power granted or reserved. The Constitution was adopted in a period of grave emergency. Its grants of power to the Federal Government and its limitations of the powers of the States were determined in the light of emergency and they were not altered by emergency... ~ in *Home Building & Loans Association v Blaisdell*, 1931

We need to run to the waiting arms of the Constitution! The above decision by SCOTUS puts 'emergency' in proper perspective.

2.8 COG, REX-84, STATE PARTNERSHIP PROGRAMS, FEMA

Given that the cabal is our enemy, it behooves us to study its plans. Consider the plan for **Continuity of Government.** Senator Inouye, at a 1988 hearing, famously asked Rep Brooks to hush up on the subject – thus acknowledging that such a 'COG' plan exists. All Americans should have leapt to ask if this were treasonous. The Framers gave Congress the authority to establish an Order of Succession if a president dies. (See that list in Ch 8.6) Why then are we building bunkers for additional Continuity-of-Government personnel? Doesn't it look just like preparation for a *coup d'état?*

> **Operation Garden Plot** of 1984 (Declassified)
> Department of Defense Civil Disturbance Plan 55-2, Section 3:
> This plan could be implemented in any of the following situations:
> **(1)** Spontaneous civil disturbances... may exceed the capacity of local civil law enforcement agencies to suppress.... This would most likely be an outgrowth of serious social, political or economic issues which divide segments of the American population.
> **(2)** Planned acts of violence or civil disobedience, which, through arising from the same causes as (1) above, are seized upon by a dedicated group of dissidents who plan and incite purposeful acts...
> **(3)** SITUATION. Civil disturbance may threaten or erupt at any time in the CONUS [continental US] and grow to such proportions as to require the use of the Federal military forces to bring the situation under control... A flexible weather support system [!!] is required to support the many and varied options of this Plan.
>
> *Note: This was obtained by uhuh.org, via Freedom of Information Act. Hooray!*

The above plan, called Rex-84 ('readiness exercise') got as far as to be printed in military manuals. The targets were the people of Los Angeles, especially 'negroes.' Today it may be protestors of HAARP. Plenty of internment facilities have been prepared. A contract to build $385 million worth of camps was recently awarded to KBR.

One more of the cabal's plans needs to be mentioned here: the State Partnership Program. See Appendix Z, which is a map of the US showing the location of foreign troops on our soil today. Jim Keith reported, in *Black Helicopters over America* (1995), that NATO had **worked a deal** with many of the 50 **state governors** to host foreign troops at their National Guard installations. His book was dismissed as conspiracy nonsense, but if you look up NATO's 'partnership programs' you'll find it. So let us ask: Is this constitutional?

The Founding Fathers refused to provide the feds with police power. Policing is the job of the states. The Constitution did, however, designate four crimes: <u>treason</u>, at Art. III, Sec 3; <u>counterfeiting</u>, at Art. I, Sec 8 [6]; and crimes committed <u>at sea</u> and offenses against the <u>Law of Nations</u>, at Art. I, Sec 8 [10]. These could give rise to some sort of federal cops. But what about Blackwater's being called in to New Orleans to disarm registered owners of guns? That is about as unconstitutional as you can get, yet the soldiers acted confidently as though their behavior could not pu t them in jail. Self confidence about breaking the law must mean that the criminals know for sure that mechanisms in politics and courts stand ready to get them off. I say this is totally un-American and **we can end it.**

The Katrina mercenaries' employer perhaps told them that everything was cricket because of the Homeland Security Act, the HSA, *under whose auspice*s the Federal Emergency Management Agency, currently exists. For years preceding the HSA, FEMA was unchartered, yet had a budget of tens of billions of dollars!

It was a vague, bureaucratic entity in which could be ensconced a secret police. Note: the German word *Gestapo* is an elision of <u>*Geheim Stadt Polizei*</u>, secret state police. **There is no reason for us to tolerate a Gestapo in the United States.** Heed the following:

Although world government had been plainly coming for some years, although it had been endlessly feared and murmured against, **it found no opposition prepared anywhere**.   [emphasis added]

~ H.G. Wells, *The Shape of Things To Come* [fiction] (1933)

A Pause To Discuss Credibility and Disinformation. This book's subject, treason, is one that people, understandably, don't want to contemplate. (It's pretty traumatic stuff!) Do I really think we can get some prosecutions going in the US? Yes, definitely. (I think it can also happen in my other home country, Australia. Only one person, the Queen, is above the law; all others are indictable and, in citizen initiatives for prosecution of treason, the Director of Public Prosecutions is not allowed to involve himself in the case!)

So what are some hurdles? There is the big one already discussed in Ch 1.5, to wit, the DoJ, unlike Australia's DPP, can thwart the bringing of the case. There's also the **silence of the legal profession**; do you know of any lawyers who even speak out against the OKC affair, or 9/11? (By the way, pilots, architects, and engineers have signed collectively to challenge the 9/11 deceits.) The public waits naively to see action by proper sources, particularly law professors and Congresspersons. When these do nothing, *that itself* contributes to the feeling of doubt. "I guess there isn't any treason going on, as someone would surely be putting the traitors on trial."

Another hurdle is the human being's nearly total **aversion to offending the 'elite.'** It just doesn't seem safe to cast aspersions on famous persons unless you have a watertight case – in advance! It is as though Americans who have watched courtroom shows on TV assume that anything less than 'proof' is worthless as evidence. Not that they would think that about an ordinary Joe, but about top dogs. This is ridiculous. The facts about the OKC deaths of Yeakey, Chumley, Wilburn, and Trentadue are strong evidence, and a jury could be reminded that any one of those deaths (except Trentadue's) may, of course, have been the *digitum dei* (the finger of God). Juries are a big weight in the Constitution; they carry society's wisdom.

Next we have the problem of disinformation. For me the worst kind is the 'tone of voice' kind. Apparently there is a cottage industry of paid bloggers who tell the Internet how they feel against whistleblowers (especially how whistleblowers are emotionally disturbed). In Appendix R, you can see comments by Kay Griggs, followed by the typical 'tones of voice' used against her. Often one person writes all the comments, using different names and arguing with himself.

To give this book credibility, I'm: A. quoting the law; B. marshalling such evidence as I can locate; C. cautioning readers where the evidence is skimpy; and D. pointing to similar historical events. I realize that, for prosecution, a court may need more, but it's a start!

2.9 AIDS, AUTISM, AND VACCINATIONS

In the 1980s a lawyer working as an actuary for a Health Maintenance Organization was asked to plot out the likely spread of the then-new disease, Auto Immune Deficiency Syndrome, AIDS, so that outlays from health insurance policies could be projected. He – Ted Strecker – asked his brother Robert, a physician, to help him.

Dr. Robert Strecker soon saw from the peculiar pattern of contagion that this was not the way an infectious disease usually works. Eventually he caught on to **the fact that AIDS had been bio-engineered** in a laboratory. Soon his brother Ted, the actuary, was dead: of 'suicide' (as was a state politician who worked on this).

Dr. Alan Cantwell was told of "the Strecker memo" (which can be viewed on YouTube) and put two and two together. Cantwell had been involved in the 1979 experimental hepatitis-B immunization of gay men in New York City and realized that most recipients of that vaccine were now dead from AIDS. Although up to that time Cantwell had been privy to all information about the study, government suddenly **refused to give him data**. In 1995 he published *Queer Blood,* cautiously putting forth his suspicion that there had been a deliberate genocide of gays. Today he says "There is no question" that it was done via the hep-B shot. (Cantwell is my hero, but it annoys me that mere truth-telling needs to be called *heroic.*)

Next, Leonard Horowitz, a dentist, published *Emerging Viruses: AIDS and Ebola* in 2001. It will surely come to be seen as the definitive work on the elaborate program called Special Cancer Virus project, started in 1969 at the request of Henry Kissinger, to find a way of knocking out the human immune system. Please read it!

Horowitz says the project involved the Rockefellers and Litton Industries and that AIDS may have been passed to Africans by the World Health Organization in smallpox vaccines. He believes it was deliberate. In the thirty years of AIDS's existence, **15 million people** in Africa have died of it. I am persuaded AIDS is genocide. That said, perhaps I should sign myself into prison. If the American government is committing genocide, I am as responsible as anyone, right? The people rule the United States, via their representatives.

What about autism? My late husband, Professor George M. Maxwell, a pediatrician, used to tell me how puzzled he was that new diseases were appearing (legionnaire's Alzheimers, ADD, AIDS) and that they were manifested 'patchily' around the world. Normally a disease takes centuries to present itself, as the bacteria or virus has to evolve some sort of relationship to the human host. Autism has been around only since the 1940s. Most Americans think autism is a problem for the psychiatric specialist (the IQ of autistics vary from genius to retarded, and there is a component of unsociability; for example the person does not make eye contact, and shuns physical affection.) But as gastro-enterologist Professor John Walker-Smith reported in *The Lancet* (Feb. 28, 1998), those mental symptoms are in many cases relieved by **treating the gut.**

I speculate autism was loosed on the population deliberately. This may have been for the purpose of studying the workings of the normal mind, obliquely. Or perhaps to cause distress in families. Causing distress is part of Tavistockian **'strategy of tension'** -- see Ch 3.7. No illness can match the strain on parents and siblings that accompanies the autism of a child. (See YouTube's *Autism Every Day* for a shock. But for encouragement, see *Autism Moms: the Final Cut.*)

I certainly hope my remark strikes you as crazy. It's a sad day when one can accept that cruel diseases are spread deliberately. However, it is seems to be true. Let me lay out two tales of coverup, regarding autism, that a jury would recognize as evidence that there must be something to cover up! First Kennedy, then Wakefield.

Robert F. Kennedy, Jr. has worked for many years as an environmental lawyer, particularly to save the Hudson River. When reading about mercury he happened to hear mothers' reports that mercury could be the cause of autism. Thimerosal, a preservative used in vaccines, contains mercury. RFK, Jr. investigated and wrote:

The CDC paid the Institute of Medicine to conduct a new study to whitewash the risks of thimerosal**, ordering researchers to "rule out" the chemical's link to autism.** More than 500,000 kids currently suffer from autism.... Truckloads of studies have shown that mercury tends to accumulate in the brains of primates and other animals after they are injected with vaccines – **and that the developing brains of infants are particularly susceptible.**
Internal documents reveal that Eli Lilly, which first developed thimerosal, knew from the start that its product could cause damage – and even death – in both animals and humans. In 1930, the company tested thimerosal by administering it to twenty-two patients with terminal meningitis, **all of whom died within weeks of being injected** – a fact Lilly didn't bother to report in its study declaring thimerosal safe. ~ RFK, Jr. in www.Salon.com 6-20-05

Manufacturers of vaccines typically distribute one-dose syringes that require no preservative, but also sell bottles of vaccine from which a clinic can draw many doses. The latter require a preservative. When granting approval, the Food and Drug Administration looked at the product (the vaccine) but not the preservative, Thimerosal. These mercury-containing shots have been given to babies as young as six weeks, when their brains are very vulnerable.

In 2005 Robert F Kennedy, Jr. was scheduled to discuss the mercury-autism link on ABC-TV, but **the program was pulled at the last minute.** He says that *as early as 1977 Russia found the autism-vaccine connection and banned the use of mercury, as did other nations* including the UK and Japan in subsequent years. (Note: in China the mercury-based vaccine is still used; many kids get autism.) So here we have the coverup of the ABC program not shown on air.

Well, keeping parents in the dark was not enough. The evil-doers (if such there be) had also to keep doctors in the dark. This was done by choosing one doctor, Dr Andrew Wakefield, in London, as the scapegoat. He is a gastroenterologist colleague of the Walker-Smith. Please read Wakefield's marvelous book *Callous Disregard* (2010). He saw that some kids who got a combined Measles, Mumps & Rubella vaccine developed bowel disease which then progressed to encephalopathy and autism. As a caution, he recommended that people choose the *separate* measles vaccine, not the 'MMR jab.' Britain then took the separate one off the market!

A journalist, Brian Deer, went to UK's General Medical Council with a complaint that Wakefield was 'unethical.' I surmise Deer was hired to do this, in order to smear the doctor. Still, you would think that the GMC, whose disciplinary board consists of three doctors and two laypersons, would arrive at the truth. They did not. In 2010, after years of twisting words and pressuring doctors to lie, the GMC revoked the medical licences of Wakefield and Walker-Smith. And *The Lancet* meekly retracted their seminal Feb 28, 1998 article.

Note: amateurs like me and thee may not be qualified to give opinions about medicine but we *are* qualified to deduce the function of smearing. I am sure that the punishment of Wakefield is meant as a signal to other doctors. Oh, by the way, do you wonder what courts have had to say to parents who bring lawsuits concerning Thimerosal or the MMR jab? Well, despite all adjudication being a public matter, you are not to know. As Wakefield's book observes, *there are secret vaccine courts in the US paying compensation.* Fathom it: *secret!*

2.10 WHAT TO DO? DENOUNCE NULLABLE LAWS!

Despair is not called for. It's perfectly possible for the population to **call a halt to unconstitutionality by government.** The US has a well-established method of voiding laws repugnant to the Constitution. Typically this is done by the court (when it declares a portion of a law null and void.) But if the court is 'out to lunch,' it is sensible to ask local police to refrain from enforcing unconstitutional laws. This is very hard for cops to do, however, because of the magic word *legal.* Police are authorized to enforce all laws passed by state or federal legislatures – that is the very definition of what is legal.

Isn't it odd that we lack a useful word to describe something that is 'on the books' and so must be obeyed, but is unconstitutional? That word would raise the question: **Should you, in good conscience, obey a law that conflicts with the supreme law of the land?** The answer can only be No. (See Appendix F.)

When putting your request to police, it would be handy to have a simple adjective that gets the point across. Let's go for 'nullable.' (The proper word is nullifiable, but that takes five syllables, nullable takes only three, and life is short.) It should be assumed that the average policeperson does not like enforcing outrageous laws and **would be relieved if the public started to demand** "Support the Constitution: Do not enforce laws that are nullable."

In Marbury v Madison (1802) Chief Justice John Marshall wrote:
"A law repugnant to the Constitution is void."

A Pause for a 'Clarifying' Interview with the Author.

Clara: That sounds cute, saying we should use words to solve our big problems, but it will never work.
Author: All right. Make a better suggestion.
Clara: [Long silence]
Author: You've been watching too many late-night movies, Clara. You think the denouement is going to be dramatic, but it's not.
Clara: Why do you think there is a lack of strong leaders today?
Author: There is a very low glass ceiling. When I first moved to Australia in 1980 I was aware that local talent could rise up to high positions, but a few years after that, the big multi-nationals came in, and so an Australian lad could not expect to become a somebody. The HQ's were in America. But now the same is true of America. A

person who is a born leader – male or female – will not be allowed to rise up. Only a Yes-man is appointed CEO. It's so emasculating.

Clara: I see this book has a Part Two "Why Do Our Brains Seem To Be Missing?" Have you considered that you might be paranoid?

Author: Yes. Therefore I am not paranoid. A person in that state is sure that he is right. No doubt I *will* be proven wrong on some of my beliefs, but I try to apply common sense. For the earthquake in Haiti, I ask if it is an act of man. *I admit it may have been an act of God.*

Clara: You sound paranoid when you say 'man' can quake earth.

Author: No, no. That is standard technology. HAARP can do it. The List of Patents reveals a lot.. As for chemtrails I was a skeptic, but Prof Vermeeren's talk at Delft University is fairly persuasive.

Clara: I heard that way back in 1973, Sen. Claibourne Pell managed to get a resolution passed prohibiting environment modification.

Author: Yes, in those days Pell headed the Foreign Relations Committee. Can you imagine the occupant of that position today 'daring' (as they say) to sponsor it? Anyway, a resolution passed by only one chamber is not law. A Joint Resolution *is,* but it needs Prexy to sign.

Clara: How can you be so sure that Katrina was man-made?

Author: I can't be sure. But I'm sure of some other 'mischief.' Perth and Melbourne's CBD's recently had crazy hailstorms, precisely at rush hour. And a tornado hit *downtown* Atlanta in 2008. How odd, as that part of Georgia is topographically featureless! Have a glance at *The Encyclopedia of Volcanoes and Earthquakes* by Ritchie and Gates. It mentions a Peking earthquake in 1773. In huge China only that one pinpoint gets the blast? I'll bet it was done with explosives. And Iceland's recent volcano followed that nation's defiance of the IMF.

Clara: I once heard that the Spanish *Armada* was done in by a man-made storm way back in 1588, but surely that is rubbish. Anyway, how can people get trustworthy information about weather control?

Author: Go to the Net. One of the scholarly websites is hosted by Prof Chossudovsky at U. Ottawa. He found out that the US Army's SOUTHCOM just happened to be rehearsing, in Miami, for 'disaster relief in Haiti' exactly one day before the 2010 quake. It seems there is *always* an exercise that parallels the terrorist attack.

Clara: If men are so wicked as to destroy Haiti, we are doomed.

Author: We are definitely not doomed. We all need to talk about these things., to overcome our inhibitions, our fear of being *impolite.*

Clara: OK. I'm not going to give those monsters any more slack.

Author: Goodonya, Clara. Well begun is half done.

List 2a.   What Is the International Monetary Fund For?

IMF was founded by a coterie of bankers. To control whole nations they must lure each country into debt, then give it a bad credit rating so no one wants to do business there. Then they come to the rescue by offering loans on nation-destroying terms.

The IMF provides low-interest loans along with an 'austerity package' in which governments are routinely required to:

$ **Cut back on welfare** spending; employ fewer civil servants

$ Repeal any worker-protections; **disallow labor unions**

$ Make natural resources available for **sale to foreigners**

$ Earn income, even if this uses **arable land for exports**

$ Take out **new loans for production of infrastructure**

$ Impose a **sales tax**, which will affect even the poorest

$ **Lift restrictions on investors**, such as the requirement of 51% local ownership

$ **Privatize** publicly-owned assets, including **water supply**

$ **Devalue the currency** on world market if appropriate

$ Cancel any **environmental protections** that hurt business

$ **Allow imports, charging no tariff** (This is called anti-protectionism; it is also known as **free trade**.)

Note: The United States is currently the largest debtor nation, owing more than $13 trillion (in 1980 it was $1 trillion).

SOURCES: Kevin Danaher, *Fifty Years Is Enough* (1994),
John Braithwaite and Peter Drahos, *Global Business Regulation* (2007)

List 2b.   Events That Somehow 'Cause' Legislation

The following events had the effect of enabling new laws e.g.
(SOVIET NUCLEAR TESTS, 1949 led to **1950 Civil Defense Act**):

KOREAN CONFLICT, 1950-1953
1954 International Economic Emergency Act
President can declare emergency "whose source is partly outside the US."   See 50 USC 1701-7

ELECTRICITY BLACKOUT, 1965 AND HURRICANE BETSY, 1965
1974 Stafford Disaster Relief and Emergency Assistance Act
Federal funds for disaster-hit States   See 42 USC 5121

SENATE FINDS OLD EMERGENCY STILL IN FORCE, 1973
1976 National Emergencies Act Makes president sole decider as to emergencies; allows DoD participation. See 50 USC 1601

SPREE KILLER, 101 CALIFORNIA ST., SAN FRANCISCO, 1993
1994 Handgun Violence Prevention Act, a.k.a. The Brady Bill

IMPRESSIVE CATCH OF DRUGS BY AUTHORITIES, 1980s
1994 Violent Crimes Control Act Lets troops assist in drug raids. It amends Posse Comitatus Act of 1878. See 10 USC 371

RIOTS WHEN RODNEY KING'S COPS ARE FREED, 1992
1994 Anti-terrorism Act passed; Civil Defense Act repealed

BOMBING OF MURRAH BLDG IN OKLAHOMA CITY, 1995
1996 Defense against Weapons of Mass Destruction Act*
and the 1997 Terrorism Incident Annex   See 50 USC 2301

2600 PEOPLE DIE IN NY SKYSCRAPERS, Sept 11, 2001
2002 Homeland Security Act   "Your papers please"

MUSLIM PUERTO RICAN (PADILLA) WITH DIRTY BOMB, 2002
2006 Military Commissions Act   US citizen, if called 'enemy noncombatant,' can lose all rights, including habeas corpus.

Now consider whether any of the events were cooked up to enable those laws.

*10 USC 175: Whoever ... develops, produces... or possesses any biological agent, toxin, or delivery system for use as a weapon [can be] imprisoned for life... There is extraterritorial Federal jurisdiction over an offense committed by or against a national of the US.

List 2c. US Issues Patents for Celestial Tampering

- April 24, 1951 - Process for Controlling Weather

- October 13, 1959 - **Method for Dispersing Fogs and Clouds**

- October 20, 1970 - Control of Atmospheric Particles

- December 28, 1971 - Generating Aerosols, Particularly Suitable for Cloud Modification and Weather Control and Aerosolization

- June 4, 1974 - **Rocket Having Barium Release System To Create Ion Clouds in the Upper Atmosphere**

- May 6, 1975 - Communications System Utilizing Modulation of the Characteristic Polarization of the Ionosphere

- July 29, 1975 - For **Triggering Their Precipitation** and for Hindering the Development of **Hail-Producing Clouds**

- November 30, 1976 - **Broadcast Dissemination of Trace Quantities of Biologically Active Chemicals**

- December 7, 1982 - Artificial Modification of Atmospheric Precipitation [and] compounds with a dimethyl sulfoxide base

- September 6, 1983 - **Atmosphere Modification Satellite**

- August 11, 1987 – Method & Apparatus for Altering a Region in the Earth's Atmosphere, Ionosphere, and/or **Magnetosphere**

- October 17, 1989 - Nuclear-sized Explosions without Radiation

- August 13, 1991 - **Method for Producing a Shell of Relativistic Particles at an Altitude above the Earth's Surface**

- August 15, 1995 – Tropical Cyclone Disruption

- January 23, 1996 - Measuring Device and Image Forming Apparatus [something to think about: holograms in the sky?]

SOURCE: a five-times longer list by Lori Kramer (providing patent numbers) available on the Net and in Jerry E Smith's Weather Warfare *(2009: 341).   Smith's book is a treasure trove. He spent many years documenting the activity of HAARP.*

Chapter 3

Plus Ça Change...   **Yesterday France, Today America**

To plunder the nation of their privileges as freeborn men was the act of a parricide [one who kills his parent]. The nation lost under his successive encroachments, what liberty the ancient government had left them, and all those rights, which had been acquired by the Revolution. **All France was one immense army, under the absolute authority of a military commander subject to no control or responsibility.**

In that nation, so lately agitated by the nightly assembly of thousands of political clubs, no class of citizens under any supposable circumstances had the right of uniting in the expression of their opinions. **Neither in the manners nor in the laws, did there remain any popular means of resisting the errors or abuses of the administration.**

...Whilst Napoleon destroyed successively every barrier of public liberty, while he built new state prisons, and established high police, which filled France with spies and jailors... To lay the whole universe prostrate at the foot of France, **while France, the Nation of Camps, herself had no higher title than to be first of her own Emperor's slaves,** was the gigantic project at which he labored with such tenacious assiduity. ...

In his public capacity, he had so completely prostituted the liberty of the press, that France could know nothing whatever but through Napoleon's own bulletins. The battle of Trafalgar was not hinted at till several months after, and then it was totally misrepresented.... **The hiding of the truth is only one step to the invention of falsehood.** As a periodical publisher of news, Napoleon became so eminent for both, that, to "lie like a bulletin," became an adopted expression, not likely to lose ground soon in the French language....
[emphasis added]

Sir Walter Scott, *Life of Napoleon Buonaparte*, 1828

3 Tribe

With glowing hearts we see thee rise,
The True North strong and free!
From far and wide, O Canada, we stand on guard for thee.
– Sir Adolphe-Basile Routhier
and Robert Stanley Weir, *O Canada*

*Pakistani businessman Saifullah Paracha, speaking at his Combatant
Status Review Trial at Guantanamo Bay:*
You are not master of the Earth, sir.
– *Associated Press*, December 2004

3.1 'NATION AMERICA' – TO STAY AS IT IS

We want to keep our nation. All people have to belong to a group whose culture they can internalize in childhood, so as to make sense of the world. The truly natural groups, i.e, ones that are diagnostic of the species *Homo sapiens,* are the family and the tribe. A nation, though not natural, can function as an oversized tribe. We have seen the US work very well. Large nations came about only centuries ago, replacing principalities, isolated villages, empires, etc. *Nation-states* depend on there being an identifiable government. Today almost everyone lives in one of the 194 nation states.

Thirteen British colonies declared their independence from King George III's reign on July 4, 1776 and became 13 states. Then on Nov. 15, 1777, they wrote up their 'Articles of Confederation and Perpetual Union,' making them not yet a nation but a loose confederation of states. Later, in 1789, the Articles of Confederation were replaced when the people ratified the Constitution.

Perhaps because of our geographical isolation from Europe, and also because of the intellectual excitement about the Constitution, we started to become tribe-like. Although we can't claim descent from one ethnic ancestral group, **we became the American tribe** by growing up amongst 'Americans.'

The first 13 states were Pennsylvania plus those on the Atlantic coast from South Carolina up to New Hampshire. In 1803, the US purchased Louisiana from Napoleon's France and eventually, through wars with Mexico and land grabs from Indian tribes, we expanded our territory from coast to coast, making a nation of 48 states. In 1958 we added the state of Alaska, from territory that had been purchased from Russia, and in 1959, Hawaii, which we got in 1898 by the most common means of getting territory—conquest.

In the late nineteenth and early twentieth centuries, there developed the famous 'melting pot.' Millions of immigrants contributed the customs and personality types of their respective homelands. Also, millions of Africans, who immigrated here involuntarily, supplied many talents, not least the power of observation about power-wielders that comes of being tricked and brutalized. As for what Native Americans can share with the 'newcomers,' we've been a bit slow on the uptake, but are getting there.

So, should we now stop being a tribe? Should we do away with borders? Should we retire the Constitution? Should we turn our backs on **rule of law**? Of course not. To give up any of those things is to become vulnerable to attack, and to chaos. Our enemy wants to break us up. We must stick together, to best use the Constitution.

Suggestion: Have you heard that globalization is inevitable? Don't believe it. Some things are inevitable, like the revolution of the earth around the sun, or the circulation of blood when the heart pumps. And thanks to 'human nature' many things are predictable, including a drive toward empire. But the only human nature factor that can really get us to globalize is the tendency to accept uncritically the propaganda that "Local rule is outmoded." What rubbish!

3.2 GUIDE TO THIS CHAPTER – *TRIBE*

National sovereignty is this chapter's issue. Some persons (to be referred to as 'the cabal') are on a mission to destroy sovereignty and establish world government. 3.3 offers a startling corrective about the Cold War. 3.4 recounts how European nations lost their sovereignty to the supra-state known as the EU. 3.5 then discusses a 'North American Union.' In order to reclaim our nation we must learn a revised history, since so much of what we were told in the 20th century was 'disinfo.' Hence the topics: 3.6 Mixed Militaries, and 3.7 Gladio (a surreptitious entity related to NATO, which is itself pretty surreptitious!). 3.8 deals with the open conspiracy of World Government, and 3.9, the CFR. The What To Do section, 3.10, recommends that we pin down the past. There is a veritable cornucopia of Appendices to go with this chapter: I through P.

3.3 COMMUNISM AND THE COLD WAR

From the Fifties through the Eighties, we and other democracies were presented with a neat dichotomy: the West was 'the free world,' its dire enemy was Communism. Growing up in the West we were taught that the Soviets 'behind the Iron Curtain' did not allow private ownership of most things, did not recognize freedom of religion, and tortured anyone who disputed the Party line.

We were allowed to feel sorry for the nations of Eastern Europe (e.g., Poland, and Hungary) that had 'somehow' become controlled by Russia. Little did we know that President FDR (Franklin Delano Roosevelt) and the UK's Winston Churchill had all but handed those countries to Stalin, at their 1945 summit in Yalta. Then, after the USSR 'got the bomb' in 1948, we all had to give top priority to avoiding a nuclear war between the two so-called superpowers.

The neat dichotomy was public relations. It seems that all US presidents – you will be astounded if you haven't already heard this – were in effect **building up the USSR's economy and military might, for decades, behind our back**. (Antony Sutton provided proof, and I mean proof, back in 1973 in *National Suicide – 3 volumes*.)

Indeed, as early as the '70s, conservative Cleon Skousen gave lectures wherever he could, quoting the following incident that Professor Carroll Quigley of Georgetown University had published:

"Meet me at the Waldorf"

"I think the Communist conspiracy is merely a branch of a much bigger conspiracy!" [said] Dr. Bella Dodd, a former member of the National Committee of the U.S. Communist Party. [She] first became aware of some mysterious super-leadership right after World War II when the U.S. Communist Party had difficulty getting instructions from Moscow on several vital matters requiring immediate attention. The American Communist hierarchy was told that any time they had an emergency of this kind they should contact any one of three designated persons at the Waldorf Towers.

Dr. Dodd noted that whenever the Party obtained instructions from any of these three men, Moscow always ratified them. What puzzled Dr. Dodd was the fact that not one of these three contacts was a Russian. Nor were any of them Communists. In fact, all three were extremely wealthy American capitalists! [She] said, "I would certainly like to find out who is really running things."

~ Carroll Quigley, *Tragedy and Hope* (1966)

The answer to Bella Dodd must be: a cabal of Americans and others are 'running things,' and one of their hangouts is Wall Street. That refers to a set of 'Establishment' law firms and private banks. Amazingly there is also evidence, exposed by Sutton and by British historian Nesta Webster, that Wall Street kick-started Bolshevism. Sutton discovered that a member of Yale's Order of Skull and Bones, Thomas Day Thacher played a particular role:

> Fortunately we have a copy of the memorandum written by a member of The Order, summarizing intentions for the 1917 Bolshevik Revolution.... Thacher's address was 120 Broadway.... In 1917 Thacher was in Russia with William Boyce Thomson's Red Cross Mission. [He] was then sent to London to confer with Lord Northcliffe about the Bolshevik Revolution. The Thacher memo...[urges] military assistance for the Soviet Army and intervention to keep the Japanese out of Siberia until the Bolsheviks could take over.
> ~ Antony Sutton, *America's Secret Establishment* (2002) p. 138

One can even find, amongst old books, Nesta Webster's 1922 report that financing for the 1917 Russian revolution came straight from NY! She said Wall Street's Paul Warburg sent $20 million to Lenin, and his brother Max Warburg *literally sent Lenin!* – Max being the head of German's secret service that protected the famous sealed train in which Lenin and others traveled to Moscow.

Fast forward a half century to the 1970s when Sutton researched Soviet technology for the conservative Hoover Foundation. Sutton found more than he bargained for! He discovered that Averell Harriman, our ambassador in Moscow, was well aware that the Russians lacked technology. Yet he pushed the line that we needed to fight them. As Sutton crisply notes, **the correct thing for Harriman to recommend was that we not provide the Soviets with technology** – but we did just that.

I thought I 'knew my America,' but was startled by two books: In 1948 a whistleblower, Major G.R. Jordan, published *From Major Jordan's Diaries*. He had been on duty in Montana supervising the Lend-Lease arrangement whereby we sent help to our Soviet allies during World War II. We donated planeloads of goods, and the planes themselves, to the USSR. Jordan was not amused to find the following items, by the ton, being packed into those planes: *the blueprints of all US patents, the street maps of all US cities,* and – wait for it

— machines for printing the equivalent of US dollars!! Major Jordan fingers Henry Dexter White as the traitor at State who organized this.

The other book is *I Saw Poland Betrayed* (1952), by Arthur Bliss Lane who was US ambassador to Poland. He bravely exposed our support of Communism. The US had issued The Atlantic Charter in 1944 calling for free elections in Europe and fair dealing with Poland's claims to certain territory. Churchill, FDR, and Stalin had said, at Potsdam, that all would honor this after the war. General Dwight Eisenhower was greeted by throngs in Poland; they hoped for America's support. But Lane, on his arrival at the embassy in 1946, saw that the Russians meant to install a puppet regime in Poland, as they had in Bulgaria, and that they controlled the media.

Lane tried to get his bosses in Washington to do the right thing, but found that 'Foggy Bottom' (location of US State Department) had no interest in stopping Communism! (See the movie *Katyn*.) It is devastating for us older persons to learn that we were so monkeyed with for much of our lives. But consider the upside: it may be that nations don't destroy one another in the way we used to think of it!

The big picture seems to be that the cabal was determined to get rid of any strong nation. The Russian Revolution of 1917 was a way of *chopping down the strong tsarist government* and reducing people to slaves. Since the US appears to be secretly helping the cabal (or World Government – I am using those terms interchangeably here) – it turns out that **we played a part in enslaving the Russians!**

We also helped hand over China to the Communists in the late 1940s; see Kubek (1963). Wisconsin's Senator Joe McCarthy, an ex-Marine, saw the US betray China, wrote an excellent book about it, and gave his all to stop it. 'They' then resorted to the usual: they told us McCarthy was nuts. He died in Bethesda Hospital, age 49.

Now consider that this game of running both sides continued throughout the Cold War (i.e., 1949-1989). This means that the October 1962 Cuban missile crisis was a staged drama – not unlike Wells's 'War of the Worlds' on radio, come to think of it.

It also invites a horrible re-interpretation of our involvement in Latin America. As suggested by John C. Coleman (1992: 30), Elliot Abrams' mission in the US State Department in El Salvador was to stir up conflict there *for the sake of it*. Such things can't happen, you say? They happen all the time. (On events in Latin America, try BibliotecaPleyades.com. Concerning the 'enigmatic' rise of Fidel Castro, see campello.tripod.com.) Now here's a rude awakening:

> **Confusing! Wasn't the US on the Same Team As Somoza?**
> There is no doubt that Chamorro was in a conspiracy to overthrow my government... and he was aiding conspiratorial efforts in Washington... We learned that a man by the name of Flynn, who was a staff member for Congressman Edward Koch of New York, was in contact with Chamorro in an effort to get sensationalism published. All of this was to be used against me. Then I began to put the puzzle together -- Chamorro, with Koch through Flynn and Mark Schneider, and with Senator [Ted] Kennedy, represented conspiracy. As my troubles mounted Chamorro became more brazen. He became one of the key Sandinistas.
>
> What I didn't know, but later learned, was that these leaders left my office and went straight to the U.S. Embassy.... On the recommendation of the U.S. Embassy, the Conservative Party refused to join the Liberal Party in condemning the terrorists. It seems unbelievable that such a thing could happen, but it did. Actually, it was evidence that the U.S. was aiding the other side – the wrong side. ~ Antonio Somoza, *Nicaragua Betrayed* (1980) p. 110

Somoza was killed a few weeks after publishing those memoirs. If it all sounds absurd, don't forget that George Orwell wrote 'fictitiously' that people in Airstrip One (his name for the UK) would accept a reversal of logic and say "War is peace." In his dystopia *Nineteen Eighty-Four*, the proles -- soldiers from the proletarian class -- were sent off to war for no reason. There were only three parts of the world then in existence, 'in *1984*': Oceania (west Europe and America), Eastasia, and Eurasia. Africa had disappeared.

3.4 FROM THE COMMON MARKET TO THE EU

Thanks mainly to the Internet, many Europeans have found out that for half a century they have unwittingly **allowed an international force to invade their democratic governments,** clipping off pieces of their national sovereignty. This was done under mild-sounding programs. At first there was the European Coal and Steel Community whose ostensible purpose was to make the two former enemies, France and Germany, start to be friendly regarding a few economic issues. There was an early Customs union among Belgium, the Netherlands, and Luxembourg, the Be-Ne-Lux countries -- whose Brussels headquarters presaged that of the EU.

Then it was said that farmers in the smaller European countries would be at a trading disadvantage unless they formed a Common Market. Whoever was behind this creeping supra-statism should be congratulated for remembering to cast a soft glow on it, by allowing the European Court of Human Rights in Strasbourg, France to be established. That institution 'proved' to many that one could go to a higher authority than one's state to obtain justice.

Meanwhile, there was also the creation of a new assembly called the European Parliament – although it does not have the powers of a real legislature, and there is a Council of Europe. The mainstream press talks about the Council as though its function is to sort out the jealousies of the several prime ministers, but that is just for show. The EU executive branch is incrementally increasing its own power.

In 1999 the euro currency made its debut. This is of great moment as it means folks can be killed with inflation instead of with guns. More money can be put into circulation causing more demand for consumer goods, thus encouraging the producers to charge higher prices. When prices go up, those with a low income may starve. In the US War Between the States, both sides used counterfeit money **as a weapon of war**. In the 1920's, to extinguish the technological eminence of Germany, the nations that won WWI used inflation very effectively to destroy the German middle class.

In 1985, the EU introduced the European passport. It allows citizens of any member country to migrate within the EU. Naturally, this cuts down on a sense of nationality in the home state. Anyway, could it really foster *community* among 27 nations?

EU = Albania, Austria, Belgium, Cyprus, Denmark, Estonia, Finland, Hungary, France, Germany, Greece, Ireland, Italy, Latvia, Lithuania, Luxembourg, Malta, Netherlands, Poland, Portugal, Romania, Slovakia, Slovenia, Spain, Sweden, U.K.

Let us note how much the EU takeover depended on secrecy, and blatant denials of the truth. If you believe that any such takeover in the US could be halted judicially, consider how judges in England were emasculated. The following case concerns a local merchant, Steve Thoburn, who tried to sell bananas by the pound instead of by the metric measurement of kilos and grams, as European Union law required. A Sunderland district judge upheld the prosecution's argument that an EC directive could override an Act of Parliament:

> **Bananas?**   On 9 April 2001, Judge Morgan stated:
> "This country quite voluntarily surrendered the once seemingly immortal concept of the sovereignty of parliament and legislative freedom by membership of the European Union ... as *a once sovereign power,* we have said we want to be bound by Community law." [emphasis added] ~ Booker and North, *Great Deception,* 2005, p. 406

Whoops, he wasn't supposed to admit that, because the United Kingdom (i.e., Britain) hadn't yet signed over to a finalized EU. Ten months later, when similar merchants, dubbed the "Metric Martyrs," challenged a conviction, their case came before Lord Justice Laws:

> **Bananas.** On 18 February 2002, Laws rule that EU law could only override the will of Parliament because Parliament had permitted it to do so through the European Communities Act. But there was nothing in [that Act of Parliament] he explained, which allowed EU or any of its institutions: '... to qualify the conditions of Parliament's legislative supremacy in the United Kingdom. Not because the legislature chose not to allow it [but] because by our law it could not allow it ....' The EU, he explained, could not overrule Parliament, because 'being sovereign it cannot abandon it sovereignty'. ~ Christopher Booker and Richard North, *Great Deception,* 2005 p. 407

Do they also manipulate environmental events?   Booker and North (2003) report that a new strain of foot and mouth disease, Pan Asian O, was found in pigs in Essex at a time when the EU wanted the UK to sign up. "Within 10 days the virus had spread through sheep, cattle and pigs, right down the west side of England [depressing] Britain's farm industry. The core problem was that the UK farmers were unable to compete with the much more highly subsidized farmers of countries such as France."

> In a Letter to *The Times* May 29, 2003, Tom Benyon said "In 1975 I campaigned as a Conservative parliamentary candidate for a 'yes' vote in the referendum that kept us in the EC. In retrospect it is abundantly clear that I campaigned on a prospectus that was sufficiently false to ensure that, if the issue has been a public offer in securities, I would face prosecution under the provisions of the Companies act and I would lose." Cited in Booker and North, p.158

(Is the reader gasping at the thoroughness of the cabal's work?)

3.5 THE NAU AS A TRADE AGREEMENT

Now to the matter of US sovereignty. As everyone knows, we have had free trade since 1994 among US, Canada, and Mexico because the NAFTA (North American Free Trade Agreement) was supplemented by CAFTA to allow for free trade with the nations of Central America. Is there also an NAU: a North American Union? Our government boldly denies it, yet in 2006 the heads of three states, Canada, US, and Mexico, put their John Hancock's on the Security and Prosperity Partnership agreement. (Be sure to see Appendix I, and indeed all the appendices at the back of this book.)

Is that 'SPP' going to make the US lose sovereignty the way Britain lost hers to the EU? Surely the answer is yes. If Britain had only wanted some trade benefits she would not have had in place the subterfuge artists needed to make Tom Benyon (above) misunderstand it, or pressured the judge in the Metric Martyrs case to rule that Parliament had *not* signed away its rights.

In spite of the fact that our government says the NAU is not happening, it *is*. Even after the ink had dried on the 2006 SPP, presidential candidate Mitt Romney, said he knew nothing about a North American Union. Actually his denials are near solid evidence! Recall the Yeakey rule from Ch 1: If police quickly close a suspicious death case by saying it's a suicide, *we suspect* it to be murder. So let's compose a Romney rule. Mitt Romney is a former governor of Massachusetts. Is it even remotely possible that he was unaware of NAU? No. He is a member of the Council on Foreign Relations, that has been disparaging national sovereignty, openly, for generations. Per the Romney rule, denials about the NAU are confirmations that the plans for NAU are real.

Note: I herewith acknowledge a debt to Italian semiologist Umberto Eco for recommending, in his *Faith in Fakes* (1976), that we decode ✔📖, instantly, the disinformation that we receive. The Yeakey rule, the Pretend Emergency rule, and the Romney rule are rules for decoding disinformation, by using logic and experience. By the way, a lovely NAU flag has been designed, but so what.

Plans for NAFTA must have been in the works in 1972 when Congress passed 'Fast Track' that allows a president to make trade agreements without going through the procedure governing treaties. The Constitution, Article II, Section 2 says of the president: <u>He shall have Power, by and with the Advice and Consent of the Senate to make Treaties provided 2/3rds of the Senators present concur.</u>

Congress is not allowed to legislate in a way that overrides that. (To change the Constitution an amendment is required.)

NAFTA allows *corporations* to sue any of the three member states – US, Canada, and Mexico. Previously, a sovereign state had to grant leave to be sued by anyone. Moreover the suing doesn't take place in a court. Tribunals are set up at ad hoc, usually consisting of business experts. They do not publish the reasons for their decisions, and **there is no appeal!** Of course this is repugnant to the Constitution's role for the judicial branch.

It also curtails the role of Congress in that the tribunals can, and do, declare laws to be 'against trade' and may require a monetary settlement for any such suffering traders. Legislators are routinely 'chilled' by this. As Draffan (2003:140) notes, we weakened our dolphin-safe tuna fishing law when Mexico threatened to sue, and the **WTO 'struck down' a Massachusetts human-rights law** that restricted state purchases from any business trading with Burma.

Canada and US have a secret Bi-National Planning Agreement for 'deep integration.' **Harmonization of laws** is a new phrase, meaning that it is bad if trading partners have laws to limit foreign investment in real estate, or a law that specifies a minimum wage.

Canadian citizens protested the August 2007 meeting of the 'business bi-nationals' in Portobello, Quebec, but police kept them 14 miles away. (That happens at Bilderberg meetings, too.) Even a member of Parliament who tried to crash the party was not allowed!

> Driven by... an unelected group of CEOs from Wal-Mart, Lockheed Martin, Manulife Financial, Chevron and Suncor Energy... SPP's job is to decide the future of Canada and to draft governmental policy towards the final step in NAFTA – the North American Union.   ~ "TILMA," *Toronto Star,* June 7, 2007

3.6 MIXED MILITARIES

Now let us look at US participation in the UN and NATO. The founding of the 'United Nations' in 1942 was initially the re-naming of an entity known as 'the Allies' (Great Britain, Soviet Union and US), that is, the nations involved in fighting the 'Axis' powers – Italy, Germany, and Japan. Only after the war did the United Nations become the 'UN' Organization, open to all, headquartered in Manhattan. (The land for it was donated by Rockefeller.)

In the 1920s the US Senate had refused to ratify the League of Nations, which arose after World War I, but it did ratify the UN

Charter in 1945. The UN consists of a General Assembly, having only the power to make recommendations and give its opinion through resolutions; a Secretary General; and some social and economic organizations, including the World Health Organization. (WHO, like the medical institutions of the US, is Rockefeller-tied.)

Above these is the UN Security Council, UNSC, with five permanent members – US, UK, France, Soviet Union and China, each having a veto. Per Article 42 of the Charter, this Security Council can make collective security decisions, when an action by any State causes world peace to be endangered. Can you imagine it!

For the first 45 years of its existence, that is, until the Soviet Union collapsed in 1990, the UN rarely asked for military action. In 1990, when the elder President Bush wanted to attack Iraq, the UNSC permitted military action by 'a coalition of the willing' (including nations arm-twisted or **blackmailed into willingness**).

Our military now has much more involvement in NATO. The Senate ratified the relevant treaty in 1949. It contains the sweet words that typify such treaties:

North Atlantic Treaty

Article 1 The Parties undertake, …to refrain in their international relations from the threat or use of force in any manner inconsistent with the purposes of the United Nations. **Article 2** The Parties will contribute toward the further development of peaceful and friendly international relations by strengthening their free institutions, by bringing about a better understanding of the principles upon which these institutions are founded, and by promoting conditions of stability and well-being… **Article 4** The Parties will consult together whenever, in the opinion of any of them, the territorial integrity, political independence or security of any of the Parties is threatened.

In the 1990s, the US, within NATO, belied those words by taking aggressive action (generally called 'humanitarian') against the Serbs in Kosovo, *without seeking UNSC approval.*

It is OK for us to join alliances, as our Constitution provides for treaties. Art. VI: <u>This Constitution, and the Laws of the United States which shall be made in Pursuance thereof; and all Treaties made… Under the Authority of the United States, shall be the supreme Law of the Land…</u> That supreme law of the land was violated in 1997 when we [with NATO] bombed Kosovo, since we were already obliged "to refrain …from the threat or use of force against the territorial integrity or political independence of any state," per Article 2 of the UN Charter, which we ratified. However this book is not concerned with that violation as such. The point is: erosion of US sovereignty. What are our troops up to? Is someone making use of them for non-national purposes? Yes.

Note: This book deliberately omits international law. Every society can decide its own laws, and still **respect humanity.** I think global governance is a false goal, and, siding with Prof Alfred Rubin (1990), I say no legal system can work in the absence of **authority.**

3.7 **NATO's Gladio, the P2 Lodge, and the Vatican**

The aforementioned NATO military, supposedly defending the free world against the Communist East European bloc, contained a clandestine unit that partially operated out of 'P2,' a 'rogue Masonic lodge' in Italy. It worked with Gladio, a super-secret semi-official paramilitary initiative, in support of far-right political parties. They were heavily involved with psy-ops. Here are a few items summarized from Daniele Ganser, *NATO's Secret Armies* (2005: 250-58):

Austria, 1965:
Police forces discover a stay-behind arms cache in an old mine close to Windisch-Bleiberg and force the British authorities to hand over a list with the location of **33 other MI6 arms caches in Austria.**

Portugal, 1966:
The CIA sets up Aginter Press which … runs a secret stay-behind army and trains its members in assassination, subversion techniques, clandestine communication and infiltration **and colonial warfare.**

Turkey, 1971:
The military stages a coup d'état and takes over. The stay-behind army counter-guerrilla engages in domestic terror and kills hundreds. [Ganser also notes that Gladio **helps Turkey torture the Kurds.**]

Netherlands, 1983:
Strollers in the forest discover a large arms cache near the Dutch village Velp and force the government to confirm that the arms were related to NATO **planning for unorthodox warfare.**

Switzerland, 1990:
Colonel Herbert Alboth, a former commander of the Swiss secret stay-behind army P26, in a confidential letter to the Defence department declares his willingness to **reveal 'the whole truth.'** Thereafter he is found in his house stabbed with his own bayonet.

Ganser uses the term 'stay-behind' army to imply that the Allies left some of their gear and soldiers behind in Europe after World War II, in case the Commies pushed west. But isn't it obvious that there was a different reason? The **many false-flag operations** he reveals, especially the [Kissinger-inspired] kidnapping of Aldo Moro by the Red Brigades, shows that World Government did not want Italian prime minister Moro to be successful any more than it would let Somoza continue to rule Nicaragua. Nationalism is *verboten*.

It is now possible for us to theorize that *almost every one* of the many terrorist attacks of the last century was designed by the World Government cabal. It has already come out in Europe, but the news is slow to filter through our corporate-owned media, that the Bologna rail station explosion in 1980 was also 'them.' Also the Baader Meinhof in Germany is 'them.' As Ganser states (p. 120) of the Piazza Fontana massacre, a former head of Italy's counterintelligence, General G. Maletti, blamed the US, saying **the CIA, "under Nixon," had ordered that massacre** in Milan, in 1969.

Even more amazing was the terrorism in Belgium known as the Brabant massacres. People standing in line at supermarket checkouts were shot by several men wearing masks and carrying machine guns. One of them was oversized and so was named 'the giant.' This occurred on several occasions, **yet the men were never caught.** The purpose must have been to put the community into disarray, (this is called '**strategy of tension**') to soften it up for introduction to the EU. Brabant is a suburb of Brussels, the EU's HQ.

Now for a brief mention of P2 and the Vatican. Prior to the 1920s, the papal states were still political states in Italy. Mussolini then got the Church to take a monetary settlement and the lands became part of Italy. Catholics (such as myself) were taught that a few popes in the past went in for a certain amount of debauchery. We were never told that debauchery is small beer compared to the political skullduggery of the Vatican. (Much less were we invited to question why there was, of all things, a 'Holy Roman Empire.')

Some members of the Church hierarchy belong to secret societies – something for which no theological justification exists. Thus it is not hard to imagine that Vatican officials belonged to the clandestine Masonic lodge known as P2. As to Church finance, a startling allegation is made by Sherman Skolnick (2005:1), *viz.*, that all the wealth of the dioceses in the US is held by one man in Chicago, operating under Illinois law as 'corporate sole.' *Mon Dieu!*

3.8 THE OPEN CONSPIRACY OF WORLD GOVERNMENT

In 1928, H.G. Wells published, openly, a book called *The Open Conspiracy*. It proclaimed some of the cabal's goals that are well on the way to being fulfilled, or have been fulfilled. Also in the 1920s, two utopian novels – Edward Mandell House's *Philip Dru, Administrator*, and Edward Bellamy's *Looking Backward*, were madly popular (Note: mad popularity of two very dry books must have been a function of promotion! See a sample of *Dru* in Ch 8.7)

All three books depict extreme socialism. For Bellamy, the people living in Boston by the year 2000 would be eating dinner every evening in a mess hall rather than cooking in their own home. H.G. Wells spoke in philosophical terms of the end of all human nastiness. His *Open Conspiracy* rejoices in the **amalgamation of all religions** into one, and celebrates **the end of the family**.

Today it has to be admitted that Bellamy did not get the mess hall thing right, but the predictions in both books came true to a remarkable extent. Even the family is falling apart: 40% of the four million babies born in the US in 2007 were born out of wedlock.

Both authors must have had inside information. This may also be the case with British novelist Eric Blair, better known as George Orwell. In 1949, he predicted in his *Nineteen Eighty-Four* that the state could hold power by controlling the personal lives of all citizens. Big Brother would watch everyone through a tele-screen that could nearly read thoughts. The state knew the importance of language and therefore controlled it by introducing 'Newspeak.'

Winston, the main character in *1984*, works at an office putting things down The Memory Hole. It is his duty to get rid of any old magazine story that shows how life was lived before The Party came into power. Moreover, the state aimed to **cancel the study** of history, so folks would have no basis on which to criticize government.

I feel certain that both H.G. Wells and Orwell were insiders. Many intellectuals in Britain were privy to secrets. May Orwell have gone too far and got bumped off? He died in 1949 at the age of 49 from a lung ailment. His sarcasm about power was scathing, for instance in his assurance that the torture of dissidents, in Room 101, would always bring about a 'conversion.' Everyone would end up loving Big Brother. (See Appendix J – if you have the nerve!)

Lothian's *The Universal Church* (1938) has a revealing chapter on "The Demonic Influence of National Sovereignty," and a chapter by John Foster Dulles, espousing – are you ready? – "a warless world."

3.9 THE CFR – COUNCIL ON FOREIGN RELATIONS

The CFR is an organization of Americans who want the US to lose sovereignty. One wonders what they think life will be like for their children once we have lost it. And thereby hangs a tale: when the cabal members set out to wreck the young, they also inadvertently made it impossible for their own offspring to take up their work (despite trying to pamper them via secret society membership).

Academic historians Carroll Quigley and Antony Sutton stress the dependence of the US on Mother England. The CFR, they say, gets its marching orders from the Round Table in UK. The story starts with Cecil Rhodes and Lord Milner who, together, angled for British takeover of the resource-rich but Dutch-controlled South Africa in 1900. Probably Rothschild financed Rhodes's goldmine ventures; the income permitted payment of many servants at CFR.

There are about 3,800 members of the CFR representing all big industries plus the press, universities, and shockingly, the US armed services. (Military officers are of course not supposed to make policy but merely carry it out). CFR's lower members don't get to make policy; they trot the data from the meetings back to their companies. Presumably they are watched to detect any 'lack of enthusiasm.'

> **Know Your Place** The cut and thrust of open debate ...had no place outside those upper echelons where the wishes of the Governor of the Bank of England still had the quality of divine inspiration... It would not be pushing the analogy too far to compare the City then... to the structure of the Communist Party... Individuals who held contrary views or talked out of turn were cold-shouldered and utterly disregarded; those ill-advised enough to dissent publicly were few. The fear of losing business by offending the hierarchy and thus being labeled as wayward and unreliable was **not so strong a motive for assent as the herd instinct of attachment to a community with its own code** of understanding and loyalty. [emphasis added] ~ Andrew Boyle, *Montagu Norman* [Governor of Bank of England] 1991, p. 137

A CFR member who becomes a president or judge (e.g., Justice Bader Ginsberg) gives up CFR membership *pro tem.* CFR also has a long list of corporate members, e.g., – many of the same CEO's that attend Bohemian Grove, a summer camp where bonding takes place.

3.10 WHAT TO DO? PIN DOWN THE PAST!

How is it possible that we were kept in the dark about these facts? The answer could be a simple matter of biology. Our brain perceives our tribe's culture as all-of-a-piece; we unconsciously reject data that does not fit our expectations. And the brain just loves dichotomies! In the Fifties: Free World v Commies. In the Aughts: Christians v Muslims. Very easy to process! It isn't entirely the media's fault — they had great material to work with: us!

As to why we continue to put up with treason even when we do learn about it, it may simply be that humans tell themselves they needn't respond to a major problem 'at least for another day.' As the Declaration of Independence says, "experience hath shewn that mankind are more disposed to suffer [than to act]."

Also, have you noticed that when someone asks you to defend your 'far-out' (i.e., accurate) account of an event for which there is an official cover story, they use a double standard of evidence? If the government claims an amateur hijacker could run a 747, that's OK, but if you say something as non-contentious as "A passport can't float down from a burning building," you get a doubting look.

Again, that's neurophysiology. Your listener would like to push away the whole matter of our government being part of evil. They will feel less threatened, however, if you use only facts from several decades ago, or in small issues. Regarding false flags, remember the girl who told Congress how Saddam's troops had stolen babies' incubators hospital? It was later admitted that she was the Kuwaiti ambassador's child, and the script was from Hill & Knowlton 'PR.'

It also helps to be ready to name your miscreants. While reading Chaitkin's book, *Treason in America,* I was impressed by the ease with which it deals blame for particular events. Chaitkin makes a tight case for Averell Harriman having helped the Nazis before 1941 (when it was still legal to do so) and after, when it fit the Constitution's definition of treason: "adhering to [the US's] enemies."

We need to pin down the past. The history that we were taught regarding 20th century events is rapidly being jettisoned. In Europe some scholars are being sent to prison for 'thought-crime,' thanks to the cabal's need to prevent research into the secrets of its wars. **Just knowing of their unease has an empowering effect!** Of this I am sure: as soon as we pin down facts, everything changes. The big boys may remain deluded, but they will be facing the ex-deluded.

And hell hath no fury like that of the ex-deluded!

A Pause To Play Make-Believe Lord Palmerston. This book can only make guesses about the cabal. It seems they often 'run' both sides in a war. To conjure up a picture of just how easy it may be to do that, please read the following summary of an essay entitled "Lord Palmerston's Multicultural Human Zoo," published in 1994 by Webster Tarpley. As I lack the ability to check out Tarpley's facts, I can't ask you to take them as true, but just pretend you are 'Pam,' the man in this story, and imagine how **you'd** carry out such work.

Pam is the nickname of Lord Palmerston, who was UK Foreign Secretary or Prime Minister for most of a 35-year span. That suffices to tell us he must have been a leader within the cabal. Or its best servant. (Kissinger and Rockefeller, they say, are but servants today.)

Pam had "three stooges" – Mazzini, Napoleon III, and Scottish labor leader David Urquart. At Pam's request they did whatever was needed **to keep Europe weak so Britain could control the world**. The main tasks for the stooges were to stir up local populations, and to create wars. Hence the 1848 Paris Commune, the Crimean War, and the disunity of Italy! (Imagine all that!) According to Tarpley:

"Starting with Lord Byron's Greek Revolution in the 1820s, British policy had been to play the card of national liberation against each of these rival empires [Metternich's Austria, Russia, and the Ottoman Empire]." In 1848 Pam arranged "an insurrection in Sicily, using British networks that went back to Lord Nelson. That started the great revolutionary year of 1848, and in the course of that year, every government in Europe was toppled." Pam was also waging the opium wars against China, using the hands of the British East India Co [says Tarpley]. After the Crimean war, Pam and "John Stuart Mill at the British East India Co [started] the Great Mutiny in India..."

North America, too, was in Pam's sights. The British "backed Napoleon in his project of putting a Hapsburg archduke on the throne of an ephemeral Mexican Empire. [This helped] Palmerston's plans to eliminate the only two nations still able to oppose him – the Russia of Alexander II and the United States of Abraham Lincoln. Lord Palmerston [was] the evil demiurge of the American Civil War, the mastermind of secession, far more important for the Confederacy than Jefferson Davis or Robert E. Lee." Gosh!

Do you think as Pam you could do all that? Look at the CV of Harriman to see how one man held enough posts to represent the cabal 'everywhere' *as a US official*. He was seen to act on **our** behalf:

"Mr. America to the World"   Averell Harriman (1891-1986)

Years in which he began certain jobs, as shown in Wikipedia.com:

1913 -	graduated from Yale, member of Skull & Bones
1915 -	VP of his father's railroad company (Union Pacific)
1917 -	at age 26, founded a shipbuilding corporation
1920 -	Chairman, W.A. Harriman & Company (banking)
1925 -	Partner, Georgian Manganese Concessions in USSR
1930 -	married Marie Norton, ex-wife of C. Vanderbilt Whitney
1931 -	Senior partner, Brown Brothers Harriman & Co (bank)
1933 -	THE BIG EMPTY BOX * (i.e., the year 1933 is not listed in the Wikipedia article)
1934 -	Administrator, FDR's National Recovery Administration
1935 -	Co-founded *Today* (merged with *Newsweek* in 1937)
1937 -	Chairman, Business Advisory Council
1941 -	Chief of Management, US War Production Board
1941 -	US Ambassador to UK, and 'special rep' to Churchill
1943 -	US Ambassador to the Union of Soviet Socialist Republics
1946 -	Cabinet member: US Secretary of Commerce
1948 -	US Coordinator of Marshall Plan, in Europe
1950 -	Special Assistant to President Harry Truman
1951 -	Director, Mutual Security Agency (a forerunner of NATO)
1952 -	Candidate, Democratic nomination for US President
1955 -	Governor of NY (replaced in 1958 by Nelson Rockefeller)

*1933 — 'unmentionable.' He with his bank, and John Foster Dulles with his law firm, Sullivan and Cromwell, were busy pushing Adolf Hitler into power in Germany! Harriman continued to help the Nazis after war was declared by the US in Dec 1941 — that is treason. Source: Anton Chaitkin, *Treason in America* (1999).

Note: this one page more or less stands for my whole book. — MM

List 3a.   CFR Members in High Places since 1947

The US National Security Council is comprised of these officers:

President and VP	Secretary of Defense	Secretary of State
Harry S. Truman	James Forrestal*	George Marshall*
1947-53 (D)	Louis Johnson	Dean Acheson*
VP: Alben Barkley	George Marshall*	
(starting in 1949)	Robert Lovett	
Dwight Eisenhower*	Charles Wilson*	John F. Dulles*
1953-61 (R)	Neil McElroy	Christian Herter*
VP: Richard Nixon	Thomas Gates	
John F. Kennedy	Robert McNamara*	Dean Rusk*
1961-63 (D)		
VP: Lyndon Johnson		
Lyndon B. Johnson*	Clark Clifford	
1963-69 (D)		
VP: Hubert Humphrey		
Richard M. Nixon*	Melvin Laird*	William Rogers*
1969-73 (R)	Elliot Richardson*	
VP: S. Agnew, G. Ford		
Gerald R. Ford*	James Schlesinger*	Henry Kissinger*
1973-77 (R)	Donald Rumsfeld*	
VP: Nelson Rockefeller		
James E. Carter*	Harold Brown*	Cyrus Vance*
1977-81 (D)		Edmund Muskie*
VP: Walter Mondale		
Ronald Reagan	Caspar Weinberger*	Alexander Haig*
1981-89 (R)	Frank Carlucci*	George Shultz*
VP: GHW Bush		
George H. W. Bush*	Richard Cheney*	James Baker III*
1989-93 (R)		L. Eagleburger*
VP: Dan Quayle		
William J. Clinton*	Les Aspin*	W. Christopher*
1993-2001 (D)	William Perry*	Madeleine Albright*
VP: Al Gore	William Cohen*	
George W. Bush	Donald Rumsfeld*	Colin Powell*
2001- 09 (R)	Robert Gates*	Condoleezza Rice*
VP: Richard Cheney		
Barack H. Obama*	Robert Gates	Hillary Clinton*
2009- (D)		
VP: Joe Biden*		

[D-Democrat; R-Republican]

*These 54 were members of the Council on Foreign Relations

List 3b.   Alleged Members of Rogue Masonic Lodge

(per list seized in police raid on member of P2 Lodge, Rome)

* Silvio Berlusconi	former Prime Minister of Italy
* Osvaldo Brama	Dakar, **Ghana**
* Roberto Calvi	'banker of God' (of the Vatican bank)
* Antonio Calvino	Buenos Aires, **Argentina**
* Franco Colombo	ex-correspondent of RAI in **Paris**
* Maurizio Costanzo	Italian journalist and TV anchorman of [Berlusconi's] Mediaset programs
* F. Umberto d'Amato	leader of an intelligence cell; was chief of the police under Mussolini
* Cesar De la Vega	**Argentina**
* Massimo Donelli	director of TV Sole 24 hours
* Giancarlo Elia Valoria	president, Assoc. industriali di Roma
* Victor Emmanuel	Prince of Naples
* Roberto Gervaso	Italian journalist and writer
*Gen. Vito Miceli,	former chief of Italian Army Intel.
Arrested in 1975 on charges of "conspiration against the state"	
* Paolo Mosca,	was director "Domenica del Corriere"
*Gino Nebiolo,	then director of Tg1, has been now sent to direct RAI in **Uruguay**
* Dott. Hatz Olah	Melbourne, **Australia**
* Judge Giovanni Palai	
* Claudio Perez Barruna	**Costa Rica**
* Judge Giuseppe Renato Croce	
* Angelo Rizzoli	owner of Corriere della Sera, cinema producer
* Guido Ruta	**United States**
* Gen. Giuseppe Santovito	[Italian Army]
* Jorge de Souza	**Brazil**
* Randolph K. Stone	Los Angeles, **United States**

Note: 950 names were published but another 1000 remain under wraps! The rumor is that the Church hierarchy is well represented.

SOURCE: Wikipedia.com. *Caution: Wikipedia articles are unsigned.*

List 3c.   What Professors Say about National Sovereignty

"Only by pushing the envelope of what we assume to be natural or inherent can we hope to envision and create a genuinely New World Order." ANNE-MARIE SLAUGHTER, *A New World Order* (2004), p. 35 – Dean of Public Affairs at **PRINCETON**

"Nationalism as we know it will be obsolete. All states will recognize a single, global authority." STROBE TALBOTT, *TIME* July 22, 1992 – President of **BROOKINGS** Institution, former Director of **YALE** Center for the Study of Globalization

"I predict that we will see ever more delegation to international institutions to make, interpret, and adjudicate law. Sovereignty is not dead but its meaning is being radically redefined." - Webchat at America.gov August 8, 2006. – Law Prof JOSE ALVAREZ, **COLUMBIA; President, American Society of International Law**

"The principle features of a model system would include... an international police force balanced appropriately among ground, sea, air, and space elements consisting of 500,000 men recruited individually wearing a U.N. uniform and controlling a nuclear force..." – LINCOLN BLOOMFIELD, "A World Effectively Controlled by the United Nations," memo for State Dept., 1962 (Later, Emeritus Professor of Political Science at **M.I.T.**)

"My central argument about America's role in the world is simple: America's power, asserting in a dominant fashion the nation's sovereignty, is today the ultimate guarantor of global stability." *The Choice: Global Domination or Global Leadership* (2004), p. vii – Prof ZBIGNIEW BRZEZINSKI, **JOHNS HOPKINS**

"The Moon Is a Land without Sovereignty: Will It Be a Business Friendly Environment?" article by Prof HENRY HERZFELD, Space Policy Institute of **GEORGE WASHINGTON U.**

Yoo-Yoo-hoo in there, Academia, anybody home?

END OF PART ONE *("TRAITORS, COME OUT")* **– A CHRONOLOGY**

1492 Columbus sails the ocean blue; nightmares and dreams ensue

1787 55 silk-hosed men in powdered wigs summer in Philadelphia

1789 Plotters of a World Revolution produce French Revolution

1882 Goldmining Cecil Rhodes recruits Scholars to direct world

1898 Lord Milner's Kindergarten gives rise to Round Table, CFR

1922 Nesta Webster clearly reveals Bolsheviks as re-run of Babeuf

1942 Against Axis powers, US sends Lend Lease to Europe, USSR

1944 New Zealand professor studies how to make tsunami for war

1948 George Orwell writes *1984*. How can it be so accurate?

1958 US helps Fidel Castro in Cuban revolution versus Batista!

1970s Drug laws help to militarize police; prison breaks up families

1976 Big promotion of swine flu vaccine dropped when many die

1979 Carter's 'Executive Order' 12148 organizes secretive FEMA

1984 REX-84 (intended as the big coup?) fizzles out in California

1995 OKC bombing involves German Strassmeier, FBI, and BATF

1992 Italians, but not Yanks, learn US killed Aldo Moro, their PM

2001 Paula Zahn hypes anthrax scare on CNN; later invited to CFR

2005 Blown levees cause flood after Katrina; mercenaries are bosses

2006 Fox, Harper at Bush ranch: Security & Prosperity Partnership!

2008 Romney, Giuliani, stumping, deny knowing of N. A. Union

2008 Army Dr. Sue Arrigo uploads AIDS vaccine recipe: rense.com

2008 By now everybody and his cousin is calling 9/11 a 'false flag'

2009 'Underwear bomber' hoax leads to nude airport photosearches

2010 Ignorant of 4th amendment, women permit such violations

2010 Andrew Wakefield gets struck off the register for doing right

ΨΨΨΨ

Welcome to Part Two: Why Do Our Brains Seem To Be Missing?

Chapters: 4 Bio-spirit
5 Masculinity
6 Menticide

from *Judges* 11:1, 30-34:

Jephthah the Gileadite was a mighty man of valour. ….And it came to pass that the children of Ammon made war against Israel…and they said unto Jephthah, Come, and be our captain … **Jephthah vowed unto the Lord and said, If thou shalt without fail deliver the children of Ammon into mine hands, then it shall be, that whatsoever cometh forth of the doors of my house to meet me when I return …shall surely be the Lord's, and I will offer it up for a burnt offering.**
So Jephthah passed over to fight against the children of Ammon; and the Lord delivered them into his hands. And he smote them….
And Jephthah came to Mizpeh unto his house, and behold, his daughter came out to meet him with timbrels and with dances.
And she was his only child.   [emphasis added]

Chapter 4

Ode to Autumn
-- John Keats

Season of mists and mellow fruitfulness,
Close bosom-friend of the maturing sun;
Conspiring with him how to load and bless
With fruit the vines that round the thatch-eaves run;
To bend with apples the mossed cottage-trees,
And fill all fruit with ripeness to the core;
To swell the gourd, and plump the hazel shells
With a sweet kernel; to set budding more,
And still more, later flowers for the bees,
Until they think warm days will never cease,
For Summer has o'er-brimmed their clammy cells.

...

Where are the songs of Spring? Ay, where are they?
Think not of them, thou hast thy music too, --
While barred clouds bloom the soft-dying day,
And touch the stubble-plains with rosy hue;
Then in a wailful choir, the small gnats mourn
Among the river sallows, borne aloft
Or sinking as the light wind lives or dies;
And full-grown lambs loud bleat from hilly bourn;
Hedge-crickets sing; and now with treble soft
The redbreast whistles from a garden-croft,
And gathering swallows twitter in the skies.

Keats wrote this when he was 25, the year before he died.

4 Bio-Spirit

Two are better than one; because they have a good reward for their
labor. For if they fall one will lift up his fellow;
But woe to him that is alone when he falleth; for he hath not
another to help him.
-- *Eccliastes 4: 9-10*

Heaven is my father and earth is my mother and even such a small
creature as I finds an intimate place in their midst. Therefore that
which extends throughout the universe I regard as my body....
All are my brothers and sisters....Respect the aged...Show affection
toward the weak....Even those who are tired and infirm, those who
have no brothers or children, wives or husbands, all are my brothers
who are in distress and have no one to turn to.
– Chang Tsai's *Western Inscription*, quoted in W.T. DeBary,
Sources of Chinese Tradition

4.1 LOVE

Can The Great Republic, fallen into trouble, rise again? **Of
course it can, because the same human race that made it work
well in the past is alive today.** The behavioral traits of our species
are as biologically given as the anatomical ones. Both our nasty and
our pleasant traits will always be 'available' for cultures to work with.

People naturally love their family, their friends, and their tribe.
Such love is provided for physiologically; it can even be seen in a
few species other than ours where evolution has 'arranged' that the
species be a social one. Social species have instincts for *altruism,* a
word derived from Latin 'alter' meaning 'the other.' (Maxwell: 1991)

Typically, society-formation in mammals adapts otherwise
selfish individuals to work together for group predation, such as ambush, or group defense against predators. In some bird species the
evolutionary explanation for the pair-bond, the basis of the family, is
the need for care of offspring by two parents where, say, snakes
would get at the nest if a sole parent went away to collect food. An
instinct to engage in *reciprocal altruism* encourages the doing of favors.
It probably underwrites human trust as well as our desire for justice.

Love is experienced as a sensation of pleasure. You might feel love during a hug, but just as easily you may feel it when making a sacrifice on behalf of a friend in need. The idea of sacrificial love is a reminder that love is not only a sensation but is a great motivator.

Neuroscientist Jan Panksepp, in his article "Altruism" in the 1989 *Yearbook of Neurobiology*, theorizes that all kinds of love owe their biological origin to maternal love. In the brains of female birds it has been found that oxytocin is the chemical that keeps a hen in touch with her chicks. If oxytocin is experimentally removed from the brain, all mothering behavior stops.

She hears her chick but does not respond to its cry. In humans, when a woman touches her baby's skin, this stimulates oxytocin in her, and also in the baby. Hence, to caress or to be caressed is to experience the sensation of love. It also contributes to bonding.

For purposes of choosing a desirable social arrangement, we would want one that gives vent to love, rather than blocks its expression. Consider the ancient Greek city-state of Sparta. The ideal Spartan life was practically barracks life. Few creature comforts were allowed and family ties were discouraged! (Perhaps this was seen as necessary for survival, to make the men warriors.) By contrast, Scottish people pride themselves on frugality *and* family life. Some habits can be encouraged and others discouraged. 'Words of wisdom' are used for this. Consider the importance of tradition:

> Traditions are never lost. They can be renewed or reinvented. All it takes is for them to be cherished. Cultures survive the way post-biblical Judaism survived: when they attach the highest priority to schools and teachers, and when they see at least part of the role of education as developing individuals articulate in the language of their heritage. [But] education needs more than schools. Above all, it needs families. ~ Rabbi Jonathan Sacks, *The Politics of Hope* (1997)

4.2 GUIDE TO THIS CHAPTER – *BIO-SPIRIT*

Here in this book's Part Two we are asking, Why do our brains seem to be missing? Why would a sophisticated society like ours allow traitors to do terrible things and get away with it? Have we all gone nuts? There will be a psychological investigation of that in Ch 6, but here in Ch 4 the message is anthropological: our biological nature is not being optimally used by American culture, and our evolved ways often make the cabal's life easy.

We look at traits: 4.3 avarice and predation, 4.4 the love of life, 4.5 devil-worship, 4.6 attachment and ideals, 4.7 war-making and genocide, 4.8 leadership, and 4.9 deceitfulness. The 4.10 question, What To Do, is answered "Work with nature." That does not mean "Capitulate to every instinct." Nor am I recommending that we design a culture and social-engineer everyone into it. Rather, this chapter tries to shake out, for inspection, any underlying 'biological' cause of our current problems. Then we can work on those.

4.3 AVARICE AND PREDATION

The human instinct to accumulate huge wealth is an outgrowth of the healthy selfishness characteristic of our species. Hoarding is practiced by some bird and mammal species. Omitting the interesting example of the magpie that collects shiny pieces of junk to decorate her nest, most riches that an animal accumulates are for its needs. Early humans probably gathered and stored more nuts and berries than the family needed at the moment. Being provident for the next day is good.

Still, it can get out of hand. The provident instinct is probably **the real cause of greed:** our subconscious calculator tells us that we may not have enough for the future, or our heirs' future. It's a rare person who says "I have enough." As Juliet Schor shows in her marvelous 2004 book, *The Overspent American,* our own culture in particular has turned greed into a virtue. For example, for the sake of profit we encourage built-in-obsolescence, i.e., wastefulness.

Also, **humans are predators by nature** – just watch a 3-year-old grab a toy from her brother. Presumably we would all take what we could get, all the time, but for society's deciding that there is a better way. Relatedly, we are parasites, living off the labor of work animals such as oxen and honeybees, and the labor of enslaved or exploited humans. We may even parasitize a fellow human via an organ transplant. (Cannibalism for food seems to be relatively rare.)

A major instrument of human predation is modern government. As 19th century sociologist Max Weber said, the state has a monopoly on legitimate violence. (Because of the 20th century decline of religion, **the state more or less monopolizes *legitimacy!*)** As seen in the sovietization of Russia – a 'soviet' being a work team – a Party controlling government can force everyone to work. That Party may say it has 'the good of all' as its goal, but few believe it. The leaders fall into the human habit of 'feathering their own nests.'

Another predatory institution, besides the state, is 'debt slavery.' It makes a man work not by threat of jail or the whip but by advancing money to him when it is obvious he will not have the means to repay. He is forced to work for *any* pay. Nearly everyone today can be forced to work by this method, as very few people now live on the land growing their own fare, and/or hunting or fishing for food.

> **Shrimp.**   *In the 1960s the government built embankments around the coastal area to stop the tail-line waters from coming in, to gain more land from the ocean. The coastal areas were the surplus food areas where a lot of grains grew. One fourth of the population of Bangladesh lives in the coastal areas. In the late 1970s and the 1980s, the World Bank said, "Go for shrimp." And some rich people ...leased a lot of land from the local people and said they were going to cultivate shrimp. The local people didn't know what was going to happen: their fields were flooded with salt water and used by the shrimp cultivators to grow the shrimp. They catch the shrimp right from the ocean and put it in these flooded areas, inside the land. When the shrimp reach a certain size, the cultivators sell them to outside markets.*
> *People are living on bamboo huts on top of the water because they have no place to go. They are sort of like hostages to the shrimp cultivators [who] hire goons to intimidate the local people. The women working those shrimp areas must go in the ocean to catch shrimp, and they are in the cold water from eight to ten hours each day.*
> ~ *Kevin Danaher, ed.* Fifty Years [of the IMF] Is Enough *(1994) p. 130*

A Pause To Mention 'Socialism.'   In living memory, a fifth of the world's population was put under an economic system, called socialism or communism. It was sudden and 'alien;' Marxist-Leninism had come off the drawing board. Nevertheless, in pre-history people were rather communistic. It is routine for society to help the sick and the poor, and the family always acts as an economic unit.

A coercive socialism now appears to be planned for the US. As described in the chapter on Fear, the IMF directs the economy of debtor nations. In 2010 the 'cashless society' began to be experimented with, in Greece. A new law there makes it mandatory to use plastic cards, not cash, for any transaction over 1500 euros. This may lead to Special Drawing Rights. Big Brother would be able to control how many times you could 'draw' from your ration for food. Worse, if you get a mark on your electronic I.D. card for being, say, a dissident, you could have your rations cut off completely.

I note that US civil society gives little attention to 'distributive justice,' and for a nation of law, rarely legislates against usury.

4.4 LOVE OF LIFE ('BIOPHILIA')

It's relieving to know that even if we mess up, culturally or politically, God provides nutrition for all humans, at least on a vegetarian basis, by putting seeds into every plant and thus there will be a harvest every year. Right? Sorry. Humans are messing that up too. Agribusinesses create, in a lab, seeds that produce a harvest once only. The crop yields seeds inadequate for reproduction!

Hmm. No farmer would buy those seeds, right? Wrong. American farmers in the 20th century started to lose independence when their suppliers merged into a handful of huge firms. Those suppliers decide what seeds to distribute, how much pesticide the farmer will need to apply, from whom she will buy her tractors, etc.

How could this happen in America? Where is the legislature? Isn't there a Sherman Antitrust Act? Yes, we have a Congress that could fix the problem of the one-season seeds. Why don't Congresspersons (a term that includes both representatives and senators) act? Some say they are corrupt but I say they are mind-controlled. Wouldn't they be at least as mind-controlled as the rest of us?

Luckily there is a new book, *Seeds of Destruction,* that tells how far we have strayed from the biblical 'time to sow and a time to reap.' Not that there is any lack of books about mistakes (see bibliography!), but inventing seedless crops is just so blatantly cuckoo!

Hog Heaven – *Not!* When Cargill acquired the grain-handling operations of Continental in 1998 [it got] 40% of national grain elevator capacity. The Justice Dept. approved the merger. Four large agro-chemical/seed companies – Monsanto, Novartis, Dow, and DuPont – control more than 75% of the nation's seed corn sales...

As traditional farmers abandoned their family land in the 1980s ...what was termed a revolution in animal factory production began. From birth to slaughter a factory pig would be in a cell only as large as the animal. [She] would never be able to lie down, and ...never see daylight. ...Under the George W Bush Administration, the EPA, at the request of agribusiness, repealed a rule that held corporate livestock owners liable for damage caused by animal waste pollution.

~ F. William Engdahl, *Seeds of Destruction* (2007) p. 138

Speaking of 'why our brains seem to be missing,' the foregoing quote demonstrates perfectly how a minority of people, who are able to manipulate the culture of a whole society for their own purposes, can bring about a hypertrophy (extreme overgrowth) of a particular aspect of human nature. In regard to breeding pigs in minimum-size cages, we see a sort of fulfillment of the human drive for money. Similarly, because movies about sex and violence do well at the video shop, inevitably their producers churn out more of same, finally reducing the plot of movies to no plot at all.

Compare the thinking of a culture that raises pigs in cages, and makes movies that stimulate killing, with the psalmist's far more balanced picture of the magnificent world we live in:

Psalm 104

You stretch out the heavens like a tent, ... the clouds [are] your chariot... From your high halls you water the mountains, satisfying the earth with the fruit of your works; for cattle you make the grass grow, [and plants to make] wine to cheer the people's hearts...

Then there is the sea with its vast expanses, teeming with countless creatures, creatures both great and small...and Leviathan whom you made to sport with.... Glory to Yahweh forever! May Yahweh find joy in his creatures! I shall sing to Yahweh all my life, make music for my God ...   ~ *New Jerusalem Bible*

Conservationist E.O. Wilson, via his popular books on human evolution, always plays up the psalmist's joy about Nature. His book *Biophilia* (1984) advises us to inquire into the innate and little-understood human sense of connection to and affection for other species. Wilson is horrified that our technology is causing the extinction of species to whom we have not yet even been properly introduced, so to speak, many of whose services we may one day desperately need:

Attention Americans Who Wear 'Plus Sizes'

Consider the case of the natural food sweeteners. Several species of plants have been identified whose chemical products can replace conventional sugar with negligible calories and no known side effects. The katemfe (*Thaumatococcus danielli*) of the West African forests contains two proteins that are 1,600 times sweeter than sucrose and are now widely marketed in Great Britain and Japan. It is outstripped by the well-named serendipity berry (*Dioscorephyllum cumminsii*), another West African native whose fruit produces a substance 3,000 times sweeter than sucrose.   ~ E. O. Wilson, *Biophilia* (1984) p. 133

A warning: the next section is unpleasant. Anyone who suffered sexual abuse as a child is advised to skip over to section 4.6.

4.5 DEVIL-WORSHIP (THE LUCIFER/LUCRE MIX-UP?)

Did you know that satanism, witchcraft, and 'paganism' are all the rage at the moment? Are you aware that the lyrics to many popular songs have themes that are, to put it politely, occult? This is pitched as part of anti-modernism: "Why be rational? Satan is cool."

In a pre-scientific era, alchemy was likely to have come about – as folks would naturally hope that base metals could be transformed into gold. And before astronomy there was astrology: people always desire an explanation for their fate, and a means to foretell it! As soon as a few claimed to know the key, they attracted followers.

Since the 'Scientific Revolution,' however, Westerners began to explain the world on a provable basis. Indeed a scientist is required to express her theory in a way that is 'falsifiable' so others can know when they have proved her wrong. From this, a 'body of science' gets built up. Now, in the New Age, there is once again a push to take things on faith. Science is scoffed at. (Never mind that the scoffer drives a high-tech car or chooses coronary bypass surgery.)

Who is Satan? The Bible's book of *Genesis* describes the creation of the first humans, Adam and Eve. God instructs them not to eat the 'fruit of the tree of knowledge of good and evil' (the apple). Soon, God's rival, Lucifer (a.k.a Satan), appearing as a snake, tempts Eve to disobey. She bites the apple and thus has to quit Paradise.

> Allah
> There is no compulsion in religion; truly the right way
> Has become clearly distinct from error; therefore,
> Whoever disbelieves in the Shaitan and believes in Allah
> He indeed has laid hold on the foremost handle....
> ~ The Koran, *Surah 2, Section 34, Verse 256*

Fast forward to around the birth of Christ, or the reign of Augustus Caesar, and we find several of the world's tribes creating explanations for sin. Some began to worship a god of sin. Some Christians argued that Lucifer will eventually come out on top.

The name 'Lucifer' comes from Latin *lux*, light, and *fero*, bear, and thus means light-bearer. In the Middle Ages we find secret groups treating Lucifer as the man-in-charge. Why the secrecy? Satanists generally twist the natural temptations into virtues, demonstrating that those who succumb to these "virtues" are the elect. Of course, it has always been easy to justify behaviors (especially profitable ones) by saying that the instructions came from a Higher Being.

Anyone researching World Government today finds frequent allusion to the occult. Around the early twentieth century there were expositors such as Aleister Crowley (British Intelligence agent who promoted himself as "the most evil man in the world"), Madame Blavatsky of the Theosophical Society, and Alice Bailey.

Were they true believers? I doubt it. I postulate that they were deployed by the cabal to paper over the social harm it caused, by insinuating that something mystical was afoot. As for Crowley's "sex magick," one can only admire his sense of humor. (For a less dismissive point of view, see David Livingstone's ancient-to-modern history of occultism, *Terrorism and the Illuminati*, 2009).

While the point of this chapter is to look at the biology underlying several traits, including devil-worship, I use the occasion to note that the First Amendment's separation of church and state has a way of preventing criticism of 'satanic religion.' Anton LaVey got tax exemption for his Church of Satan, and US Army Col. Michael Aquino, in 1975 founded the Temple of Set, which was listed in a 1978 handbook for chaplains in the military! Only in America!

A Pause To Categorize Pedophilia and SRA, Satanic Ritual Abuse. The activity known as (sexual) child abuse has unexpected tie-ins with mind control and with political corruption. I propose a practical division of pedophiles into three types. First, there's the ordinary type in which a man (or, occasionally, a woman) is drawn to children as sex objects. It appears to be an addiction, but people are generally not sympathetic with it, as they are with addictions to gambling or alcohol. In this category of pedophilia the victim may be a relative, and the perpetrator does not participate in related crimes such as pimping, trafficking, kidnapping, or the sale of kiddy porn.

In a second category, one or more of those crimes may be involved. Here, the 'pedophile' may not even have the addiction, but is in the business because it is lucrative or because he has been pressured into it. **Many police seem to be caught up in this way.**

A third category of pedophilia is Satanic Ritual Abuse. I did not think it was real when I first heard of it, but it has been practiced for centuries. You can find numerous reports of ritual torture ('ritual' in the sense that it is performed at a 'rite') at which Satan is invoked. A group may gather in someone's basement wearing black robes and holding candles while a victim, often a baby, is abused and/or ritually murdered. Ritual itself may put people in a trance. (This stuff protects the murderers, as people find victims' reports incredible.)

78

Many victims of childhood mind-control (Hersha: 2001) report that it was the SRA in which they saw other children killed – or were required to do the killing themselves – which traumatized them into splitting their personality. The experience is extremely painful, and as the child is not even allowed to scream, she 'runs away' by creating in her mind another personality. She then *dissociates*.

Her dissociative disorder is in fact the desired result, since one of her other selves – her 'alters' – can be accessed quite easily by a skilled manipulator. This controller then instructs the alter to perform criminal missions, without the real self ever knowing about it.

Perpetrators ('perps') would normally be arrested and tried, yet almost never are because they are in high positions. One may think it is against the mathematics of probability that many prestigious men molest kids, but it needn't be a factor of chance: **pedophiles are put into high positions** by the cabal -- for mutual protection. In Belgium, it took tens of thousands of citizens protesting in public to get the arrest of a pedophile who was murdering girls in his basement (McGowan 2003). Note: the case of Holly Greig, complete with a lawyer being gagged, is possibly distractive disinformation. I suggest *Dunblane Unburied* (Uttley 2006) as a model of documenttation of court-suppression of facts. Uttley shows, to my satisfaction, that the massacre of first graders connects to pedophile police!

Suggestion: Honor the Dead. Thousands of American children, particularly sons and daughters of military personnel, were cruelly experimented on by the CIA from 1950 to 1970 (see Ch 7.10) – *some after they had been deliberately softened up by pedophilia, torture, and SRA!*

Many universities took part. Unbelievably, so did many doctors. It's now our responsibility to help the living and remember the dead. Neil Brick runs a website SMART (Survivors of Mind Control and Ritual Trauma. In Canada, Lynne Moss-Sharman, author of *Go Boy!*, has assisted men in prison who are victims of menticide. The Sullivans, a couple that survived CIA cruelty, maintain a memorial garden near Chattanooga to honor many victims who did not make it.

4.6 ATTACHMENT, BELONGING, AND NATIONAL IDEALS

Our brains tend to take us in the direction of the universal. We can, at least in some circumstances, relate to all our fellow human beings. (Indeed one may feel 'high' doing that.) This may be why some, who don't understand the terrible price of globalization, think we shall inevitably move towards world citizenship. Ever since the

Greek philosophers, it has been accepted that our common humanity exists because we all have reasoning. Yet our reaching toward the humanity of all isn't based on rationality. It is a further development of our reaching out to our tribe. We need 'our own' and this is well provided for in our evolved psychological predispositions. One may love one's spouse as much as one's self. Most mothers love their newborn baby *more* than themselves. We even find that a request for money is hard to turn down if it comes from a niece or cousin. This is called 'kin altruism.'

Per Darwinian theory of evolution by natural selection (only the fittest survive) we shouldn't be inclined to help every member of the tribe. We should only help when it pays. (Genetically, it pays to help kin, and it pays to make favor-exchanging relationships.) However, it seems that, when we have enough to spare, or when people are in dire straits, there is a spillover of love to any member of the group.

An alternative evolutionary explanation for tribalism or ethnocentrism is that, in evolutionary time, fights with hostile humans were fights to the finish. They were Darwinian, so to speak: only those who won lived to produce descendants. If those winners won on the strength of their ability to 'love us/hate them,' this may account for some in-group solidarity, jingoism, racial prejudice, etc.

Jingo is defined in *The American Heritage Dictionary* (1976) as: One who vociferously supports his country, especially one who supports a belligerent foreign policy; a blatant patriot; chauvinist. From the refrain of a music-hall song sung by those in England ready to fight Russia in 1878: *We don't want to fight, but by jingo! if we do! We've got the ships, we've got the men, and we've got the money, too!*

Singing the Jingo song has the immediate physiological effect of uniting the team. It makes one feel proud of one's group. The goose-pimples-when-you-see-the-flag phenomenon is excellent evidence that we have an **innate capacity for identifying with our society and its needs**. All Dutch children learn about this hero:

The Leak in the Dike by Phoebe Cary (1824-1871)
...And the boy! He has seen the danger, / And, shouting a wild alarm, He forces back the weight of the sea/ With the strength of a single arm! ... [He thinks] how, when the night is over, /They must come and find him at last /But he never thinks he can leave the place/ Where duty holds him fast.

Other examples of inspirational nationalist statements are as follows:

> ~ Thucydides, *Pericles' Funeral Oration*, Trans. by B. Jowett
> [From our ancestors] we have received a free state.... And we our-
> selves assembled here today, who are still most of us in the vigor of
> life, have carried the work of improvement further ... a spirit of
> reverence pervades our public acts .... We have a peculiar power of
> thinking before we act, and of acting, too, whereas other men are
> courageous from ignorance but hesitate upon reflection. I would
> have you day by day fix your eyes on the greatness of Athens, until
> you become filled with the love of her; and when you are impressed
> by the spectacle of her glory, reflect that this empire has been ac-
> quired by men who knew their duty and had the courage to do it....

> from Bill Moyers, *The Secret Government* (1988) pp. 108-9
> It is hard to maintain a constitutional order. We are asked to be
> much more truthful, reasonable, just, and honorable than the letter
> of the law. The government, too, must live up to this exacting
> standard. The Constitution implies equality not only in the
> protection of the law of the least of us, but in the demands of its
> morality upon all of us, including those with the greatest power.

In my junior year at college, 1967-68, everyone was looking for a way to get in on the action – the action consisting of such things as having integrity and courage (I am not kidding). Role models at that time were Rev. Martin Luther King, Jr. and the man who had been US Attorney General before JFK died – namely, his brother Robert.

Public speeches were very stirring and did not sound like they had come out of a speech-dispensing machine. Encouragement to work for the poor was so normal that graduating from law school was practically synonymous with working *pro bono* for human rights. Doctors and priests could be counted on to participate in anti-war rallies. People enjoyed Ralph Nader's consumer-rights ideas.

Unfortunately in the Seventies 'political correctness' started to replace spontaneity, as far as attachment to the nation was con-cerned. In the Eighties 'individualism' reasserted itself. (The U.K.'s Margaret Thatcher informed us "There is no society.") By the Nine-ties, various Rupert Murdochs had re-designed mass media: different worldviews were parceled out to particular groups instead of all of us watching the same channels and reading the same paper.

4.7 WAR-MAKING AND GENOCIDE

Since 'three three' (Art. III, Sec 3) of the Constitution associates treason with 'levying war,' let us inspect the war-making instinct. In evolutionary terms it is both a *form of predation* and a form of defending the life of one's tribe. In cave-man days it must have been normal for one group of humans to regard other groups of humans as their predators who may attack them. Two tribes in one territory can be peaceful, but only if there are sufficient resources.

Could war break out on the basis of pride? Does one group go at another because it feels insulted? Since we know that a modern gang of boys may be easily provoked into action on that basis, the answer is probably yes. But if, in early days, a fight started over name-calling, it was probably the last straw — more than likely a situation of competition for resources had been brewing for some time. (Note: Women are typically one of the 'resources' contended for.)

Useful information comes to us from sociobiology. Richard Wrangham and Dale Peterson note in *Demonic Males* (1996) that in only a few species do animals kill adult members of their own species. Rivalry may lead to two individuals duking it out, but the winner would not gain much by killing the rival. (It suffices that he establish his superiority.) However, a few species have 'gangs' that knock off their rivals *as a group*. Spotted hyenas, chimpanzees, and honeypot ants have such gangs.

Spotted hyenas, in which the warriors are female, appear to size up the neighboring population. When one's group can see that it is numerically superior, it goes on the attack. It does so, the authors say (relying on Hans Kruuk, *The Spotted Hyena,* 1972), simply **because it pays.** The bigger group will not suffer many casualties, and will win two prizes: the territory of the decimated group, and freedom from the daily bother of small economic rivalry.

We were taught that there was only one major genocide in history, the one in Germany, and that it was fueled by a philosophy of racial purity. That is wrong; **genocide is commonplace** in the human species. Of course that statement doesn't mean we should give vent to our genocidal tendencies: many of society's rules and values have everything to do with suppressing instincts.

Even Hitler's philosophy of racial purity was not essential for stimulating genocide. Just think how the American settlers used 'Manifest Destiny' to justify the brutal extermination of native tribes. MD meant that our 'destiny' was manifest, i.e. it was plain to see, that our country would stretch from the ocean on which we arrived – the Atlantic – to the other ocean, the Pacific. Another 'MD,' the Monroe Doctrine, does an equally succinct job of glorifying the unglorifiable by saying that North America is the guardian of South America. **Our guardianship is even at this moment genocidal.**

Most genocides are economically motivated. The West's desire for resources has recently caused Iraq and Afghanistan to experience war. Africa is suffering for apparently the same reason: people in the Congo and Sudan have recently died by the millions in 'civil war.' Zimbabwe has been the trial area for use of the kick-them-off-the-land approach, while in So. Africa, Haiti, and Brazil the AIDS genocide has brought death to millions (and has orphaned millions).

Now consider Thomas Barnett's 2004 book, *The Pentagon's New Map*. The first page is an actual world map on which many nations appear as blanks. He politely refers to the 'core' countries – Europe, North America, China, Russia, etc., and the 'gap' countries. The latter 'won't be able to make it.' They include most South American countries, many South Asian nations other than India, and all of the Middle East. (Yes *all*; Israel will not survive.) Barnett worked on his scheme as part of a project for Cantor Fitzgerald, Inc., a global financial services provider' **with offices onsite at the Pentagon**.

Was Barnett forced to come up with this? He makes frequent mention of the plight of his little daughter who, from the age of two months, has had an extremely rare disease. Perhaps her survival will depend on Dad's cooperating with the powers that be?

Today we seem to be under threat of a worldwide (!) genocide from the cabal. They have openly stated a depopulation policy while cloaking their rationale in sensible talk about the earth's limits. These individuals, who have in mind to control 'every corner of the globe,' need to keep numbers down *for their own convenience.*

Naturally I condemn these horrific plans. We citizens must act swiftly against any plans to commit genocide anywhere. Humans are not spotted hyenas. We rise above genes in many ways. Obviously it is every civilized person's responsibility to oppose genocide.

At the same time, though, it should be emphasized that there *is* a population problem. **Good leaders will address this.** During the lifetime of my Dad (1899-1981) world population *tripled*. The current number of souls is about 7 billion. This is disastrous. The nations that leave a big ecological footprint are the most worrying. They not only take more resources and pollute, they strain Nature's services.

In the animal kingdom, population crashes occur every now and then when a species finds its food supply cut back. It may result from bad weather, destruction of its habitat, encroachment by a rival species, or mere overpopulation. I believe that ecologists know that humans are courting a crash. (See *Scientific American,* 9/1976 edition).

Suggestion: We need a moratorium on human breeding. It is far more humane to prevent an increase of population than to offer early death as the 'solution.' Societies are capable of much better than that! So what if it is a difficult thing for people to give up their reproductive rights? China did it by coercion but no one has even tried yet to reason people into it. **And who made up the rule** that if something is difficult we should avoid thinking about it?

Recently a speech by a biologist, Eric Pianka, was sensationalized, with articles on the Net indicating that he wanted everybody to be killed off. What he actually said, however, was reasonable:

Prof Eric Pianka. We are going to have to make some tough decisions now and live extremely frugally if we want civilizations and humanity to have any chance of enduring long into the future. Failure to take action now could well result in our extinction or near extinction as well as the loss of our civilizations, cultures, and human knowledge. The very future of humanity itself is at stake!

First, and foremost, we must get out of denial and recognize that Earth simply cannot support many billions of people, at least not in the lifestyles we would all like to live. There is a trade off between quantity and quality. This planet might be able to support perhaps as many as half a billion people who could live a sustainable life in relative comfort. Human populations must be greatly diminished, and as quickly as possible to limit further environmental damage.

~ Speech as award recipient, Texas Academy of Science, 3/2006

Finally, in this section on genocide, 'race' needs to be discussed. I will try to keep a straight face talking about such things, but I do not believe in race. It took me till about the age of 48 to wake up to this. The joke is that that there cannot be separate kinds of humans. People are all the same. They have the same needs, the same hopes.

Sure there are personality differences within any group, and it is to be expected that particular personality types may be drawn out more by one culture than another. But rarely does a group have a trait that other groups completely lack.

Sociobiologist Pierre van den Berghe argues persuasively in *The Ethnic Phenomenon* (1981) that we do not have a genetic drive to hate or persecute the out-group. If we treat them cruelly, he says, it is because the stranger is excluded from the protection we give our own. Foreigners don't come under our natural umbrella of altruism.

'Black-white relations' in the US have been manipulated for over a century with the direct objective of stirring Americans up against Americans. Why has there been a calculated effort to keep groups apart and afraid of one another? **To make sure the natural feeling of unity can't form among us**, else we'd be strong in fighting our true enemy, the traitors within!

Divide-and-rule is also applied within the African-American population itself. Recall that the FBI was *helping* Malcolm X when it looked like he was harming black unity, but, according to his autobiography, the FBI opposed him as soon as he moved in the direction of unifying the brethren. The desire of the great singer Paul Robeson (his undoing) was to unite *the workers of America and the workers of the Soviet Union!* What could he have been thinking!

Possibly the put-downs of blacks in the US are also part of the plan to assure Americans that it is OK to wipe out the inhabitants of Africa, as that continent is so resource-rich. Recently, the biologist James Watson, who co-discovered DNA, claimed that the idea "that equal powers of reasoning were shared across racial groups was a delusion." (*The Independent*, UK, 17 Oct 2007). He then apologized!

To add to our collection of Umberto Eco-style decoding rules, here is one to help answer the question "When is a war motivated by economic genocide?" The ⌐ rule is as follows: Whenever the media and academia say that two peoples are fighting each other for racial, or ideological reasons, *their theories* are coverup. It's rivalry by outsiders who covet their resources. Call it the Huntington rule.

4.8 LEADERSHIP (AS DISTINCT FROM HIERARCHY)

Think about this interesting question for a moment: in animal species that live in groups (a herd of elephant, a school of fish) what is the best ratio of leaders to led? And how do the led know which leader to turn to for direction? Also, what makes a leader, a leader?

In a letter to *Nature* (Vol. 433) dated 3 Feb 2005, biologists from Princeton, Oxford, Leeds, and Bristol reported that different factors in different species make for leadership. These include age or dominance, possession of information – such as traveling routes for migratory birds – and an inherited propensity to lead.

Among humans, some individuals are born bossy, or born with 'vision,' or born with a sense of responsibility for the fate of the group. (That, of course can be perfectly selfish; one who invests in improving her society will then enjoy that improvement.) Age counts, too, as does 'possession of information.' Personality traits such as self-confidence, trustworthiness, and decisiveness can bring a person from obscurity to the pinnacle of his school or her nation.

Leadership can be distinguished from ambition – though, as Machiavelli showed 500 years ago, ambition alone can win a man a high position – and top-grade ruthlessness will virtually guarantee it.

To rise in a human hierarchy is something we all are 'wired' for. And we all have wiring for submitting to those above us. Playing the deferential role *and* the superior role is part of everyone's life. A person might hold a high rank in his profession but rank low rank in his clan, or be high in her club, but humble outside of it.

Today we need leaders and the lack of them is making us all feel very vulnerable. (I believe one reason for the dearth of leaders is that young promising individuals are **picked off** – yes, killed or disabled by the cabal, but I have no proof.) In any case, without resorting to such extreme measures, the cabal can purge leaders from our midst by co-opting them. Many people are glad to receive what looks like a high position – even in name only. A fat paycheck? Even better.

Another thing is that companies and governments have become so big and so standardized that the managers only get to pass on the instructions from on high. They don't develop a reputation as someone who can be relied on in all areas thanks to being leader-like. In his 1903 book *Political Parties*, Robert Michels wrote "Who says organization says oligarchy." We can add: "Who says oligarchy says perverted culture." The few at the top (*olig-archy* means 'rule by the few') become more and more preoccupied with rule itself and can't add anything to the culture. Worse, they obstruct the natural accidental development of culture, forever snuffing out bright local ideas.

Suggestion: Think of the person you would go to in a crisis. Go to her now, and ask if she would please put out her shingle as a leader.

A Pause To Talk about the 'Rational Mind' and Hypnosis. I'm no brain surgeon, and aspire only to provide some thoughts on why our brains seem to be missing . Even Ch 6, concerning menticide, will not look inside the brain. However, before tackling the issue of deceit, below, it behooves us to try to envision non-rational activity.

86

Picture yourself and your dog lying down asleep. There are a lot of things going on in both of you that require no conscious intervention. The lungs take in oxygen, the protein that you consumed goes to build new tissue, the body thermostat keeps you warm. That's the autonomic system; it never needs the cerebrum – the 'upper' part of the brain that enables conscious decision-making.

Both you and the dog then happen to be awakened by, say, thirst. Off to the kitchen go you and the dog, each taking a drink – him from his bowl and you from a glass. Voluntary muscles drove the legs of both you and the dog. Filling the glass with water requires your knowing how the tap works, but it doesn't take much cognition. You have performed the drink routine for years so it's 'second nature'. Even **voluntary action can bypass the cerebrum**.

Psychologist Paul Verdier notes that a hypnotist gets "A" to obey an instruction while A's cerebral cortex is switched off. Hence, the hypnotist can send instructions for voluntary movements directly to the sub-cortical brain. These will be carried out instantly because A is not using the part of the brain, the cerebral cortex (the folded surface of the brain) that considers what to do. By contrast, data coming to us through the five senses are acted on *only after we spend time* processing them (including by comparing them to past experience and by applying value choices). Any motor response is prevented until we process all that. **The cerebral cortex always delays, i.e., inhibits, the motor response**. Under hypnosis, that inhibitory function is deactivated. Your cerebrum *doesn't* block direct connections between incoming and outgoing. You 'obey.'

So how does the hypnotist get you to that point? Assuming he has not used sodium amytal, or some newer method, he has got you to deactivate the cortical block simply by having you use either the *visceral sense* system or the *muscles sense* system. It would not be ethical for him to employ the visceral sense system, but let's say you have given permission. He need only create shock in you. ("Your sister has just been murdered," or "You have just won the sweepstakes," or "Nuclear bombs are raining down on America.")

As soon as your viscera (guts) react, their own senses do what evolution prepared them to do – by sending messages to the autonomic system. Your heart beats faster, thanks to adrenalin, you sweat, you may become oblivious of your environment, and **you can't think.** Because your cortical block is off, the hypnotist could then instruct you, in a calm, helpful tone, to do anything -- and you would do it. It seems odd that his *words* can pass the cortex and go right to your lower brain, since human language is a 'higher' development of the brain. But words *can* be heard in the lower brain.

In any case, that shock method is rarely used by hypnotists. (It is used in torture; see Appendix J). For our purposes it is enough to say that when a hypnotist asks you to raise your hand, or look above eye-level at his watch, the muscles you use (in your arm or eyelids) may cause your cortex, and with it your memory-storer – to switch off. Thus you become, temporarily, a robot, or a slave, and you will be unable to remember later what you did for your 'master.'

Non-memorizing also occurred when you poured that tap water. Or when you lock the door upon leaving the house. Later you worry because you don't remember if you locked up. When an action is second nature, it's sub-cerebral and usually you don't 'memorize' it.

For our later discussion of menticide, please keep in mind the slavishness of the hypnotized subject and the fact that **words can bypass the thinking brain**. (Dogs respond to words, don't they?)

4.9 DECEITFULNESS

The topics in this chapter run in positive-negative order: avarice followed the topic of love, genocide followed attachment and ideals, devil worship followed love of life, and now, to follow leadership, we have 'deceitfulness.' Certainly the human habit of deceiving is not all negative. When I apply lipstick I am trying to fool everyone, including myself, about my true age and beauty, and that's just fine!

That said, in Part Two we are endeavoring to find out why our brains are letting us down. Like members of some other species, we are deceivers. When X wants something from Y she can command or cajole Y to give it to her, or she can get it by lying to Y. (Animals can tell lies without language.) It is so normal to get one's way by lying that everyone understands it and adjusts for it. When your child says she needs to use the computer all weekend for 'home-work' you know she is up to something of a non-academic nature.

If our brains are letting us down today it is not because we are fooled -- for example about 9/11. A critical mass of Americans now sees that 9/11 was an inside job. So it must be **self-deception** that is preventing us from prosecuting those who demolished the towers. We subconsciously calculate that it's safer to keep a lid on things.

Granted, the big, big lie of the past hundred years, as to who really runs things, kept us genuinely in the dark. But many who now have access to the facts push those facts away **subconsciously**. The reader of this book, and the author, are, of course, exceptions. We know that the **subconscious is not to be relied on**. Our subconscious serves us well much of the time; think how cleverly it evaluates personal relationships – that's good animal wisdom! But we give subconscious inklings the heave-ho in favor of reasoning, as a scientist dumps superstitions when experiments invalidate them.

Back to the analysis of lying. As animals we lie for two purposes -- **to puff ourselves up, and to get goods.** Note that the puff-up deception category can be lumped *into* the get-goods category (as looking big or nice may get you more goods). Thus all lies are really for the purposes of 'getting!' Another type of lie is *giving false leads to your rival*, but that, too is for 'getting goods.' Note that humans often appear to make power grabs just for the sake of it, but of course the evolutionary point of increasing one's power is to get goods.

I can think of **only one other reason** to deceive, and it is probably restricted to humans and chimpanzees: **we lie to evade blame**. Granted, when one successfully hides one's blame, one lives another day to pursue goods-getting. But it seems worthwhile heuristically to say that blame-evading is a major activity for its own sake. Every human dreads punishment, and the emotion of shame is painful.

This can help us recognize the **real function of truth-seeking**. It's an attempt to restore balance between individuals in a situation of palpable unfairness. People can tolerate a social ladder and unequal exchange of goods. But a very unbalanced world 'gets to you.' Truth-seeking erupts! Society starts to crack down on its predators.

Today's massive disinformation industry is all about hiding the blame of cabal members – both so they can continue grabbing goods, and so they never have to face court. Think of all the fancy-footwork involved in hiding their guilt, even unto controlling the writing of history textbooks so that the real story doesn't come out. But it *has* now come out and they will face court. (Or face a mob!)

Here is a story that shows how well suited the English language is for dodging acknowledgement of guilt even when the evidence is rock-solid. Nathan Rothschild 'helped end the slave trade' by lending the British government money to pay compensation to slave owners. The *Financial Times* recently stated that his loan was so massive that it "dwarfs today's efforts to shore up financial institutions"!! *FT.com* also said that a journalist discovered that Nathan 'owned' (as collateral) 88 slaves in Antigua, and when the client defaulted, Nathan applied for compensation himself under the scheme:

Commenting on the assertion that NM Rothschild made a claim as a mortgagee of slaves under the compensation system, a Rothschild bank spokesman noted: "Nathan Mayer Rothschild was a well-known and prominent campaigner for equality and civil liberties in his day. His circle of friends included many like-minded individuals who would have been influential opinion-formers of the time. Against this background, these allegations appear inconsistent and misrepresent the ethos of the man and his business."
~ Carola Hoyos, "Paper Trail Loosens Shackles on Hidden Past," *Financial Times,* June 26, 2009   (also at ft.com)

4.10 WHAT TO DO? WORK WITH NATURE!

There is nothing more self-genocidal than deliberately wrecking the ecosystem. Don't believe anyone who says we can repair it later. **Of course we cannot repair such a thing!** We are acting in mistaken ways. We desire something, such as wealth or security, and stupidly end up making terminator seeds. We 'eat the seed corn.'

To make sensible plans for society nowadays means being realistic about our Nature *and* also about the world we have set up *via our institutions and beliefs.* The registering of patents is such an institution. The republic that we created in 1776 is also one. We use institutions for reasoning and sensibility. There's no need to panic:

The pilgrims' plan to cross the ocean had been full of worry: "persons worne out with age and travile could never be able to endure [the long voyage] ...And the miseries of the land which they should be exposed unto would be hard and lickly to utterly ruinate them. For ther they should be liable to famines and nakedness.... The chang of aire, diate and drinking of water, would infect their bodies with sore sickness and greevous diseases..."   quoted by Daniel Boorstin in *The Americans, the Democratic Experience* (1974)

In place of panicking we could be urging imaginative people to get on the case. Being assertive about the correct action to take for Earth, instead of worrying about the bad usage now being made of it, may make the cabal's misbehavior seem much less daunting.

We also need to admit that our vulnerability is based on a true demographic problem. Because we are not hunter-gatherers we cannot control our individual supply of food, and there are far more **jobseekers** than there are jobs. This will result in chaos and cruelty, but can be headed off by intelligently addressing the need to share.

List 4a.   **Universal Social Behaviors**

Inter-personal Acts Found in Every Culture:

Age statuses
Attachment
Childhood fear of strangers
Coalitions
Collective identities
Conflict
Cooperation
Coyness display
Customary greetings
Dominance/Submission
Empathy
Envy
Ethnocentrism
Family (or household)
Food sharing

Gift giving
Gossip
Groups that are not based
  on family
Healing the sick (or
  attempting to)
Hospitality
In-group, bias in favor of
Judging others
Kin, close distinguished
  from distant
Language employed to
  manipulate others

**Language employed to
  misinform or mislead**
Leaders
Males dominate public and
  political realm
Males more prone to lethal
  violence
Promises
Proper names
Property
Rape
Rape proscribed
Reciprocity, negative
(revenge, retaliation)
**Resistance to dominance
  and to abuse of power**
Self-image, awareness of
  (concern for what others
  think)
Sexual attractiveness
Sexual jealousy
Sexual modesty
**Socialization expected
  from senior kin**
Statuses, ascribed, achieved
Territoriality
Tickling
Trade
Visiting

Note: Items are of interest to the book at hand are bolded.

SOURCE: Items culled from Donald E. Brown's list of human universals, compiled in 1991, quoted in Steven Pinker, *The Blank Slate: The Modern Denial of Human Nature* (2003)

List 4b.   Banks with Breathtaking Audacity

EXIM -- export-import bank (gives US-backed financing to construction firms)
"Kearns was echoing the [Bechtel] refrain 'for the US to be involved in as many nuclear plants as possible.' [When a loan to Bechtel] pushed the bank over the $1 billion threshold ... Kearns threw a party to celebrate. At the Bank's expense [i.e., the taxpayers' expense], 150 of the world's top energy officials were flown to Washington for a black-tie dinner presided over by Vice President Spiro Agnew."
        ~ Layton McCartney, *Friends in High Places* (1989) p. 160

SILVERADO (one of many Saving and Loans that failed) "... financial disaster... happened quietly, secretly... [we failed to see the] massive transfer of wealth from the American taxpayer to a select group of extremely rich, powerful people [who had] symbiotic relationships to the Mafia and the CIA, and to the two [Texans, former] President Bush and Senator Lloyd Bentsen."
        ~ Pete Brewton, *The Mafia, CIA, and George Bush* (1992) p. 1

FEDERAL RESERVE SYSTEM "On Dec. 15, 1911, Congressman Lindbergh rose before the House of Representatives and took careful aim: 'The Aldrich Plan is the Wall Street Plan. It is a broad challenge to government by the champion of the Money Trust. It means another panic, if necessary, to intimidate the people."
        ~ G. Edward Griffin, *The Creature from Jekyll Island* (1994) p. 448

NUGAN HAND bank (in Australia, run by CIA's Wm. Colby)
"Lernoux says the bank controlled the $100 million "Mr Asia" heroin syndicate which arranged a number of contract murders.... In Saudi Arabia Nugan Hand handled the large outlays of Bechtel Corp. ...The Australian Federal Bureau of Narcotics refused to investigate [Nugan Hands drugs, and then, under increased public pressure] the Bureau disbanded in 1979!"
        ~ Eustace Mullins, *World Order: A Study in the The Hegemony of Parasitism* (1985) p. 123

List 4c.   The Thrust of the British Empire
(It's Easier To See UK's Imperialism Than Our Own:)

Mark Curtis, in *Web of Deceit (2003)* lists actions of Britain as:

1948 Begins 12-year war in **Malaysia** to defend rubber industry

1952 Establishes concentration camps in **Kenya;** 150,000 die

1956 Invades **Egypt**, tries to assassinate pan-Arab leader Nasser

1957 Bombs villages in **Oman** to support a repressive regime

1958 Fabricates a coup scenario in **Jordan** to justify intervention

1961 Enters **Kuwait** by fabricating threat of Iraqi invasion there

1962 MI6 and SAS work covertly in **North Yemen;** 200,000 die

1965 Secretly aids **Indonesian** Army in its slaughter of 100,000

1968 Removes the population of **Diego Garcia**, Chagos Islands

1986 MI6 gives **Afghanistan** rebels shoulder-launched missiles

1991 With US, begins bombing **Iraq** re its invasion of Kuwait

1994 During genocide in **Rwanda**, reduces UN forces there

1996 Trains **Saudi Arabia's** Nat'l. Guard to protect Saudi royals

1996 Backs assassination/coup attempt against **Libya's** Qadafi

1999 With NATO, bombs **Yugoslavia,** stimulating genocide

During the same 50 years the US intervened in Iran, Guatemala, Cuba, Indonesia, Vietnam, Dominican Republic, Laos, Cambodia, Chile, Angola, Grenada, El Salvador, Nicaragua, Jamaica, Panama, Haiti, Iraq, etc. In no case was the motive 'to help the people.' Today we are in Afghanistan, Colombia, Sudan, and many other places that US citizens are not told about.

Chapter 5   The Man from Snowy River

There was movement at the station, for the word had passed around
That the colt from Old Regret had got away   And had joined the wild
bush horses; He was worth a thousand pound,   So all the cracks had
gathered to the fray....   There was Harrison who made his pile
When pardon won the Cup, the old man with his hair as white as snow,
But few could ride beside him when his blood was fairly up,
He would go wherever horse and man could go.
And Clancy of the Overflow came down to lend a hand,
No better horseman ever held the reins;
For never horse could throw him while the saddle-girths would stand,
He learnt to ride while droving on the plains....

> And one there was, a stripling [you may] doubt his power to stay,
> And the old man said, "That horse will never do
> For a long and tiring gallop -- lad, you'd better stop away,
> Those hills are far too rough for such as you."

[but Clancy said] "He hails from Snowy River, up by Kosciusko's side,
Where the hills are twice as steep and twice as rough,
Where a horse's hoofs strike firelight from the flint stones every stride,
The man that holds his own is good enough."

> So he went [and at the] summit, even Clancy took a pull,
> It well might make the boldest hold their breath,
> The wild hop scrub grew thickly, and the hidden ground was full
> Of wombat holes, and any slip was death....

And the man from Snowy River never shifted in his seat --
It was grand to see that mountain horseman ride....
He sent the flint stones flying, but the pony kept his feet,
He cleared the fallen timber in his stride.

> Then they lost him for a moment, where two mountain gullies met
> In the ranges, but a final glimpse reveals
> On a dim and distant hillside the wild horses racing yet,
> With the man from Snowy River at their heels....

And he ran them single-handed till their sides were white with foam.
He followed like a bloodhound on their track,
Till they halted cowed and beaten, then he turned their heads for home
And alone and unassisted brought them back....And down by Kosciu-
sko, where the pine-clad ridges raise   Their torn and rugged battlements
on high...   The man from Snowy River is a household word today
And the stockmen tell the story of his ride.

-- Banjo Paterson, 1886

5 Masculinity

And how we burned in the camps later, thinking: What would things
have been like if every Security operative, when he went out at night to
make an arrest, had been uncertain whether he would return alive... Or
what about the Black Maria sitting out there on the street with one
lonely chauffeur – what if it had been driven off or its tires spiked?
– Aleksandr Solzhenitsyn, *The Gulag Archipelago, Vol. I*

His brow is wet with honest sweat,
He earns whate'er he can
And he looks the whole world in the face,
For he owes not any man.
– Henry Wadsworth Longfellow, *The Village Blacksmith*

5.1 MASONS AND OTHERS, E.G., SKULL AND BONES

When anthropologists first started to do field research in the 19th
century they found that some social institutions are universal – e.g.,
marriage, law, religion, rites of passage, and groups whose
membership is exclusively male. Some such groups keep secrets
from the women and children but are not 'secret societies.' Later in
history, men developed clubs whose members promise not to divulge
the club's business, and may even deny its existence.

This section is about two such groups. One officially dates its
start to 1717 as the Freemasons, in London, only partly related to the
guild of stone-workers (masons) that worked in many European
cities in the Middle Ages (i.e., 1100-1500). The other is The Order of
Skull and Bones, whose origins can be traced to Germany.

Assume that up-and-coming individuals in England got word of
the new Masonic organization. On inquiring, they would have been
impressed by the 'brochure' claiming, in so many words, "Join us and
you will have incredibly good support; stay away and you will never
reach a high position in your career. We have our hand in every
important endeavor...." After a while, members' sons are
automatically invited, and talent scouts look around to recruit non-
sons. Before you know it, the 'brochure's' prophecy has come true.

95

Pay no heed to the Freemasons' claim to be nonpolitical. It is a ridiculous claim – the top men in all walks of life do not allow simply anybody to make the laws and choose the rulers. For example, in 1910 the Masons created a republic in Portugal:

In 1907 a grand master, Magalhaes Lima, went to Paris and gave in the lodges a lecture series called "Portugal, the Overthrow of the Monarchy and the Need of a Republican Form of Government." Some weeks later King Carlos and his eldest son were assassinated....
The mason Furnement said at the sitting of 12th February 1911: "In a few hours the throne was brought down, the people triumphed, and the republic was proclaimed. ... **We knew the marvelous organization of our Portuguese brothers, their ceaseless zeal. We possessed the secret of that glorious event.**"
[emphasis added]

~ *Bulletin du G: O de Belgique 5910*, 1910, quoted in Vicomte Leon de Poncins, *Freemasonry & Judaism* (undated, reprinted 1994) pp. 60-61

What was done by Freemasons in Portugal – and in many other places: Hungary, Italy, Turkey – appears to have been done in 1776 on another continent. The date was July 4th. Many of the signers of the Declaration of Independence were Freemasons. As early as 1734 Benjamin Franklin was a Mason – indeed he formed his own group, the Leather Apron Society, but it fizzled out.

Later, when the site of the federal government was chosen to be Washington DC, that city was laid out by Pierre Charles L'Enfant in the shape of a square and compass, the sign of the Mason's craft. In a startling book called *Lost Symbols?* (2009), David Ovason goes up and down the streets of our capital city identifying many occult Masonic symbols, especially zodiacs. (The same could be done in Tel Aviv: Rothschild funded the parliament building, the Knesset, which is decorated with occult art, including the all-seeing eye.)

1776 was also the year in which, on May 1st, Adam Weishaupt in Bavaria created the Perfectibilist Society, which was soon renamed the 'Illuminati.' It is speculated nowadays that the meetings of the higher-degree Masons were a standard venue for the Illuminists. The 'Blue Lodges' – where apprentices, companions, and masters meet – may know nothing of what goes on upstairs, so one has to be careful not to blame Masons, as such, for the Illuminist program. (I add: the same is true of Jesuits, very few of whom are 'in it deep.')

Our Great Republic is great and deserves our protection. Since it appears today that some secret society is planning our destruction, **we had better be aware of the way in which one famous group**, the Masons, **has been able to run governments.**

Now to the other group, Skull and Bones, a secretive fraternity at Yale University. It calls itself "The Order" and is a branch of a German society that was brought across the Atlantic by William Huntington Russell, scion of America's premier opium-trading company of the day (significant, eh?). The group appears to use occult practices and symbols, and has had tremendous power in America.

In 1986 historian Antony Sutton published *America's Secret Establishment* in which he theorizes that such groups as the CFR and the Trilateral Commission are merely the outer circle, while **Skull and Bones is the inner core**. He believes that the world is run by a coalition of secret societies and that The Order, based at Yale, is one part of it, while England's Roundtable inner core, 'The Group,' based at Oxford, is another.

> And on their breasts they wear a sign
> That tells their race and name
> It is the ghastly badge of death
> And from his kingdom came
> The son of Satan, son of sin
> The enemy of man."
> (so said an editor of *The Iconoclast* at Yale in the 1870s, about
> The Order of Skull and Bones) ~ quoted by Antony Sutton,
> *America's Secret Establishment* (2002) p. 22

Each year 15 seniors at Yale are 'tapped' for membership. Once they join, they may end up as Wall Street **investment bankers or partners in the big law firms**. They may also end up marrying daughters of The Order. Sutton found that, of the nearly three thousand Bonesmen, *only twenty families* account for the most power, and that these are mainly families that settled in New England in the 1600s! He found that 2% of The Order joins the Protestant clergy.

Bonesmen who have played major roles in American foreign-policy-making, while serving as government officials, include: Pres Wm Howard Taft, Senator Prescott Bush, his son Pres George H.W. Bush and grandson Pres G. W. Bush, Cabinet members McGeorge Bundy, Robert Lovett, Henry Stimson, Jock Whitney, Averell Harriman, and Winston Lord (a president of the CFR).

5.2 GUIDE TO THIS CHAPTER – *MASCULINITY*

This chapter covers things that tend to be in 'the male preserve.' 5.3 is about the military. 5.4 sketches Machiavelli's prince. 5.5 deals with *Vive la difference!* 5.6 covers the ruling on federal police power in the *Morrison* case. 'Manchurian candidates' (mind-controlled assassins) are described in 5.7, and mutiny in 5.8, while 5.9 is about mafias. The answer to 5.10's What To Do? is: "Men, defend us!" Appendices that may affect testosterone levels are: G, L, M, and N.

5.3 THE MILITARY OF THE UNITED STATES

Since 1789, when the Constitution came into effect, two branches of government have shared the 'war powers' – as they are called. The president's war power derives solely from Article II, Section 2 of the Constitution which says: <u>The President shall be Commander in Chief of the Army and Navy of the United States, and of the Militia of the several States, when called into the actual service of the United States.</u> It is reasonable to conclude that he can make decisions about weapons, the location of bases, and the promotion or demotion of officers.

If we are in war, our president can make decisions (with help of experts, naturally) about strategy and tactics in the battlefield. In another of his presidential capacities, that of conducting foreign relations, he may conjure up alliances with other nations, but a two-thirds ratification by the Senate is required for a treaty of alliance.

That said, most of the US military power lies with the legislative branch. Four of Congress's 18 powers concern the military. (See Appendix Q of this book for all of Congress's powers.) The four are:

[11] <u>To declare War, grant Letters of Marque and Reprisal, and make Rules concerning Captures on Land and Water.</u> In other words, we don't go to war without our elected representatives say-so, and we don't even commit acts of retaliation – 'reprisal' – against another nation without that say-so. *(Note: a letter of marque is a permit to kill);*

[12] <u>To raise and support Armies, but no Appropriation of Money to that Use shall be for a longer Term than two Years;</u>

13] <u>To provide and maintain a Navy</u> [later this included Marines];

[14] <u>To make Rules for the Government and Regulation of the land and naval Forces.</u>

The US Military (which also encompasses the Canadian Royal Air Force via NORAD) is divided into commands, known as *COM's*. PACCOM is our command in the Pacific and Asia. NORTHCOM and SOUTHCOM are for the Americas, EUCOM is for Europe, and CENTCOM (based in Florida) is for the Middle East. Strategic command, STRATCOM, at Offut Air Force Base, Omaha NE, used to be for nuclear weapons but now includes space-based weapons.

In 2005 a change was made to each name by adding 'US,' hence they are now called USPACCOM, USCENTCOM, etc. Perhaps it became too obvious that it is really an arm of World Government? In 2007 a new one was created: USAFRICOM. (Recall Thomas Barnett's book *The Pentagon's New Map*, that suggests Africa is slated to 'disappear.') As no African country has yet shown willingness to host this new COM, it is headquartered in Stuttgart, Germany.

Three current features of our Army not authorized by the Constitution (and against the thrust of the parchment as a whole) are:

1. The use of mercenaries: This has been lowering troop morale, as regular soldiers are aware that privatized forces get much higher pay.

2. "Mixed militaries," such as the participation in NATO, and

3. Pentagon's practice of establishing Special Operations Groups. These are warriors on clandestine missions, such as assassination detail. (As noted above, letters of marque are a Congressional not an executive power.) **The very existence of SOGs tells us that someone is running a secret government within our nation.**

5.4 MACHIAVELLIANISM IS NOT APPROPRIATE FOR THE US

See the frontispiece of Ch 2 above, for Machiavelli's famous idea of how to be the Smartest Guy in town. Want to become a senator? Why bother to campaign and await election – you can get all that by killing a bunch of senators – as did Agathocles, one of Machiavelli's heroes, and grab power wholesale.

Every male mammal has within him the notion of becoming the alpha. In some species, such as the fur seal, the alpha enjoys a local monopoly on mating; thus the genes of this aggressive male get inherited by every member of the next generation.

In the US there must be a certain number of alpha-gotta-be's who find our Republic frustrating. However, there must be millions of males who are pleased to know that our culture does not support an Agathocles-style takeover, thus they need never worry about being slain by an Agathocles. Also, they need not be resentful about a small number of top dogs monopolizing the females.

> Males have evolved to possess strong appetites for power because with extraordinary power males can achieve extraordinary reproduction..... Harems of at least several hundred women have been the norm for the emperors of all major civilizations: Aztec, Babylonian ... Indian, and Roman. During the golden age of Chinese civilization from 618 to 907 A.D., so many women lived in the emperor's seraglio that meticulous bookkeeping was needed to keep track of menstrual cycles.... The date of a concubine's coupling with the emperor would be stamped on her arm in indelible ink: her ticket to an imperial inheritance should she give birth nine months later. It's probably fair to say that men with absolute power have routinely fathered several hundred children – rather in the manner of a successful bull elephant seal.
>
> ~ Wrangham and Peterson, *Demonic Males* (1996) p. 234

One person who seems not to have picked up on this is Michael Ledeen, a member of the American Enterprise Institute who has been associated with the P2 Masonic Lodge in Rome. (See List 3b.) He was on the federal payroll as a foreign-policy adviser to President Bush from 2001 to 2009. It may have been his 1999 book that got him the job. Its title? *Machiavelli on Modern Leadership: Why Machiavelli's Iron Rules Are As Important Today As Five Centuries Ago.*

In that book, Ledeen says "Change – above all, violent change – is the essence of human history." He then cites as "Machiavellian" President Clinton's use of the Internal Revenue Service in 1997 to undertake audits on 20 non-profit organizations that criticized Clinton's policies. Perhaps Ledeen is unaware that one of the Articles of Impeachment prepared against President Nixon (but not used; he resigned) concerned Nixon's political abuse of IRS records.

In any case, the biological laws of political behavior were well noted by the sagacious Florentine, and these should be carefully watched. For example, Chapter 6 of Machiavelli's *The Prince*, entitled "Of New Dominions" says "There is nothing more difficult to carry out, nor more dangerous to handle than to initiate a new order of things. For the reformer has enemies in all those who profit by the old order." (such as, say, us three hundred million Americans...)

5.5 MARS IS NOT VENUS

Some women, present company included, have masculine traits. In fact all humans, irrespective of gender, have at least a tiny dose of all human behavioral traits. Statistically, females have *more* of the so-called female traits of caring, coyness, and the urge to train children.

The average male has more of the 'masculine' traits, such as ambition and aggression, and wants to submerge himself in teamwork.

A culture may then step in, to urge females to strive for the feminine ideal, and urges the males to be 'masculine.' As noted in Ch 6, entitled Bio-spirit, **the raw material that every culture must work with** is the set of innate traits that humans possess.

In the US, some clandestine group along the lines of Tavistock has been trying to break up the family. (Recall H.G. Wells's plan!) One way to do this is simply to put many men in jail. Another way is to 'equalize' the two sexes. Lately there is even a trend toward encouraging parents to see their child as unisex. Of course the sales pitch for this is 'equality of opportunity.'

Generally speaking, women's liberation has been a benefit to individuals (especially in nations where the woman is legally chattel) and it helps societies as a whole because new talent is able to emerge. There is also the new acknowledgment that lesbians and gay males are as worthy of a place in society as anyone else.

Nevertheless, human society is biologically underwritten, and there is such a thing as a female role (homemaking, nurturing,) and a male role (he protects and provides). Let ladies be protectors and providers as much as they wish, but the *image of masculinity* in those endeavors must still be offered to boys – at least as an option.

As John Gray says in *Women Are from Venus and Men Are from Mars* (2007), we are not identical to the opposite sex. (Thank God.)

5.6 THE MORRISON CASE AND THE LOPEZ CASE

According to the Constitution, **the US has no police power**. (The 50 states do.) For a long time the Supreme Court went along with such deviations as the FBI and DEA, usually basing this on Art. I, Sec 8, clause 3 known as the commerce clause – the clause creating federal regulation of interstate trade. In 1995, however, the defendant in *US v Lopez*, accused of possessing a gun near a school, was found not to be afoul of any federal law. The Court said that relying on the commerce clause would do away with the "distinction between what is truly national and what is truly local."

Then in 2000 the Supreme Court, in *US v Morrison,* struck down the part of the Violence against Women Act that allowed women to sue in federal court for actions in which there was an apparent gender-based motive for violence. SCOTUS ruled that the effect of that criminal conduct on interstate commerce did not qualify it for

Congressional legislation. Indeed, the Court said it could think of **"no better example of the police power, which the founders denied the National Government and reposed in the States, than the suppression of violent crime."** [emphasis added]

Justice Clarence Thomas, in a separate but concurring opinion, recommended that the Court use any future case that may arise, to 're-visit' this whole issue – in effect, to criticize its past overuse of the commerce clause. SCOTUS is never bound by precedent, not even from its own bench; an about-face will cause no loss of face.

5.7 MANCHURIAN CANDIDATES

The US Military speaks openly of its futuristic high-tech plans to create the cyborg soldier. (See, for example, J. Moreno, *Mind Wars*, 2007.) 'Cyborg' has to do with connecting the soldier's brain to his ammunition for instantaneous fire – or something like that. Yet the Pentagon hides the fact that members of the Special Forces, such as DELTA and SEAL, are already subjected to brain manipulation.

One of the products of MK-Ultra, which began around 1950, is the attempt to create a 'Manchurian candidate.' That's a person, traumatized and hypnotized into submission, who can then carry instructions in their brain which could be triggered weeks, or even years later, by such things as simple as hearing a certain tone over the telephone. (Persia had assassins nine centuries ago who obeyed orders after dosing high on hashish. I wouldn't rule out that Japan's kamikaze pilots were similarly unfree – and most suicide bombers?)

Such a person rushes to do his duty – such as to kill an appointed target – and then immediately forgets he has done it. Hence he is safe from spilling the beans under interrogation, or implicating others. This one invention has **greatly** changed our nation.

CIA agent Gunther Russbacher, who also worked for Office of Naval Intelligence, became remorseful and stated to the public that the US is able to produce various levels of mind-control. 'Level 3' is often **voluntarily** entered into, he claims, by our ambassadors or Cabinet members. Not to make them commit a crime, but to get their thinking aligned with the party line. Perhaps this is how politicians get trained to answer questions smoothly and evasively. The highest level, Russbacher says, is called Clear Eyes. (See Ch 6.7.)

At the time of this book's writing there is a lawsuit in federal court filed by Vietnam Veterans of America. One of the plaintiffs, Frank Rochelle, says he was subjected to experiments at Edgewood

Arsenal in Maryland, including LSD experiments. Some veterans had their brain implanted with electronic receivers for radioed commands. Their case will be considered with others in Ch 7.10.

5.8 THE M WORD (RHYMES WITH 'SCRUTINY')

Soldiers and sailors have, in the past, occasionally mutinied when they should not have done so. At other times they have failed to mutiny when that would have been the right thing to do. *The Law Dictionary* (1986) defines *mutiny* as "unlawful resistance to a superior officer." Mutiny is a rare event and one that is frowned upon, with good reason. It is essential that military personnel, especially in the theatre of war, submerge their individual wills into the will of the group – as expressed in the commands of the leader.

Servicemember's Legal Guide, by LTC Jonathan P. Tomes 2001

Entering the service, whether you enlist or accept a commission, means that you take on the responsibilities to **remain fit**, to **be present** for duty, to **perform your duties well**, and to **obey lawful orders**.... What is the difference between a lawful order and one that is not? A lawful order must relate to the performance of military duties and have a proper military purpose, [including] to keep unit members able to perform their duties, such as an order to take a flu shot to prevent illness. An order is illegal if it is unconstitutional or against the law, if it is unrelated to military duties, [or] if it is unrea-sonable.... **An example of an unconstitutional order would be an order to torture a suspect** as a means to make him confess to a crime. [emphasis added]

The Uniform Code of Military Justice is available on the Net. Needless to say, the UCMJ does not offer advice about disobeying a bad leader. Seeking guidance from chaplains won't help, either. They will recommend that you obey now and argue it out later.

As the above quote from the Servicemember's Legal Guide shows, it is uncontroversial to teach soldiers that doing something against the law is wrong. But that is only a tantalizing principle. Discussing how to disobey an illegal order could cause a soldier to be suspected of disloyalty. Anything **related to the *group's* claim on the individual is emotion-filled**, so this could prove traumatic.

The question being pursued here is: What can a soldier do if his superiors are engaging in unconstitutional actions? When the government in Washington DC is acting generally lawlessly, as today, a soldier takes his life in his hands by questioning authority. Did Pat Tillman do that? We don't know. We do know, thanks to the book *Boots on the Ground at Dusk,* that 'the brass' **arranged for him to die.**

AP 7-27-07 U.S. Army medical examiners were suspicious about the close proximity of the three bullet holes in Pat Tillman's forehead and tried without success to get authorities to investigate whether the former professional football player's death amounted to a crime.

The doctor said he took the unusual step of calling the Army's Human Resources Command and was rebuffed. He [also asked] the Army's Criminal Investigation Division [to open] a criminal case. "He said he talked to his higher headquarters and they had said no."

Pat's mother, Mary, is the author of that 2008 book. A report she uncovered quotes an officer saying that an Afghan man (our ally) "was to be south" of Pat, implying that the scene was scripted before it began. She also noted that the order was given for Pat to be at his destination *at dusk,* when what was meant was *dawn.* "Why not say '6 hundred 40 hours' per usual military jargon?" she asks.

Let us establish a 🖎 decoding rule, naming it after General Stanley McChrystal who initially claimed Tillman died heroically in battle in Afghanistan. The McChrystal rule is: **when the Army changes its story under pressure, there has been crime** *ab initio.* More will be said later about the US killing its own soldiers.

Now let us look at the case of Army Lt. Ehren Watada, who refused to be deployed in 2006 to Iraq, on moral grounds. Watada decided to disobey orders and take the consequences. He remained at Fort Lewis in Tacoma WA, while his men flew to Iraq. In his free time, dressed in civilian clothes, he spoke publicly in San Francisco about his dilemma, five days before his Army hearing.

It is possible that this whole affair was a scripted psy-op -- for the purpose of creating in other soldiers' minds the notion that Watada's cry would result in a breakthrough. In other words, his case, which took three years, kept other persons from bothering to prove the same point. Perhaps because of this the Iraq battlefield did not host any American mutinies (at least not as far as we know!).

Watada was charged with missing movement, and contempt. Then he was additionally charged, for the San Francisco speech, with 'conduct unbecoming an officer.' His first case was dismissed on a technicality and his second on arguments about double jeopardy. So there was no ruling on the merits. This is extremely unfortunate.

Intermission! Time for Popcorn, Ice Cream, Happiness, Love, etc.

Good news for the reader (unless the reader thrives on depression): the situation is much better than it looks!! We are at a turning point!

Sure we are getting into some sad topics in this book but the message is that we have *misunderstood* many events and if we can now ken them correctly we can enter a veritable Golden Age. Think about it: we start by refusing to take what a few crazy individuals have been dishing out to us, and we end up realizing that love can multiply our capacity for good.

'Love' and *'good'* are more or less the same thing, biologically. Our DNA holds instructions that bring out generous, tolerant, idealistic behavior (see Ch 4) when the situation calls for it. We are free now to **create** those situations, where previously we could only hit upon them by luck.

When EO Wilson was asked by *Discover* magazine (12-1-01) "If you could travel back in time, what would you change about this planet?" he said "If I could go way back, I'd have humanity reach at least its current level of self-understanding and appreciation of the environment before our species moved out of Africa. How great it would be to explore and embrace the untrammeled living world without destroying it."

I am saying "We did leave Africa too soon; we did mess up the planet. We also took our species' propensity for hierarchy and deceit down many painful paths. Millions suffered; we can't change that. But oh how great it will be now to re-think our arrangements!" Just consider this: For many individuals it's routine to devote their life to helping society. What if they could now be egged on, instead of being roadblocked?

Dear Reader, this upbeat Intermission page reflects my having recently become a founding member of the Truth and Reconciliation Coalition that Kathleen Sullivan had the genius to propose. (See her Foreward to this book). This TRC is profoundly affecting my outlook. Probably I was a cock-eyed optimist beforehand, stating frequently that the Constitution can get us through. But I was only envisioning a return to the status quo ante. Now I'm hell on wheels thinking about new opportunities for America. (See unitedstatestrc.com)

*Most of the the founding members were 'recipients' of MK-Ultra torture; their contribution is **forgiveness**. For me it was first a necessary intellectual and legal step to figure out how to prosecute the cabal. (Not to prosecute is to condone.) But since the situation is so far gone, and since I consider all of us Americans responsible for much of what took place, the beauty of 'reconciliation' is starting to have an appeal. I hope you may feel this way too. — MM*

p.s. You live in another country? You can start a TRC of your own. Why not?

Watada. Today, I speak with you about a radical idea … that to stop an illegal and unjust war, the soldiers can choose to stop fighting it. Now it is not an easy task for the soldier. … The soldier must realize that this is a war not out of self-defense but by choice, for profit and imperialistic domination. WMD, ties to Al Qaeda, and ties to 9/11 never existed and never will.

The oath we take swears allegiance not to one man but to a document of principles and laws designed to protect the people. Enlisting in the military does not relinquish one's right to seek the truth; neither does it excuse one from rational thought nor the ability to distinguish between right and wrong. "I was only following orders" is never an excuse.

If soldiers realized this war is contrary to what the Constitution extols — if they stood up and threw their weapons down — no President could ever initiate a war of choice again. When we say, "… Against all enemies foreign and domestic," what if elected leaders became the enemy? Whose orders do we follow?

The answer: the conscience that lies in each soldier.

Examine his remark "Ties to Al Qaeda … never existed and never will." It seems that Watada did not believe we should be occupying Iraq, which we have now been doing for a long time — seven years as of 18 March 2010. It is awful for a young person in uniform to have to carry such heavy responsibility as to try to evaluate the national policy; Congress and civilians should do that.

Watada used selective legal reasoning. Could he have said he was refusing to deploy because he would be made to commit war crimes? Probably not, because if he thinks the war is an imperialist one, his complaint is based on *jus ad bellum* principles — whether there was justice in our undertaking the war. The US's law of war has to do, instead, with *jus in bello* — concerning particulars such as "Don't fire on a hospital tent." See pegc.us. (You could make a *jus ad bellum* case from our having ratified the UN Charter's Article 2.)

As this book deliberately omits international law, we are not talking about the new International Criminal Court (It is hopelessly compromised by the fact that its prosecutions need approval from the UN Security Council). The Aforementioned American war crimes law (codified at 18 USC 2441) refers to, and incorporates, the Geneva Conventions of 1925 and 1945. Here is an item that quotes John Ashcroft replying to a question about war crimes.

> REP. HANK JOHNSON: As the Attorney General, you were the President's senior law enforcement officer, were you not?...
>
> JOHN ASHCROFT: The military tribunals try war crimes, and the Attorney General has no authority to try war crimes. He deals with the laws enacted by Congress. *House Judiciary Committee Hearing*, 2008

Wow. Ashcroft didn't know that war crimes were in his jurisdiction! Just shows you how the DoJ has internalized its own disinformation! Or maybe it is *policy* for any war crimes committed by lower ranks to be transmogrified into UCMJ crimes and thus be met with a discreet court-martial rather than an open trial.

Consider Pvt. Javal Davis who, like Spc. Charles Graner (of Abu Ghraib photo fame), was court-martialed. He threatened to blame higher-ups and was then able to cop a plea, accept a gag order, and go free. This happens all the time. So the war crime provisions of 18 USC 2441 are kept under the rug. So, too, is the UN Charter's Article II: "[We will] refrain from the use of force." Yet recall that our Constitution's Article VI says: <u>all Treaties made... shall be the Supreme Law of the Land and the Judges in every State shall be bound thereby...</u>.

Harking back to Watada – his question, **"What if elected leaders became the enemy?"** is the very pith of this book. Rule of law is imperiled by even a small amount of lawlessness in government. You may have heard that every grunt in the US Army has seen Kay Griggs on youtube, explaining how her Naval officer husband, when drunk, let out the most outrageous secrets of the military. Her words are now altering the power equation. (I have put them next to the Bill of Rights in Appendix R as a salute to all whistleblowers.)

Suggestion: COMU. This is a lengthy section. The suggestion is that we find ways to develop counter-mutiny – 'COMU' as they might call it in military bureaucratese. (You may remember that the FBI called its 1960s counter-intelligence program 'COINTELPRO')

I personally think that the US should reinstate the draft – a Selective Service Act was in force from 1940 to 1973 – then we citizens would be talking about "all of our guys" when we refer to the military. As you can see in Rep Henry Gonzalez's Articles of Impeachment of President Bush, Sr. – Appendix G of this book – there is noticeable unfairness concerning the burden of defending the US. I think it should be an honor, not a punishment, to do this job.

107

That said, we must go with the army we have, one in which the typical soldier is not free to argue with the boss or he will lose his job. My suggestion is that we, on the more comfortable outskirts of battle, take up his cause. We can meet as Counter-mutiny clubs — perhaps at the premises of Veterans of Foreign Wars posts. There **we could discuss very openly the predicament of our military.**

The following two are Rest-in-Peace examples of what happens if a soldier protests on his/her own:

- Alyssa Peterson of Utah was a US Army Arabic-language interpreter in Iraq. She complained of the abuse of prisoners there, including putting people in a closed box with insects. (When I read of that practice in *The Gulag Archipelago* by Solzhenitsyn, I could never have dreamed Americans would do it!) Alyssa then died of a rifle wound.

- Col Ted Westhusing was a Professor of Military Ethics at West Point who volunteered for duty in Iraq. While there he was told of financial corruption (involving a contractor connected to the Carlyle Group). He investigated, really dug into the matter. He was soon found inside his trailer, shot dead.

It is reasonable to say that these two souls are crying out to us from beyond. They were each on a mission and *got thwarted*. I say *let's make a mission out of that* — it's a national calamity. Your COMU group could informally name itself after Alyssa. It would be such a mistake let her sterling effort be forgotten! If many COMU's do identical work, that's no problem. Our penchant for expecting resolutions to problems to take place on a grand scale is mistaken. Real human things occur face-to-face. My mantra is "Keep it small and local."

First, let us note that mass media *did not report* the above incidents, much less make an issue of them. The Pentagon closed each case immediately by saying the death was a suicide. By the way, FBI and CIA have the ability to produce letters written in anyone's handwriting, so 'suicide notes' have little probative value any more.

Second, note that in calling these particular deaths suicides, the Pentagon opened itself to the Yeakey decoding rule. Whether it be Yeakey, Peterson, or Wustinghus, we know they did not end their life 'by their own hand.' It is insulting to say that a patriot working to expose our rogue government would duck out like that.

One more suspicious death in the military is that of Air Force officer David McCloud at age 53. He ran his Cessna into a tree on the AF base in Alaska. *Did he?* More likely somebody doctored his plane. To the credit of his fellow officers they at least 'murmured' that McCloud had logged thousands of hours in fighter jets and so was not much of a candidate for wrecking a Cessna. (What of Rep John Murtha's death in April 2010 following gall bladder surgery at Bethesda Naval Hospital? As head of the House Defense Appropriations Subcommittee, he used his voice on behalf of soldiers.)

The bigger story is this: **Since the Pentagon is putting out the suicide lies, the Pentagon did the killing.** To our Counter Mutiny clubs, that is grist for the mill. After all, such deaths could motivate the pals of the deceased persons to take vengeance. We do not want such mutinies to occur. (and I condemn fragging.) Rather, the reality needs to be aired: Pentagon As Killer of Our Own!

In turn these episodes prove that, logically, **the Pentagon can't be working for the US.** If it were, it would not kill the aforementioned persons -- plus Pat Tillman. Hence, the Pentagon must be the servant of some other entity. As far as I can guess, and I realize I may be wrong, that other entity is World Government. Right now one of our top military men, General McChrystal, holds the title Commander of ISAF, within NATO. And what does that acronym stand for? "International Security Assistance Force." Oh, come on!

If the boss is not the US, our Congress does not have a say in the decision-making, does it? Strangely, Congress seems to *prefer* not having a say (as will be analyzed in Chs 7 and 9). Congress also has constitutional responsibility in the matter of subjecting the army to DU, depleted uranium. It is tempting to say "Well, soldiers get into harm's way regularly – it's their duty." Hold it! There is no need to shut off one's thought processes like that.

Each nation can *decide* if it wants to use a weapon overseas that contaminates its personnel even after they come home. In the US, citizens who stop to give it some thought **would surely demand that their Congressperson legislate against the use of DU.**

Another policy in which the citizen should be in the know concerns the aforementioned privatization of the military. There is a letter displayed on the Internet (authenticity not guaranteed) that shows two former Cabinet members, Frank Carlucci and William Perry, writing to Defense Secretary Rumsfeld on February 15, 2001:

> Dear Don. Thanks for the lunch last Friday. It was great seeing you in such good spirits even if you are "all alone." We thought it useful to follow up on discussions on the need for reductions in the infrastructure of the Department....

That was written on the letterhead of the Carlyle Group! It was mentioned in Ch 4.7 that Thomas Barnett has been working, as a civil servant, with Cantor Fitzgerald, Inc., at the Pentagon. His task is related to identifying 'the core nations versus gap nations.' It sounds as much like a plan for global genocide as one could get away with saying above a whisper. Barnett's book *The Pentagon's New Map* has literally got a map in it that shows **many countries conspicuously missing!** Again I say, genocide is a crime in US law and carries the death penalty. If Congresspersons instruct our military to commit genocide, will they be hanged?

Here is what some Israelis have said on behalf of soldiers:

Open Letter from 358 Faculty Members In Israel, 1/08/2007
We, faculty members from a number of Israeli universities, wish to express our appreciation and support for those of our students and lecturers who refuse to serve as soldiers in the occupied territories. For thirty five years an entire people, some three and a half million in number, have been held without basic human rights. The occupation, and oppression of another people have brought the State of Israel to where it is today.

…the present war is not being fought for our home but for the settlements beyond the green line….We hereby express our readiness to do our best to help students who encounter …difficulties as a result of their refusal to serve in the territories.
~ Seruv.nethost.co.il/UniversitySupportEng.asp

5.9 MAFIAS ARE GENETICALLY PREDICTED

We will always have mafias, or attempts to form mafias. Each human being carries within him a calculator of his own best interest. It motivates him to be honest, mainly for reputation's sake, and to be dishonest, if the stakes are high. (George Washington noted in his *Moral Maxims,* "Few men can resist the highest bidder.")

To visualize how natural it is for mafias to form, lay a bunch of paperclips on your desk to represent members of society. Spread them out so that friends and relatives are somewhat clustered and many individuals are isolated. Next, place your stapler in their midst, to represent a local church, and use another object, such as a paperweight, to be the police station. Assume that the society has long since established those institutions to teach people to be honest and to help catch and punish thieves.

Now imagine that two of the 'paperclips' decide to extort money from a third. Instead of filching his wallet, they force him to hand over $20 a week to them, warning him *if he reports this arrangement to anyone they will break his legs.* He decides to pay this 'protection.'

Such a system came about in Sicily (naturally, it added some justifying theme about being beneficial to society). This Italian mafia was imported to the US around 1910, and by 1940 had a Jewish offshoot led by Meyer Lansky. On the west coast, Chinese immigrants brought their Triad system of bullying: three men who, as individuals, could not scare a flea, can together terrify everyone. Will we always put up with mafias? Most people will not risk a broken leg and so take no action. Don't the 'paperweight' and the 'stapler' get in there and help society? No. The mafia anticipates the problem of the paperweight by corrupting police with a share in the take. As for the stapler, religion tends to be silent in the face of power grabbers: the Church claims that its sole business is in souls.

Can it be that there is no way to stop the terror? Society would need to be cognizant of the biological parameters of sin and the way in which *any coalition of 'paperclips'* is likely to amass power. Think of how paperclips Rockefeller and Brzezinski formed the Trilaterals:

> The Trilateral Commission is intended to be the vehicle for multinational consolidation of the commercial and banking interests by seizing control... [It will] consolidate the four centres of power – political, monetary, intellectual and ecclesiastical. [!!] What the Trilateral Commission intends is to create a worldwide economic power superior to the political governments of the nation-states involved. As managers and creators of the system, they will rule the future. ~ Barry Goldwater, *With No Apologies* (1971)

5.10 WHAT TO DO? MEN, DEFEND US!

Veterans, and other real men, you know who you are. Did we gals give you the impression we don't want your protection? Sorry. That was just a fad. *Of course we want your protection!!* Help! Help! This chapter formed part of the investigation of why our brains seem to be missing. Well, it's not just brains if you know what I mean. How utterly stupid of our culture to downgrade strength.

Appendix Z shows – as validated by Michigan's government website – that most of the 50 states are now hosting foreign troops. No need for anyone to believe the nonsense that these visitors are

111

here to learn the American way of democracy! They are part of NATO, so surely they are here to serve World Government. They will aid in the violent removal of our constitution – mark my words.

Also, Men, please contemplate how Haiti's quake occurred, and imagine us as the next target. Visit List 12c, which says that manliness is being held back by the most ridiculous psychological factors. Please become a true hero. Thank you!

Civilian protection of the welfare of soldiers is also urgent. Law professors and military Judges Advocate General, please read:

KBR. The U.S. Army is under fire for reversing a decision to have three companies compete for more than $500 million worth of work in Iraq, and instead keeping it under an existing contract without any bidding. The $568 million contract for support work in Iraq stayed with contracting giant KBR [formerly Kellogg Brown and Root] under the existing sole-source contract. ~ CNN Senior Pentagon Producer Mike Mount, May 11, 2010 (globalpolicy.org)

Suggestion: Get with the law. While we must wait for legal concepts to be inventoried in Ch 7, and Congress's treason to be looked at in Ch 9, it is important to say now that **today's lawlessness in the Defense Department cannot be tolerated.** As it is, persons with hands in the till don't even get confronted. Rumsfeld chose late afternoon Sept 10, 2001 to announce that $2 trillion was missing from his shop (let's see, why didn't he think it would be explosive?).

We pay mercenaries $99 per bag for laundering battlefield clothes. Regarding no-bid contracts, the law – of course – says there must be bids. Believe it or not, that law says *"except in time of war."* Thus the (endless) war on terror makes bid-free the order of the day. See 'afghaniscam' at corpswatch.org. Any senior officer with commonsense should bring this to the attention of the public and insist that there is no reason whatsoever to rebuild Iraq bid-free.

As far as I am aware, it is a similar wording in the fine print of recruitment contracts that causes soldiers to be press-ganged into extensions of their overseas 'tours.' Stoploss is a ridiculous breach of the essence of contract law. Deceptive contracts, or ones made under duress, are unenforceable. *Everybody knows that.*

As for the murder of Pat Tillman – and remember it's not a maybe, it's a definite – **the relevant officers should be arrested** immediately. The family of the Afghan man who was used as a prop should also bring suit. Murder is a crime and this was premeditated.

Veteran's benefits applications are also to be responded to with care and respect. They aren't requests for a *gift*. One hears that the amount of paperwork required of families is so daunting that many soldiers can't face it. This is an outrage; it desecrates the flag. Also, J. Kors in *The Nation* 4/7/09 says that men are discharged from the service with a diagnosis of 'personality disorder' so they can't claim disability. Hmm, then shouldn't we discipline the recruiters who wrongly hired them and the doctors who let them pass a physical?

We also have Neutrality Acts, from the 1930s (mostly obsolete), but with the following part still intact in the United States Code:

> Whoever, within the United States, knowingly begins or sets on foot or provides or prepares a means for or furnishes the money for, or takes part in, any military or naval expedition or enterprise to be carried on from thence against the territory or dominion of any foreign prince or state, or of any colony, district, or with whom the United States is at peace, shall be fined under this title or imprisoned not more than three years, or both. ~ 18 USC 960

Which part of that don't the soldiers of fortune understand?

Then we hear from Major Doug Rokke that he was forbidden to keep records of the anthrax-vaccinations he gave to Army personnel and that the boxes in which they arrived called for cold storage but they were not refrigerated. (Johnson 2001: 118) Why follow such orders? Is it legal for soldiers to be used as guinea pigs?

Yes, it is, per majority opinion, written by Scalia in *US v Stanley* (1986). It quotes a 1959 Staff Study by Army Intelligence on the "administration of LSD to soldiers," and rules that Stanley could not make a damages claim for "service-related injury"!! However, Brennan's dissent to the Court's ruling says: "Severe violation of the Constitutional rights of soldiers must be exposed and punished."

A Pause To Revisit The Ancient Legal Concept of Outlawry. All societies, however primitive, have standardized ways to deal with members who violate the rules -- i.e., they have retributive justice. Furthermore, all have been forced to think of ways to deal with the problem of some members being able to buck that legal system. In England, a person who did not respond to a summons by the court could be deemed an outlaw. In Norse villages, which did not have prisons, and so could only assign fines, a person who would not pay the fine could be 'outlawed' and consequently ostracized by society.

113

> **OUTLAW**: In the common law of England, a "Writ of Outlawry" made the pronouncement *Caput gerat lupinum* ("Let his be a wolf's head")... equating that person with a wolf in the eyes of the law: Not only was the subject deprived of all legal rights because the law no longer deemed him human, but others were permitted to kill him on sight as if he [were] a wild animal. Outlawry also existed in other legal codes of the time, such as the ancient Norse and Icelandic legal code. To be declared an outlaw was to suffer a form of civil or social death. The outlaw was debarred from all civilized society. No one was allowed to give him food... The possibility of being declared an outlaw for derelictions of civil duty continued to exist in English law until 1879.... ~ Wikipedia, as of May 16, 2010

Recently South Australia's legislature reinstated a kind of outlawry but that was found unconstitutional by the High Court in 2009: *Totani & Anor v State of South Australia.* It would certainly be unconstitutional in the US, thanks to a citizen's right to due process. Still, recall from Ch 2.10, SCOTUS's phrase "The Constitution is not a suicide pact." Also recall my phrase "The law is not an ass."

A main chore of this book, *Prosecution for Treason,* has been to identify the many ways traitors can, and do, evade the law. They can control laws and executive actions in such a way as to spare themselves from indictment. If someone threatens to speak against them, that person may suddenly be jailed. And don't forget the pardon power. The first President Bush pardoned Caspar Weinberger *before* trial, which meant nothing could come out against Bush at that trial.

I suggest that a band of well-respected Americans get together and write up, in a strictly tentative way, some ideas for a constitutional amendment that would break the impasse. If I were in the group I would talk plain talk and say "I saw my beloved die of cancer and now I hear – from however reliable or unreliable a source – that the Rockefeller Institute has the cure for cancer locked away. I demand that past officials of that organization be called for questioning and if any refuse, may their heads be those of wolves."

You know that others in the group would be able to articulate an amendment to deal with that sort of thing, right? Earlier I also mentioned the concept of *hostis humani generis.* These **intellectual tools** help, because it is psychologically almost impossible for any group to acknowledge that its own leaders are acting against it. A new theory of Imposture will be added to the collection, in Ch 8.10.

List 5a. Men's Societies That Value the Occult (the Hidden)

(Typically only a group within the group follows the occult agendum.)

Shriners – related to Masons, wear fez; Harry Truman was one

Rosicrucians – contributed alchemist influence to secret lore

Opus Dei -- papally approved Catholic cult, W Colby was in it

Mafia – begun in Sicily, has code of honor, shakes people down

Skull & Bones - German 'exchange' with Yalies since 1830s

Ancient Egyptian, Jewish **Qabalists** - find numerology inspiring

Masons – 5 million in America; many are police, judges, lawyers

Illuminists – Voltaire, Weishaupt, Hamilton. Outlawed in 1787

Mossad – "By deception shall we do war." British influence

Knights Templar – 11th century 'warrior monks,' very wealthy

The Fellowship – politicians' prayer breakfasts; prison ministry

Jesuits – educators since 1571, run Georgetown University

FBI– produces evidence of crime at Quantico VA

Modern **Kabalists** – wear red; Hollywood females now joining

Sufi – Islamic mystics whose rituals are used in Freemasonry

SOURCES: A. Daraul, *History of Secret Societies*
Clarence Kelly, *Conspiracy Against God and Man*
Vicomte Leon de Poncins, *Freemasonry and Judaism*
Rodney Stich, *FBI, CIA, the Mob, and Treachery*

List 5b. Vital Statistics of US Veterans and Soldiers

What is the number of:

1. Vets collecting disability for **Gulf War Illness?**
   - UNAVAILABLE
2. Vietnam War vets now **homeless?**
   - UNAVAILABLE
3. **Fragging** incidents in Gulf War, Iraq War?
   -UNAVAILABLE
4. Persons in US Army uniform who are **not American?**
   -UNAVAILABLE
5. Dollars spent by military families on **body armor?**
   -UNAVAILABLE
6. **Suicides** of discharged soldiers after Iraq tour?
   -UNAVAILABLE
7. Iraq War deaths attributed to **'friendly fire'?**
   -UNAVAILABLE
8. Soldiers currently under **gag orders?**
   -UNAVAILABLE
9. **Desertions** from US Military since 2000?
   -UNAVAILABLE
10. Soldiers recruited from **jails?**
    -UNAVAILABLE
11. Vets complaining of exposure to **Depleted Uranium?**
    -UNAVAILABLE
12. Vets **addicted** to drugs?*
    -UNAVAILABLE
13. Soldiers seeking discharge because of disagreement with **aims of war** in Afghanistan?
    -UNAVAILABLE
14. Soldiers who **refused to return** to Iraq?
    -UNAVAILABLE

* "Conservatively estimated, each one of the **twenty thousand or so GI addicts** in Vietnam spends an average of twelve dollars a day on four vials of heroin." ~ U. of Wisconsin Professor Alfred McCoy, *The Politics of Heroin in Southeast Asia* (1972) p. 183

List 5c.   Fantastic Promotions for the Class of 1986

Later Positions of Persons Who Worked in the Reagan White House during Iran-Contra Scandal (circa 1986):

Mr. Eliott Abrams ✈ Under-Secretary of State, 2001-09

Mr. Richard Armitage* ✈ Assistant Secretary of State, 2001-05

Vice Pres. George Bush* ✈ US president 1989 to 1993

Mr. Jeb Bush ✈ Governor of Florida 1999 to 2006

Dr. Michael Ledeen ✈ Adviser to Pres. G. W. Bush

Marine Col. Oliver North ✈ Host of 'conservative' talk show

Adm. John Poindexter ✈ Head of Pentagon's TIA, 2002-2003

Army Gen. Colin Powell ✈ US Secretary of State, 2001-05

Mr. Otto Reich ✈ Assistant Secy. of State for Latin America

Mr. John Roberts ✈ Chief Justice of the United States

Mr. Lawrence Silberman ✈ Federal Appeals Judge

Gen. John Singlaub ✈ Consultant, GeoMiliTech

Secy of State G. Shultz ✈ Recruited B. Netanyahu for Israel

CIA Gen. Counsel Stanley Sporkin ✈ District Court Judge

Secy of Defense C. Weinberger* ✈ Pardoned before Trial

*These also availed themselves of a knighthood of the British Empire.

SOURCES: Al Martin, *The Conspirators;* Wayne Madsen, *Jaded Tasks*

Chapter 6   Testimony at Presidential Hearings, 1995

Good afternoon. I'm Chris De Nicola born July of 1962...My parents were divorced around 1966 and Donald Richard Ebner, my natural father, was involved with Dr. Green in the experiments .... Dr. Green performed Radiation Experiments on me in 1970 focusing on my neck, throat, and chest, 1972 focusing on my chest, and my uterus in 1975. Each time **I became dizzy, nauseous** and threw up.... Dr. Green was using me mostly as a Mind Control subject. From 1966-1973 his objective was to gain total control of my mind and train me to be a spy/assassin. The first significant memory took place **at Kansas City University** in 1966. Don Ebner took me there by plane when my mom was out of town. I was in what looked like a laboratory and there seemed to be other children.

I was strapped down...Dr. Green had electrodes on my body including my head. He used what looked like an overhead projector and repeatedly said he was burning different images into my brain while a red lighted flashed, aimed at my forehead. In between each sequence he used electric shock on my body**... while repeating each image would go deeper into my brain, and I would do whatever he told me to do.** I felt drugged because he had given me a shot...I was 4 years old...

The rest of the experiments took place in Tucson, Arizona out in the desert. **I was taught how to pick locks, be secretive,** use my photographic memory to remember things and a technique to withhold information by repeating numbers to myself. He often tied me down in a cage, which was near his office. Between 1972 and 1976 he and his assistant were sometimes careless and left the cage unlocked. [Hence I got] into his office and found files with reports and memos addressed to CIA and Military Personnel ...[about which] I have submitted in written documentation... **I ask that you keep in mind that the memories I've described are but a glimpse of the countless others** that took place over the ten years between 1966 and 1976. **Please help us by recommending an investigation** and making the information available so that therapists and other mental health professionals can help more people like myself...   [emphasis added]

6 Menticide

Truth shall spring forth from the earth.

– Psalms, 85

Had I not started that healing journey in 1991, I would not have
been able to break the [suicide] programming that was installed in
me for the Ides of March 1999. It was a pathetic program to be
sure, installed by pathetic men when I was only 16…. They hoped to
move another piece of the power puzzle that only they
truly understand.

– Carol Rutz, A Nation Betrayed

6.1 THE CRIME OF MENTICIDE

This chapter is about: mind control, mind manipulation, thought
control, psychological warfare. This stuff is criminal. Although there
isn't yet a 'crime of mind control,' perpetrators of non-consensual
mind control are at least committing the crime of assault and battery. Per most states' laws, individuals can commit assault without
physically touching someone; they only have to cause apprehension.

To commit battery one can 'batter' another's mind, their
emotions, their stability. Thus there are many criminals waiting to
be collared, in universities, hospitals, prisons, and on military bases –
the sites of unbelievable experimentation with people's minds.
(Much of the battery was physical, of course – unbelievably so.)

One can additionally arrest the conspirators, the accessories
before the fact, and persons who cover up the crime. In the US,
with regard to federal crimes, it is a felony to refrain from reporting
an indictable crime that you know about! That felony is misprision:

Misprision [rhymes with vision]
Whoever, having knowledge of the actual commission of a felony,
cognizable by a court of the US, conceals and does not as soon as
possible make known the same to some judge or other person in
civil or military authority under the US shall be fined under this title
or imprisoned not more than three years, or both. ~ 18 USC 4

Editors, TV producers, and school administrators involved in mind
control, not to mention psychiatrists, may be looking at jail time.

There have been a few successful lawsuits claiming damages for these despicable acts, but no prosecutions. After all, most of the evidence has been kept under wraps. I think the MK-Ultra program clearly meets the Constitution's criteria for treason. In that secret program, which was carried out by the US government, **war was levied** against citizens, particularly children. One of the survivors, Carol Rutz, has aptly named her autobiography *A Nation Betrayed*.

Please don't ever take the fact that there have been no convictions to mean that no one is guilty. As mentioned earlier, we have rarely indicted Americans for treason, but evidence has now surfaced — as it was always bound to surface — that many of our compatriots betray us. The perpetrators can be indicted any day now. Here is what we used to do to traitors:

Treason… Laws of Maryland at Large 1638 *Hurst* 71–72

All Offences of Treason to be punished by Drawing, Hanging and Quartering of a Man, and Burning of a Woman; …and to forfeit all his Lands, Tenements, Goods, &c. to his Lordship. But Punishment of Death to be inflicted on a Lord of a Manor by Beheading.

6.2 GUIDE TO THIS CHAPTER -- *MENTICIDE*

I will begin with something you may often have wondered about at the checkout counter when seeing the magazine headlines, *viz.*, why do the TV stars allow cameras to 'document' their private lives? Section 6.3 will claim that Hollywood celebs (at least some of them) are 'programmed.' Then there will be a two-page summary of a published article by a now-deceased CIA man, in 6.4, advising us how a new personality can be created. You may think it is science fiction. I am pretty sure it is accurate, or at least in the ballpark, but it will be followed by a 'softer' subject, 6.5, on education.

Actually it is not soft at all, and young adults may go through the roof with anger when they hear what has been done to them. 6.6 then shows how we were warned specifically over 40 years ago by Dr Day. 6.7 is about intellectuals and think tanks. 6.8 is about sex, music, and drugs. 6.9 asks why we all fell for the ruse about 'Muslims' on 9/11. The What To Do? section offers, well — what do you think it might offer as the antidote to mind-control? — Turn off the TV? No, but that's a good idea. Please supply your own answer before reading 6.10. Appendices related to this chapter are L, M, R, and S, while J gives a step-by-step guide to breaking the will of any human. It is strongly recommended that you read J for starters.

6.3 CELEBS AND ROBOTOIDS

Have you ever noticed that famous music performers never – never, ever – hit a wrong note, either with their voice or on the instrument they play? Is it possible that the heavily promoted stars of Hollywood, TV, and the recording studios, have undergone mind enhancement? I think so. The technique may also help athletes, or mathematicians, and has perhaps been quietly in use for decades.

It's also reasonable to guess that the celebs whose intimate lives are forever being reported on the cover of magazines are in some way 'owned' by the media. Whether they are singers or soap-opera stars, their performances both onstage and offstage are intended as lessons for the young. Let us establish a decoding rule ✍, calling it the magazine-cover rule: Whenever a face appears on the cover of several magazines at once, the story involved is media-created.

Cheryl Hersha, who was used in the CIA's MK-Ultra program, tells how children can be controlled from infancy by the use of trauma – a trick known for centuries, apparently. Hersha, like Cathy O'Brien and Brice Taylor, explains how she was made into a sex slave, with an eye to the 'servicing' of diplomats, legislators, or anyone who could thereby be filmed and blackmailed. Reportedly the Mafia now regularly creates prostitutes through programming.

Occult Sex? I was programmed and equipped to function in all rooms at Bohemian Grove in order to compromise specific government targets according to their personal perversions. Slaves of advancing age were sacrificially murdered in the wooded grounds of Bohemian Grove, and I felt it was simply a matter of time until it would be me. Rituals were held at a giant, concrete owl monument.... These occultist sex rituals occur because slaves require severe trauma to ensure compartmentalization of the memory, and not from any spiritual motivation.

~ Cathy O'Brien, *The Trance Formation of America* (1995) p. 170

Brice Taylor (1995) says the making of a human robot is now a trade secret sold by the US military to private buyers. She was often 'demonstrated' under hypnosis so that corporate directors would catch on to how well such a robot might service the needs of their firm. For example, their sales personnel may be given "training."

Since corporations paid huge sums to buy this technology, they no doubt put it to use! Maybe Christian preachers use it too. Certainly military boot camps do.

6.4 How a New Personality Can Be Created By the CIA

(This section is a summary of allegations by Gunther Russbacher, 1996) Our people canvass the county hospitals and immigration centers in order to find viable candidates. We locate and select people who have no close family or friends.// The subject will be "recalled" and taken to a location of our choice. Further tests for vulnerability will be conducted at this location. If he passes these tests, he is then brought to <u>Level 2 hypnosis</u> where specific instructions are "written" via hypnotic commands and suggestions, into his personality and he is given diverse small orders.// If the subject, upon release, shows that he has retained the instructions and if he carries out those small duties, he will receive a "recall service notice."// If the subject was not given a "trigger" word, a handler will use a quick and powerful form of hypnosis similar to Neural Linguistic Programming. The subject will be told when and where to report. He will have no memory of being given these instructions, he will just report on time to the proper location. The next step is <u>Level 3 hypnosis</u>, where the subject will become an **"overwrite"** upon his own personality. An **overwrite** is a new identity or personality. It is similar to having multiple personalities, except the original personality is repressed or hidden under the "overwrite" and will not surface for a set period of time. The "overwrite" is not a complete new identity. Just enough information will be written in for the operative's alias and story to be believable by everyone, including law enforcement officials...// For the field operative who is being prepared for a deadly covert mission, a Level 3 "overwrite" can eliminate all fear and nervousness. All operatives have to go through these 3 Levels before being fielded! During Level 3 sessions, the new subject **is told that anything his "friends," i.e. programmers, ask him to do, is okay, even though it may be against all laws of the land.** At Level 3, the subject is also made to believe that he must and can do everything his "friends" (programmers) ask him to do.// If his IQ is high enough, we will study his abilities and our needs, and determine how the subject can be further used. Once this determination is made, the subject will be taken to "The Farm" or one of our numerous facilities throughout the US and Canada for further and final programming. **(Doctors Hospital in Dallas, TX is one of our main centers!)// There he gets <u>Level 4 hypnosis</u>, a place where he no longer differentiates between right and wrong.** The subject will be told he is a Super Human and all laws are written for other people. This is the Level that turns a subject into a 'Clear Eyes,' i.e., a fully programmed "sleeper" assassin, who can commit murder, and later have no shame, guilt, or remorse.// The Super Human "overwrite" also

gives the subject the feeling of immortality and invincibility. If he has to perform a particularly suicidal or important assignment we do our job at Stoney Mountain facilities.// At Level 4, diverse programs can be written or overwritten into the brain. Any command is accepted at this level. At Level 4 you can give the test subject a completely new personality and history. You are able to make him believe anything required for the accomplishment of the desired project. In this case, a new person is being created, not just a partial personality as in Level 3.// Once the Level 4 programming is complete, the subject will be a different person with no memory of his former life. He will not be an amnesiac, **he will have memories. Ones which we gave him**. He will be relocated to a new state and town and given a new life. Everything to complete the construction of the new person will be provided. Items such as driver's license, car, bank accounts, passport, credit cards, and birth certificate will be created or supplied by us and will be valid and legal.// The subject will also be provided with all the small things that ordinary people have in their lives, such as photos of his family. His family won't really exist, but he won't know this. He will have all the feelings of love, hurt or anger that normal family members feel for each other.// The photos of family and friends will be of deep cover agency personnel. If a mission goes "sour" and the news media starts looking for his family, the "agency-created family" will be produced for a news conference. They are trained actors and actresses. **They will tell folks that the "Clear Eyes" subject has always had a deeply troubled, violent past.** The media will present the "Clear Eyes" as a nut case who went on a tragic and senseless rampage. If the subject is going to be used to infiltrate a patriot group, religious commune, political campaign or environmental movement, the subject will be given all the knowledge and beliefs that are commonly held by people in his targeted group. The subject will believe that his fervently held opinions are his own. He will be believable to other members of the group.// **Many politicians and government officials on a world-wide level have been given "new agendas"** by Level 4 programming. Their own beliefs are replaced with the agenda of the programmers. They are given super human talents such as a photographic memory, and the ability to lie convincingly. Mr. _____* is an example of a world leader who has been programmed with this technique.// Once the future government leader is programmed, he will be recalled on a yearly basis and given hypnotic reinforcement. *End of Gunther Russbacher, "Operation Open Eyes"* (in Rayelan Allan, *Obergon Chronicles*, 2001, and for free download at rumormillnews.com).

*Name omitted by Maxwell; possibly the name of any leader would do!

Ch 7.10 has much to say about prosecuting people who have created Manchurian candidates, but the urgent thing is to get them to reveal the secrets of de-programming. Some of the victims have been given 'beta-programming' to make them commit suicide later:

The letters "XBGUMIDUTYBX" were found scribbled on the white surface of a cigarette pack that was in Castillo's possession at the time of his arrest [for attempting to kill Philippine President Marcos in 1967]. Placing Castillo in a trance, the hypnotist called out the series of letters…Castillo did not react.

He then tried calling out the letters, pausing at different places. He found that when he paused between the G and the U, saying "XBG, UMIDUTYBX" Castillo would reply with "I am myself to kill." In another session the hypnotist experimented with saying "Luis Castillo" as a command. The hypnotist reported "A pathetic sight takes place after this. The subject turns his pistol to his own temple and squeezes the trigger, as many times as his name is repeated."

~ Walter Bowart, *Operation Mind Control* (1978) p. 179

6.5 What Schools Do

Oh boy, what schools are doing to our babies! You'd better have your smelling salts handy if you have not heard of this before. And if you are a teacher, please don't think we blame you. This scheme came down from on high, as admitted here:

BET THIS NINETY-SOMETHING BLOKE IS NOT LYING

Norman Dodd has said, in an old film now on youtube.com:
In 1954, Alan Gaither, who was, at that time, President of the Ford Foundation, [said to me] "Mr. Dodd, all of us who have a hand in the making of policies here, have had experience **operating under directives**, the substance of which is, that **we use our grant-making power so as to alter life in the United States** that it can be comfortably merged with the Soviet Union."

[emphasis added]

The fascist project of Mussolini's Italy and Hitler's Germany, and the communist project of the Soviet empire were never nationalist, in the sense of being native to their respective cultures. They were imposed by one supra-state power. Let's see how that power also got their weevils in there to wreck our kids' ability to think.

1984: "You haven't a real appreciation of Newspeak, Winston," he said almost sadly... "In your heart you'd prefer to stick to Oldspeak, with all its vagueness and its useless shades of meaning. You don't grasp the beauty of the destruction of words... Don't you see that the whole aim of Newspeak is to narrow the range of thought? In the end we shall make thought crime literally impossible, because there will be no words in which to express it... Every year fewer and fewer words, and the range of consciousness always a little smaller" ~ George Orwell (1949)

How's that for Orwellian? And now from John Gatto:

The children I teach are indifferent to the adult world. This defies the experience of thousands of years. A close study of what big people were up to was always the most exciting occupation of youth...The children I teach have almost no curiosity and what little they do have is transitory. **They cannot concentrate for very long, even on things they choose to do.** The children I teach have a poor sense of the future, of how tomorrow is inextricably linked to today...they live in a continuous present: the exact moment they are in is the boundary of their consciousness.   [emphasis added]
~ John Gatto, New York City teacher, *Dumbing Us Down* (2002)

Perhaps you have seen the two-minute spot, "Lost Generation" on YouTube. It is good to hear a young citizen say that she believes in the future. She also says she intends to make her world. I would like to underscore the importance of *knowledge* for that.

Two generations ago American kids were routinely taught the 3 r's, history and geography, science, basic moral principles, and great works of art, music, literature (called *the classics*). I can't say that this is the only 'valid' way – many ways are valid. But I can say, personally, that my training makes me feel secure and free – free in the sense of control, of making my world. The opposite sensation is felt when I lack knowledge. For instance, I am clueless about cars. When I go to a garage mechanic, the most 'control' I can muster is to say to him "Please try not to charge more than a grand."

Now let me describe some of the changes in American education that occurred between my time in school and now. The thing to realize is that each of them was billed as something quite other than it really was. (Yes, that means it was sinister.) In the Sixties I noticed the new math because I found myself unable to help my little brother with it. (He was learning about 'sets' instead of numbers!)

Naturally it was presumed that some responsible scholar had developed this 'new math' to give kids a better deal. It was *entirely beyond our ken* to imagine that some idiot would be trying to prevent children from learning arithmetic. Yet now we hear, through the good offices of Charlotte Iserbyt (who actually has the audiotape of Mr. Nelson saying the following), that, yep, it was perfectly sinister:

In 1928, I was asked to [give a talk]. We were 13 at the meeting... Drs. John Dewey and Edward Thorndike, from Columbia University, were there. I checked later, and found that all were paid members of the Communist Party of Russia. The sole work of the group was to destroy our schools! We spent one hour and 45 minutes discussing so-called 'Modern Math.' At one point, I objected because there was too much memory work, and math is reasoning; not memory. Dr. Ziegler turned to me and said, "Nelson, wake up! That is what we want... a math that the pupils cannot apply to life situations when they get out of school!"

~ A.O. Nelson "Young Parents Alert" quoted in Iserbyt (1999) p. 14

Holy Toledo! Earlier in this book the question was put: How did H.G. Wells and George Orwell make such accurate predictions about our new society? Most likely they were informed by the inner circle. Now let's change the query to: "How did those predictions then *get carried out*?" Someone had to perform a Herculean task – doing away with time-honored teaching methods in all subjects. To learn how cabal members think (and they really deserve medals for cleverness), please make the effort to answer these questions yourself:

1. How would one get around the constitutional barrier that Congress has no grant of power to legislate in the area of education?

2. How will textbook writers be informed of the new themes if it is all so clandestine?

3. Won't teachers unions stand in the way?

4. How to get past any resistance from parents and grandparents?

Honestly, it will pay to dwell on the above before turning the page....

Not easy, eh? But for the cabal it was a breeze. In 1958 they got Congress to pass the National Defense Education Act, allegedly in reaction to the Soviets beating us in the space race. Section 101 says: "The present emergency [i.e., Sputnik] demands that more educational opportunities be made available." (We *all* fell for that!)

Seven years later – the public having become conditioned – Congress passed the Elementary and Secondary Education Act. As noted by Iserbyt (1999:72), by the end of the 1980s, state departments of education would be receiving 60% to 75% of their operating budget from the US Deptartment of Education. Amazing. That department came into being in 1979 under Carter; it is Cabinet level.

Textbook writers were not a problem, since they had, for some time, been drawn from a group of scholars who, though they may not have been in the big loop, were at least in enough loop to know that they had to take their cue from the publisher, who knew to take her cue from...etc. As for teachers unions, they were the main – how can I say this politely – snake-oil salesmen. They linked to state legislatures by, say, asking for increases in teachers' pay for 'new training.' They also had **the task of intimidating any resistant teachers**, many of whom simply took early retirement.

As for parents and grandparents, they were not allowed to catch onto the changes. At most they knew the kids were being asked to resolve ethical problems, such as whom to save on a lifeboat.

[If] you said that a person had principles or that someone stood by his or her principles, it was a compliment. Not anymore. A person who stands on principle is "arbitrary", "inflexible", and "authoritarian." While youngsters may or may not hear the word 'relativism,' they will be taught that there are no moral absolutes and that right and wrong are highly dependent on the situation.
Beverly K. Eakman, *Cloning the American Mind* (1998) p. 328

In 2002 the controversial No Child Left Behind Act was passed, making it possible for children to be diagnosed *and treated* at school for 'mental disorders' (with Medicaid paying for most of the medications). Since 1997 there is also an Employment Training Act that views children as future workers. It has to do with the 'school-to-work pipeline,' which Dean Loren claims is paralleled in New York City by a school-to-prison pipeline. Please see his lawsuit and his jaw-dropping interview with Molli Cheshire on YouTube.

Former teacher Beverly K. Eakman tells us about a test administered in several states, called EQA. It contains enough academic questions to be credible, she says, but the purpose is to mine the child's opinions and values from his answers. Somebody wants to know which children — and their parents? — are 'politically incorrect.'

One of the Educational Quality Assessment questions is this:

> There is a secret club at school called the Midnight Artists. They go out late at night and paint funny sayings and pictures on buildings. I would JOIN THE CLUB when I knew...
>
> [a] my best friend had asked me to join;
> [b] Most of the popular students in school were in the club;
> [c] my parents *would ground me* if they found out I joined.

And now you will see why Eakman refers to her book, *Walking Targets,* as "an examination of how educators and provocateurs drive a wedge between parents and their children." Dear Parents, in case you missed it, the 'club' referred to is one that does grafitti.

> The Midnight Artist question was clearly a "fishing probe": it assumed that the child *would* join the club under some circumstances, including the peculiar desire to provoke parents [!!!]
>
> Subsequent questionnaires, under the cover of mental health, have been asking pupils what it would take to make them shoot their classmates and teachers. [Dear Reader, have you passed out?]
>
> Test creators have always maintained, of course, that they are not trying to plant suggestions in youngsters' heads... But triggering conflict and strife is exactly what these hypothetical questions and self-reports wrought. Most adults could see through such a ploy right away [so] they were never permitted to see these "tests."...
>
> Once a child selects an answer that sends up an alarm bell, anything can happen, from mandatory counselling, to placement in Special Education classes, to drugging and even removal from the home.... [EQA] was testing for the child's "focus of control"...
>
> Answer "**b**" to the Midnight Artists question was preferred because it reflected a "willingness to conform to group goals"....
>
> ~ B. K. Eakman, *Walking Targets* (2007) pp. 19-20

6.6 Dr. Day (of Planned Parenthood) Gives a Report

In 1969, during a medical conference at the Pittsburgh Academy of Pediatrics, a physician named Richard Day, of Planned Parenthood, gave an after-dinner speech that let loose many secrets. This speech took place 3 years after Carroll Quigley of Georgetown University had published *Tragedy and Hope* (1966).

Both Day and Quigley admitted to being insiders regarding the plans that were being made for humankind by the 'big guys upstairs.' Neither acted like a whistleblower, saying "We can't let this continue." Each instead offered a rather tranquilizing "Here's the way it's going to be, Folks, there is no stopping it and indeed it will work out for the best."

In 1989 a pediatrician named Lawrence Dunegan went public about Dr. Day's speech; see 'The New Order of the Barbarians' (not his title) published by Randy Engels on the Internet. The predictions Day made forty years ago do not shock us now, as they have indeed come into effect. For instance, he said abortion will cease to be a crime; it will be accepted as normal. Our culture has accepted these changes. We have assumed that they were the outcomes of scientific development, economic corruption, or consciousness-raising.

For instance, we were told that The Pill, once invented, led naturally to a change in mores (i.e., customs). Did any teacher ever say, in college, "This was all planned by the big guys upstairs"? No. What really got Dunegan's goat was Day's remark that the **churches were going to assist world-orderists** in doing away with religion. That is what led to Dunegan speaking to Randy Engels.

For Day's very prescient remarks on sports, see Ch 11.5. The following tells why 'Plymouths' might have gone off the market:

There was some discussion of steel and... I remember [Day] saying that automobiles would be imported from Japan ...but the Japanese product would be better. Things **would be made so they would break and fall apart** -that is, in the United States- so that people would tend to prefer the imported variety. You'd get a little bit disgusted with your Ford, GM, or Chrysler product — because little things like window handles would fall off more... Your patriotism about buying American would soon give way to practicality... **Patriotism would go down the drain.** [emphasis added]

~ *Dr. Lawrence Dunegan, interviewed by Randy Engels in 1989*

Among Day's quiet bombshells was notification that someone was going to try to make us fat. And why? Apparently 'we' (Rockefeller's Planned Parenthood?) were interested in identifying the worthies (the one's who dieted) for 'survival of the fittest' purposes!

Dunegan continues his recollections: "[Dr Day] said something about diet information, about proper diet, would be widely available, but most people, particularly stupid people who had no right to live anyway – they would ignore the advice and just just go on and eat what was convenient and tasted good."

Among other predictions by Dr Day were:

1. People will have to get used to change, so used to change that they'll be expecting change; nothing will be permanent.
2. More men will be transferred to other cities, and in their jobs, more men would travel. This would tend to make the marriage relationship less stable and, therefore, tend to make people less willing to have babies.
3. **The cure for cancer already exists and is locked away in the Rockefeller Institute.**

What?

The reader will be wondering why someone didn't put upon the speaker, right then and there. A large part of the answer must be the setting. Dr. Day was among colleagues and medical students. The gathering was fancy and formal. He introduced his topic by implying that he was going to help doctors adapt to future events by giving them a sneak preview. Also, the guests had been drinking. (Perhaps Dr. Dunegan was a teetotaler?)

But three more factors, ones that affect each of us, mattered a lot: First, he presented his facts with an overall justification – in this case, the population problem. In fact he stated "There's just no other way" – as if the whole thing were a humanitarian vision instead of the harass-and-murder mission that it is.

Second, Dr. Day stated – frequently – that it's too late now to stop the plans: they are already materializing. "Everything is in place (1969) and nobody can stop us now." Of course that remark could have been challenged by somebody in the audience yelling "I never heard such nonsense in my life," at which point the lecturer probably would have quit rather than be pushed into revealing the reasons for his certainty. But as soon as a few minutes went by with no one yelling out, everyone became more likely to accept the lot (and as we know, it is extremely hard to be the only one yelling out).

130

Third, for those who felt moral distress, there was always a path to denial. Day advised that the elderly would have the option of taking a 'demise pill.' In order to let the elderly know that they had become *too* old, a paler color of ink was going to be used in forms that they needed to fill out – at, say, a department store. The moral person in the audience would say to himself "Impossible! The owner of the store has elderly parents and would not contemplate such a thing!" Little would that person know that in future hardly any independent stores would exist. But for the moment, the implausibility could prompt denial.

6.7 SEX, ROCK MUSIC, AND DRUGS

Next we examine changes in popular culture, such as rock music and drugs. But first to sex.

Sexual intimacy can bond two individuals like nothing else. Until quite recently, what a couple does is their own business and both the man and the woman keep it private. World Government has now decided that won't do. **Persons must not be allowed such bonding as it would make the couple a strong entity.**

What is promoted instead is freedom from commitment. This is aided by the commoditization of sex: one can ask to have one's pleasure buttons pushed in exchange for cash rather than for love.

> [Ah, the lost art of talking dirty]:
> Had we but world enough, and time,/ This coyness, Lady, were no crime/ We would sit down and think which way/ To walk and pass our long love's day.../ A hundred years should go to praise/ Thine eyes and on thy forehead gaze;/ Two hundred to adore each breast,/ But thirty thousand to the rest; ..../ Now therefore, while the youthful hue
> Sits on thy skin like morning dew, And while thy willing soul transpires/ At every pore with instant fires, ...Let us roll all our strength and all/ Our sweetness up into one ball/ And tear our pleasures with rough strife/ Through the iron gates of life/ Thus, though we cannot make our sun / Stand still, yet we will make him run.
> ~ Andrew Marvell (1621 - 1688) *To His Coy Mistress*

Also, one can have many short-term partners. Divorce and abortion, difficult to obtain fifty years ago, can now be had on demand. Abortion in the form of the morning-after-pill can be obtained by some from the school nurse, without the student having to feel embarrassed. Condoms are dispensed for free by schools,

131

which is sure to make a boy feel inadequate if he is not 'doing it.' Also, it appears that lowering the age of sexual maturity is a goal. In fact, childhood is being wiped out with teenagehood available to all. Sex education curricula cover such 'vital' topics as oral and anal sex.

Stand by for an announcement: the report by Alfred Kinsey, published in the 1950s to great titillation, was cooked up. Contrary to media hype, the book referred to as '*The Kinsey Report*' was not a survey of the public (who would answer such questions?). Rather, it was the mind manipulators using psychological warfare methods to changing our expectations. Open today's magazines for 13-year-olds and you will find Kinseyesque questions such as "How often do you do_____?" How dare those creeps try to ruin the intimacy of sex!

List 6b shows the way in which rock 'n' roll of the 1950s, up through to MTV of the 1990s, expanded the limits of what was mentionable. A similar list of clothing fashions would show the expanding limits of how much skin should be displayed. While it is possible to interpret these changes as liberations from the prudishness of the Victorian era, there also exists the likelihood that **the changes were introduced carefully and deliberately.**

In his 1969 speech, Dr. Day forecast (at a time when "Burn the bra" was ascendant) that bras would make a comeback, but that instead of being stiff they would be softer and more able to show the natural movements of the body. What else can we gauge from this but that our planners are so connected with industry that they can control women's fashions. Haven't they anything better to do?

It is now well documented that Dr. Day's 'friends' are the ones who expanded the drug culture. The purpose of this was to make a buck, but equally **to wreck American society**. Soldiers in Vietnam were captive prey for government heroin dealers, but that wasn't enough. New 'recreational' drugs were foisted on the educated class by being distributed for free on college campuses; then, the media gave LSD prominence with interviews of Timothy Leary.

In 1975 Senator Frank Church ran hearings that outed the role of the Army's Ft. Detrick in giving LSD surreptitiously to unwitting people. A new book about that, by Hank Albarelli, *A Terrible Mistake* (2009), documents that in 1951, Ft Detrick spiked, with LSD, the bread in Pont-St-Esprit, France, resulting in five deaths. The famous death of Frank Olson (by defenestration) may have been because he knew too much about it. In other words, Olson was murdered. I gather he was *not* flying on LSD, as has been believed for years.

132

As for the connection between rock-music and drugs, that hardly needs explanation. The [stage-managed] counter-culture of the 1960s provided both at the same venue. Cathy O'Brien (1995: 122) states that country-music road-shows, also, were begun because they aided in drug distribution. (John Lennon's 1975 *Playboy* interview makes only a vague reference to LSD, contrary to rumor.)

An additional purpose of rock music is that apparently it makes people more obedient. Even the earliest human societies seem to have figured out that a drumbeat induces the feeling of tribal unity.

John C. Coleman attributes many of the bright ideas about rock music's potential to Aldous Huxley (author of *Brave New World*) and says Ed Sullivan's show was used to push rock groups. All this new culture, according to Coleman, was coming from think tanks. "How mortified [kids] would have been if they discovered that most of their 'cool' habits and expressions were deliberately created for their use" (1992: 86).

> The Beatles were brought to the United States as part of a social experiment, which would subject large population groups to brainwashing. Tavistock brought the Beatles [as] an integral part of "The Aquarian Conspiracy," ... which sprang from "The Changing Images of Man." **URH (489)-2150** Policy Research Report No. 4/4/74. Policy Report prepared by the Stanford Research Institute.
> ~ John C. Coleman *The Conspirators' Hierarchy* (1992) p. 88

6.8 TREETOPS PROPAGANDA

Predictably there is now centralized control of intellectuals, and social leaders too. (Congratulations to the cabal for understanding the power of ideas!) The late Alex Carey, an Australian union leader, coined the useful term 'treetops propaganda' (opposite of grassroots) for the way in which think tanks send messages down:

> The [American] Roundtable organized a national distribution of cartoons, pamphlets, ads, and newsletters in opposition to the Consumer Protection Agency (CPA)...[They] hired a public relations agency to distribute canned editorials and cartoons to 1000 daily newspapers and 2800 weeklies...Portions of the distributed material were published – without any indication of source. The Roundtable also sponsored a fraudulent poll which claimed to show 81 percent of Americans opposed to the CPA...~ Alex Carey (ed by Andrew Lohrey), *Taking the Risk Out of Democracy* (1993) p. 94

The Foundations' concern to blanket the air with only a narrow agenda requires that they send out 'talking points' every day for columnists and radio show hosts – both liberal and conservative.

Do you recall the posters of Smokey the Bear on city buses and trains: "Only you can prevent forest fires?" It seems that Congress required the Ad Council to give 5% of its space free to a cause, and it's better to go with Smokey than to allow real ideas. When you think of it, we have been reading for years that some tiny percentage of people owns more than half the wealth in the US. Was there ever reason for us to believe that those folks would *not* try to control us?

George Draffan (2003: 55) says the Brookings Institution in the1990s "promoted market-based incentives to replace regulation, increases in military spending, and 'free' trade." Brookings' board of trustees included the corporate CEO's and directors of Bechtel, Booz Allen, Kissinger Associates, AT&T, State Farm, Times Mirror, Aetna, US Airways, and the directors of many universities. These individuals know each other. **I wonder if the intellectuals feel embarrassed** as they look around at all their fellow rubber stamps.

A separate issue, regarding the brains of society, is the financial control of education that is exercised by the largest foundations such as Ford and Carnegie. In 1951 the Cox Committee of Congress cleverly articulated this question: "Through their power to grant and withhold funds, have foundations tended to shift the center of gravity of colleges and other institutions to a point outside the institutions themselves?" The answer must be "Yes, definitely." Is there any university dean or high school principal who has the sense of being her own boss today?

Worse, scholars are no longer encouraged to criticize the system, and teachers are required to pass to their students the party line:

The free university, historically the fountainhead of free ideas and scientific discovery, has experienced a revolution in the conduct of research. Partly because of the huge costs involved, a government contract becomes virtually a substitute for intellectual curiosity.....
The prospect of domination of the nations scholars by Federal employment, project allocations, and the power of money is ever present. ...we must also be alert to the danger that public policy could itself become the captive of a scientific-technological elite.

~ Pres Dwight D. Eisenhower, *Farewell Address,* January 17, 1961

6.9 TAVISTOCK (BRITISH MILITARY INTELLIGENCE) AND ISLAM

Tavistock concerns itself mainly with *mass mind control.* Social psychologists had discovered that persons in groups are far easier to influence, because the group setting brings out mental behaviors that an individual on his own does not manifest. Then, Tavistock realized it could 'create the environment' in which the people may show those behaviors! For instance, it can, by ordinary terrorist tactics, make a nation 'go mad.' Less dramatically, one can interfere with the brain by overwhelming it with constant changes: when confused, one's decision-making center calls it quits. **The key is to know the mind's natural processes,** especially non-rational ones.

Much can be gained by understanding the way in which the human brain evolved to accommodate culture. The child must be able to pick up, effortlessly, the viewpoints of her community. How is this done? Simply by absorbing the bits that are repeated most often. "Aha! says Tavistock, so then we must have propagandists (i.e., media) deliver the message over and over." Right! It works!

How many times have we been advised that Arabs are talented hijackers? Look at List 8c. See the episode of Arab-Japanese terrorist collusion? If that had been calmly inspected it would never have passed the giggle test. Indeed if any TV reporter had displayed a comparative chart, like List 8c, the game would have been up. Still, we're so *conditioned* it's hard to accept the truth. David Livingstone (2009: 141) argues that it was the British who started the Muslim Brotherhood as a divide-and-rule strategy and that the UK is the creator of both Islamic fundamentalism and the Wahabi movement!

That echoes a book by Robert Dreyfuss, *Hostage to Khomeini,* written under the auspices of Lyndon Larouche in 1978. (I do not know where Larouche gets his excellent inside information. He has good ideas, in my opinion, but I am wary of him as he has a 'cult.')

Dreyfuss's theory is as startling as the revelations that the Cold War was a hoax. He says our enmity with Iran, over the Ayatollah Khomeini's *coup* against the Shah in 1979 – supposedly an Islamic fundamentalist revolution, can't be real as it was the US that trained and supported the Ayatollah. John C. Coleman (1992:41) credits two professors at Princeton with having installed the Ayatollah. (Coleman states that while working for the British in Angola he had access to top secrets.) I do not feel confident of either the Dreyfuss or Coleman theory, but offer them for consideration. If true, we should presume today's Iranian leaders are also Western-controlled!

6.10 WHAT TO DO? PRAISE REASONING!

Reasoning means applying the test "If A then B." Even an ape has enough reasoning ability to notice "If my trainer puts a pink cup to the left of the blue cup, the candy will be under the pink cup." But apes cannot go very far beyond that level of reasoning. They cannot calculate: "I don't like the way society is organized. I'm going to apply some compelling principles to formulate a new way."

The praises of reasoning have been extolled over the ages. The 'gold' in the Golden Age of Greece was human rationality. Today it is vital to acknowledge that we can call on our brains to "do their stuff" when addressing various crises. It may even pay for individuals to defy the standard worry about boasting and announce at the beginning of their preaching that they thank God or_____ (substitute a name) for the human capacity to solve problems.

Here are words from historian Anthony Kubek, whose book laments the US secret support of communism in China in the 1940s:

> Acquisition of knowledge by man implies the drawing of conclusions, the passing of rational judgments, the determination of courses of action. False knowledge leads to false conclusions, irrational judgments, and wrong courses of action.... Barring complete descent of an anti-knowledge curtain, it is anticipated that further data will become available in the future. It is reasonable to assume that additional evidence will only contribute further to an indictment of our war and postwar foreign policy. Otherwise there would be no conceivable reason for its continued suppression.
> ~ Anthony Kubek, *How the Far East Was Lost* (1963) p. 441

A big cause of human's superiority to animals is that working together intellectually allowed members of our species to increase their smarts a millionfold. However admirable the lonely Robinson Crusoe (who survived by his wits after a shipwreck) may seem, we do better by interacting. My theme, in this book, is that small groups are what we most need today. The 19th and 20th centuries were wonders of coordination of knowledge, and the 21st, thanks to the Internet, has enabled us to tear down a lot of 'false knowledge.'

Now we need to get in there and exercise our cerebra. We need to become bold problem solvers, either in disregard of the bigger institutions or in cooperation with them, **but not as spectators**. Paraphrasing the Bard: Some persons are born great and others have mini-greatness thrust upon them in neighborhood or clan meetings!

Suggestion: Do not 'ancestralize.' That is a term coined by Prof Charles Crawford, a sociobiologist, that helps us picture what may occur if modern society collapses. Namely, he thinks we will go back to the earliest human behaviors (those of the Pleistocene era), as that is all we are equipped for. Consider the following sketch:

1. Most human behaviors are based on genes that were already formed in our ancestral hunter-gatherer days. (The mapping of the human genes was recently completed. It is accepted by scientists that our DNA has much in common with that of chimpanzees.) Such things as eating, sleeping, finding a mate, running from danger, cooperating, gambling, bowing to leaders, are givens of our species. (Granted, you may consciously decide *what* to eat or *when* to sleep, but you can't avoid eating and sleeping.)

2. Because of our innate propensities as animals, we, as humans, **will invent some traditions that are obviously based on those innate traits.** For instance, as soon as society is complicated enough to have a leader higher than the father of a family, he will be revered. Eventually, he will wear fancy costumes, will hold titles – will inspire patriotic self-sacrifice, will be considered 'above law.' It is our *human nature* that *creates* kings. Likewise, females will develop traditions of exchanging hints about men, or advise each other on dress. Because we evolved naked, it can't be that the interest in kingly costume or female couture is genetic. Rather we're set to produce anything that makes a leader admirable, or that helps the mating game be played.

3. We are still creatures of the Pleistocene, albeit we have become sophisticated and our environment is largely one that we ourselves create. Today the landscape consists of buildings; social relationships are structured by 'the market;' the speed of movement (55 miles per hour) is determined by politicians, etc. We no longer live in the Pleistocene – yet biologically we remain Pleistoceners!

4. So what will happen if rapid changes occur in the created environment? If the aforementioned parts of our environment can't carry on (e.g., if we lack materials to maintain the buildings, or if the market turns social relations into 'slaves and dictators'), how will humans cope? Charles Crawford claims we will revert to natural, Pleistocene-appropriate behavior. **We will ancestralize.** "What else *could* we do? It's all we've got." he says (personal communication, 2010). If our culture collapses, its many excellent restrictions on bad behavior won't be honored. Thus we will act for our own survival. Crawford (2001) first noticed ancestralization in regard to minor changes, not social collapse. For example, polygamy, rather than monogamy, was our Pleistocene norm, but Western culture has, for centuries, promoted marital fidelity. In other words, culture ruled, and those who wanted extra-marital sex had to get it on the sly. With 1960s liberalization, the urge for many sex partners reasserted itself. People 'ancestralized' back to Pleistocene behavior.

When sociobiology was introduced by EO Wilson in 1975, the very mention of humans having genetic propensies (for anything!) was considered outrageous. Many academics seemed to feel safer believing that we get all our guidance from without, not from within. Today, though, hardly anyone denies that the human brain is wired a certain way and that we have instincts. And Crawford's observations help show the interplay between social change and instincts.

I find this crucial for our decisions as to how to handle the constitutional crisis being narrated in this book. Just think how extremely dependent we are on our 'civilization' and particularly on rule of law an environment where less that 2% of the people grow the food they eat. If 'authority' gets cancelled out – by cynicism or by any other means – and we decide to let the jungle rule, we will be mighty hungry watching it rule. No amount of fighting among neighbors in big cities will result in the arrival of food!

So, yes, we might start to ancestralize, but to what avail? Thanks to density of population we are in trouble. Thanks to a huge Nanny state (which started in the New Deal era of 1934) we stopped looking to local leaders in favor of an imaginary national 'fix.' In Ch 4.8, I claimed we are deprived of young leaders by murder. Historically that's normal. All junior officers in Poland's army were secretly massacred in Katyn in 1941, and 'someone' has lately killed many professors in Iraq. Can you even name some persons who can lead?

Now think back to Crawford's plaintive cry "What else have we got?" The answer is: We've got our social institutions. We should keep any of them that are keepable during this time of insecurity. Tradition is a stabilizing force, and our Constitution is like a friend.

Such creations from the past were worked out largely by **talk.** Do you know that **folks used to have their own town hall meetings?** It is still possible. I once paid $75 to rent a civic premises in Townsville, Queensland, and later the money was refunded to me because the nature of my meeting was in the pubic interest! Was I ever gobsmacked when I opened that envelope.

Use the institutions that we have. Do not ancestralize!

List 6a.   'Ideological' Agenda of the Public Schools

(These policies have been implemented by state laws!)

-- from *Deliberate Dumbing Down* by Charlotte Iserbyt (1999):

To let him know he is being trained as a worker:
1. Tell everyone the primary function of the school is training for life, especially for the workforce.
2. Accept that schools have natural ties to business corporations
3. Explain to the community that all this is necessary to keep jobs from fleeing this country.

To fiddle with his personality:
4. Show children how to do groupthink, that is, how to arrive at decisions by consensus
5. Teach the child that thinking for himself is not good – it disrupts the class and may even hurt others' feelings.
6. Give him cognitive dissonance; it frustrates decision-making.

To keep the child uneducated:
7. Deprive the student of capability in arithmetic by not teaching him to memorize tables of multiplication and division.
8. Deprive children of the well-established key to reading that is based on phonics, (not 'whole language' or 'look-say.')
9. Gear the lessons to the less bright students.
10. Teach him that all stories have equal merit; if the author's work has been loved for centuries that does not matter.

Note: Iserbyt returned to the US after 17 years abroad, in 1971. Thanks to the items that her young sons brought home from school, she quickly noticed the radical changes that had taken place in curriculum and said "I was shocked to find public education had become a warm, touchy-feely, soft experience with its purpose being socialization, not learning." Iserbyt has now been an activist for 39 years, decrying all these abominations. Her book is a compendium of the work of other activists, plus incriminating documents and speeches by the planners. Her articles appear on the website newswithviews.com. Every parent needs to hear about this!

List 6b.   Sex in Songs, Movies, and Cultural Fashion

From the Days of Hubba-Hubba until Now!

In the 1940's, actress Mae West, was the symbol of naughtiness, using double meaning phrases as "Come up and see my etchings." Starting in the 1950s, the following rapid departures from the then-accepted social mores took place, *each raising scandal* at first.

☞ the hip-grinding musical style of Elvis Presley, and, later, the Twist

☞ the phrase "courtin' too slow" in the song *On Top of Ol' Smokey*

☞ the movie *Lolita* about what was not yet widely known as pedophilia

☞ the bikini, and the decolleté of Raquel Welsh and Gina Lolabrigita

☞ 'shacking up' (formerly 'living in sin') made possible by 'The Pill'

☞ topless waitresses, preceding by many years, pole and table dancers

☞ rape of male in *Deliverance*; male-female anal sex in *Last Tango in Paris*

☞ topics on the *Donahue* talk-show including intimate bedroom details

☞ explicit description of various sex acts in magazines for girls age 13

☞ Madonna and others on MTV channel portray sex as part of music

☞ at age 16 Britney Spears as sex-object-in-school-uniform, on MTV

☞ *Brokeback Mountain,* about male lovers; the Sydney Mardi Gras

☞ Janet Jackson's revealing of a breast on TV during '06 Superbowl

☞ clothing for little girls now styled the same as for young women

☞ plans for a metal sculpture in London Tube of a couple mating

☞ Home Box Office promising full-frontal male nudity in 2010

☞ Next on the agenda: live sex shows (You heard it here first.)

List 6c.   Tax-Exempt Foundations and Think-Tanks

Shown with a few of their major interests, that indicate how they influence politics, economics, and American culture:

American Enterprise Institute: DEFENSE, NEOCON IDEAS

The Heritage Foundation: EDUCATION POLICY

Guggenheim Foundation: MODERN ART, SCULPTURE

Carnegie Endowment for Peace: WAR, DIPOMACY

Ford Foundation: WOMEN IN DEVELOPING NATIONS

World Wildlife Fund: GLOBAL LEADERS for TOMORROW

Rockefeller Foundation: MEDICINE, EDUCATION, MEDIA

RAND Corp: KEEPS RECORD OF SPREAD OF AIDS

Cato Institute: PRIVATIZATION OF PUBLIC LANDS

Olin Foundation: SUPPORTS RAND, CATO, OTHERS

Scaife Foundation: CONSERVATIVE JUDICIAL CASES

Brookings Institution: SOCIAL AND ECONOMIC POLICY

Lucis* Trust: UN, GREENPEACE, AMNESTY INTERNAT'L

Stanford Research Institute: BEHAVIOR, MIND CONTROL

James Baker III Institute for Public Policy: MIDDLE EAST

*formerly the Lucifer Trust, started by occultist Alice Bailey in 1922; publishes for schools, on spirituality. See Constance Cumbey (1985)

Note: It is within Congress's power to alter the relevant legislation.

SOURCES: George Draffan, *The Elite Consensus (2003)*
Rene Wormser, *Foundations (1958)*

END OF PART TWO *("WHY BRAINS MISSING")* **– A CHRONOLOGY**

1090 Assassins in Persia create mind-controlled *agents provocateurs*

1902 Pavlov rings dinner bell; dog thinks 'New York sirloin'

1902 General Education Board set up as charity by Rockefellers

1918 Schoenberg's music is intended to be unbeautiful, harsh

1920 Tavistock founded, propagates arrogant idea of social control

1926 Freud's nephew, Bernays, helps Madison Av & PR industry

1928 Wells' *Open Conspiracy* is true: the conspiracy is indeed open

1930 Marriage of CBS to CIA; William Paley wears hat of each

1940s Walt Disney produces Bambi while Sandoza produces LSD

1950s TV starts quiz shows, sitcoms, soap operas, subliminals

1950 Congress of Cultural Freedom hobnobs with Europe's artists

1954 Norman Dobbs initiates scrutiny of methods of foundations

1965 Beatlemania, Age of Aquarius. These later revealed as psy-ops

1966 Unbelievably, it is the gov't that is pushing recreational drugs!

1969 Planned Parenthood's Dr. Day spills all beans to fellow MD's

1970s *NYT Book Review* easily controls which books get promoted

1970s Inner cities: some banks arrange redlining, add to white flight

1970s PLO, IRA, constantly in news, hence new 'security' at airports

1980 Brice Taylor demo'd for commercial sale as mind-files robot

1980 Reagan 'insider,' Charlotte Iserbyt, aghast at Education policy

1990 Oregonians allege symptoms of electromagnetic wave attack

1994 Neil Brick, survivor of ritual abuse, creates S.M.A.R.T. group

1997 UK Home Secy requires that judges register if they're Masons

2000 No Child Left Behind Act includes psychiatric diagnosing

2000s Commercial patenting of life forms (seeds and DNA) allowed

2007 extreme-abuse-survey.net draws 1400 responses worldwide

ΨΨΨΨ

Welcome to Part Three:

Long Live This Marvelous Constitution!

Chapters: 7 Judiciary
8 Presidents
9 Congress

from Justice Madden, *Lovett v United States,* 1946:

It may well be that under our Constitution and under any constitution which may be devised for a free people, one branch of the Government could, temporarily at least, subvert the Government.

> The judges might refuse to enforce legal rights or convict criminals.

> The President might order the Army and Navy to surrender to the enemy.

> Congress might refuse to raise or appropriate money to pay the President …

But any of these imagined actions would not be taken pursuant to the Constitution, **but would be acts of subversion and revolution.**

[emphasis added]

IN EMINENTI
(A Papal Bull Excommunicating Freemasons)

Since the divine clemency has placed Us, Whose merits are not equal to the task, in the high watchtower of the Apostolate with the duty of pastoral care confided to Us, We have turned Our attention, ... to those things through which the integrity of Orthodox Religion is kept from errors... Now it has come to Our ears...that certain Societies, ...called in the popular tongue Liberi Muratori or Francs Massons
...are spreading far and wide and daily growing in strength.... But it is in the nature of crime to betray itself ...Thus these aforesaid Societies have caused in the minds of the faithful the greatest suspicion and all prudent and upright men have passed the same judgment on them as being depraved and perverted....

We therefore, having taken counsel of some of Our Venerable Brothers among the Cardinals of the Holy Roman Church, and also of Our own accord ... do condemn and prohibit them.
Wherefore We command ...that none, under any pretext or for any reason, shall dare or presume to enter, propagate or support these aforesaid societies, ...or to receive them in their houses or dwellings or to hide them, be enrolled among them, joined to them, be present with them, give power or ...help them in any way, ...but they must stay completely clear of such Societies, under pain of excommunication ...

Given at Rome, in the year 1738 of Our Lord
Source: www.papalencyclicals.net

7 Judiciary

Punishment for being Quakers in Massachusetts:... [in 1656]...
Wm. Brend [was put] into Irons, Neck and Heels, lockt so close
together...and was kept in that way for 16 hours, without food
after having been whipped.
— James Truslow Adams, *The Founding of New England*

Roma locuta est. Causa finita est. (The Church has spoken. Case closed)
— paraphrasing St Augustine, circa 416 BCE

7.1 UBI SOCIETAS, IBI JUS (WHERE SOCIETY IS, THERE IS LAW)

Under the Judiciary Act of 1789, every federal judge must take
this oath of office: "I do solemnly swear that I will administer justice
without respect to persons, and do equal right to the poor and to the
rich; and that I will faithfully and impartially discharge all the duties
incumbent on me as ____, to the best of my abilities and
understanding, agreeably to the constitution and laws of the United
States."

It would be marvelous if members of modern society were
'grabbed' by the feeling of solemnity that used to accompany the
swearing of an oath, but they are not. As was noted 75 years ago:

Mutilation for Perjury!!

Under Charlemagne a convicted perjurer would have his hand
struck off; ...some of the Anglo-Saxon kings imposed heavy fines
or mutilation... The oath [is now] secularized.... The religious
faith in the direct visitation of God's anger on him who swore
falsely has decayed so as to exert little influence on those to whom
truth-telling is not a normal rule of conduct....

The time will come when we shall have to deal seriously with the
question of inventing new ways of persuading people to tell the
truth.... So far we have not even begun to face this problem or give
it serious consideration, with results in our Courts of law [in Britain]
which it is impossible to view with satisfaction.

~ William Robson, *Civilization and the Growth of Law* (1935) pp. 158-9

The Constitution's Article III, about the judicial branch, is short:

Art. III, Sec 1. <u>The judicial Power of the United States, shall be vested in one supreme Court, and in such inferior Courts as the Congress may from time to time ordain and establish.</u> [Note: Congress did establish other courts, such as Federal district courts, immigration court, and the outrageously corrupt bankruptcy court.] <u>The Judges, both of the supreme and inferior Courts, shall hold their Offices during good Behaviour....</u>

Section 2. <u>The judicial Power shall extend to all Cases, in Law and Equity, arising under this Constitution, the Laws of the United States, and the Treaties made, or which shall be made....</u>
<u>In all Cases ...in which a States shall be Party, the supreme Court shall have original jurisdiction. In all the other Cases before mentioned, the supreme Court shall have appellate Jurisdiction, both as to Law and Fact, with such Exceptions, and under such Regulations as the Congress shall make. The Trial of all Crimes except in Cases of Impeachment, shall be by Jury....</u>

Some judicial responsibilities are also seen in the Amendments:
Am 5. <u>No person shall be held to answer for a capital, or otherwise infamous crime, unless on a presentment or indictment of a grand jury.... nor shall any person be subject for the same offense to be twice put in jeopardy of life or limb; nor shall be compelled in any criminal case to be a witness against himself....</u> [Hence the phrase 'he took the fifth']

Am 6. <u>In all criminal prosecutions, the accused shall enjoy the right to a speedy and public trial, by an impartial jury of the state and district wherein the crime shall have been committed... and to be informed of the nature and cause of the accusation; to be confronted with the witnesses against him; to have compulsory process for obtaining witnesses in his favor, and to have the assistance of counsel for his defense.</u> ['Compulsory process' means he can have those witnesses summoned by the Court.]

Am 8. <u>Excessive bail shall not be required, nor excessive fines imposed, nor cruel and unusual punishments inflicted.</u> [Note: that wording came straight from the English Bill of Rights of 1689.]

146

7.2 GUIDE TO THIS CHAPTER -- *JUDICIARY*

Section 7.3 is about Jose Padilla. 7.4 presents a 'Law Showcase' as a quick guide to a dozen types of law that Americans are legally obliged to obey. 7.5 laments the epidemic of fake court cases. 7.6 is a rhapsody on the mechanisms for justice. 7.7 thanks Sherman Skolnick for doing his best. 7.8 comments on the Judicial Conference and names our Supreme Court Justices. 7.9 displays ways to control courts. 7.10 What To Do? says Prosecute menticide! See Aps A through D, plus Y, and – urgently, for impeachment of judges – V.

7.3 NO WAY, MR PADILLA

Probably the most significant prosecution ever to reach the Supreme Court of the US, as far as citizens' rights are concerned – or as far as the strength of the parchment is concerned, was the case of Jose Padilla, the man supposedly found entering the US in December 2001 from Pakistan. He allegedly carried plans to use a 'dirty bomb' to blow up an apartment building in Chicago.

Not a trace of evidence was ever produced, but then it did not have to be produced, as the Executive, in the person of Atty Gen Ashcroft, said that Padilla was not protected by *habeas corpus*. That's the rule by which a family member of the prisoner can ask for a Writ that is sent to the jailer saying "You have the man; make sure you bring him before a judge within 48 hours to be charged."

According to the Justice Department's creative wording, Padilla was not exactly a citizen; he was an *enemy non-combatant*. Not being a military person he could not get a court martial, and not being a foreigner he could not come under the Geneva Convention's protection of prisoners-of-war. Padilla was a US-born citizen who had converted to Islam. (Believers in Islam are known as *Muslims*).

Here was the big chance for SCOTUS to deal with the outrages of the Bush administration. Indeed, Justice Scalia did the right thing the first time the Padilla matter came up, in *Hamdi v Rumsfeld* (2004). Padilla was a defendant along with Hamdi, a 21 year-old born in the US. The majority ruling sent Padilla's case back to a lower court.

Dissenting Scalia said there's no need to invent new ways to deal with emergencies (he decried the "Mr. Fix-it mentality" of the ruling written by Justice Sandra Day O'Connor) because, he observed, the Framers had already taken that into consideration. Scalia said Padilla should be charged with something, *perhaps treason*, and tried in the normal way. Ah, wouldn't a treason trial have been eye-popping!

The Court did not want any such putting at ease of the American people as may have resulted from a genuine trial of the accused. On a flimsy technicality, Padilla's case was remanded. We then had to wait more years for the case to once again reach the top.

Finally, when the SCOTUS case was due to begin, President Bush withdrew the allegation of the dirty bomb, depriving everyone of seeing how the court would handle the 'enemy non-combatant' thing. Our Justices did not have to fall for this routine. They could have ruled on the matter even though it was moot. After all, in 1973 they continued to rule on a woman's right to abortion in *Roe v Wade* long after the baby was born. That baby is now about 40 years old.

The law professors of the US, of whom there are thousands, did not go berserk over the chicanery surrounding the Padilla case, and needless to say, the media did not inform the public of what was going on. We were simply 'informed' of the new charge that Padilla had engaged in *conspiracy,* and he was subsequently convicted of that. (I guess that means the DoJ goes in for conspiracy theory. 'lol.')

7.4 LAW SHOWCASE

This section shows 12 types of law that Americans obey. Each mentions the group to whom it is addressed, followed by *the sanctions (punishments) for those who disobey,* and the way to locate the law.

1. *Common law* applies to every member of society. *Fines, jail, death.* It is the body of law accumulated from judges' decisions.

2. *Statutes* apply to all Americans if the statute was enacted by Congress, or to all persons in the state, if part of state law. *Fines, jail, death.* Many federal statutes are codified in the USC (United States Code). State laws can easily be found by an amateur Internet search.

3. *Military law* applies to armed services personnel, and to POW's. *Demotion, forfeiture of pay, loss of benefits, dishonorable discharge, fines, jail, death.* The Uniform Code of Military Justice is found at 42 USC 21.

4. *Rules* apply to those who join a group, such as a corporate board, a club, or the US Senate. *Reprimand, censure, suspension from the group, expulsion.* Ask your group to show you its rules or 'by-laws.'

5. *Executive orders* apply to anyone targeted by the particular order. *No punishment, since executives by definition do not make law; they see to its execution. However, the EO is usually based on statutes, and these may*

have sanctions. EO's are published in the Federal Register. (Some are called Presidential Decision Directives and other names.)

6. ***The laws against torture and genocide*** apply to every human, as they have been declared open to 'universal jurisdiction.' Thus, an American could be tried for them by another country, even 'in absentia.' *Fines, jail, death.* See The Convention against Torture and 18 USC 2340A. For genocide, see 18 USC 1091 (and Appendix O).

7. ***Ethics codes of certain professions*** apply to their members, as the state has allowed them to be partially self-policing. *Loss of licence to practice law, medicine, nursing, accountancy, etc.* Codes are kept in public libraries and can be inspected at, say, the American Bar Association.

8. ***Regulations*** apply to persons who participate in certain things, such as 'all users of this publicly-owned skating rink.' *Fines, administered by the 'statutory body' that oversees the place, such as the state's Department of Recreation. (When a person receives notice of the fine she can appeal this to the administrator, and ultimately to a court.)* US government regulations are codified in the Code of Federal Regulations.

9. ***Private law*** applies to parties who have contracted with each other, or to members of society who have a particular duty toward certain others. *Courts enforce private law by awarding damages to the aggrieved party, or by ordering the performance of some duty.* The laws of contract and of torts are found in common law and in statutes.

10. ***Civil rights enforcement laws*** (which are inherently redundant!) apply to all, notably police, who mistreat citizens. *Fines, jail, death (or award of damages if victim files a civil suit).* 18 USC 241.

11. ***Court orders*** apply to persons with relation to a particular case, as when a judge awards custody of a child to the grandparents. *Fines, jail - for contempt of court.* The specifics are written on the order.

12. ***Constitutions*** differ from laws; they grant legitimacy to laws by stating how or why particular of government officials are allowed to wield power. *Our Constitution does not specify penal consequences for wielding power wrongly, but Congress can use impeachment, reprimand, and censure. Citizens use voting and moral pressure to discipline elected leaders. This book emphasizes that criminality by government officials (be it treason, theft, or war crimes) needs to be met by the normal remedy:* ***criminal prosecution.*** The crime of treason is spelled out in Art. III, Sec 3 of the Constitution.

Court cases are on the Net. Active federal cases are viewable, pay-per-page, at PACER. To locate law, search the topic plus 'USC.'

When a bill is being considered in the House of Representatives it has the prefix HR; for Senate it is S. If the bill passes and is signed it becomes a PL – Public Law Number Such-and-Such. The Patriot Act is PL **106-56,** meaning the 56th Act of the 106th Congress. (The first Congress sat in 1791, so the one elected in 2008 was 111th.) Public laws get codified into the 50 titles of the USC.

7.5 **Fake Cases Galore**

The serial killer myth is a ploy to get us to fear our neighbor. Mentally sick persons do *not* go on rampages. It follows, then, that the trials of the various accused were handled in a dishonest way. Or trial is *avoided*, by having the man plead guilty. Please look at List 7a.

Also, the terrorist case related to the 1993 bombing at WTC must be phony. Perforce, I believe the related trial of Lynne Stewart had to have been a set-up **for the purpose of 'chilling' other attorneys.** She was convicted of helping the 'blind sheikh' in prison. AG Ashcroft took the peculiar step of announcing on Dave Letterman's TV show that Lynne had been arrested. Investigators had carried 12 boxes of attorney-privileged papers from her home!

Many *dissents* by SCOTUS Justices arouse my skepticism. They express the law so perfectly that one must wonder how the Justice failed to prevail on his colleagues. Could it be that dissents are written to mask a radical deviation by the Court? They cause people to hear familiar words, which stave off alarm. See the ones by Jackson in *Korematsu*, or Harlan in *Hurtado* – so heartfelt, so comprehensive (Justices Brennan and Holmes were called 'the great dissenters').

Your humble author is the Maxwell in *Maxwell v Bush*, an antiwar suit. Did I ever get an eyeful when collating previous cases of the same type! Appendix W is a list of those cases. I reckon most of them were set-ups – to create the 'custom' that a president, not Congress, declares war. (Oh, don't ever listen to Bruce Ackerman who says that Constitution changes according to custom. Heresy!!)

The modus operandi is that a war-powers case gets dismissed by a lower court and the Supreme Court resolutely refuses to hear the final appeal. A decoding ✍ rule is called for, no? Look at the past cases listed in Appendix W and ask why the dismissal was never followed up by the plaintiff. This can be called the Conyers rule: if someone files suit and lets the matter drop, it may be a fake case.

7.6 PERFECT JUSTICE, ALMOST HEAVEN

Lest anyone think the foregoing section bespeaks a need for new law, no -- just a need for better behavior. Anglo-American law, as it has developed over the centuries, **is a wonder of the world.**

This may be because it attracts deep thinkers who love to handle abstractions. It may also be that the concept of justice, which sits atop our evolved emotion of reciprocal altruism, is always pushing toward completion. People want problems resolved fairly. As expressed by the symbol of the lady holding the scales of justice, balance is the desired outcome. Here is a sample of legal notions:

Abuse of process: You must not abuse the judicial system by, say, bringing a fake case, or using lawsuits as a means to harass someone.

Access to the court: As stated in *Chambers v Baltimore & Ohio* (1907) "The right to sue and defend in the courts...is the alternative of force. In an organized society it is the right conservative of all other rights and lies at the foundation of orderly government. It is one of the highest and most essential privileges of citizenship."

Amicus curiae: Those not parties to the case can help the court to understand some issue, by filing a brief as a 'friend of the court.'

Antitrust: Congress passed the Sherman Act in 1890 to outlaw huge corporate trusts. Competitors use antitrust law to sue one another but the DoJ has responsibility for prosecuting, as in *US v Microsoft.*

Bench warrant: Judge can issue an arrest warrant when she receives sworn statement, and good evidence, that X has committed a crime. Yes, this means we are not dependent on federal or state executive!

Civil rights: 18 USC 241: "If two or more persons combine to injure, oppress, threaten or intimidate any person in any State ... in the free exercise or enjoyment of any right or privilege secured to him by the Constitution or laws of the US ... they shall be fined..." DoJ rarely undertakes such prosecutions. See O.J. Simpson case.

Compelling a witness: If you are accused and you know of persons that could speak in your favor, the court is required to assist you by subpoenaing them. They can even be arrested as witnesses for you.

Criminal Complaints: Anyone can go to a police station and file a report, then carry a Police Incident Report to a courthouse (**e.g. in**

Boston it is at 124 New Chardon St) and make Application for Criminal Complaint. Per mass.gov/courts: "When completed, a hearing will be scheduled and the defendant will be notified by mail. The burden of probable cause rests solely on the complainant."

Declaratory Judgment: A plaintiff may seek to have a judge rule before any injury has occurred. The judge simply issues an opinion declaring the rights of the parties. In 1934 Congress enacted the Declaratory Judgment Act.

Discovery: You have a right, in trying to win your case, to demand information from the defendant. He must produce what you need.

Discretion: Every judge is given his head.

Exculpatory: If the public prosecutor possesses information that tends to show innocence of the accused, he must reveal it.

'Fraud upon the court': Little used but vital. If any part of the court cheats, a judgment may be vitiated. See Anant Tripati's Arizona case.

Judicial notice: "The acceptance by the court of certain notorious [i.e., noticeable] facts without proof" (*The Law Dictionary*, 1986).

Jus cogens: Concept that set crimes such as piracy, slave-trading, and torture are recognized by all nations: and that the criminals are *hostis humani generis:* enemy of all mankind. Vienna Convention on Treaties (which the US quit in 2005) says any treaty condoning those is void.

Jury nullification: No matter what instructions the judge gives, jurors may vote their conscience. Bringing in a verdict of 'not guilty' when the jury clearly knows the person committed the crime, is taken to be a proper protest that the law itself is unfair. However judges sometimes tell a jury that there is no such thing as jury nullification. This subject has – predictably – never reached the Supreme Court.

Legal aid: In all criminal prosecutions the accused shall enjoy the right…to have the Assistance of Counsel for his Defense. So promises the 6th Amendment, and states have provided the realization.

Maxim: A maxim is a general principle, such as: "Fraud vitiates every transaction into which it enters." Per a ruling in *The People of Illinois v Fred Stirling* (1934) this "applies to judgments… thus a court ruling that sprang from fraud must be void." What import in those words!

152

Miranda's: "You have a right to remain silent. Anything you say may be held against you …" Per 1966 Supreme Court ruling in favor of Mr Miranda, who was not informed of his rights, interviews with suspects could be ruled inadmissible in court. But *Berghuis v Thomkins* (2010) says the accused must articulate his wish to remain silent.

Misprision: 18 USC 4. It is a felony to fail to report crime. Socially, tattling is frowned on, but for the crime of treason please do it, now.

Mittimus: ('we send.') A Justice of the Peace, or legislature, informs police or jailer that a suspect is being sent to them, to be kept until a hearing, e.g., because their remaining free is a danger to the state. [!]

Obstruction of justice: Shredding documents, bribing jurors, etc. Can be by omission. Some judges commit this crime routinely.

Outlaw: A person who cannot be controlled by law is 'outside the law,' hence is subject to violence by any member of society. (archaic)

Protective custody: You know something about the baddies and thus fear they will get you? You can ask to be jailed prophylactically.

Pro se filings: Anyone can walk into Federal District Court and lodge her pleadings (lawsuit) without benefit of attorney. She is thus a *pro se* litigant, meaning 'for herself.' The filing fee (currently $350) can be waived in cases of hardship. (You can send info to tips.fbi.gov.)

Remedies: If someone has done you wrong, the court can set things right, as expressed in the maxim *Lex semper dabit remedium.*

RICO: It is hard to pin a Mafia boss with the actual carrying out of a crime. The Racketeering and Corrupt Organizations Act deals with this by requiring that only a *pattern* of crime be demonstrated. You can bring a civil action along this line (see *Rodriguez v Bush* in Ap C).

Special Prosecutor: Congress or state legislatures can appoint one!

Unjust enrichment: Using principles of the old courts of Equity a judge may order a person who has made unfair gain to 'disgorge' the money. In *Snepp v US* (1980) SCOTUS ruled that Snepp had to disgorge his ill-gotten gains! See Constitution Art. III, Sec 2 re equity!

Witness Protection Program: In exchange for your testimony against criminals, you may be offered a new passport, a new nose, etc.

Victoria, by the Grace of God, of the United Kingdom of Great Britain and Ireland Queen, Defender of the Faith, To J. K., Keeper of our Gaol of Jersey, in the Island of Jersey, We command you that you have the body of C. C. W., detained in our prison under your custody, as it is said, together with the day and cause of his being taken and detained, … in our Court before us, at Westminster, on the 18th day of January next, to undergo and receive all and singular such matters and things which our said Court shall then and there consider of him in this behalf; and have there then this Writ.

[a Writ of Habeas Corpus, dated 1845]

---

23 November 2002 OFFICIAL LOG OF INTERROGATION AT GUANTANAMO (The prisoner's name is 'Detainee 063')

0225 [a.m.]: The detainee arrives at the interrogation booth at Camp X-Ray. **His hood is removed [!!!] and he is bolted to the floor.** Sgt A and Sgt R are the interrogators. A DoD linguist and Maj L (BSCT) are present. 0235: Session begins. The detainee refuses to look at [female] Sgt A "due to his religion." This is a rapport building session. 0240: Detainee states he's on hunger strike. Sgt A explains the effects of a hunger strike on the body.

Sgt A runs "love of brothers in Cuba" approach. 0320: The detainee refused to answer whether he wanted water. Sgt R explained with emphasis that not answering disrespects Sgt A and embarrasses him. The detainee said no, he didn't want water. The detainee continues to say he's on hunger strike. Interrogation resumes. The detainee refuses food and water. 0540: Sgt A begins 9/11 theme. The detainee asks to pray and is refused. 0550: Detainee drinks bottle of water and states after this he is on strike, he refuses food. 0620: Interrogators take break to discuss theme. 0630: Interrogation resumes. **Sgt A continues with 9/11 theme.** 0700: Sgt R emphasized his frustration over detainee's refusal to speak. Sgt R denies detainee's request to pray. [emphasis added]

[Question: What effect is this task having on Sergeants A and R?] *See Scalia's excellent dissent in* Boumediene v Bush. *Such POW's deserve Geneva-Convention treatment, not habeas corpus.*

7.7 SKOLNICK, OUR RABBI

The Alabama case of the judge having to remove the Ten Commandments from the Courthouse is one that feeds into 'culture wars.' How far we have gone in misinterpreting the First Amendment's prohibition of a state religion! All societies have as their basic rules the ten – more or less – commandments, to restrain us from the anti-social things we are naturally inclined to do: lie, steal, hit, be adulterers. The put-downs of religion today make one think of Sherman Skolnick and his utter dedication to American law. (He managed to get *judges* behind bars for their crimes-in-court.)

He got this from his Americanness but as a religious Jew he also got it from the Judaic tradition of rabbinical courts. Loss of religion is a serious problem if it means loss of a reference point for righteousness. Today who can trust whom to have noble motives for anything? Skolnick credited his parents for his strong moral sense. He used a cable channel once a week for his *Broadsides* show. His *The Overthrow of the American Republic* came out after his death:

Citizen's Committee To Clean Up the Courts (Skolnick's base of operations in Chicago): Your Honor, tell us what happened.
Chief Judge: I went to the top officials of the DEA and FBI. I gave them specific details. Instead of helping me they joined with the criminals to threaten me. So now the dopers are running my courthouse.
Citizen's C'tee: Maybe I can suggest someone who would publicize this.
Chief Judge: For the sake of my family, I want no publicity. I need help.
Chief Judge [when we met again]: I resigned. **My family was in danger**.

7.8 THE JUDICIAL CONFERENCE

The Framers intended that the rare bad judge be dealt with by impeachment (Art. II). Additionally, Congress created the Judicial Conference where federal judges can discipline their own. They could have disciplined Justice Scalia, when he failed to recuse himself in a case in which VP Cheney was the plaintiff, and Scalia and his daughter had just been on a hunt with Cheney. Sadly, the 34-page agenda of the 2007 Judicial Conference makes no mention of any of the ethical or criminal issues raised in this book.

Today's 9 SCOTUS justices are John Roberts (Chief), Antonin Scalia, Stephen Breyer, Anthony Kennedy, Clarence Thomas, Ruth Bader Ginsberg, Samuel Alito, Sonia Sotomayor, and Elena Kagan.

A Pause To Discuss Cruelty. Ch 4 sketched our tendency to greediness, war-making, and deceit. Those traits account for the vicissitudes of life (whether within the tribe or between tribes) – in addition to the vicissitudes of hunger, illness, and personal disappointment. You may have gathered that I do not believe in 'evil forces' as such. What can look like an evil force is the accumulation of bad traits, particularly in a ruling class (Note: the US is seen to be the ruling class that determines the fate of many nations!) In Dickensian London, children had to show up for work before dawn. This was caused **by elegant families, not by persons who resembled werewolves.** The fine folk probably turned their face away from the children's suffering, or made up a justification for it, including that "it's for the best." Here is one such comment:

> The men of the New Republic will not be squeamish either in facing or inflicting death.... **They will have ideals** that will make killing worthwhile.... They will hold that a certain portion of the population **exists in sufferance** only out of pity and patience...and I do not foresee any reason to suppose that they will hesitate to kill when that sufferance is abused. [emphasis added]   ~ H.G. Wells, *Anticipations of the Reaction to Mechanical and Scientific Progress Upon Life and Thought,* as quoted in Carol White, *The New Dark Ages Conspiracy: Britain's Plot To Destroy Civilization* (1980) back cover.

Recall Wells's seemingly civilized argument (1928) for changing over to a universalistic religion and life without families. Think, too, how easily we Americans honor the principle that business *must* make a profit. The 'bottom line' justifies mad ecological destruction!

> "How does one man assert his power over another, Winston?"
> Winston thought. **"By making him suffer,"** he said. "Exactly. By making him suffer. Obedience is not enough... Power is in inflicting pain and humiliation. Power is in tearing minds to pieces and putting them together again **in shapes of your own choosing**.... Do you begin to see, then, what kind of world we are creating?... A world of fear and treachery and torment, a world of trampling and being trampled upon.... The old civilization claimed that they were founded on love and justice. **Ours is founded upon hatred.** In our world there will be no emotions except fear, rage, triumph and self-abasement. ~ George Orwell, *1984* (1949) p.31 [emphasis added]

Still, as noted in the above quote, deliberate cruelty is used for controlling people. Tellingly, Orwell followed his remark, about the new world differing from one based on justice and love, by having O'Brien say: "Already we have **cut the links between child and parent,** between man and man, and between man and woman."

So let us consider again what it is in our power, and our talent, to do. *Theoretically* we can reform both our society and our culture. Those two are intertwined: to change social structure, one would change demographics, economics, and relationships, but to do that, one would use cultural means of encouraging particular behaviors. So it's **culture that we can deliberately modify.** That modification needs to show deference to natural propensities. In this book I have been celebrating America's great cultural gift, the Constitution. That scheme of government surely has an eye for natural propensities!

Yet it failed to prepare us for a reign of sociopaths. Judging from some of the events narrated earlier, we should now include in our social planning a greater awareness of systematic cruelty. Now that we see what a secret cabal can achieve, and **what public ignorance can support,** we know that better mechanisms for confronting major malice are needed. Those mechanisms include teaching folks about the standard human habit of 'going into denial.' And we should be much more upfront than we have been about the inherent tendency of bureaucracies and 'noble institutions' to cover up evil.

Today, what if the oil spill were found to be not accidental but a sociopath's attempt to destroy the planet? Personally I would say it's open season on the oil-spillers. Isn't it a pity some Americans didn't go feral **as soon as they realized** the JFK assassination was an inside job? And that the media promoted the cover story (Oswald) in a manner that could only have been collusive? Hand-to-hand combat at that stage would have been enlightening to persons like myself who didn't have a clue. (By the way, I now think the sole purpose of JFK's killing was 'trauma' – to swat America's self-confidence and her at-that-time-genuine generosity of spirit.)

Sadism itself is a feature of human nature. Taking pleasure in another's pain must be in some way underwritten in our genes. (Cruelty has been noted in chimpanzees, but only when 'in battle.') Sadism is an awkward subject to discuss, but shouldn't leaders act responsibly to protect our planet from it by whatever means? When desperate we can say *Necessitas non habet legem.* But first let's go legal.

I'm pretty sure we can succeed if we *really use* our legal resources.

7.9 CONTROL FROM THE TOP

As we saw earlier in the Padilla case, policy decisions are made by higher-ups. Courts – even SCOTUS? – may be pressured into following them. As we saw in Ch 1, regarding 'the DoJ problem,' decisions to refrain from prosecuting are often very political, not to say criminal! The media, too, has ways of controlling the outcome of cases, and so does the legal profession. Here are some items from the bag of tricks that are frequently used to frustrate justice:

Bar Associations: Like the American Medical Association, the American Bar Association seems to be one of World Government's controllers of the professions. In the old days such organizations were proud to take a stand against social evils; today, not. 'Barring': From what was said earlier about *access,* it is hard to see how a US judge could ever bar a citizen from coming to court, but three law-abiding Americans say that precisely that has happened to them. They are Eustace Mullins, Sherman Skolnick, and Rodney Stich. It may mean they were deemed 'vexatious' – *q.v. (quod vide:* which see). Clerk as gatekeeper: The clerks-of-court sometimes prevent judges from seeing certain information. In 2009, Attorney Orly Taitz met Chief Justice Roberts at a book-signing and asked about the case she had filed regarding Pres Obama's birth certificate. The judge's reply indicated that he had not seen the case. Taitz then instigated a complaint against the clerk of court. Court-appointed lawyer: An accused often has no say in who will defend him. In the Brian Nichols case in Fulton County, Georgia, it was obvious from the trial, which was televised in full, that the accused had no say in anything. He was zombied out. Declining to hear: Supreme Court's chronic declining to hear cases on a certain issue such as war powers is tantamount to a ruling. Deep-pocketing: An affluent litigant can keep his case running until the other side has to quit for lack of funds. FBI: When the FBI has exclusive custody of the evidence, anything can happen. FISA: The Constitution does not provide for secret courts, yet we do have the Foreign Intelligence Surveillance Act courts. If all that is needed is protection of classified documents, this can be done by any judge *in camera* [in his/her chambers]. Forfeiture: Gains to be made out of asset forfeiture incite some police to overdo it. Gagging: What could be more unconstitutional than this? (In Australia, David Hicks won't tell of his 7 years in Gitmo. Was that case conjured to remind colonials of their place?) Headnote: A headnote is written by a court reporter describing a judge's ruling. Headnotes have no legal authority, and yet one was used in the *Santa Clara* case to create a radical new interpretation of the Fourteenth Amendment. The man who wrote it was J. C. Bancroft Davis, a former railroad president. (Update: In 2010 SCOTUS honored that headnote again in the case *Citizens United v Federal Election Commission*). He-men: some police, and many lawyers too, feel the need to be aggressive; they think civility or courtesy is a sign of weakness. Intimidation: Courts are scary, as they should be, because they carry the wrath of society against wrongdoers. During the initial trial of Death Row prisoner Troy Davis, his relatives were told not to appear in court. They later saw that the reason for this trick was so the jury would not realize the accused had a loving family. This seems to constitute fraud-upon-the-court. Methinks executions should be stayed. Until fraud is sorted out we need 'caretaker government.' Plea bargain: Ever wonder why so many people do not receive the constitutional benefit of a jury trial? It is because they have 'copped a plea.' In exchange for promise of a light sentence they agree to plead guilty to a lesser charge. Precedent-worship: Lawyers exaggerate the importance of precedents. They should look at Maxim 18 in Ap C: *Judicandum est legibus, non exemplis.* Settling out of court: A plaintiff can be paid off to close the case, so that no precedent will be set. SLAPP suits: These Strategic Lawsuits Against Public Participation are filed by corporations to harass activists. It is a disgrace that the courts do not do something about this 'abuse of process' Standing: Until the 1920s it was understood that every American had 'standing' – the right to sue in regard to protecting the Constitution; since the 1962 case *Baker v Carr,* there are specific requirements -- the cabal uses these to shield our eyes from the status quo ante. Environmentalists have won some easing up of this in *Lujan v Laidlaw* (1986). 'State secrets' privilege: Per *US v Rey-nolds,* plaintiff may not be allowed to sue if national-security secrets would come out at trial. Tax-whisper: Courts do not want to hear challenges to the Internal Revenue Service. Best to only whisper about that touchy subject. See the fate of Sherry Peel Jackson, and the murder of Gordon Kahl. Vexatious litigant: There are a few nutcases who take up court's time, but *caveat* this designation. Widow's son: Every Mason must help a brother in trouble, including one in trouble with the law. If a defendant makes the cryptic gesture "Who will help the widow's son?" and the judge is a Mason, what is a judge to do? See E. Mullins *Rape of Justice* (1989).

7.10 PROSECUTE MENTICIDE!

> Medical Consent ...[N]o investigator may involve a human being as a subject in research covered by this policy unless the investigator has obtained the legally effective informed consent of the subject or the subject's legally authorized representative. An investigator shall seek such consent only under circumstances that provide... sufficient opportunity to consider whether or not to participate and that minimize the possibility of coercion or undue influence.
> *—Code of Federal Regulations Title 45 Public Welfare, Revised June 23, 2005*

As Part Two showed, the 20th century development of mind-control techniques has had an enormous effect on our lives. Now we laypersons can push for the prosecution of menticide. It was noted in Ch 6.1 that getting into another person's head to make them do something they do not voluntarily choose, can constitute assault, per state law. (Also there is federal law against transporting a child across state lines for prostitution. See 18 USC 1591 and 18 USC 2421-2423. That is the fate of many mind-controlled children.)

The claim that our military needed to experiment to protect our soldiers against enemy brainwashing is no excuse. It is now wildly clear that whatever our military was doing in the mind-control field was for the sake of learning new techniques to be used offensively.

Mind control victims would be grateful for your taking up their cause on this matter. Needless to say, they carry many psychological burdens and so cannot easily initiate a court case. Also, many of them are in hiding, because even after they have been liberated, there is substantial risk that they will be 'accessed' once again.

Some pre-2010 legal actions and some sources of evidence:

1. As of 2009, the veteran Frank Rochelle is suing in Federal Court to win identification of all soldiers who were experimented on. (*US v Stanley, 1987,* said suing is not available to military experimentees.)

2. For many years, employees at the American embassy in Moscow were subjected to a harmful electromagnetic signal called 'the woodpecker.' The US discovered it, yet let the Russians continue!

3. CIA Director Stansfield Turner confessed MK-Ultra to the Senate in 1977; the LSD affair came out via the 1975 Church Committee.

4. In the 1990s, Val Orlikow, the wife of a Canadian Member of Parliament, sued for damages following her admission to the Allan

Memorial Hospital in Montreal for depression. She was treated by CIA psychiatrist, Ewen Cameron. His invention was called 'psychic driving.' After placing the patients in isolation and sensory deprivation, he tried to give them a new personality. She won the case.

5. Here's a case that I bet was 'planted.' A patient reported incestuous sexual abuse. The therapist was then successfully sued for a large sum of money on the allegation that she had planted false memories in her patient. The outcome of this case was well-publicized by the media, with two results: 1. Other therapists were discouraged from taking the part of clients who reported incest. 2. Citizens and teachers got the erroneous impression that many a child, such as those at McMartin preschool, had made the whole thing up.

That lawsuit was a terrible blow to all mind-control victims, who already had a very difficult time getting people to believe them. Much worse was their distress when a group, called False Memory Syndrome Foundation, sprang up to discredit and mock them. Some (or all?) of its members, **such as Dr Martin Orne, were coverts.**

6. There is a little bit of jurisprudence on the subject of reduced responsibility for murder on the part of a 'Manchurian candidate.' During Patty Hearst's trial for bank robbery the defense lawyer said that she was brainwashed by her cult. (remember 'the Symbionese Liberation Army'?) Walter Bowart (1978: 281) says there is much of interest in the Hearst court transcript including testimony by Martin Orne, 'head of Office of Naval Research Committee on Hypnosis.'

7. As seen at Ch 6's frontispiece, Chris deNicola got a chance to mention her MK-Ultra torture at the 1995 Presidential Hearings – because she was also a nuclear experimentee. Failure to follow up on her case, or on the many published exposés may render Congressmen indictable for coverup. **They did cover it up.** (See franklinfiles.net)

8. Carol Rutz and three colleagues posted a questionnaire on the Internet, to which 1400 mind-control survivors from several countries responded. See the results at extreme-abuse-survey.net. If the respondents knew a court would take them seriously, they would no doubt give evidence, as well as confess to crimes they committed!

Mind control victims can sue both a technician that ran the offending laboratory of a university, and the head of that university.

Invasion of privacy is a recognized action in tort. See Federal Tort Claims Act. For crime, DA's can write the necessary arrest warrants. A few states, such as KY, still allow private prosecutions.

Would it be unfair to surprise a perpetrator with this new crime, 'menticide'? After all, Article I, Section 9 of the Constitution says: No... ex-post facto law shall be passed. No, it would not be unfair; *menticide* is only a new name; the crime of assault has been around for ages. Slavery, too, is against federal law, per the Thirteenth Amendment: Neither slavery nor involuntary servitude...shall exist in the United States...Congress should have power to enforce this article by appropriate legislation.

If mind control took place long ago, the Statute of Limitations may bar litigation. (This varies by state: 1 to 2 years for civil actions and 5 years for crimes is rather typical. California allows adults 3 years *after they discover* they were abused as kids). There is never a time limit on murder or treason – and MK-Ultra involved plenty of both.

Another way to bring perpetrators to book is via the crime of obstruction of justice. Some 'false memory' groups have as their main mission **to save persons accused of sexual abuse from being convicted**. If their mission is not genuine, they'll be up for obstruction of justice. Keep in mind that being an accessory after the fact of a felony is also a crime – **and so is cover-up!**

Additionally we need to deal with the diminished responsibility of criminals who were 'under instruction.' Dr Paul A. Verdier (1968) advised us in relation to the Charles Manson murders. He made up a checklist of indicators that a person had been mind con-trolled and recommended that a numerical weighting be given to each of these. For example, we should ask whether the person had been subjected to sleep deprivation, torture, or humiliation. If she was, it may mean she was deliberately **deprived of her normal self** in order to open her up to indoctrination or hypnotic command.

Dr Verdier calls his scheme CRIB: Conditioned Response Index for Brainwashing. His book was aimed at families of persons that had been kidnapped into cults. Verdier (1977: 100) says CRIB may "bring into clear public focus the insidious and ominous forces that are warping the minds of the young."

Naturally, a major stumbling block to the prosecution of menti-cide is our fear of being made a fool of, by false stories. Probably a few that claim to be MK-Ultra are fakes. If you fall for them don't take it too hard! Stay on board for the genuine ones and for the US.

List 7a.   Famous Killers (or patsies as the case may be)

Note: to read the transcripts of these cases is to see that the authorities 'knew.'

Convicts Now Deceased:

Albert deSalvo   ('The Boston Strangler') Killed in jail.

Richard Speck   (killed 8 nurses without a gun. Died in jail, age 49.

Henry Lee Lucas   (many murders) Pardoned by Gov. G. Bush.

Ted Bundy   (many young women killed) Executed.

Jeffrey Dahmer   (Gruesome killing of males) Died in jail, age 34.

Otis Toole   (chopped off victims' extremities) Died in jail, age 49.

James Earl Ray   (M. L. King). Died after 30 years in jail, age 70.

Timothy McVeigh   (OKC bomber, 168 died) Executed.

John Allen Muhammad   ('The Washington Sniper') Executed.

John Couey (death of Jessica) Died in jail awaiting appeal, age 54.

Convicts Still Alive

Ted Kazinski   ('Unabomber' -- 3 died over 2 decades) In jail.

Wayne Williams   (the 'Atlanta child murders') In jail.

David Berkowitz   ('Son of Sam' – Satanic cult) In jail.

Sirhan Sirhan   (RFK assassination) In jail, recognizably *MK-Ultra*.

Martin Bryant   ('retarded' Aussie, 35 shot dead in a café) In jail.

Charles Manson   (actress Sharon Tate death and others) In jail.

Mark Chapman   (John Lennon's killer) from Tavistock. In jail.

Brian Nichols   (5 carjacks, death of Judge Barnes) In jail.

SOURCES: David McGowan, *Programmed To Kill* (a compendium)

Maury Terry, *The Ultimate Evil* (re son of Sam)

Max Call, *Hand of Death* (Lucas revealed a cult; police would not look)

Michael A. Hoffman *II, Secret Societies and Psychological Warfare*. Hoffman says these are 'psychodramas' produce to sicken, and distract, the public.

List 7b. CANONS OF JUDICIAL ETHICS

– as recommended by The American Bar Association, as adopted by Montana Supreme Court, May 1, 1963 (abridged):

3. **It is the duty of all judges to support the federal Constitution and that of this state; in so doing, they should fearlessly observe and apply fundamental limitations and guarantees.**

4. A judge's official conduct should be free from impropriety and the appearance of impropriety....

10. A judge should ...require, and, so far as his power extends, enforce on the part of clerks, court officers and counsel civility and courtesy to the court and to jurors, witnesses, litigants and others having business in the court.

11. **A judge should utilize his opportunities to criticize and correct unprofessional conduct of attorneys** and counselors.

15. A judge should not permit private interviews, arguments or communications designed to influence his judicial action, where interests to be affected thereby are not represented before him, except where provision is made for *ex parte* ...

16. In disposing of controverted cases, a judge should indicate the reasons for his action in an opinion showing that he has not disregarded or overlooked serious arguments of counsel.

17. A judge should be mindful that his duty is the application of general law to particular instances, **that ours is a government of law and not of men... He should administer his office with a due regard to the integrity of the system of the law itself, remembering that he is not a depositary of arbitrary power, but a judge under the sanction of law...**

19. A judge should ... not utilize information coming to him in a judicial capacity for purposes of [financial] speculation....

22. [A judge should] in pending or prospective litigation before him be particularly careful to avoid such action as may reasonably tend to awaken the suspicion that his social or business relations or friendships constitute an element in influencing his judicial conduct.

23. **He should deal with his appointment as a public trust.**

[emphasis added]

List 7c. Women Who Survived the MK-Ultra Program

I (MM) make the following paraphrases of the claims published by these wonderful persons:

BRICE TAYLOR   *Thanks for the Memories* (1995)
I was purchased by Bob Hope and contracted out to Henry Kissinger to be used as a mind-files robot. Also trained in a program of swimming with dolphins. Venues: Barking Sands Missile Base, Point Mugu Naval Base, UCLA Neuropsychiatric Institute, USC School of Dentistry. I am the niece of Charles Horn.

CHERYL HERSHA   *Secret Weapons* (2001)
My sister Lynn and I were ordered to torture other children with electroshock; I refused. From age twelve I piloted helicopters to make drug pick-ups in Mexico. We were mind controlled at Army National Guard Camp Greyling, Carlsbad Army/Navy Academy, and Kansas City U. My sister has not recovered.

CAROL RUTZ*   *A Nation Betrayed* (2001)
In 1951, when I was 4, my grandfather got immunity from prosecution as a pedophile for handing me over to US military. I was tortured by Dr. Sidney Gottlieb of Fort Detrick. When Gottlieb died, my programming began to lose its grip on me.

KATHLEEN SULLIVAN*   *Unshackled* (2003)
I was subjected to satanic ritual torture and forced to kill babies, at the direction of my multi-generational pedophile family. Some of this took place in cults in the basement of Christian churches in Marietta, GA, and in a Masonic hall near Reading PA. The Mob also used my services, as did the CIA.

ANN DIAMOND*   *My Cold War* (2007)
My Dad reluctantly agreed to let his employer, Canadian MI, work on me starting in 1956 when I was 5, with Dr.Cameron at McGill U. Orphans were treated much worse than others. Dad pulled me out of the program when I was 12, but that cost him his life.

* I have met these three women and hereby gladly vouch for them.

Chapter 8
The 'Northwoods Memo' [Discusses a Hoax Plane Crash To Prepare for US Invasion of Cuba]

For: the Secretary of Defense   March 23, 1962
From: Gen. Jay Lemnitzer

... Joint Chiefs of Staff are to indicate brief but precise description of pretexts, which they consider, would provide justification for US military intervention in Cuba.... **World opinion, and the United States forum should be favorably affected by developing the international image of the Cuban government as rash** and irresponsible, and as an alarming and unpredictable threat to the peace of the Western Hemisphere...

a. Sabotage ship in harbor; large fires – naphthalene.. **Conduct funerals for mock victims...** c. Commence large-scale ... military operations.... **A "Remember the Maine" incident could be arranged in several forms...**

4. We could develop a Communist **Cuban terror campaign in the Miami area, or other Florida cities and even in Washington...** We could sink a boatload of Cubans en route to Florida (real or simulated). **We could foster attempts on lives of Cuban refugees in the United States even to the extent of wounding** in instances to be widely publicized... C-46 type aircraft could make cane-burning raids at night. **Soviet Bloc incendiaries could be found...**

7. Hijacking attempts against civil air and surface craft should appear to continue as harassing measures condoned by the government of Cuba...

8. It is possible to create an incident, which will demonstrate convincingly that **a Cuban aircraft has attacked and shot down a** chartered civil airliner en route from the United States to Jamaica.

a. An aircraft at Eglin AFB would be painted and numbered as an exact duplicate for a civil registered aircraft belonging to a CIA proprietary organization **[It] would be loaded with the selected passengers, all boarded under carefully prepared aliases. The actual registered aircraft would be converted** to a drone.

b. At precisely the same time that the aircraft was presumably shot down **a submarine or small surface would disburse F-101 parts, parachute, etc....**

[emphasis added]

166

8 Presidents

Hail to the chief, who in triumph advances!
Honor'd and blessed be the evergreen Pine!
Long may the tree in his banner that glances
Flourish, the shelter and grace of our line.
 – Sir Walter Scott, *The Lady of the Lake*

Andrew [warned me] "If we go through with this you will be
physically destroyed... please be careful." We had been living in a de
facto separation for years, and the caring we shared would endure.
I was divorcing the Firm, however... As any student of British
history can tell you, women leave the Royal Family in only one
mode: with their heads cleaved from their shoulders.
 -- Sarah Ferguson, *Sarah the Duchess of York: My Story*, 1996

―――――――――――

8.1 THE PRESIDENT'S JOB IS SMALLER THAN YOU'D THINK

In an arrangement that preceded the Constitution by 12 years,
'the presidency' was such a small job that it sat inside Congress:

> Article IX of the Articles of Confederation, 1777
> The United States in Congress assembled shall have authority to
> appoint a committee, **to sit in the recess of Congress**, to be
> denominated 'A Committee of the States,' and to consist of one
> delegate from each State; and to appoint such other committees and
> civil officers as may be necessary for managing the general affairs of
> the United States under their direction – **to appoint one of their
> members to preside**, provided that no person be allowed to serve
> in the office of president more than one year in
> any term of three years. [emphasis added]

Eventually there came to be an unconstitutional arrogation of
power, with American presidents touting the responsibility of
'leading the free world.' In his second inaugural address in 2005,
our 43rd president made the arrogant and ludicrous statement that
America "proclaims liberty throughout all the world."

> ....We have seen our vulnerability -- and we have seen its deepest source. For as long as whole regions of the world simmer in resentment and tyranny .... There is only one force of history that can break the reign of hatred and resentment, and expose the pretensions of tyrants, and reward the hopes of the decent and tolerant, and that is the force of human freedom.... We will encourage reform in other governments by making clear that success in our relations will require the decent treatment of their own people.... All who live in tyranny and hopelessness can know: the United States will not ignore your oppression, or excuse your oppressors. When you stand for your liberty, we will stand with you. ... America, in this young century, proclaims liberty throughout all the world, and to all the inhabitants thereof.
>
> ~ Pres. George W. Bush, *Second Inaugural Address*
>
> January 20, 2005

The 'job description' of the president occupies all of Article II of the Constitution. The main points are as follows:

Article II, Section 1. The executive Power shall be vested in a President of the United States of America...
No Person except a natural born Citizen...shall be eligible to the Office of President; neither shall any person be eligible to that Office who shall not have attained the Age of thirty-five Years, and been fourteen Years a Resident within the United States.

Section. 2. The President shall be Commander in Chief of the Army and Navy of the United States, and of the Militia of the several States, when called into the actual Service of the United States;
And he shall have Power to Grant Reprieves and Pardons for Offences against the United States...
and he shall nominate, and by and with the Advice and Consent of the Senate, shall appoint Ambassadors... Judges of the Supreme Court, and all other Officers of the United States.

Section 3. He shall from time to time give to the Congress Information on the State of the Union, and recommend to their Consideration such Measures as he shall judge necessary and expedient; he shall take Care that the Laws be faithfully executed...

8.2 GUIDE TO THIS CHAPTER – *PRESIDENTS*

The claim of this chapter is that the executive branch of the US is out-and-out run by World Government (I think it started with Teddy Roosevelt in 1901). 8.3 and 8.4 discuss assassinations. The next two sections concern the criminality of government: 8.5 deals with drugs, and 8.6 with covert agencies. 8.7 lists the order of succession. 8.8 abandons all hope of presidential immunity. 8.9 opines that privatization has gone too far. What To Do? 8.10 offers the theory of imposture. See many Appendices: E through I, M through P, and U through Z. That last one, a truly weird graphic, says it all.

8.3 ASSASSINATIONS AND COUPS D' ÉTAT IN THE US

Eight American presidents have died in office, of which only four: Garfield 1881, Lincoln 1865, McKinley 1901, and Kennedy 1963, are spoken of as assassinations. The others died from 'natural causes:' Harrison 1841, Taylor 1850, Harding 1923, and FDR 1945, the likely reason being that they threatened to go off the reservation. Lone gunwoman Squeaky Fromme shot at President Ford in 1975.

John Hinckley shot Reagan soon after he took office in 1981. Hinckley then spent 25 years, without trial, as a mental patient in St. Elizabeth's Hospital, Washington DC, at taxpayer expense. The fact that Hinckley's oilman father is a friend of the then Vice President, George H.W. Bush, was announced on the day and then suppressed.

For our purposes it is enough to assume that assassinations are almost always done by the World Order cabal. We should wake up to the commonsense fact that lowly citizens, especially mentally disturbed ones, could not do such a thing. **Thus, all the expensive 'security' is a joke.** To rub this in, let's make a comical decoding ⌁ rule. Hinckley said his reason for shooting President Reagan was to impress the actress Jodie Foster. The 'Jodie Foster' rule will mean any such implausible excuse. It can be applied to any event.

Also, First Ladies suffer. For example, Betty Ford acquired a drug addiction, and Pat Nixon had a stroke after her husband's resignation. If, perchance, these illnesses were imposed on them, it is very cruel. It's also possible that family members are 'killed off' to soften the man up to obey the cabal. Teddy Roosevelt's wife and mother both died suddenly. In UK, Prince Albert's dying at 42 weakened the monarch, Victoria. As widow(ers) know, the loss of a spouse is devastating. Loss of a child is worse. In her 1994 *Memoir,* Barbara Bush seems to cry out to us about her daughter Robin.

Two US *coups d'état* must be catalogued here. First, Watergate. A person nicknamed Deep Throat allegedly leaked to *Washington Post* reporters Carl Bernstein and Bob Woodward that Nixon's re-election team stole some data from the Democratic Party at the Watergate Hotel in DC (since then all scandals are called '-gate').

Watergate now appears to have been a CIA/Military intelligence doing — both the bungled burglary and the 'leaking' of it. It was to pry Nixon out of the White House so Secretary of State Kissinger could rule 100% via the successor, Pres Gerald Ford instead of only 90% as he had done while Nixon was there. In order for Ford to get the VP job, the serving VP, Spiro Agnew, had first to be taken out:

How They 'Got Agnew First'

His remark sent a chill through my body. I interpreted it as an innuendo that anything could happen to me; I might have a convenient "accident." What had Haig meant when he said "anything may be in the offing"? I was close enough to the presidency to know that the office could exert tremendous power. …I was told, "Go quietly -- or else." I feared for my life. If a decision had been made to eliminate me -- **through an automobile accident, a fake suicide,** or whatever, the order would **not have been traced back to the White House**… The American people should know that in the last hectic year or more of his residence in the White House, Richard Nixon did not actually administer all the powers of the presidency. As I have stated earlier, **it was General Haig** [an officer of NATO] **who was the de facto President.** [emphasis added] ~ Spiro Agnew, *Go Quietly…or Else* (1980) p. 190

The next coup is known as the October Surprise. In 1980, President Carter, seeking a second term, was hampered by looking impotent during the Iranian siege of the US Embassy in Tehran. 52 Americans were still being held there, by revolutionary 'students.' In October 1980 George Bush, a VP hopeful, visited Paris. Was it to fix a deal whereby the hostages would stay put until after the November election? Indeed, Iran released the hostages on Reagan's Inauguration Day! (See Robert Parry's consortiumnews.com.)

Later, Congress made some effort to air that accusation, but Lee Hamilton stood firm, saying there was not enough evidence. In fact there's plenty of evidence, plus the (usual) sudden deaths of several witnesses. (See Paul Hoffman's *Lions of the Eighties,* 1982.)

8.4 CLOSURE REGARDING THE ASSASSINATION OF JFK

House Select Committee on Assassinations, the HSCA, was set up in 1978, partly at the insistence of MLK's widow, Coretta Scott King and Congress's Black Caucus, to resolve the deaths of JFK, RFK, and MLK (and the 1972 shooting of Governor G. Wallace).

Richard E. Sprague, apparently no relation to HSCA counsel Richard A. Sprague, wrote *The Taking of America* (1979, which gives a good account of how the House Rules Committee had tried to thwart the formation of HSCA. He shows how the media, especially the *New York Times*, stepped in to be sure the public did not become aware of the excellent evidence being unearthed. (Few Americans even now know that Congress's final report says JFK's assassination looks like conspiracy!) Hmm, why would the *NY Times* do that?

Shortly after JFK died in 1963, President Lyndon Johnson appointed then Chief Justice Earl Warren to head a group that would make sure to label Lee Harvey Oswald the culprit. Members of the Warren Commission could have been expected to suppress data about the conspiracy since they were part of it: John McCloy, Allen Dulles, and Gerald Ford. A doubter, Hale Boggs, died mysteriously.

The Warren Commission staff member who authored the preposterous single-bullet theory is Senator Arlen Specter. His deceptions were recorded in Sylvia Meagher's *Accessories after the Fact* way back in 1967. It should take no more than a simple interrogation of this man to learn exactly who terminated JFK:

Specter: *Could that missile have made the wound on Gov Connally's wrist?*

Dr. Humes: *I think that this is most unlikely....This [bullet] is basically intact; its jacket appears to me to be intact, and I do not understand how it could possibly have left fragments [in the governor's wrist]* (file 2H 374-5)

Specter: *Could it have been the bullet which inflicted the wound on... wrist?*

Dr. Finck: *No; for the reason that there are too many fragments described.*

Conclusion: "All the evidence indicated that the bullet found on the Governor's stretcher could have caused all his wounds."
~ The Report of the Warren Commission

(Note: Specter can also be seen on YouTube haranguing Anita Hill to assure the 1992 confirmation of Clarence Thomas as a Justice.)

171

8.5 CONTROLLED SUBSTANCES

Thanks to the simple fact that something in the human brain can addict an individual to a substance, such as a narcotic or a stimulant, there is a great market for such substances. **Quite possibly science has already found the key to all addictions** (including gambling) but isn't 'allowed' to use it beneficially. Since neuroscience has made fantastic advances, and the human genome is now fully mapped, it would be a surprise if addiction were still a mystery.

Time was, you could buy any medicinal or 'recreational' drug on the open market; no doctor's prescription needed, no cops arresting you for possession or drug dealing. By 1920 most addictive substances (including alcohol, for a while) were outlawed. Possibly our legislators did that outlawing under supervision from the biggest dealers, including the Delano family of China and New York, in order to raise the street price. (One thinks of comedienne Elaine May's joke "I try to be as cynical as possible but I just can't keep up....")

In any case, trade in opium, when processed into morphine, was and is a huge business since the early 1800s, and cocaine from Latin America has been large business since the 1960s. John C. Coleman (1992:117) alleges that the World Bank traffics in drugs, too.

Affidavit　　[emphasis added]

I, Dois Gene Tatum, declare: I was a helicopter pilot for the United States Army ... **I witnessed activities** [including] rampant drug smuggling into the US involving people in control of the CIA, the Drug Enforcement Administration, the armed forces of the US. I have documented some of these activities on military flight plans... I *was present* while there were discussions as to where drug money was being siphoned on the Panama to Arkansas run. Present at this meeting were Manuel **Noriega**; William **Barr**; Joe Fernandez; Mike Harari; General Gustavo Alvarez. Participating in this meeting via satellite telephone was VP George **Bush**, Oliver North, and William Jefferson **Clinton**, then governor of Arkansas.

After I refused to perform a mission that I felt was beyond my willingness to execute, I notified my handlers that **I wanted out** of the operation, which at that time was known as Operation Pegasus. Their response was to warn me that **no one leaves the operation.** I declare under penalty of perjury that the above facts are true...

　~ quoted in Rodney Stich, *Defrauding America* (1998) p. 459
　Note: Although signed and sworn, this affidavit has so far not found a 'home.'

Relevant points about the drug business are:

1. More than one million Americans are incarcerated today over drugs. This breaks up families.
2. Drug-caused violence helps justify a police state.
3. Many of our soldiers are "hooked" on drugs deliberately.
4. The wealth garnered through this black-market corrupts our system and allows those in the shadows to direct our affairs.

A Pause To Discuss Gary Webb's Work: An old-school journalist, Gary Webb, was mad as hell when he discovered that, in connection with the CIA's Iran-Contra business, drugs were delivered to gangs such as the Crips and the Bloods, for distribution to poor neighborhoods. He did in-depth investigations for the *San Jose Mercury News*. Subsequently, that newspaper came under pressure and 'retracted' what Webb had written.

Meantime, his work had sparked a Congressional investigation. In 1998 Rep Maxine Waters was a leader in this, but she has since faded out. Had she not chosen that option she would be dead. Rep Julian Dixon, also involved, died of a 'heart attack' in 2000 and Gary Webb died of 'suicide' in 2005. On the Internet you can search for 'suspicious deaths/Clinton/Bush' and find a long list of persons that could have given testimony about the CIA's importation of drugs to a small airport at Mena, Arkansas, but they did not live to tell.

A relevant meeting of the House Committee on Intelligence was held on March 16, 1998. It had an incredible irony: **the chairman of that committee was Rep. Porter Goss of Florida, himself a CIA man** involved in these affairs since the 1960s (Hopsicker: 2001).

8.6 ARE COVERTS 'LEGAL'?

As Fred Hitz, Inspector General of CIA, admitted to Congress, US Attorney General William French Smith had permitted the CIA to 'look the other way' in regard to drug trafficking. (Oops, misprision and conspiracy!) In general, Congress eschews its duty to oversee the intelligence agencies. Unfortunately the average citizen assumes that secret agencies have important missions to carry out and should not be called on the carpet to account for drugs.

Insurance companies employ a handy term, *moral hazard*, to indicate situations in which it can be realistically anticipated that people will cheat. Thus, for example, insurers usually do not cover collisions between two cars driven by members of the same family, as that could tempt a family, in need of money, to defraud.

Without using the exact term, the Framers of our Constitution made many acknowledgements of moral hazard. Certainly it never embarrassed them to mention the facts of life concerning power and dishonesty. Had the Framers been asked about the wisdom of setting up a secret office of government, one that enjoyed off-the-books funding, they probably would have laughed out loud. That said, let us see what we can find about the legality of our coverts. (The noun *covert* means "a covered place or shelter; a hiding place.")

Turning to the question of the CIA's legality, it is customary for academics to point to the National Security Act of 1947, in which Congress truly did license an intelligence agency. In historical reality, however, the CIA did not spring full-blown from that 1947 Act.

Rather, it had two foreign sources. In the 1940s an 'Office of Strategic Services,' ostensibly part of the US War Department (later called 'Defense') was run in the RCA building in New York — a major player was William Stephenson of Britain's MI6: Military Intelligence. (Incidentally, our first Secy of Defense, James Forrestal, died of defenestration in 1949. See biography by Cornell Simpson, 1966)

OSS was lampooned as being an acronym for 'Oh So Social' or 'Oh Such Snobs,' as many persons in the upper crust were asked to belong or to become informants. (We can thus assume the incipient CIA was a protector of the interests of America's upper class.)

By 1944, a second foreign source 'contributed' to what would become the CIA. This source was a contingent of Nazi officers who knew that Germany would lose the war. Some of them, under Operation Odessa, moved smoothly to Argentina and a few other Latin American nations. Some, under Operation Paperclip, moved seamlessly into the US, via a group called the Gehlen Organization.

This was led by General Richard Gehlen of the German Intelligence organization, Abwehr. Amazingly, he was allowed to swap his Nazi uniform for a US military uniform. The pretext for the US accepting him was that he had info on the Russians. The real reason was that **transferring German weapons experts to America was planned prior to 1940.** 'Operation Paperclip' has been declassified for decades but is still not mentioned in history textbooks!

This censorship must stop! Recall from Ch 3.6 that 'Bolsheviks' were funded by Wall St. Nazis were funded too. Doesn't that suggest a cabal hand behind World War II? See some research hints on this in the Bibliographical Essay. Recall, too, that a 'Nazi' was caught in OKC. And an Aryan Brotherhood is now hot in US and Sweden.

174

Suggestion: Cast a skeptical glance at the word 'findings.' In 1991, partly in response to Iran-Contra, Congress passed the Intelligence Authorization Act. It allows the president to begin a covert action on his own and report his finding (as to why it was needed) to Congress, promptly. So far, so good. But Section 503 (5) says "A finding may not authorize any action that would violate the Constitution or any statute of the US." Clever wording. It does not say he must not break the law, just that he must not authorize it in the finding.

We can assume the drafter of the Act was well aware that the CIA permits itself to do anything under the sun – and with plausible deniability, to boot! And thereby hangs the tale. **You can't have rule-of-law where there is implicit approval of law-breaking on the part of certain individuals.**

Our CIA *does* do one of the things we want it to do, namely, collect information. It publishes, for example, 'national estimates' that are full of data on the world's 194 countries. But it also does many bad things. To name just one, **it meticulously covers up the crime of pedophilia in high places.** Observe this casual admission by a man who was both a CIA and Naval Intelligence officer:

> I worked out of the consular general's office in Genoa.... I worked with and against the Baader Meinhof...and [Italy's] Red Army faction. I sanitized areas in Germany, Austria and East Berlin during the pedophile crisis. **There were no arrests.** [emphasis added]
> ~ Gunther Russbacher, in R. Allan, *Obergon Chronicles* (2006) p. 338

Don't forget, too, that to 'finance' its operations, a covert can simply steal money. They have a general 'free ticket' against arrest, (or if arrested, against trial). The theft could be an actual bank robbery, or – as we saw in the 'Savings and Loan Scandal' – it could be ...uh...an actual bank robbery! Al Martin (1995) argues that the reason money disappears from the Department of Housing and Urban Development is that CIA can so easily embezzle it.

> Frank Carlucci and Dick Armitage set up an export company, Blackstone Investment Group, operating ostensibly for the CIA to purchase potentially wayward nuclear materials out of the Soviet Union. This also involved some technology that people aren't aware of. The stuff was getting repacked and then surreptitiously sold back to China. ~Al Martin, *The Conspirators* (2002) p. 192 *[Are they all in it together: Iran, China, US? Has World Govt already begun? See Appendix X]*

> ### The Famous Executive Order 12,333 dated Dec 4, 1981
> *[Recall that presidents are not lawmakers, but can 'fill up the details' of law]*
>
> 1.4 The agencies within the Intelligence Community shall, in accordance with applicable United States law … conduct intelligence activities necessary for the conduct of foreign relations and the protection of the national security of the United States, including: …
>
> (c) Collection of information concerning …terrorist and international narcotics activities, and other hostile activities directed against the US by foreign powers, organizations, persons,…
>
> **(f) Such other intelligence activities as the President may direct from time to time.** *[Note: a claim so broad has no legal value]*
>
> 2.7 Contracting. Agencies within the Intelligence Community are authorized to enter into contracts or arrangements for the provision of goods or services with private companies or institutions in the US and **need not reveal the sponsorship of such contracts or arrangements for authorized intelligence purposes.** Contracts or arrangements with academic institutions may be undertaken only with the consent of appropriate officials of the institution. …*[This reflects Derek Bok's complaint to Congress that as President of Harvard University he did not know how many of his staff were coverts. – In Ivy League and most law schools they are rife.]*
>
> 2.11 **Prohibition on Assassination.** No person employed by or acting on behalf of the US Government shall engage in, or conspire to engage in, assassination. *[But see Donald Freed's book Death in Washington re Orlando Letelier's death.]* Ah, events have overtaken us: President Obama now prescribes, not proscribes, assassination.

8.7 ROADS TO THE WHITE HOUSE

The US government is controlled by outsiders. In all cases, including Carter who was billed as a 'peanut farmer,' the man who becomes president **is selected years before** and then is given the necessary publicity by the media. Any undesirables, such as Michael Dukakis in 1984 or Gary Hart in 1976, get smeared by the media.

Dukakis' smear was that, as Massachusetts governor, he had approved of prisoner furloughs and this 'led to' a prisoner named Willie Horton going on a 'murderous rampage.' (The seeds for the furlough and the manhunt for Horton were possibly laid years earlier.) Al Gore used it in the Democratic primary, then Bush used it.) Dukakis's wife Kitty had to endure ridiculous smearing as well.

Philip Dru, Administrator **(1922) by 'Col.' E. Mandell House**

HOW SELWYN DID IT

Masterful and arrogant wealth, created largely by Government protection of its profits... had sought to corrupt [both parties] and to that end had insinuated itself into the primaries, [so] no candidates might be nominated whose views were not in accord with theirs.

...[Selwyn solicited] a thousand multi-millionaires, each one contributing ten thousand dollars. He forged a subtle chain with which to hold in subjection the natural impulses of the people ... There was no man in either of the great political parties that was big enough to cope with him or to unmask his methods.

His first move was to confer with John Thor, the high priest of finance, and unfold his plan to him, explaining how essential was secrecy. Thor's influence throughout commercial America was absolute [thanks to] the capital he could control through the banks, trust companies and industrial organizations, which he dominated.

...Thor was to send for each of the thousand and compliment him by telling him that there was a matter, appertaining to the general welfare of the business fraternity... Selwyn then transferred these amounts to the private bank of his son-in-law [to be paymaster].

Not only did Selwyn plan to win the Presidency [for his man Rockland], but he also planned to bring under his control both the Senate and the Supreme Court. He selected one man in each of thirty of the States, some of them belonging to his party and some to the opposition, whom he intended to have run for the Senate.

...Honest officials who were in the way were removed by offering them places vastly more remunerative... He began by eliminating all states he knew the opposition party would certainly carry. He also ignored the states where his side was sure to win...

Drunk with power and the adulation of sycophants, once or twice Rockland asserted himself, and acted upon important matters without having first conferred with Selwyn. But, after he had been bitterly assailed by Selwyn's papers and by his senators, he made no further attempts at independence. He felt that he was utterly helpless in that strong man's hands, and so, indeed, he was.

[This novel endorsed a socialist utopia. It would be led by the altruist 'Philip Dru' who would counteract Selwyn's plan by a kindly coup d'état.
House was President Woodrow Wilson's close advisor. Yet he was even closer to President Taft, according to Antony Sutton (1986: 96). Taft's father, Alphonso, co-founded The Order of Skull and Bones (and later was US ambassador to Russia). Sutton claims the Philip Dru book in some way **encodes** *the Order!]*

As for an unplanned vacancy in the White House, the Constitution makes the VP president and grants legislative power for arranging additional successors. Congress passed such laws in 1792, 1886, 1947, and most recently in 2006 to include Michael Chertoff, head of the newest department, Homeland Security:

The Order of Succession to the Presidency [Ignore 'COG'!]: The VP, Speaker of the House, President pro Tempore of the Senate, Secretary of State, Treasury, Defense, Attorney General, Secretary of Interior, Agriculture, Commerce, Labor, Health and Human Services, Housing and Urban Development, Transport, Energy Development [!], Education, Veterans Affairs, Homeland Security. *Each must also meet presidential eligibility criteria.*

During the younger Bush's presidency a movie was released showing in fiction that he was shot dead. Around that time the media also came up with the preposterous notion that Muslims in Canada were going to behead the Prime Minister, but "were foiled." (Can you imagine anyone getting close enough to do that hands-on?) Fact is, presidents need our protection and we should do for them what they cannot easily do – get the killers **out of their inner circle**.

See the 25th Amendment. It says that if the president dies or is disabled, or is accused of being unable to discharge his duties, others can take steps to remove him. Thus, as well as our having to be alert for beheading, we have to be alert for a menticide of the president. (Speaking of the 25th amendment, also known as the Rockefeller amendment, it is likely that the cabal instigated it. Maybe they did *all* of the last 17 amendments. We should be careful.)

Pres Reagan's daughter recalls: I remember first noticing the men who would remain attached to [my father] for years: Mike Deaver, Ed Meese, Bill Clark. What happened after a while, though, was that these men seemed to converge into one.... Even when he was president, and Jim Baker melted into the equation, the same thing would happen to me. I'd see a newspaper photo or watch a soundbite on the evening news and moments later, I'd wonder, "Wait, which one was it?" There was something so similar about all of them; maybe it was the way they related to my father – warmly, almost paternally, but tentatively, as though they weren't sure who he was. ~ Patti Davis, *The Way I See It* (1992) p. 114

8.8 PRESIDENTIAL IMMUNITY? IT DOES NOT EXIST.

That was the bad news (Sections 3-7). Now the good news. In our American Republic we don't put up with people strutting around Washington DC acting like they own the place. *We* own the place and our governmental servants will do as we tell them. Right?

At all times members of the executive branch are subject to law and if they break the law they are subject to its punishments. There are no exceptions. Let us quickly dispose of the matter of *immunity*.

If – to take the most sensitive case – a president, VP, or First Lady were suspected of a crime, should they be treated differently than Tom, Dick, and Harry? Yes, of course. The 'arresting authority' would, we hope, be as discreet and as deferential as possible. Indeed, the president should be given a chance to resign quickly so that the nation never has to see handcuffs on our 'chief.'

Is it OK to *excuse* his behavior, for the sake of the nation? Absolutely not. In 1998 the Supreme Court even went beyond that and said that a mere civil case brought against President Clinton (by Paula Jones) had to start promptly. An argument could easily have been made that Ms Jones would not lose any rights to damages if the case were put off until the end of Clinton's term. Surely a court should balance an individual's interest (Paula's) against the interest of the nation. Our interest, even strictly for military reasons, is to have a strong president in office, not one who is being mortified.

There is another, separate matter called *sovereign immunity* (also called *state* immunity). It refers to the state, and reflects the real-world fact that one state (that is, one country) cannot subject another to its courts. How would it get the other party to show up? If you personally wish to sue the Prime Minister of Portugal, in his official capacity, what court could you go to? In an American court the judge will not issue a summons to that person. By custom, only a *state* is allowed to sue a state. (Note: the US withdrew from the World Court in 1989 when Nicaragua sued us for mining its harbor.)

Can you sue our own government? As just mentioned, Paula Jones was able to sue the president, but that was in his personal capacity. If you have a claim for damages, such as "The postman's truck knocked down my fence," you can sue, because Congress's Federal Tort Claims Act legislatively waived the traditional sovereign immunity of the US for these sorts of matters. Also, as noted in Ch 3.4, our surrender of sovereignty, via NAFTA and WTO, means we can be sued over free-trade issues by corporations and governments.

As for arrests, Sherman Skolnick alleged that numerous 'flag officers' (i.e., generals and admirals, attempted to arrest Commander in Chief Bill Clinton for treason. Skolnick implied that this is a special duty or prerogative of the military. True, high officers in the military can be arrested on base only by other high officers, but a criminal president could be arrested by any cop with a warrant. Skolnick claimed Admiral J. Boorda was killed for attempting it! Also, Waynemadsenreport.com said that some US military officers boarded a plane while it was in Australia to arrest Cheney, but failed.

Can a US government official be arrested by other nations if she be in that territory? Yes. But that nation, typically, will fly her home to be tried. (Note: the US went into Panama, arrested Gen Manuel Noriega in 1989 and made him serve 17 years in a Florida jail.) All *ambassadors* have immunity in the host nation, per the Vienna Convention (1961). and state immunity protects *heads of state* from arrest.

However there's the matter of universal jurisdiction, which some nations claim to exercise over torture, genocide, and war crimes. Spain demanded that the UK extradite Augusto Pinochet, Chile's 'senator for life,' so he could face charges in Madrid for torturing a Spanish citizen in Chile. England's court ignored the senator-for-life tag, and agreed to the extradition, but left the actual removal to the discretion of the Home Secretary, Jack Straw. (Straw demurred.)

In 2009 when Bush was no longer president, a Mohawk activist attempted to citizen-arrest him in Alberta, Canada. That man, Splitting the Sky, was himself arrested, as can be seen on YouTube. Canadian Broadcasting Corporation has refused to report this. *Suppressio veri, expressio falsi,* CBC!

This brings up the matter of police officers, even here on US soil, attempting to arrest any high mucky-muck. Don't 'personages' have security guards? Would they allow access? Legally it's not for the security guards to decide. If you employ a bodyguard to keep police from arresting you, those guards could be arrested.

Henry Kissinger is wanted for questioning in Spain, but in June 2010 when he attended a Bilderbergers meeting in Madrid, Spanish police left him alone – and he holds no diplomatic post. I think a case can be made against Kissinger (Nobel laureate!) for treason regarding AIDS, and he could be brought in for police questioning in any of the 50 states in which a person had died of AIDS.

On July 15, 2010 the International Criminal Court declared that *starting* an illegal war is a *war crime*, but this comes into force in 2017.

8.9 PRIVATIZATION GONE MAD

Although I was brought up very American, I have spent half my life in other countries. I often notice a big difference as to what a nation considers to be publicly-owned goods. But it's really quite a fuzzy legal concept. In the US we didn't need to articulate it until the trend toward privatization of government services began.

In the early Eighties, President Reagan, imitating Prime Minister Margaret Thatcher in Britain, began to sell off the assets of government. In the US this was given ideological cover of an almost Jeffersonian flavor: "Make government smaller." One way to make government smaller, at least on the books, is to convert a public service, such as prison management, to a private business. There was also an alleged 'ideological' thrust toward deregulation: "Stop burdening business with rules." "We don't need a watchdog."

In the light of our new awareness, it appears that asset-stripping is just one more part of the plan to bankrupt governments and weaken societies. Somewhat separately, the privatization of police and spy operations prevents folks from identifying and punishing those who are doing great harm. Consider this: prisons are now being run as businesses, complete with proprietary control over information. If the DoJ informs us that a particular person has been sentenced to 20 years, do we really know that he is in prison? Would we know if he's paying a large monthly 'rent' for luxury conditions?

There are also some leave-you-limp conflicts of interest regarding the US's national security. Tim Shorrock, writing *Spies for Hire* (2008: 303), mentions the company Argon. Its CEO worked for a dominant supplier of surveillance equipment for the CIA and DIA (Defense Intelligence Agency), such as anti-submarine patrol planes. The CEO then hired Peter Marino, ex-director of CIA's Technical Services and Maureen Baginsky who had been NSA's lead analyst for the SIG-INT (Signals Intelligence) director. What will these Argon employees do if a foreign customer seeks Argon's help?

Privatizers are giving a whole new meaning to the term 'the withering away of the state.' Have you always assumed that when material is 'classified' by the US executive branch that it's stored by federal personnel? It may or may not be. Even documents sealed from the public eye can go to private firms. If they happen to have a fire or flood, oh well, that's that. Note: ChoicePoint has custody of the evidence from the 9/11 attacks, such as 'DNA.' And there are many private-business-protection aspects of our military actions:

I suspected I was just part of a racket at the time. Now I am sure of it. Like all the members of the military profession, I never had a thought of my own until I left the service. My mental faculties remained in suspended animation while I obeyed the orders of higher-ups…. I helped make Mexico, especially Tampico, safe for American oil interests in 1914. I helped make Haiti and Cuba a decent place for the National City Bank boys to collect revenues in. **I helped purify Nicaragua for the international banking house of Brown Brothers in 1909. I brought light to the Dominican Republic for American sugar interests in 1916. In China I saw to it that Standard Oil went its way unmolested**.
~ Major Gen Smedley Butler, USMC "On Interventionism," 1933

It may be that we are unleashing unaccountable killers overseas via Special Operations Groups. As with the mercenaries who interrogated Iraqis at Abu Ghraib, they are not as indictable back home as our own soldiers would be. By the way, isn't the entire game of interrogating prisoners just a pretext for torture? 'Truth drugs' suffice for eliciting information. Might it not be that the US trains anyone – including prisoners – to qualify for the job of torturer? If you wish more on that, please search the Net for Harold C. Funk.

In Australia, under the Westminster system, parliament can hold the executive accountable during Question Time. Hence we heard:

Simon Kearney, "SAS Naked and Bound in Training" Aug 20, 2005. Soldiers are being blindfolded, stripped naked and menaced by savage dogs for up to three hours in extreme training exercises… Defence Minister Robert Hill has confirmed interrogators are authorised to use threats of physical and sexual abuse during simulated interrogation sessions…   [I]n a written response to a parliamentary question from federal Labor MP Daryl Melham, Hill said trainees were blindfolded for much of the exercise "In no circumstances are RTI trainees kept naked for a period longer than three hours in aggregate during the RTI exercise." *~The Australian*

Lastly, here is an interesting clue for Aussies re Martin Bryant's case. The premises of the Broad Arrow Café, where 35 people were shot dead had been *purchased by* the government just months before the event. Nudge nudge, wink wink – the opposite of privatization. The Tassie police also purchased a 'morgue truck' capable of toting many bodies, and then sold it soon after the 1996 killing spree. Gee.

182

8.10 WHAT TO DO? DETECT IMPOSTORS!

Now to imposture. Think about all the crimes that this book has been attributing to the CIA, the police of Oklahoma City, or the army as in the case of Pat Tillman's murder (three close gunshots in the forehead, not exactly random!). At times the blame here has been attributed to 'World Government' – but its orders always have to come down to someone for hands-on. **That someone gets a federal paycheck once a fortnight and** *can be located.*

The person(s) who actually pulled the trigger on Pat Tillman must surely be known. They were given specific instructions to do it. The army won't release any names? The hell they won't! They *will.* They have to, as soon as they are subpoenaed by the court.

They won't answer a subpoena? Get the US Marshals – it is their line of work, their *raison d'etre.* But arrest of officials at the Pentagon would be bad for army morale? Tch Tch – they should have thought of that before. Anyway, is there anything worse for soldiers than knowing they are fair game for *Pentagon-directed* snipers?

I now propose a theory of imposture: **When an officer of the US government uses his position to perform a crime on behalf of someone else** (say, the cabal), **he is not being a US employee.** He is acting outside of his job description. Two legal concepts – vicarious liability and frolic – should first be eliminated here:

1. *Vicarious liability.* The carpet cleaner ruins your rug by using the wrong chemical, out of ignorance, but who should take the blame? His employer! The worker was the *agent* of the employer, so really the employer ruined your carpet. By law, she is vicariously liable.

2. *'On a frolic of his own.'* The bank teller mixes up some cash that he is to give you, and pockets $500 for himself. Is the employer (that is, the bank) liable? No, because stealing, unlike cleaning a carpet, is not what the boss ordered. The teller was on a frolic of his own.

Now back to *imposture.* Assume that someone got our president to sign a form authorizing a strike on a foreign state, 'Ruritania.' (Constitutionally he needed Congress's approval but went ahead without that approval.) To make this case easy, say that the motive was money. A third country wanted someone to strike Ruritania and offered a huge bribe for the US to do it. Of what is our president guilty? Officials who take bribes tend to get indicted for *corruption* (if they get indicted at all). In this case, though, the president has done more than just pocket some money for himself. His action may cost American casualties, environmental destruction, foreign backlash.

That is what we need to look at. He must be made to answer for what he has done, of which depriving the Treasury of a few million dollars is not very crucial. One might say "He'll get his punishment by not being re-elected." That is beside the point. He needs to feel the brunt of the law. When he doesn't feel it, our nation collapses.

Anyway, when a US president carries out unlawful actions it is rarely the frolic-of-his-own type (for $$). He was placed in the White House by others so *they* could commandeer the nation's resources. His mind may be manipulated or he may be threatened, and thus he is *not* really acting freely as our leader. He works for 'the man.'

Now try looking at such a president as **an impostor**. (This is my own theory.) Wouldn't it be better for all of us if we said, "Look, there's someone sitting at the president's desk in the Oval Office who is a puppet for outside forces. He's *not* the real president. He's an impostor"? Similarly, if a judge is committing crimes every day by misinterpreting evidence deliberately or citing the law incorrectly (at the behest of, say, the Mafia), she's an imposter, not a 'real judge.'

Please note that my scheme is only for mental exercise; I do not want a new law against 'impostoring.' Once the mental exercise is performed, we won't be as inhibited as we normally are about recognizing our leaders' sins. We'll be able to identify the appropriate criminal charge and make arrests. It's painless to arrest an impostor.

There is semi- relevant jurisprudence from Iran-Contra. Military and CIA persons diverted the Pentagon's weapons to Iran. Allegedly they did so to get money with which to help right-wing Nicaraguans, the 'Contras,' fight the Sandanista's (Communists). Congress had passed the Boland Amendment forbidding funds for those Contras.

One of the men involved, Albert Hakim, was convicted of theft of weapons from the Pentagon. Actually it was not himself but his firm, Lake Resources, that got fined by the judge, but the point is: **he used Pentagon weapons unlawfully, thus he committed ordinary crime.** That is what I recommend (if treason is too hard).

Let us restore the ideal of our republic. After all, a republic *is* mainly an ideal. It is an imaginary projecting of society's good onto a fictional entity, the state. We have done it to great effect in the past. Other nations saluted our success at this. *We claimed* our republic meant justice for all. And so it did – because we idealized it. If we now trash it, by saying "Oh, you know how politics works these days," there is *nothing* left to make justice happen. Our *expectations* are a controlling force. **We need to expect that the law works.**

184

List 8a.   Assassinations and *Coups d'État* in the Republic

Palace intrigue in the 20th century?

Insiders can eject a president without citizens knowing it has happened. It may have happened in these cases:

1901 "Deranged anarchist" shoots Pres. McKinley at an Expo.

1919 Pres. Wilson has stroke. 'Col.' House appears to take over.

1923 Pres. Harding dies suddenly on the way back from Alaska.

(**1935** Gen. Smedley Butler approached by business leaders to lead a military coup. He refuses, and reports it to Congress.)

1945 Pres. FDR gets an unexplained illness (Stalin blames it on "the Churchill gang"), dies in April of cerebral hemorrhage.

1963 Pres. JFK shot by someone other than the patsy, Oswald.

1968 Pres. LBJ possibly ordered not to seek re-election, retires.

1974 Kissinger and Haig set Pres. Nixon up for the Watergate debacle, pressure him to resign, and thus make possible the presidency of Ford and vice-presidency of Nelson Rockefeller.

1980 CIA team of Casey, Gates, and Bush bribe Iran to hold 52 American hostages for 3 more months to deter reelection of Pres. Carter (This has been proven by R. Parry's investigation).

1981 Pres. Reagan inaugurated in January. In March he is shot at but not noticeably hurt. It is conceivable that he was merely kidnapped to hospital, to be reminded who the real bosses are.

1998 Pres. Clinton impeached by the House (though not convicted by the Senate). The Monica affair may have been a typical 'sting.'

(Most Americans are unaware of these ejections, except for 1963)

List 8b.   'Defense' Plans for Smallpox and Nuclear War

Note: the **'Spanish flu' that killed one-third of Europe** in 1918 was recently bioengineered by DNA and is now **privately patented!**

From DoD Smallpox Response Plan 18, of Sept. 29, 2002: "The Smallpox Coordination Cell will coordinate with smallpox response staff at the Military Services, the CDC, and other agencies, synchronize information exchange for military chain of command... the Cell will coordinate with FEMA...   Smallpox symptoms (e.g., high fever, fatigue, headache, backache) begin 7 to17 days after exposure... Smallpox kills about 30% of those infected.

Smallpox has been eradicated; the last natural case occurred in 1978.   However, smallpox remains a biological threat, because of remaining viral stocks. **Smallpox virus could be released either in military or civilian settings**... [There are] two internationally approved storage facilities..."

Bulletin: The Danish firm Bavarian Nordic has shipped to the DOD the first million of 20 million doses of smallpox vaccine on July 14, 2010 with an **option to send 60 million more doses**. (Imvamune) The website of that manufacturer says "The threat of bioterrorism is real. The **September 11, 2001 attacks** on New York show the willingness of terrorists to murder large numbers of people arbitrarily."

Prof. Michel Chossudovsky, *Targetting Iran:* "This military adventure in the real sense of the word threatens the **future of humanity.** While one can conceptualize the loss of life and destruction resulting from present-day wars including Iraq and Afghanistan, it is impossible to fully comprehend the devastation which might result from a Third World War, using "new technologies" and advanced weapons, until it occurs and becomes a reality." globalresearch.ca 8/13/ 2010

From the Pentagon's *Doctrine for Joint Nuclear Operations:* "...it is essential [that] US forces **prepare to use nuclear weapons** effectively and that US forces are determined to employ nuclear weapons if necessary to **prevent** or retaliate against WMD...."

[Note: don't worry if you find these things absurd. Worry if you don't!]

List 8c.   How We 'Learned' that Arabs Are Terrorists

'68: Robert F Kennedy assassinated by **Palestinian**, Sirhan Sirhan.

'70: Plane blown up in Zurich Airport. All 47 died. Credit claimed by **PFLP (Popular Front for the Liberation of Palestine).**

'70: Jordan: simultaneous 3 plane hijack. **PFLP** blamed, released.

'72: Lod Israel Airport. 26 killed by **PFLP & Japanese Red Army.**

'73: Athens airport. 3 killed by **'Black September Suicide Squad.'**

'75: **PFLP with freelance terrorist Carlos the Jackal** kidnap 11 oil ministers at OPEC meeting in Vienna, get ransom, escape.

'76: Entebbe: **PFLP & Baader-Meinhof** hijack. Israel rescues 258.

'81: Italian liner, *Achille Lauro*. Man in wheelchair thrown overboard. **Abu Abbas** convicted, then freed by Israel, then captured in Iraq by US, then died in custody.

'85: **Arabs** simultaneously attack Rome, Vienna airports. 18 died.

'86: Explosion in Berlin disco. 2 US soldiers died. **Libya** blamed.

'88: Lockerbie, Scotland TWA flight explodes. 270 died. Sue **Libya**.

'92: Argentina: **Islamic Jihad** bombs Israeli Embassy. No arrests.

'93: **Arab** gunman kills 13 tourists, himself, on Empire State roof.*

'93: World Trade Center basement bombed. 6 died. **Sheik Abdel Rahman** convicted, then died; **Hamzi Yousef** is in jail.

'95: Oklahoma City Federal Building bombed. 168 died. McVeigh convicted but **Iraqi immigrants** are also found to be involved.

'98: Kenya: US Embassy bombed. 213 died. **Ali Mohamed** pleaded guilty. Three others, prosecuted by Patrick Fitzgerald, got life.

* This episode brought about New York's first Joint Terrorism Task Force.

Chapter 9
The Sherman Antitrust Act of 1890

Every Contract, combination in the form of trust or otherwise, or conspiracy, in restraint of trade or commerce among the several States, or with foreign nations, is declared to be illegal. Every person [doing these illegal things] shall be deemed guilty of a felony, and, on conviction thereof, shall be punished by fine not exceeding $10,000,000 if a corporation, or, if any other person, $350,000, or by imprisonment not exceeding three years, or by both said punishments, in the discretion of the court.

Every person who shall monopolize, ...any part of the trade or commerce among the several States, or with foreign nations, **shall be deemed guilty of a felony, and, on conviction thereof, shall be punished ...**

The Several district courts of the United States are invested with jurisdiction to prevent and restrain violations of sections 1 to 7 of this title; and **it shall be the duty of the several United States attorneys, to institute proceedings in equity to prevent and restrain such violations ....**

Any property owned under any contract or by any combination or pursuant to any conspiracy... mentioned in section 1 of this title, and being in the course of transportation from one State to another, or to a foreign country, **shall be forfeited to the United States,** and may be seized and condemned by like proceedings as those provided by law for the forfeiture, seizure, and condemnation of property imported into the United States contrary to law. [emphasis added]

[The above is good law as of July, 2010, in Title 15, USC]

9 Congress

9.1 CONGRESS'S POWER IS TOPS

Dear Reader, how many bonbons did I eat? Please think about that question and the answer will emerge later.

The Framers gave almost all the power of government to the legislature. The Executive branch is practically dispensable, and there is little need for a federal judiciary since 50 states have courts. Without so much as a by-your-leave, Congresspersons can cancel the existence of three unsolicited bureaucracies: Housing and Urban Development; Health and Human Services; and Education. Today.

They can state that the US is a sovereign nation with no intention of merging into any supranational group. They can order the release of all evidence concerning 9/11. They can forbid any further mind manipulation of our Special Forces. They can look at the evidence showing the New Orleans levees were exploded and arrest the guilty. They can eminent-domain the patent-holders of seeds. Right now.

Are the media making it difficult for politicians to reach their constituents on the airwaves? No problem. All media law in the US comes from Congress, as does the statutory body, FCC, that grants broadcast licenses. Congress can make new laws limiting renewal.

Anyway, thanks to the commerce clause, Congress also controls the merger of corporations and can rule against the concentration of media in the hands of a few. In fact it can treat trust barons as felons (only timidity stays government's hand from using the Sherman Act).

189

Will big foundations stand in the way? Whoops, there go the tax laws that permit the foundations to exist. Are the President or the Justices imposing unfair barriers? Whoops, it's impeachment time.

A quick glance at Article I of our magnificent Constitution (printed in full in Appendix Q of this book) will reveal that none of the above is even controversial. It's plain, ordinary, legitimate power. It may be arrogant of Congresspersons to act so aggressively, but they would not be found to be *ultra vires* – acting beyond their power. They *have* the power. The queer thing is, they don't use it!

9.2 GUIDE TO THIS CHAPTER -- *CONGRESS*

Section 9.3 sketches a day on the Hill. (Why not supplement this with a visit to your state legislature in session, O Citizens?) 9.4 looks at oversight responsibilities. 9.5 describes 'guarding the purse.' 9.6 views the Federal Reserve Act as scandalous. 9.7 alleges treason. 9.8 is about Congress's duty to 'restrain the dogs of war.' 9.9 is about martial law 9.10 What To Do? says: Protect Congresspersons! The appendices that match this chapter are E through L, and V.

9.3 THE LEGISLATIVE HOPPER

The public hadn't heard the word *hopper* for a long time. Then Rep Cynthia McKinney, on her last day in Congress, filed Articles of Impeachment against President George W. Bush, whereupon we learned that when such an item lands in the legislative hopper, all House action is supposed to stop while that urgent matter is attended to. Each chamber has rules. For example:

Resolved by this House: That the following shall be the rules to regulate the proceedings of the House of Representatives for the 2007 and 2008 sessions: ...

SEATS

32. Immediately after the adoption of these rules the speaker shall appoint a committee of four, who shall assign seats to all members of the House. 33. The seats assigned to members shall be their seats for their term of office.

Whence cometh the rule that each chamber makes its own rules? From Art. I, Sec 5: <u>Each House may determine the Rules of its Proceedings</u>. And what if the members get into a fight about this? <u>Each House may...punish its Members for disorderly Behavior, and with the Concurrence of two thirds, expel a Member.</u>

Does a member ever get expelled? There was a famous court case in which Rep. Adam Clayton Powell objected, successfully, to an attempt by Congress to refuse him a seat when he returned after his 1966 election. (The clause above does not allow the House to refuse to take a member.) In 2002, James Traficant of Ohio was expelled.

That said, what happened to the Impeachment Articles in the hopper? Nothing, because **each Congressperson is not treated equally.** Humans have a penchant for hierarchy, and for specialization. These have developed in Congress and work towards the weakening of the Constitution. Rep McKinney was not one of the 'big guys.' To be a big guy you have to be a committee chair, or have a title such as Minority Leader, party whip, or Deputy Speaker.

Note: **the party system gets no mention in the Constitution.** It often leads to foolishness, such as "We can't impeach a Democrat because we are a Democrat-majority Congress." (Is that foolish?)

The powers that have been arrogated by the speaker hierarchy can similarly end in absurdity. Democrat Speaker Nancy Pelosi amazingly decreed that any Bush/Cheney impeachment was "off the table," meaning she would not allow a vote to come to the floor. It goes against nature that she did this! Bush/Cheney had only a year left in office; she would almost certainly have become US president.

The **committee system,** however, is what really gives some Representatives more power than others. First a bill is proposed, then it is referred to a committee. The committee can 'report it out' for a full vote, or can let it die. If reported out and it passes, it then would have to go to the other chamber i.e., the Senate if it started in the House. Assuming the two chambers disagree, the bill goes to a Conference, where members from both chambers 'iron out the wrinkles.' Much can happen during that ironing out. Things get added and subtracted and Congresspersons are wont to say they voted on the 'final bill' **without noticing the small-print changes.**

Here's a prediction made by a very prescient conspiracy theorist 18 years ago, in regard to a secret 'Westminsterization' of Congress:

> Carter's legal counsel, Lloyd Cutler, and committee of constitutional lawyers [!] has been working to change the US Congress into a non-representative parliamentary system.... **Members will not be responsible to their constituents** but to party whips and will be told the way they are to vote... [emphasis added]
> ~ John C. Coleman, *Conspirators' Hierarchy* (1992) p. 170

9.4 OVERSEEING THE GOVERNMENT

Didn't You Know Rummy Was a Legislator?

In March 2002, a presidential commission …recommended that three key Pentagon-financed intelligence agencies – the National Security Agency, the National Reconnaissance Office, and the National Imagery and Mapping Agency – be placed under the control of the director of the CIA. This was a serious challenge to Rumsfeld's empire. On June 21, 2002 Secretary Rumsfeld responded with what *U.S. News & World Report* called a "brilliant stealth attack." **He quietly inserted in a Senate defense bill the authority to create a new undersecretary of defense for intelligence….** The new undersecretary position is a bureaucratic coup that accomplished many Pentagon goals in one fell swoop…. [emphasis added]

~ Chalmers Johnson, *The Sorrows of Empire* (2005) p. 127

As to the question "How many bonbons did I eat?" The answer is "I ate eighteen." Just my way of remembering the location, in the Constitution, of an oft-missed point. Go to Art. I, Sec 8, Clause 18 ("I-eight-18") and there you find: [The Congress shall have power] to make all Laws which shall be necessary and proper for carrying into Execution the foregoing Powers [i.e., 1 through 17] and all other Powers vested by this Government of the United States, or in any Department or Offices thereof.

Hence, if the judiciary or the president needs a law made for the operation of its branch, it has to get that law from Congress. In its very first session Congress gave the courts a Judiciary Act and in 1934 added the Rules Enabling Act. In Ch 3.5 it was mentioned that most Executive Orders fail the test of legality. Now we can answer more definitively the question "Why is a presidential directive or executive order not a law?" It is because *I ate eighteen.*

Congress is also said to have 'government oversight'. It is responsible for reviewing, if necessary, the results of its legislative creations. This leads to hearings, for instance, on soldiers' complaints about Gulf War Illness. (The army itself is the legislature's creation.) Congress also assumes a more general investigative function. It can hold hearings **on any complaint** that has a federal connection. One often hears that members of the executive, such as Karl Rove, refuse to testify. But they can be forced to. Moreover, if they "willfully falsify or cover up" information they can be imprisoned up to 5 years. Amazing but true: see 18 USC 1001.

Congress can cite for contempt if invitee refuses to give evidence: "a legislative body cannot legislate wisely or effectively in the absence of information.... Experience has taught that mere requests for such information which is volunteered is not always accurate or complete; so some means of compulsion are essential to obtain that which is needed." ~ US Supreme Court in *McGrain v Daugherty* (1927)

Congress's switchboard is 202-224-2131

9.5 GUARDING THE PURSE

Congress has not been a good guardian of the purse, and since 1980 it hardly even makes a pretense of it. When Ronald Reagan won the presidential election that year, the government's debt was negligible; it is now thirteen trillion dollars. That means we owe, and are paying interest on that amount. A separate matter is the current budget deficit. Under the first Obama budget, the amount of planned expenditure is two trillion dollars greater than the funds available!

Among the 18 powers granted to the federal government, on which Congress can make law, several relate to money. They are shown here with an inserted clause number (there are no actual clause numbers *in* the Constitution) from Art. I, Sec 8: <u>Congress shall have Power... [1] To lay and collect Taxes, Duties, Imposts and Excises, to pay the Debts and provide for the common Defence and general Welfare of the United States; [2] To borrow Money on the credit of the United States; ... [4] To establish uniform Laws on the subject of Bankruptcies throughout the United States; [5] To coin Money, regulate the Value thereof, and of foreign Coin.</u>

In the section immediately after Section 8's enumeration of the 18 grants of power to the federal legislature, we find this gem:
Art. I, Sec 9. <u>No Money shall be drawn from the Treasury, but in Consequence of Appropriations made by Law; and a regular State-ment and Account of the Receipts and Expenditures of all public Money shall be published from time to time</u>.... ["I'm like Huh?"]
Drafting of the budget is nowadays done by the Executive. There is a huge bureau, The Office of Management and Budget, for this.

How is it that Congress has for 60 years exempted such organizations as the CIA, NSA and NASA – and now the Department of Homeland Security – from supplying receipts, or even supplying information about how they spend some of their 'appropriations?' The Constitution gives no scope for such practice.

I Did Not Make This Up!   June 28, 2010

Incredible! Congresspersons reporting to each other about what they can glean from *Vanity Fair, Wall Street Journal,* and the BBC, as to HOW MUCH US IS SPENDING ON MILITARY -- MM

Congressman Dennis Kucinich (D-OH) today made the following statement on the floor of the House concerning an expected vote on a $33 billion supplemental war funding bill:

"In a little more than a year the United States flew $12 billion in cash to Iraq, much of it in $100 bills, shrink wrapped and loaded onto pallets. Vanity Fair reported in 2004 that `at least $9 billion' of the cash had `gone missing, unaccounted for.'

"Today, we learned that suitcases of $3 billion in cash have openly moved through the Kabul airport. One U.S. official quoted by the Wall Street Journal said, `A lot of this looks like our tax dollars being stolen.' $3 billion. Consider this as the American people sweat out an extension of unemployment benefits.

"Last week, the BBC reported that "the US military has been giving tens of millions of dollars to Afghan security firms who are funneling the money to warlords." Add to that a corrupt Afghan government underwritten by the lives of our troops.

"And now reports indicate that Congress is preparing to attach $10 billion in state education funding to a $33 billion spending bill to keep the war going.

"Back home millions of Americans are out of work, losing their homes, losing their savings, their pensions, and their retirement security. We are losing our nation to lies about the necessity of war."

~ Published at kucinich.house.gov   Yes, that is an official website. Also published by Patriot, on 6-30-2010, at America-hijacked.com

Where is the check on Congressmen allotting money, single-handedly, to federal projects in their district by a scheme called 'earmarking'? There is a General Accounting Office, the GAO, that perhaps sounds as though it may function to supervise spending. But no, it is an arm of Congress and Congress does not have to answer to it. Indeed, this is an instance of an institution making us believe that its mere existence sets things right. Let us develop a decoding ✒ rule here, calling it the GAO rule: If something has a name that can lull us, watch out!

9.6 THE 'FEDERAL' RESERVE ACT

Now we turn to the most outrageous deed ever performed by Congress in regard to *not* guarding the purse. In 1913, near Christmas, when many Congresspersons had gone home, some men with an eye on the main chance moved in for a vote on the Federal Reserve bill. Among the results of their action were: our current debt, the Great Depression of 1933, and the ease of funding a war. It also was a steppingstone toward the Bretton Woods Institutions of 1944 (IMF and World Bank) and thus, of World Government.

Here is the one instance when bringing "the Jews" into the story is appropriate. Since medieval times, when the Church forbade the practice of usury (charging high interest on loans), Jewish money lenders occupied this trade more or less exclusively, for example in Venice. Some of them formed the Venetian Black Nobility that later migrated to Hamburg and then Amsterdam. After the battle of the Armada in 1588 (in which Catholic Spain, complete with the Inquisition, lost Holland as a territory), the Dutch formed a republic.

By the 1660s the Dutch were able to gain sufficient power in London to install William of Orange as co-monarch with his Scottish wife, Mary. By the 1700s, the Oppenheimers, Warburgs, and other banking families in Germany had become tremendously wealthy, mainly from the business of making loans to governments for war expenditure. Some bankers worked behind the scenes to *foment* such profitable wars, as do the weapons manufacturers today.

The Bank of England – which is not part of Britain's government despite its name – won financial control in 1694, six years after the Glorious Revolution that put the Oranges on the throne. Its 'governor,' – presently it is Mervyn King – stays out of the limelight.

Sen. Nelson Aldrich, Paul Warburg, and a few others had a secret meeting on Jekyll Island, Georgia in late 1910 to work out a plan for

Congress to legitimize an astonishing scheme. Henceforth the banks would be allowed to 'produce' money, as it were, and at the same moment cause the US to borrow that amount at interest.

Granted, the Constitution gives Congress the power to borrow, but it does not allow anyone but Congress to 'coin' money. In the 1960s we heard that LBJ was 'printing money' to finance the war in Vietnam. It was worse than that: he was letting 'the Fed' 'print' it.

Carroll Quigley (1966) and the Eustace Mullins (1985) demonstrate how the Federal Reserve here is related to the Bank of England. The biggest owner in both is 'the House of Rothschild.' Mullins' indefatigable research demonstrated that even big names like Morgan, Rockefeller, and Carnegie were front men for the Rothschilds in the 1910s. Since our concern here is with Congress, suffice it to say that the dastardly deed of 100 years ago needs to be overturned by our current legislators. Repeal of the Federal Reserve Act has in fact been proposed many times by Rep. Ron Paul.

Suggestion: Let's stop saying that "the Jews" are running Congress. Every time Ron Paul proposes that we axe the Fed he is voted down by most of his 434 colleagues, 90% of whom identify their religion as Christian. Can we please be logical? Can we please say 'up' is not 'down,' and two plus two is four? It is *Congress* that controls our financial fate – not the Jews, not Wall St, not Boeing or Raytheon.

It is Congress that has the sole power to determine our financial system. Why be tongue-tied about saying so? Ring 202-224-2131 and explain to the senator or representative that he/she is wonderfully powerful. (You can leave a voicemail after hours.)

9.7 TREASON ON THE HILL

Horrible treachery has been occurring here for over a century. Let's review the things that supposedly prevent us from stopping it.

Firstly, recall the discussion of governmental immunity in Ch 8.10. The state itself (the nation-state, the US) is immune from lawsuit – unless it grants leave to be sued. Also, the law frees judges and legislators from civil suit for decisions they make on the job. This is a practical matter: what judge or legislator could make tough decisions if she stood to lose her life savings? Note: civil servants have 'qualified immunity,' too, but only because courts, **by policy**, presume good faith on the part of government. (The plaintiff in *Harbury v Deutsch* (2001) got that policy set aside: she had been deliberately misled by the CIA about the kidnapping of her husband.)

196

Secondly, Congresspersons aren't liable for libel for things they say 'at work.' Art. I, Sec 6: <u>They shall in all Cases, except Treason, Felony and Breach of the Peace, be privileged from Arrest during their Attendance at the Session of their respective Houses, and in going to and returning from the same; and for any Speech or Debate in either House, they shall not be questioned in any other Place.</u>

Thirdly, every American enjoys freedom of speech. Some states have laws against obscenity – but not against 'political' speech. Twice we had Sedition Acts, in 1798 and 1918, but these violated the First Amendment. What about speaking (not acting, but speaking) against the Constitution itself: is that allowable? Sure! How else would amendments get started? It is even proper for a Congressperson to say "We need a whole new kind of government. Let's have a debate." But she must not proffer an apparently benign bill that is really aimed at making constitutional government collapse!

Treason is a crime, per the Constitution. The Framers pared it down from what it was in England at the time. Protection of the King had become so hyped up that even a word of threat, made humorously, could be punished by death. It is said that the owner of the Crown Pub once boasted that his son would inherit the crown, and was hanged for treason! Mostly, the Framers wanted to be sure no one would be convicted merely on words he or she uttered, not even if the words reek of treasonous thought. Thus they required that Treason must consist of an act. (Note: in law, *writing* is an act.)

Per Art. III, Sec 3, treason against the US shall consist only in *levying war* against them or in *adhering to their enemies,* giving them aid and comfort. Does a senator **who proposes anti-constitutional law commit treason,** under either part of that definition? There is hardly any case law to guide us. The first part, "levying war," may apply to that senator. But let's deal with the second part, "adhering to the US's enemies, giving them aid ...." – as it is easier to prove.

At this point in the book we know who the enemy is: 'World Government.' It is those who direct the three missions of a historic conspiracy, which are: **destroy all governments, get rid of all religions, and reduce people to slavery.** These are similar to the missions the Elector of Bavaria caught the Illuminati performing in 1784. They are the same ones H.G. Wells talked about – approvingly – in his book, *The Open Conspiracy,* eighty-two years ago (see Ch 2.8).

We educated Americans have never been able to get a handle on this because the intrigues of the cabal are hidden from us and, when

197

discovered, are emphatically denied. To my knowledge no one who aided the cabal has ever been brought to court and made to risk perjury by denying, under oath, that he or she worked for them.

In March 2010, Senators McCain and Leiberman proposed a bill, S.3081, that essentially denounces habeas corpus. In my opinion – and I will be happy to hear an opposing view – **their action was intended to aid the cabal and both men are therefore indictable for treason.** I realize that is a strong statement but haven't many people declared the Patriot Act to be treasonous?

It would be helpful for us laypersons to make it a rebuttable presumption that legislation that **flies in the face of the Constitution** is traitorous. (In law, 'presumptions' are handy; they let you start without proof, and the other person has to show that your presumption is wrong. I suggest only that we do it *informally*.)

I recommend that we waste not another minute watching our birthright, the Constitution, be decimated by Congress. Let's indict the sponsors of treasonous bills. But might this get out of hand, with folks applying the word 'treason' to any bill they dislike? No. We have brains enough to attack only the bills that deserve it.

Often the White House or an interest group is the originator of a bill. For instance, the Patriot Act was drafted by Michael Chertoff and Viet Dinh, both DoJ employees at the time. But they did not commit the treason of making it into law – only legislators could do that – Rep Jim Sensenbrenner was the proposer of the Patriot Act. Don't be concerned that since most representatives voted for the Patriot Act, the task of prosecuting would be overwhelming, and would leave us without a parliament. The smallest list (how about 'McCain and Lieberman'?) would make Congress reform overnight.

It is imperative that Americans understand that treason is criminal and that our leaders **are never immune** from criminal prosecution. What would you do if someone stole your car or assaulted your elderly Mom? Call the police, right? Same thing for traitors. Your senators and representatives live in your state for at least part of the year, so local police can make the arrests.

If police won't help, citizens will have to do it. Look up your state law concerning citizen's arrest – it *is* legal but has risks. (Be aware that, in citizen's arrest, it may be lawful for you to use reasonable force, but the arrestee – *if he believes the arrest is unlawful* – may also use reasonable force to out-do you.) Isn't it reasonable to say that a **danger of coup d'état** justifies our acting in self-defense?

198

> **Self-Defense.** This [legal] strategy makes the claim that it was **necessary** to inflict some harm on another **in order to assure one's own safety** in the face of near-certain injury.... The amount of defensive force used must be proportionate to the amount of force or perceived degree of threat that one is seeking to defend against. Hence, **reasonable force** is that degree of force that is appropriate in a given situation and is not excessive. [It] can be thought of as the minimum degree of force necessary to protect oneself, one's property, [or] a third party... in the face of a substantial threat. **Deadly force**... is considered reasonable only when used to counter an immediate threat of death or great bodily harm.
> [emphasis added]   ~ Frank Schmalleger, *Criminal Justice* (2001) p. 101

It's even possible to imagine an *en masse* arrest on the Hill. In New Hampshire in late 2006, *The Concord Monitor* reported that the district's newly-elected member of Congress arrived to find his desk in Washington looking rather bare. He stated that he had been given only a pen, a telephone, and **the card he would use for voting**.

Wait a minute! Is there software involved here? Do some representatives secretly give party leaders advance permission to fiddle with their 'decisions' about legislation. In New Hampshire's state legislature, each member has a green light and a red light on his desk so citizens in the gallery can easily see who voted Yes or No. But could our (mind-controlled) Congresspersons be unaware of their own vote? I unexpectedly found the answer. In 2008 I ran into a woman friend who is a CIA agent and remarked "It's disgusting the way they use plastic cards in Congress, so they don't even know how they are voting." Madame CIA, apparently did not realize it was a secret, so she defended the practice: "It is quite sensible. A member from Iowa may not know how to vote about ship-building, while one from Rhode Island knows nothing about grain storage." *Arrgh!*

Constitutionally, that probably does not rise to treason (though I think a judge could stretch it that far). But as usual with governmental misbehavior, a lesser crime can be invoked. It is fraudulent for Congress to pretend every member is voting independently if that is not the case. The standard of **fraud** in federal law is:

> If two or more conspire...to **defraud** the United States...in any manner or for any purpose and one or more of such persons do any act to effect the object of the conspiring, each shall be fined under this title or **imprisoned not more than five years.**   ~ **18 USC 37**

PRES. GEORGE WASHINGTON: 6TH STATE OF THE UNION MESSAGE, NOVEMBER, 1794 (THE WHISKEY REBELLION)

[W]ith the deepest regret do I announce to you that during your recess some of the citizens of the United States have been found capable of insurrection.... In the four western counties of Pennsylvania a prejudice, fostered and imbittered by the artifice of men who labored for an ascendency over the will of others ...produced symptoms of riot and violence.... The very forbearance to press prosecutions was misinterpreted into a fear of urging the execution of the laws, and associations of men began to denounce threats against the officers employed. ... [We acted] against the rioters and delinquent distillers... They fired upon the marshal, ...seized his papers of office, and finally destroyed by fire his buildings... Upon testimony of these facts an associate justice of the Supreme Court of the United States notified to me that "in the counties of Washington and Allegheny... laws of the United States were opposed, and the execution thereof obstructed, by combinations too powerful to be suppressed by the ordinary course of judicial proceedings or by the powers vested in the marshal of that district".... ...My proclamation of the 7th of August last was accordingly issued.... They were authorized to confer with any bodies of men or individuals. They were instructed to be candid and explicit in stating the sensations which had been excited in the Executive, and his earnest wish to avoid a resort to coercion;.... Pardon, too, was tendered.... I ordered the militia to march,... In this uncertainty, I put into motion 15K men, ... **Thirty days from the commencement of this session being the legal limitation of the employment of the militia,** Congress can not be too early occupied with this subject.... It has been a spectacle... to behold the most and the least wealthy of our citizens standing in the same ranks as private soldiers...the army of the Constitution undeterred by **a march of 300 miles over rugged mountains** ... The devising and establishing of a well regulated militia would be a genuine source of legislative honor ... I therefore entertain a hope that the present session will not pass without [establishing] the power of organizing, arming, and disciplining the militia, and thus providing, in the language of the Constitution, for calling them forth to execute the laws of the Union, suppress insurrections, and repel invasions. Gentlemen of the House of Representatives: Let us unite... in imploring the Supreme Ruler of Nations to spread his holy protection over these United States ...and to verify the anticipations of this Government being a safeguard of human rights.   [emphasis added]

9.8 RESTRAINING THE DOGS OF WAR

A blatant type of Congressional treason that has been occurring for about 50 years has to do with the legislature's yielding up its responsibility for checking the executive's penchant for warmaking. In *Youngstown* (1953), as in many earlier cases, the Supreme Court did the right thing in standing up for the legislature's "I ate eleven" role. Then it beat a shameful retreat, as is vividly shown in Appendix W.

Ch 7.5 chided the Judiciary for preventing 'war powers' cases from reaching SCOTUS. But the fault lies originally with Congress. Our $174,000 a year politicians on the Hill haven't read Constitution Art. I, Sec 8 [11]. As you read this next quote you'll think "There must be a typo" – but no, there isn't. It is just shocking misbehavior:

"DeFazio Amendment Against Attacking Iran on House Floor Today,"

~ Robert Naiman in *The Hill*   [Huffingtonpost.com] *May 16, 2007*
An amendment blocking military action against Iran without Congressional authorization is expected to be voted on in the House today as part of the debate on the defense authorization bill. The amendment is being introduced by Reps. DeFazio, Paul, Hinchey, and Lee. House Democrats, **who have been divided on whether the president needs authorization from Congress to attack Iran**, suggested yesterday that they are more united on the controversial issue. But with Iran measures possibly headed to the House floor as early as today, it is unclear if Democrats have the votes **to pass legislation calling for the president to seek authorization from Congress** for a preemptive strike on Iran. [emphasis added]

What more is there to say on that subject? Put them in the stocks.

9.9 IS MARTIAL LAW CONSTITUTIONAL?

To answer the question "Is martial law constitutional?" we would normally research the jurisprudence (i.e., judges' rulings on cases and other scholarly opinions). We shall do that below. But first it is essential to note that the 'martial law' that we fear today would not be the kind to which the Constitution, or jurisprudence, gives sanction. None of us fears a legitimate effort by the US government to keep order, or thwart a rebellious group per Art. I, Sec 8 (16). If anything that's what this book is madly calling for. Rather, what we fear is a 1917 Russia-style change of government, in which people will be roughed up. To disambiguate, let's call the Constitution-sanctioned type 'lawful martial law,' and the other, 'bully martial law.'

The Constitution refers mainly to lawful martial law of the type that needs to be called up when some of *the people* are making it hard for all to enjoy the Republic. In Article IV, the Framers also arranged for the feds to go in and help any *state* that lost its republic!

Jurisprudence of martial law is based on two cases. In *Korematsu v US*, an American citizen challenged President Roosevelt's Executive Order 9066 that forbade him to travel outside his home area, in California, during WWII, because of his Japanese ethnicity. **The Court upheld martial law.** Later it was revealed that the president had known there was no risk from any Japanese-Americans.

Might it be that the restrictions were imposed *for the purpose* of setting a legal precedent for martial law? We don't know, but the constitutionality of an ethnic roundup became 'settled' via *Korematsu*. (After SCOTUS gives a clear ruling, the law is considered settled.)

Later, in the 1990s, Congress awarded $20,000 compensation to each Japanese-American that had been interned, but this does not affect jurisprudence. Americans interned today would *not* win relief in a lower court, as it is settled that internment in wartime is constitutional. However SCOTUS can always override itself.

The one other relevant case is that of *Ex parte Milligan*, dating back to 1866 ('*ex parte*' means one of the parties was not present). Milligan was accused of helping the enemy, i.e., the southern-states Confederacy, and was arrested by the military, and court-martialed.

By the time the SCOTUS heard his appeal, the Civil War had ended. The Court avoided commenting on Lincoln's declaration that the nation was at war, and merely ruled that Milligan should not have been court-martialed because the regular courts were functioning at that time. The upshot was that the term 'martial law' received an abstract definition, *viz.*, it means **"military commanders are ordering the public with no court available to hear challenges."** That definition is worse than useless. It takes up vital legal room.

Now to '**bully martial law.**' There is no jurisprudence for this. Of course there have been court rulings against police brutality. And if your litigation – as a person harmed during martial law – ever gets heard, you may well win damages. (There is also precedent, from the Wounded Knee episode, that when military take part in law enforcement they may not search you. See *Bissonette v Haig*, 1985).

But let's be sensible and say that if the cabal clamps down on us violently, we will no longer have 'rights.' The protections in the Constitution will be academic. **Thus we need to talk loudly, while**

we still can, about bully martial law. Think back to the opportunity for that which arose during hearings when Rep Brooks inquired about Continuity of Government (the 'COG' from Ch 2.8):

> *Rep. Brooks:* Colonel North, in your work at the NSC, were you not assigned, at one time, to work on plans for the continuity of government in the event of a major disaster?
> *Brendan Sullivan:* Mr. Chairman?
> *Sen. Inouye:* I believe that question touches upon a highly sensitive and classified area so may I request that you not touch on that.
> *Rep. Brooks*: I was particularly concerned, Mr. Chairman, because I read in Miami papers, and several others, that there had been a plan developed by the same agency, a contingency plan in the event of emergency, that would suspend the American constitution....
> *Sen. Inouye:* May I respectfully request that that matter not be touched upon at this stage. If we wish to get into this, I'm certain arrangements can be made for an executive session.
> ~ *Hearings on the Iran-Contra Affair* (1988) On video at youtube.com

The persons that participated in Iran-Contra were among the planners of 'martial law,' so it behooves us to **get them before they get us.** We can call senators in for questioning and, if they seem to be protecting an extra-constitutional government, may arrest them on charges of **conspiracy to commit kidnap and murder.** After all, they'll have to commit those acts during a takeover – won't they?

This book wants to turn the clock back to the time when we believed we were in charge. We still are! **Because we've got law.** Criminals really do worry about law: AG Gonzales got Congress to change the wiretap law retroactively, so Bush couldn't be charged.

If you think the Constitution will protect you, you are right. But the Constitution depends on people upholding it. If you won't participate, the outlook is grim. Orwell, who knew his onions, said: *If you want a picture of the future, imagine a boot stamping on a human face – forever.*

The reader may suspect I am on the wrong track, that I'm mixing up notions of the governing process with the notion of criminal law. Yes, I definitely am mixing them, but not because I am 'mixed up' about them. If anything, they are too sequestered in my mind (and everyone else's). I am forcing myself to put them together on a piece of paper here, to get to the constitutional meat of the matter.

I am currently in final semester of law school, in Australia. Writing this book has caused me to notice how my legal training tries to shut off thought. It instructs me to terminate an inquiry as soon as

I reach the 'black-letter-law.' Lawyers see *Korematsu* and *Milligan* cases as *the* universe of ideas to be canvassed about martial law.

If I went traipsing back to my Politics professors, they too would decline to deal with big issues. They would say (I am not joking) "We deal in political reality, not values or ideals. We can point to, say, riot-control weapons, but we do not declare them good or bad. That would be a value judgment. Our students come here to learn, not to be preached at." "Also, it is not our job to make policy. We are not..." – wait for it – "in politics."

Mind you, if I went to a priest in my Faith and said "Our rulers plan to murder whole swathes of the US," his 'advice' would go like this: "Holy Mother Church cares for your spiritual, rather than your temporal well-being. Let us pray for our leaders. *Pax vobis.*"

OK, back to analyzing *bully martial law*. Whenever the few want to conquer the many, they have to use weapons. Our internal enemy has lots of weapons, including those furnished by the taxpayer. Remember 'they' have satellite weaponry, too, including the kind that can give us hailstorms at rush hour, plus tornados, quakes, and heat waves. It goes without saying that have the gall to use them.

So what do *we* have to protect ourselves? We have an army, a national guard, and police. The trick is to figure out who has access to them. Whose side will they take? Here is what **10 USC 332** says:

> Whenever the President considers that unlawful obstructions, combinations, or assemblages, or rebellion against the authority of the US, makes it impracticable to enforce the laws of the US in any state by the ordinary course of judicial proceedings, he may call into Federal service such of the militia of any State, and use such of the armed forces, as he considers necessary to enforce those laws or to suppress the rebellion. **(But compare Constitution Article I, Section 8 [15] – urgently!)**

List 9c makes bold to tell soldiers that the *executive* branch must not use the Militia (i.e., the National Guard of each state) unless Congress calls for it, must not impose martial law (i.e., must not suspend habeas corpus) without the "Yes" from Congress, and must never disarm citizens. Period. Congress can't change the Constitution; that would require an amendment. One of the 18 grants of power, by the Framers, to the Legislature is: <u>Congress shall have power...To provide for calling forth the Militia to execute the Laws of the Union, suppress Insurrections and repel Invasions</u>. Art. I, Sec 8 [15]. Anyone can see that 10 USC fails to reflect that. Of course the USC is meant to codify federal statutes, not the Constitution. President Washington's pitch about the Whiskey Rebellion led Congress to pass the Enforcement Act of 1795, 'giving' the executive permission to call up state militias. Has this ever been challenged in court? Go to the Annotated Constitution at law.cornell.edu. You'll find, near Art. I, Sec 8 [15], a reference to *Martin v Mott,* the case of a man who didn't answer the New York militia's call-up for the War of 1812. Justice Story found that President Madison had acted properly *because he relied on Congress's I.8.15 authority.* I confess that I can't comprehend SCOTUS on this.

Note that anyone wanting to find justification for tyrannical power, in the slim Article II that gives the president his/her role, can find it. One need only emphasize the logic that *a leader cannot be left impotent.* I agree that a leader needs power to protect the nation. But is that logic supposed to make us zip up our lips as to the reality of the fact that our leaders let 9/11 happen? Now we are back to the arguments of Ch 2, which was entitled *Fear.* There it was said that 'emergency' is a psychological trick, it makes us act like idiots.

We are also back to Ch 5 and Ehren Watada's question What if the elected leaders became the enemy? If Congress is acting against us we can't use the logic that says, Give leaders the power to protect us. That would be absurd! Let's instead concentrate on the criminal-law model. There's a plan for the foreign troops in US (Appendix Z) to give us bully martial law, isn't there? That's treason. Call the cops!

9.10 WHAT TO DO? PROTECT CONGRESS!

It is a plain fact that our legislators do not feel free to speak their minds. Granted, the Constitution specifically shields them from libel suits for anything they utter from the floor. But such parliamentary privilege doesn't give the protection they most need: **Congresspersons may be killed, or see their loved ones killed, if they challenge the powerful.**

Such punitive deaths never get proven as crime – they are called accidents or natural deaths, or suicides – but correlating them with outspokenness does show that death occurs too frequently to be by chance. In 2008, Rep Dennis Kucinich, a candidate in the presidential primaries, proposed Articles of Impeachment against VP Richard Cheney. Soon thereafter his 51-year-old brother died. Not defeated, Kucinich tried again. Then his sister died, age 49.

It's now for you to take up this matter. Why not choose one from the following list and act on it howsoever you can with friends:

Among the well-known deaths of outspoken legislators are Hale Boggs, the only member of the Warren Commission who didn't buy the Lee Harvey Oswald story. Boggs disappeared on a plane, along with Alaska's Rep Nick Begich (Sr.), who 'outed' the HAARP ionospheric heater. Senators William Taft and Joe McCarthy challenged the US's pro-communist policies in the 1950s and then died young. Senator Paul Wellstone died in a small plane crash, with his wife.

(Australians wonder about Senator Jeannie Ferris, who was 'not a team player.' She died of cancer, and just before her funeral her former husband, a journalist in Canberra, died in a one-car accident.)

Among African-American legislators, Barbara Jordan died of pneumonia at age 59 (after she left Congress), and Stephanie Tubbs-Jones, a few days after she teased candidate Senator Obama about his birthplace, was in a one-car crash and died in hospital. (State legislators, too, fall off the perch. See NH for some recent cases.)

There are many more. The point is, it is very hard for one of the 535 Congresspersons to do the right thing! If they are parents they must worry that their child will be attacked. Wright Patman, who took seriously his responsibilities on the Banking Committee, lost a son. Senator John Edwards's son's car flipped over in bad weather.

Therefore we *must protect them* by showing a big interest in any such death. Yes, it could be natural causes or genuine accident, but the rebuttable presumption should, logically, be otherwise. Website politicalgraveyard.org lists the names of 116 senators who died in office from 1900 to 1949. (There were fewer than 50 states then, so this is a huge percentage.) Was it ever mentioned in our school history books? No. Write to your school principal to ask about this!

Please read this aloud with me now (from robertburns.org.):

Fareweel to a' our Scottish fame/ Fareweel our ancient glory;
Fareweel ev'n to the Scottish name/ Sae fam'd in martial story....
What force or guile could not subdue/ Thro' many warlike ages,
Is wrought now by a coward few/ For hireling traitor's wages....
O would, or I had seen the day/ That Treason thus could sell us,
My auld grey head had lien in clay/ Wi' Bruce and loyal Wallace!

Note: if it seems too difficult to 'get' anyone for the crime of treason, you can at least get them for misprision of treason (failure to report it). Does any senator *not* know 9/11 was a false flag? In Australia the penalty for misprision of treason is life. Here it is only 'up to seven years,' but that'll do. See 18 USC 2382. And how about your good self behind bars. You are now aware of treason, right?

List 9a.   House Committees and Codified US Law

The following House Committees (and similar Senate ones) reflect the powers granted to the federal legislature by the Constitution: **Appropriations, Armed Services, Budget, Energy and Commerce, Financial Services, Homeland Security, House Administration, Judiciary, Oversight, Rules, Standards of Official Conduct, Transportation, Veterans Affairs, Ways and Means**

Committees that do not have express constitutional basis are: Agriculture, Education and Labor (yes, that's combined!), Foreign Affairs, Intelligence (except as a military function regarding enemies), Natural Resources, Science and Technology, Small Business

---

The following are the 50 titles of the United States Code (USC). These reflect Congress's 222 years of producing law in fields in which it has the constitutional authority to do so, and a few areas (italicization added) in which it arguably does not:

1. General Provisions 2. Congress 3. President 4. Flag Seal, States, Seat of Gov't (city of DC) 5. Government Organization and Employees 6. Domestic Security 7. *Agriculture* 8. Aliens and Nationality 9. Arbitration 10. Armed Forces 11. Bankruptcy 12. Banks and Banking 13. Census 14. Coast Guard 15. Commerce and Trade 16. *Conservation* 17. Copyrights 18. Crimes and Criminal Procedure 19. Customs Duties 20. *Education* 21. *Food and Drugs* 22. *Foreign Relations and Intercourse* 23. Highways 24. *Hospitals and Psychiatric hospitals* 25. Indians 26. Internal Revenue Code 28 Judiciary and Judicial Procedure 29. Labor 30. *Mineral Lands and Mining* 31. Money and Finance 32. National Guard 33. Navigable Waters 35. Patents 36. Patriotic Societies and Observancesances 37. Pay and Allowances of the Uniformed Services 38. Veterans' Benefits 39. Postal Service 40. Public Buildings, Properties, and Public Works 41. Public Contracts 42. *Public Health and Social Welfare* 43. Public Lands 44. Public Printing & Documents 45. Rail transport 46. Shipping 47. Telegraphy 48. Territories & Possessions 49. Transportation 50. War and National Defense

[Search for, say, "8 USC" and you'll get all codified law on immigration.]

List 9b.   Requesting Resignations from Congress Today

1. The Constitution is the sole basis for the authority of the United States government, and must be meticulously followed.

2. It is not constitutionally possible for the US to join a suprastate. Legislators who support an NAU **should not seek re-election.**

3. Every adult American holds equal political power and equal hope of influencing legislation. Elected members of Congress speak for the people in their district, state, and the nation. **We request Congresspersons to resign today if they view their obligation otherwise.**

4. The Court is the symbol of lawfulness. **We ask the Congress to impeach any federal judge who courts disrespect.** Also, it is essential that any Congressperson or judge who is being strong-armed communicate his plight to the public. Citizens who learn of such goings-on have a **serious responsibility to try to help.**

5. It goes without saying that Americans condemn **torture, genocide,** the deliberate spreading of **disease**, invading foreign lands except in self-defense, or **manipulating the weather** maliciously.

6. It goes without saying that it is the job of parents to raise their children and that government **may not interfere in the parent-child relationship via indoctrination** or by sneakily controlling the culture. 'The State' has no role to play in family or personal life.

7. The mentioning of various evils that 'go without saying' is occasioned by recent enactment of unconstitutional laws, the signing of particular executive orders, and the apparent carrying out of covert actions pertinent to such evils. **The offending laws must be repealed right away by Congress, and Congress must halt the associated Executive practices. Impeachment or indictment of many officials is called for.**

Note: author of the above, Mary Maxwell, welcomes anyone to make use of it.

List 9c.   Martial Law? A Checklist for Constitutionality

SOLDIERS & GUARDSMEN: NOTE THAT THE CONSTITUTION TRUMPS ANY FEDERAL LAW. ALWAYS. *MARBURY V MADISON* STILL HOLDS!

Article I – *[The Article that stipulates the powers of the Legislature]*
SECTION 8 The Congress shall have Power... To declare war...; To raise and support Armies...; **To provide for calling forth the Militia to execute the Laws of the Union, suppress Insurrections** and repel Invasions; To provide for organizing, arming, and disciplining, the Militia, and for governing such Part of them as may be employed in the Service of the United States...*[rather than of the States]*

SECTION 9 The Privilege of the Writ of **Habeas Corpus shall not be suspended**, unless when in cases of Rebellion or Invasion the public Safety will require it. *[Note: The fact that this appears in the Legislature's part of the Constitution implies that it is up to Congress to suspend the privilege of Habeas Corpus.]*

SECTION 10 **No State shall**, without the Consent of Congress, ... engage in War, unless actually invaded, or in such imminent Danger as will not admit of delay.

Article II – *[The Article that stipulates the powers of the Executive]*
SECTION 2 **The President shall be Commander in Chief** of the Army and Navy of the United States, and **of the Militia** of the several States, **when called into the actual Service of the United States**... *[Note: "when called" must mean "when called by Congress" per Article I Section 8 above. Nevertheless "the Constitution" includes decisions made by the judiciary as to its interpretation, and Martin v Mott (1827) seems to allow the President to call up the National Guard.]*

Article IV – *[The Article that deals with the States]*
SECTION 4 The United States shall guarantee to every State in this Union a Republican Form of government, and shall protect each of them against Invasion; and **on Application of the** [State] **Legislature, against domestic Violence.**

Amendment II A well regulated milita, being necessary to the security of a free state, **the right of the people to keep and bear arms shall not be infringed.**

[emphasis added; nothing in the parchment is bolded]

END OF PART THREE *("CONSTITUTION")* – A CHRONOLOGY

1910 Jekyll Is.: Nelson Aldrich, P. Warburg create Federal Reserve

1919 Col. Mandell House advises, and resides with, Pres. W. Wilson

1924 J Edgar Hoover heads FBI, insists there is no organized crime

1930s Congress permits Executive to expand unconstitutionally

1941 Military makes deal with Sicilian Mafia, launches many careers

1945 Nazis form our CIA; they get safe haven in Peron's Argentina

1947 National Security Act gives fig leaf of legitimacy to covert ops

1960 Congress tries to give Rep Adam Clayton Powell the heave-ho

1968 Feds lie: 'Clay Shaw is not in CIA,' so Garrison loses JFK case

1974 Kissinger arranges VP spot for N. Rockefeller, via Watergate

1976 Pat Nixon has a stroke shortly after leaving job of First Lady

1980 'October Surprise' delays the release of 52 American hostages

1980s Reagan/Thatcher ordered to deregulate & privatize US, UK

1988 Treasurer Jas Baker assures voters S & L swindle 'no big deal'

1989 Atty Gen Smith: "CIA exempted from reporting drug crime"

1995 Al Martin claims Hell's Angels allowed to be drug distributors

2000 White House allotted to Bush, not Gore, in 5-4 decision

2001 Chertoff, Dinh draft Patriot Act; claim "Privacy done gone."

2002 Cyn McKinney pops the question to Rumsfeld, loses her seat

2003 Ashcroft on Letterman show: "Atty Lynne Stewart arrested"

2004 Kerry wins election; Bush resumes office; Congress shrugs

2006 Shocker: SCOTUS 'moots' Padilla enemy non-combatant case

2007 Maxwell's suit dismissed; she checks quiver for other arrows

2009 Congress bails out Wall Street with $700 *billion,* due to 'crisis'

2010 In a campaign finance case, SCOTUS reaffirms *Santa Clara*

2010 Greece becomes laboratory for cashless society

ψψψψ

Welcome to Part Four:

Hurry! It's Much Easier If You Act Now!

To a Historian

You who celebrate bygones,
Who have explored the outward, the surfaces of the races,
the life that has exhibited itself,
Who have treated of man as the creature of
politics, aggregates, rulers and priests,
I, habitan of the Alleghanies, treating of him as he is in
himself
in his own rights,
Pressing the pulse of the life that has seldom exhibited itself,
(the great pride of man in himself)
Chanter of Personality, outlining what is yet to be,
I project the history of the future.

by Walt Whitman (1819-1892)

Chapter 10

Magna Carta – "The Great Charter" – 1215

John, by the grace of God, king of England, lord of Ireland, duke of Normandy and Aquitaine, and count of Anjou, To the archbishop, bishops, abbots, earls, barons, justiciaries, foresters, sheriffs, stewards, servants, and to all his bailiffs and liege subjects, greetings.

Know that, having regard to God for the salvation of our soul…we have granted as underwritten…

We have also granted to all freemen of our kingdom, for us and our heirs forever, all the underwritten liberties, to be had and held by them and their heirs…forever…. **No village or individual shall be compelled to make bridges** at riverbanks, except those who from of old were legally bound to do so. All counties, hundreds, wapentakes, and trithings (except our demesne manors) shall remain at the old rents… No constable or other bailiff of ours shall take corn or other provisions from anyone without immediately tendering money therefor…. **No bailiff for the future shall, upon his own unsupported complaint, put anyone to his "law,"** without credible witnesses brought for this purpose. … To no one will we sell, to no one will we refuse or delay, right or justice. … We will appoint as justices, constables, sheriffs, or bailiffs only such as know the law of the realm and mean to observe it well. … **All fines made with us unjustly…shall be entirely remitted.**

[W]e give and grant to them the underwritten security, namely, that the barons choose five and twenty barons of the kingdom, whomsoever they will, who shall be bound with all their might, to observe and hold, and cause to be observed, the peace and liberties we have granted…so that **if we,** or our justiciar…**shall in anything be at fault towards anyone…**

and the offense be notified to four barons of the foresaid five and twenty, **the said four barons shall repair to us…and, laying the transgression before us, petition to have that transgression redressed without delay.**

And if we shall not have corrected the transgression…within forty days…the four barons aforesaid shall refer that matter to the rest of the five and twenty barons, and those five and twenty barons shall, **together with the community of the whole realm, distrain** and distress us in all possible ways, namely, by seizing our castles…saving harmless our own person and the persons of our queen and children.

[emphasis added]

10 Elections

Think what stamina and inner strength drove...dirt-poor farmers of
the late 1800s who, taking on the major railroads and banks, used
their heads, hearts, and feet... Without electricity, motor vehicles, or
telephones [they] mobilized person-to-person.
That history certainly motivated and excited me as a youngster.
– Ralph Nader, *The Good Fight*

The criminal cried as he dropped him down, in a state of wild alarm,
With a frightful, frantic, fearless frown, I bared my big right arm...
– Sir William S. Gilbert, *Mikado,* "The Criminal Cried"

10.1 YOUR FIRST WEEK IN CONGRESS

Finally, the American public woke up to the fact that since no
member of Congress, except Cynthia McKinney, had ever taken up
the astounding case of 9/11, it was necessary to replace the entire
House. You are one of the replacements, elected by the people of
your district on the first Tuesday of November. You found an
apartment in Washington in December and today, the first Monday
in January, you walk up the steps of the Capitol. A great serenity
comes over you, "the Honorable Member," as you know that the
434 others are really going to be your teammates. None of them has
a need to ridicule you. Everyone is smiling knowingly at each other.

As you enter the chamber, you see that the seats do not have
name-tags, so you sit where you please. In a few minutes your colleagues are starting to chuckle over the fact that there is no one to
greet the members or to start the formalities. Someone gets to her
feet and starts a pledge of allegiance to the flag. Everyone joins in.

Then a young person approaches the pit (Is that what it is
called?) and says "May I have the floor long enough to propose that
the Member from Nevada's second district, James Eagle, preside
over us, only for today, in order to handle housekeeping?" "I'll
second that," says a lady with a Southern drawl. "Any objections?"
None are heard. "All in favor?" A mixture of Aye, Aye's and Hear,
Hear's, and James walks to the lectern.

"We will need to compose a whole set of House rules in the coming weeks, but I suggest for the moment we follow the rules of the last Congress for a few days so there won't be chaos." "Aye, aye" shout the members. "And I propose that the Member from the 5th district of Michigan –Ruth – would she stand up, please – be the person to whom you give nominations, including self-nominations, for the position of Speaker. She should give us a synopsis a week from today, and again after two weeks on what she has received."

Objection from the floor "Why did you pick Ruth?" James: "She is the only person I know so far." (Laughter) "Well, I'd prefer you draw the name from a hat instead, so we can be sure it isn't a fix." "Good idea. Anyone who wants to collect nominations for Speaker just put your name in this hat please. And how shall we pick my replacement for tomorrow?" "Just go alphabetically by surname." "Hmm. I like that. Any objections?" None. "Those in favor?" Enthusiastic ripple of Aye, Aye's.

Suggestion: If you don't think Congress is too impressive, how about taking over? (Just one seat of course.) The opportunity to replace your Representative arises in every even-numbered year. Per Art. I, Sec 2: <u>No Person shall be a Representative who shall not have attained to the age of twenty five Years, and been seven Years a Citizen of the United States, and who shall not, when elected, be an Inhabitant of that State in which he shall be chosen</u>. Easy! (and some *state* offices are open to 18 year-olds). For Senate, see List 10a as to whether your state has a vacancy this year (minimum age <u>thirty</u>). Art. I, Sec 4: <u>The Times, Places and Manner of holding Elections for Senators and Representatives, shall be prescribed in each State by the Legislature thereof; but Congress may at any time by Law [alter such]</u>....

10.2 GUIDE TO THIS CHAPTER -- *ELECTIONS*

10.3 shows how campaigns can be done on the cheap. 10.4 sings the most essential talent of women. 10.5 is about presenting yourself as rightwing, radical, or whatever. 10.6 shows how two major parties run the show. 10.7 discusses ballot theft by software. 10.8 is about the Electoral College. 10.9 deals with Constitutional amendments.

The What To Do? section, 10.10, urges you to start the political job even before you are elected, by becoming a self-appointed ombudsperson. Note: if you want to run for office, don't delay. The same goes for recruiting others. Get on to it urgently. If you have missed a deadline for the current year, try being a write-in candidate.

10.3 A Cheap Campaign for House of Representatives

Let me tell you how easy I found it was to run in the Republican primary, in NH in 2006. (For your state's rules just go to the Net.) Particularly I want to tell you that it was inexpensive. I spent four thousand clams, all up. The guy who won the seat spent $400,000. Perhaps that proves it is expensive to *win*. Maybe, but the cost of running is not prohibitive. Media love to imply that only millionaires get into the race (and seldom say Congress's base pay is $174,000!).

The application fee in New Hampshire was $50 (in Florida it is $5,000). Right after signing up I spent $250 to attend the State Republican Party dinner in Manchester where I had my photo taken with — here it comes — Karl Rove. The emcee at the dinner chose not to acknowledge my presence, as I was running against an incumbent Republican. I suggest you focus on the Constitution's 'invitation' to run, and not let party traditions or jealousy faze you.

Is there any national rule about becoming a candidate? Yes and No. The Constitution gives the election process to the states, but the feds have got into the act via the Federal Elections Commission. When I looked up the rules I found that to be a candidate, there had to be a "Committee to elect Maxwell." By phoning FEC, however, I learned that the candidate's official bank account *is* his committee!

So I walked down the street to a bank and started an account. Be sure to follow the rules at fec.gov for reporting donations. The maximum you can collect from an individual, presently, is $2,300. That donor must be a resident of US and must be given a receipt.

My main expense consisted of: paying for website hosting (see maxwellforcongress.com); printing of campaign posters; having my mugshot portrait done twice (for $3 each), in a booth at a mall, where I was given a choice of the Michelangelo or the Rembrandt. The one on my home page is Michelangelo — *think* of it, for 3 bucks!

I also had to pay for mail-outs, and a taxi-fare to a Fourth of July picnic. The Party sold lists of Republican voters in NH and, for a nickel per name I could have used a Maryland service to update the phone #'s. I asked my potential constituents to invite me to their front porch for a lemonade. (No need to report that as a gift!)

Media coverage was entirely free. Radio shows and newspapers called me for interviews — including a radio show in California! Some people wrote me up on their blogs. I did, however, pay $120 for my first shot at a press release and later did one for which there was no charge. In both cases "PR Web" sent my statement of 700 words (actually it was an article called 'Republican Candidate Thinks Party Should Dump Cheney' or something like that) out to radio stations. ListenupNH kindly made a video of me, and YouTube'd it.

I also hired a venue with cash bar at the Holiday Inn, Nashua, for $250. The hotel provided me with a podium and a flag, which, just in case you don't know, must appear to the speaker's right, the audience's left. (If you forget, just picture where Old Glory was in the classroom of your youth – over to the left corner – remember?) In short, you can make your campaign as cheap or as dear as you like. You can rent a storefront, hire a band for an open-air concert, or use a calling service – either automated or live – to remind voters to vote for you. Check with local police for the rules of setting up a stall on the sidewalk or leafleting near the grocer (private property).

The whole thing need not be frightening. I was good 'n' scared when I began campaigning but no one attacked me or my website. Indeed there were moments when I felt like a star. You do of course run the risk of getting smeared. Purchase a credit-rating on yourself to see what's in file. Take relatives on board to let them know you will appreciate comforting if things get rough. If journalists ask about your private life, stare them down with "It is improper for you to ask that question" or "I'll take a pass on that one."

I had trouble holding up a sign but found that a plywood stick (sold at home improvement shops for a dollar) could be leaned on the ground, with my banner stapled to the top. Posters, bumper stickers, and buttons can be got from wholesalers, via the Net.

Homely hints are available for the asking from folks who have run for office and by inspecting a few of last year's websites. The thing you must get is 'name recognition.' Even if people never hear anything more than your name, that is an 'in' – because no one in the voting booth ticks the box next to an unknown name.

Have friends write Letters to the Editor with info about you. I've seen this done shamelessly, and why not? For a 'platform,' you could hand out the Bill of Rights: use Appendix S – it's ready to fly, just add your campaign details at top. It's best to have one main issue and keep harping on it, e.g., 'Today's Congress needs to go bye-bye.'

10.4 THE MATERNAL BRAIN

I'm here to say we need more women in office, but not the kind we have been getting. Today's female governors and Congresswomen seem to have all been recruited by party leaders on the basis of their willingness to obey. When I was considering a run for state office in New Hampshire, I was told that I could go for "training" and even "be told what to say." Fancy that!

The woman's position in running the nation should be similar to what it is in running the family, if society is to enjoy the great benefit of the maternal brain. Every human female, whether she wants it or not, has a strong instinct to protect her young: she looks out for their welfare, she anticipates any danger or adversity they will encounter. When you went to Scout Camp it was an embarrassment that Mom packed rainwear for you 'just in case.' Right? Well, she couldn't help it. Instinct made her do it.

Boy, do we need women in Congress – a Maternal Caucus perhaps. (Most caucuses are bipartisan.) The maternal brain excels at knowing how to ration or redistribute resources, something that may become necessary for survival. The mother doesn't want any of her own kids – or anybody else's kids – to go hungry. She also doesn't want them to be mean to one another, and tries to end (not incite) squabbles among them. Wouldn't that be a refreshing change!

Suggestion: Have a 'Maternal Draw' to nominate candidates. Without the need for any governmental permission you can start a local movement to recruit women to run for Congress. You could offer that any woman nominated by friends – or by herself – will be included in a draw.

'Sortition,' as this type of lottery is called, was actually proposed by Aristotle for the Athenian democracy in the 4th century B.C.E. ('before Common Era'). Today, sortition is constitutionally acceptable, subject to your state's approving this creative approach. People hardly ever turn down a recruitment drive – it's nice to be asked. By the way, **right now I am asking you. Please?**

If you are the maternal runner, you needn't start a new party. In most states you can march straight into the Secretary of State's office and become a candidate as a Democrat or Republican – without having to be screened by those parties. You can use their logos, if you like donkey or elephant. Or join a small party.

Search the Net as soon as possible, or phone the State House. You may find that there is a duration of, say, 6 months, for you to have registered (with the state) your association with donkey or elephant. **Some states require you to collect signatures** before you can self-nominate as an Independent. Better get a wiggle on!

10.5 ARE YOU LEFT, CONSERVATIVE, RADICAL, ETC.?

First we might ask whether the three labels conservative, right-wing, and radical are based on types of personality. John Dean, in his *Conservatives without Conscience* (2006), says the research supports the idea of a person being right-wing from childhood, even if his brother is left-wing. Such persons are favorably disposed to religious dogmatism, to the superiority of one class or group over another, take patriotism to heart, and are especially pro-military.

Of course we all have those traits, but if a person's brain has slightly less affinity for order, he may end up in a group that favors *criticism* of authority: he'll be liberal. In the US, *liberal* does not have the same sense as in the UK where it usually refers to liberation of business from regulation. (Americans call that *conservative!*). *Liberal* has to do with not judging a person by the group he comes from. It also means one is broad-minded about lifestyle. In the US, liberalism merges into leftism, but lefties are antagonistic toward the affluent.

In either case, though, your political position has to be 'out there' for voters to associate it with your beliefs and ideas. And how did those positions get out there? I am uncertain of their origins, especially after having most of my history school lessons thrown in the wastebasket lately. It seems that the French Revolution's famous banner "Liberty, Equality, and Fraternity" was placed 'out there' by cynical manipulators. The people of France didn't 'rise up' in revolt.

Yet, once people were able to consider such options they found them appealing. Liberty is an animal desire of the individual mammal – we like to run around. Fraternity is another animal desire in us – we gravitate toward kin. Equality? Well, anyone on the poor side of the tracks covets it, and the rich shun it, naturally.

In regard to running for office I think the public is disgusted with all labels; thus you would be better off campaigning free of categorization. Democrats want generous public spending and "rights." Republicans mostly claim to be conservative (as I do) meaning "Stick with our heritage, and keep government small."

Which type of rule will you declare as your preference? (or your nemesis?) Some labels are useless. Consider East Germany, which was a sovereign, Communist nation from 1960 until the Berlin wall 'fell' in 1989. It called itself GDR -- the "German Democratic Republic." But it was no democracy, as it lacked majority rule. Was it a *republic*? The word comes from Latin *res publica*, the public thing. Strictly, it indicates only the participation of citizens. Today it mainly means "not a monarchy." The GDR was not a monarchy, but was ruled by a dictator, and may be categorized as a dictatorship.

Oddly enough, one of the other Soviet 'satellites,' the republic of Romania, started to resemble a monarchy with its leader, Nicolae Ceausescu, taking on some of the symbols of a king.

Was communism the *type of rule* in those countries? No. The type of rule was dictatorship. That government happened to require that the economy be run by the state. Collectivist agriculture was forced and such things as factory wages were set by the Party rather than by the market. But communism is not a type of *government*. It describes methods of ownership of property and could theoretically be found in a democracy. The Israeli kibbutz is an example of that.

Australia and Sweden in the 1970s provided free public services: university education, hospital admission, marriage counseling, etc. and charged an income tax over 50%. Citizens were free to vote for representatives who ran on a platform of, say, an end to high taxes and an end to free hospitals, but a majority did not support that platform (since workers were not in the highest tax bracket).

What about *fascism?* – associated with Hitler, Mussolini and Franco. Is that a type of government? Yes and no. The word refers more to a way of governing, a *style* of power-wielding. We saw fascism in US during Katrina. The men in uniform pushed people around and obviously had no respect for them. Such men are trained to treat people as the enemy, deserving of degradation and violent punishment. It is sad to note how, in 1932, Italy's parliament had a **chance to put an end to fascism but blew it:**

> The black shirt and the black cap disappeared from the streets, the leaders of Fascism were in tremulous hiding, and a cry for freedom and liberty arose in the land.... The King considered... abolishing the illegal Fascist militia, restoring democratic government. But he was afraid. The Opposition parties had only to take one decisive action, but for four days they talked and talked because they foresaw two or three hundred men killed ... despite the fact they had already lost four thousand men,* dead in fighting with the Black shirts, they decided not to shed more blood but hope for peaceful evolution without action. ~ George Seldes, *Sawdust Caesar* (1935) p. 154   *As of mid-2010 we have lost 4880 troops in Iraq. Tens of thousands have come home severely disabled. Australia has informed its troops that they will be in Afghanistan for thirty years.

10.6 PARTY GRIP

The preceding sections implied that you can be what you want to be, but that is true only of Independent candidates. The two major parties exist to make sure nobody rocks the boat. Recall that, in this book, World Government sets the stage but makes it *appear* that things are directed by lower ranks. When lower ranks fight with each other it is mainly for show – see Appendix X. (We get pulled into fights by nation, by religion, by party, even by gender.)

To get a taste of the fact that one man can run both parties, re-read the excerpt from *Philip Dru, Administrator* in Ch 8.8. I assume Edward Mandell House published these details of how Selwyn controlled candidates, so his friends could learn it.

Trust me on this: the criminals overcome democracy in every way they can – **and it's easy because we're gullible.** Many of our party leaders and their party hacks appear to be either bought and paid for, compromised or out-and-out 'programmed' to have done the actions they have done. You will not be able to change that; as a candidate you can only try to get around them:

1. No matter how down-home your local party leader appears, they are on the payroll of the Democratic or Republican National Committee. These two committees are composed of persons that support many policies repugnant to the voters of that party!

2. Your local leader is not bothered by that. After all, he or she says, defeating the opposite party is the urgent task, and criticizing our own side is too disloyal for words.

3. At the party convention there is no scope for an individual delegate to contribute ideas. (Ideas? are you kidding?) The very style of the meeting – lots of noise, huge attendance – rules out debate.

4. A fundraiser for your party is pitched as "Help! We need money to defeat that awful candidate from the other party," but it seems more and more to be used to support the 'election year' circus that keeps attention off the real issues.

I think I feel a decoding rule coming on. ✍ When you hear "Support the Democrats" or "Support the Republicans" just replace that with *"Send in some money that we can spend on anaesthetizing you."* Dunegan (Ch 6.6) reported that Dr. Day made one wistful remark. He said "People are too trusting. **They don't ask the right questions**"? So ask: Why are the two parties are in cahoots?

10.7 VOTESCAM SOFTWARE

The Collier brothers, Jim and Ken, revealed in the early 1990s that the reason the TV networks are able to announce the national vote as soon as the polls are closed is that **they knew those figures even before the polls opened!** Elections involving computers can be rigged. (Lever voting and paper ballots are more secure.)

The main surprise Jim and Ken found was that the announcement made by the media was based on a private group's, count of the vote. National Election was the group's name; in 2000 it was called Voter News Service and since 2003, National Election Pool (NEP). NEP is **a private, media-owned, firm**. It is a consortium of the three major networks, plus CNN, AP, etc. Wow.

The Colliers, in *Votescam* (1992), noted that a meeting on Nov. 26, 1985 was attended by: Katherine Graham of Washington Post, Lawrence Grossman of NBC, Roone Arledge of ABC, Robert Tisch of Loews, Willam Leonard of CBS, Hamilton Jordan of CNN, Lane Kirkland, president of AFL-CIO, the chairmen of both the Republican and Democrat national committees, Sen Wendell Ford, Rep Tony Coelho, and New Hampshire Governor John Sununu. So much for competition among the parties or among the networks!

Decades ago, when Jim Collier heard on ABC news, 15 minutes after the polls closed, that 8% of New York's vote was already in, he knew it could not have been transmitted to ABC by computer, since schools and fire stations where voting took place did not (then) have computers. Through persistent questioning he learned that the numbers were called in, to a headquarters, by field workers operating under the name of the private club: League of Women Voters. (Does the GAO decoding rule come to mind here?)

Voting. [When you vote] an electronic impulse... is triggered.... The computer program immediately erases all record of the transaction except the result, which is subject to an infinite variety of switching.... It is impossible to get back to the original event, like you can with a paper ballot and start all over again in case fraud is suspected. No human eye can watch or protect your vote once it is cast. ~ Jim Collier, "Electronic Hoodwink," constitution.org

(He is also the co-author of *Votescam*, 1992)

US elections are a sham. Period. On the 'big night' in November (the Tuesday after the first Monday), the decision as to who won is made by the cabal, not by us citizens! A big legal trick involved is the right of computer firms to their 'trade secrets' – so citizens cannot discern the programs in voting machines.

Isn't it time you got nasty with your party's 'leadership?' Collier's exposé has been in print for 18 years. **Are you American?**

Funny, do you think these votes ever got counted?

In 1975, Britain had a referendum on the question: Should we remain in what was then called the common market? The turnout was huge, closely comparable to that of a General Election, but because there was only a yes/no vote, the ballots were counted not by constituencies but in one huge tally in what was then the largest indoor arena in the country.

(A touching memory comes to the surface, I recall that for ease of moving the huge bundles of votes, those in charge of the count had requisitioned three thousand super market trolleys.)

~ Bernard Levin, *The Worth of Nations* (1996) p. 1

10.8 ELECTORAL COLLEGE

The Constitution makes five points about electing a president:

1. Electors, chosen by their states, will meet in their states on a day to be set by Congress. The number of electors per state is equal to the number of Congresspersons for that state. (Art. II, Sec 1)

2. At each state's meeting each Elector has a ballot on which she writes a name for president, and another ballot for the VP name. The group puts these signed ballots into a sealed envelope and sends them to Congress. (Read Amendments 12 and 20 in Appendix T.)

3. On a day in January (shortly after you and other congressional freshmen have been sworn in!) the retiring VP presides over a joint meeting of the two Houses for the purpose of opening the sealed envelopes and counting the ballots. If any candidate got a majority (half the total, plus one) she wins the presidency.

4. If no one has a majority, the electing of the president devolves to the House, with each state having only one vote. From the Electors' ballots, the House identifies the three top candidates, and must vote again and again until one of those gets a majority of the 50 states.

5. If no VP candidate has a majority, *that* vote is done by the Senate. Elections never devolve to Congress, because the 50 states' two parties – *which are really the same party* – make sure the boat is never rocked. In 2008 there were 538 Electors (Washington DC gets three). As January 6, 2009 approached, for the opening of the envelopes, there was no nail-biting, no tension. The Electors

meetings had taken place on December 15, 2008 and all persons in-the-know knew who won simply because they knew who 'won' on Tuesday, November 4th. To put it bluntly, all Electors act like robots. This flies in the face of how the deal was advertised:

Alexander Hamilton's *Federalist 68*, written in 1788:
[Presidents should be chosen] by men most capable of analyzing the qualities… and **acting under circumstances favorable to deliberation**….Nothing was more desired than that every practicable obstacle should be **opposed to cabal, intrigue and corruption.**   [emphasis added]

(Note: The Federalist Papers, first published in newspapers, encouraged ratification of the Constitution by informing the public at a very literate level.)

Somewhere along the line, states gave the two parties full control of the Electoral College. (This *is* constitutional because the states can do what they want.)   Under what might be called a Gentleman's Agreement between Democrats and Republicans, each Elector is to cast his ballot the way the people at the polls did in November. Indeed many states make Electors take an oath to 'do the right thing.' Given the opportunity for bribery, it is striking that in all 56 elections in our history there were only 9 instances of a so-called 'faithless Elector' changing his/her vote.

In 1953, an Elector challenged Alabama's law that said the Elector must take an oath (regarding his intention). SCOTUS ruled that the state could direct an Elector (but refrained from saying the Elector must obey). One Justice, in dissenting, waxed Hamiltonian:

Gilbert & Sullivan Tune Hummed in Supreme Court

Electors, although often personally eminent… officially became voluntary party lackeys and intellectual nonentities to whose memory we might justly paraphrase a tuneful satire: "They always voted at their Party's call And never thought of thinking for themselves at all." Party control entrenched by … **exclusion of nonconforming party members is a means which to my mind cannot be justified by any end**…. The court is sanctioning a new instrument of power in the hands of any faction that can get control of the Democratic National Convention. [emphasis added]

~ Justice Robert Jackson, dissenting, in *Ray v Blair* (1952)

As you see from the Montana nomination form below, a person running for office must affirm that he meets the qualifications. Candidate Obama refused to show his *original* birth certificate. Many citizens were horrified and there were 40 lawsuits. In NH there had already been a suit by Fred Hollander challenging John McCain's eligibility. Of that suit, law professor P. Spiro told the *NY Times* (7 11, 2008) "No court will get close to it and everyone else is on board so there's a constitutional consensus, the merits of the arguments… aside." Wow. (My guess is that Obama's certificate omits paternity. My publisher opines Mr. Berg's lawsuit may be distractive disinfo.)

"I declare myself a candidate for Congress"

[For] United States Senate, United States House of Representatives, Secretary of State, Attorney General, State Auditor, State Superintendent of Public Instruction, Clerk of the Supreme Court
To the Honorable Secretary of State of Montana, and to the Members of Said Party and to the Electors of the State of Montana:
I, the undersigned citizen of the United States of America and resident of the State of Montana, declare pursuant to Section 13-10-201, Montana Code Annotated, that I am a candidate for nomination by the _____ Party for the office of _____ in the State of Montana at the primary nominating election to be held in said state on _____, and for such purpose do affirm that **I possess the qualifications** prescribed by the Constitution and laws of the United States and the State of Montana for the office herein named, and that:
1. My full name as it is to appear on the ballot is: _____ _____

Note that *lower courts dismissed all the birther cases.* SCOTUS, which thrives on hearing newly-contested Constitutional issues, refused to accept appeals. Justice Thomas admitted with a laugh (see youtube) "We try to evade that [issue]." Talk about mocking the judicial role!

Found! The Guardian of the Rule of Law

…It is confidence in the men and women who administer the judicial system that is the true backbone of the rule of law…. Although we may never know with complete certainty the identity of the winner of this year's Presidential election, the identity of the loser is perfectly clear. It is the Nation's confidence in the judge as an impartial guardian of the rule of law.
I respectfully dissent.
[Justice John Paul Stevens, Dec. 12, 2000, in *Gore v Bush*]

Sketch of the 17 Amendments after the Bill of Rights

From 1791 to 1992 the people have ratified **27** amendments, the first 10 of which comprise the Bill of Rights. They appear at the end of this book, along with the full text of the Constitution (Aps Q, S, and T). The following list categorizes amendments 11 through 27. Note: Roman numerals in original; Arabic here for convenience:

———————

Five amendments concern **"voting rights."** The Constitution had been silent, as the states alone determine which of their citizens can vote. These amendments now provide that no one will be prevented from voting because of **race** (Am. 15), **gender** (Am. 19), **youth,** if at least eighteen years of age (Am. 26), failure to pay a **poll tax** (Am. 24), or residence in Washington, D.C. (Am. 23).

Another five have to do with elections and office-holding: Ams. 20 and 25 clarify the **succession** to the presidency and vice-presidency. Am. 12 (partly updated by Am. 20) is about **Electors.**

Am. 17 makes **senate election direct.**

Am. 22 limits the president to **two terms of office.**

Two amendments have to do with **alcohol.** Am.18 prohibited the sale of it and Am. 20 repealed that amendment almost completely.

Am.13 declares the **prohibition of slavery.**

Am. 16 (whose ratification is disputed) allows **income tax.**

Am. 11 denies the Supreme Court a role in some cases in which a **state is being sued.**

Am. 27 prevents a lame-duck Congress from giving itself a **pay-raise.**

That leaves the **"equal protection of the laws"** amendment (Am. 14) that gave someone the chance to misreport that the Court, in the *Santa Clara Co.* case, extended citizens' rights to corporations. This very important matter can be corrected today by any of three means: Congress can legislate, judges can rule, or the people can amend.

– MM

10.9 AMENDING? BEWARE A CONSTITUTIONAL CONVENTION

You may wish to skip over this section but before you go please note that a sneaky move has been going on, to get a supermajority of states to request that Congress call a Constitutional Convention. It could lead to an unraveling of the Constitution, the death of our best friend! And the needed quota, 34, has almost been reached.

The American people are the ongoing authors of the Constitution in that they can change any part of it (except one):

Article V. The Congress, whenever two thirds of both Houses shall deem it necessary, shall propose Amendments to this Constitution, or, on the Application of the Legislatures of two thirds of the several States, shall call a Convention for proposing Amendments, which, in either Case, shall be valid to all Intents and Purposes, as Part of this Constitution, when ratified by the Legislatures of three fourths of the several States, or by Conventions in three fourths thereof, as the one or the other Mode of Ratification may be proposed by the Congress; Provided that *no Amendment which may be made prior to the Year One thousand eight hundred and eight shall in any Manner affect the first and fourth Clauses in the Ninth Section of the first Article; and that* [obs] no State, without its Consent, shall be deprived of its equal Suffrage in the Senate. Note: The italicization in Article V is an indicator that the part is obsolete. See Appendix Q.

After the original Constitutional convention in Philadelphia in 1787 there was no other. Note the phrase "Congress may call" one if 2/3 of the states so wish. Recently, nearly 2/3 of the state legislatures *have* signed up for one! This is no cause for rejoicing. It is a stealth move. **People will be told that the desired amendment has to do with a balanced budget**, or apple pie, but it's a trick. All the while, media is staying mum, surely a sufficient warning in itself.

In Australia on November 6, 1999 the population voted on a referendum to make Australia a republic. The wording on their ballot had been arranged at a Constitutional Convention the previous year. It looks as though the majority of Australians, who voted against the proposal, may have been in favor of a republic but were put off by the method for appointing a president.

They were offered only the chance to say yes or no to a law that would "alter the Constitution to establish the Commonwealth of Australia as a Republic with the Queen and Governor General being replaced by a president appointed by a two-thirds majority of the members of the Commonwealth Parliament." (They said no.)

226

Alert! President Obama has just signed EO 13528 establishing a Council of Governors whom he will select from the ten federal regions. To understand that, you are urged to read the following:

Mother England Is Dying. Would Somebody Please Help…
England's 48 counties are being replaced with 9 European Regions. England's 20,000 town, district and county Councilors will also be abolished. There is no democratic process here; it is being done illegally, but central government does not expect councilors to stand up for their rights, or ours. The South Eastern Region includes Hampshire to Kent; its Regional Capital is Calais [in **France!**]. The 9 Regional Capitals report directly to the 25 unelected EU Commissioners in Brussels, not to Westminster – which will very effectively **eliminate the nation of England.**

[This was] in Article 198 of the Maastricht treaty, which re-stated much of the 1957 Treaty of Rome. Its 130 unreadable pages cross refer to other treaties and documents by Article number. …it conceals its true intent and should never have been signed. It sets up the Committees of the regions, which means 444 extra UK representatives to pay for in Europe, plus their staff, travel and expenses.

John Prescott announced the plans to abolish the counties in Parliament to the horror of his backbenchers, **who wanted it kept quiet.** If you read them (our MP's didn't), the six EU treaties the Queen has signed over the last 33 years define and build an unelected dictatorship that replaces our nation. EU laws the Queen has signed give it **the powers of a police state.** For 33 years we have been denied the fundamental right to vote against the EU to keep our own nation. Please go see your councilors with this document. Tell whoever you can.　　　　[emphasis added]
~ This article by David Noakes is on Facebook, and he can be seen on youtube or contacted at eutruth.org.uk

---

The 27 Amendments in existence today, including the 10 that the Bill of Rights treats as one slate, were proposed by Congress and sent to states for ratification. The state legislates ways for this to happen, such as by referendum on voting day. There is no federal procedure for a citizen to make a ballot initiative of this kind on her own, but check your state's rules for the balloting of 'propositions.' In these peculiar times, any move a citizen can make is worth a try.

10.10 WHAT TO DO? START OMBUDIZING!

In the US it is perfectly legal for you to mimic a government function as long as you make it very clear to the public that you are not operating with authority. In Westminster-style governments, such as the Canadian and Australian ones, the 'loyal opposition' forms a shadow Cabinet. When the Labor Party has a majority in Parliament, it chooses, from its ranks, the Prime Minister and all Cabinet members, such as the Minister for Immigration. The Liberal Party then picks one of its MP's to be 'the Shadow Immigration Minister.' She will routinely publish a statement about her preferred policy of immigration. I assure you all Americans can do the same.

You are even perfectly free to call yourself the Shadow Secretary of Defense. Since few people will understand that, it might be better to call yourself an 'Ombudsperson for Defense.' That word, from Sweden, has been in vogue in the US since 1970. Usually an official position, it is the person to whom folks can take a complaint. In Japan, neighborhood Justices of the Peace officially listen to problems concerning human rights.

Should you plan to run for Congress, or some other office, and are worried about having no experience, you could get some right now by 'ombudizing.' Just hang out your shingle, claiming to be someone who will listen to problems that the government should be, but is not, working on. Even while you are campaigning you can designate part of your campaign office (front lawn, garage, etc) to ombuds-type work. It's hard to imagine your neighbors objecting.

Why not summarize your constituent's problem on a page and send it off to the proper official? Then, with permission, photocopy it for your publicity. Also you can help him research law on the Net.

Making your basement available as a holding pen — should any of your constituents wish to make a citizen's arrest of a felon — is another idea that will quickly let everyone know you are a leader. Of course you should preface that activity by inviting local police, district attorneys, sheriffs, etc., to come out and inspect the basement. Ask them what kind of trouble they think you could encounter. Gosh, talk about sending a message!

(On being reminded that it is impossible to refute Bishop Berkeley's proof of the non-existence of matter) Johnson, striking his foot with mighty force against a large stone, till he rebounded from it, answered, "I refute it *thus*."   ~ James Boswell, *The Life of Johnson*

List 10a.   Fifty States – Their Population and Flowers

(with Guide to Date of Next US Senate Election):

Pop	State	Flower	Pop	State	Flower
4.6	AL❁	Camellia	2.9	MS◇	Magnolia
0.7	AK❁	Forget Me Not	5.8	MO*	Hawthorn
6	AZ*	Saguaro Cactus Blossom	0.9	MT◇	Bitterroot
			1.8	NE◇	Goldenrod
2.8	AR❁	Apple Blossom	2.4	NV*	Sagebrush
36	CA*	California Poppy	1.3	NH❁	Purple Lilac
4.7	CO❁	Rocky Mountain Columbine	8.7	NJ◇	Violet
			1.9	NM◇	Yucca Flower
3.5	CT*	Mountain Laurel	19	NY*	Rose
0.8	DE◇	Peach Blossom	8.7	NC◇	American Dogwood
18	FL*	Orange Blossom	0.6	ND*	Wild Prairie Rose
9.1	GA❁	Cherokee Rose	12	OH*	Scarlet Carnation
1.3	HI*	Pua Aloalo (Hibiscus)	3.5	OK❁	Mistletoe
			3.6	OR❁	Oregon Grape
1.4	ID*	Syringa - Mock Orange	12	PA*	Mountain Laurel
			1.1	RI◇	Violet
13	IL❁	Purple Violet	4.3	SC❁	Yellow Jessamine
6.3	IN❁	Peony	0.8	SD❁	Pasque flower
3	IA❁	Wild Prairie Rose	6	TN◇	Iris
2.7	KS❁	Sunflower	23	TX◇	Bluebonnet
4.1	KY❁	Goldenrod	2.5	UT*	Sego Lily
4.5	LA❁	Magnolia	0.6	VT*	Red Clover
1.3	ME◇	White Pine Cone and Tassel	7.6	VA◇	American Dogwood
5.6	MD*	Black-Eyed Susan	6.3	WA*	Coast Rhodo-dendron
6.4	MA◇	Trailing-Arbutus			
10	MI◇	Apple Blossom	1.8	WV◇	Rhododendron
5.1	MN◇	Pink and White Lady Slippers	5.5	WI*	Wood Violet
			0.5	WY◇	Indian Paintbrush

* This state has no US Senate election in 2016, 2022, etc
◇ This state has no US Senate election in 2012, 2018, etc
❁ This state has no US Senate election in 2014, 2020, etc

SOURCE: census.gov   State flowers and birds are at netstate.com

List 10b.　　A Plate of Piquant Amendments

There is nothing to prevent any of the six amendments proffered here from becoming part of the Constitution should the people so desire (that desire being expressed in the form of ratification by legislatures of 38 states.)

<u>One</u>　"The United States shall not be a member of any international organization if that membership could have the effect of limiting Congress's legislative freedom."

<u>Two</u>　"Living material, such as seeds and DNA, shall not be patented and patents already issued for such are now void."

<u>Three</u>　"Threatening or attempting to blackmail a member of Congress shall be a crime for which the penalty is death."

<u>Four</u>　"Congress shall legislate the termination of the banking system created by The Federal Reserve Act of 1913."

<u>Five</u>　"The word 'persons' in Amendment XIV refers only to human beings, not to corporations."

<u>Six</u>　"The oath or affirmation in Article VI must be renewed every two years, in July, and shall not be taken by any person who belongs a secret society."

Note: Each amendment above, except Five, and perhaps One, would also need to contain the following sentence: "Congress shall have the power to enforce this article by appropriate legislation." (See, in Appendix T of this book, how that is done, and why.)

As a thought experiment, estimate the likelihood of 38 states ratifying the following changes that the US government has simply made unconstitutionally: the declaration of a war by the president rather than by Congress (war on terror); eviction of home-owners if higher-tax use can be made of their land (Supreme Court ruling in Kelo v New London); and the banning of ownership of various types of guns.

List 10c.   Write Your Own List of Suspects!

Anyone who:

1. Acted as, or hired, *agents provocateurs* to stir up riots

   _____

2. Assaulted any unwitting person by controlling her mind

   _____

3. Stole weapons from the Pentagon or embezzled funds

   _____

4. Sent a soldier on an unprotected mission as punishment

   _____

5. Fiddled with voting machines of the public or of Congress

   _____

6. Dispersed noxious chemicals or germs into sky over US

   _____

7. Threatened a legislator or a judge

   _____

8. Warned soldiers or whistleblowers not to file a report

   _____

9. Caused property damage by steering hurricanes or fires

   _____

Or anyone who: covered up the above, obstructed judicial or Congressional inquiries, destroyed evidence, or made false statements about the above

Note: They can indeed be sent to jail, and are probably quite apprehensive about their forthcoming apprehension. They may be pleased to know that leniency is often granted to those who step forward, and who show remorse.

Chapter 11   Codes of Ethics
of Journalism as a Principled Profession

In 1926, Sigma Delta Chi, a fraternity of journalists, adopted the canons of journalism drawn up by The American Society of Newspaper Editors, saying: "The primary function of newspapers is to communicate to the human race what its members do, feel, and think. [We have] obligations as teacher and interpreter...A journalist who uses his power for any selfish or otherwise unworthy purpose is faithless to a high trust."

Items from 1994 Australian Journalists Association Code of Ethics:
- ❧ To report and interpret news with a scrupulous honesty.
- ❧ Not to suppress essential facts nor distort the truth by omission or wrong or improper emphasis.

Items from the 2006 Gannett News Service Code of Ethics:
- ❧ We will not lie...[or] alter photographs to mislead readers.
- ❧ We will always try to do the right thing. [We say]: Don't be stampeded by deadlines, competition, peer pressure....
- ❧ [We] expect reporters and editors to understand the motivations of a source and take those into account in evaluating the fairness and truthfulness of the information provided.

Items from the 1994 Associated Press Managing Editors:
- ❧ The good newspaper is fair...Truth is its guiding principle.
- ❧ [It] has a special responsibility as a surrogate of its readers to be a vigilant watchdog of their legitimate public interests.

Items from the *New York Times* Ethics Code:
- ❧ Relations with sources require the utmost in sound judgment and self-discipline to prevent the appearance of partiality.
- ❧ The relationship between the Times and advertisers rests on the understanding that [each has] distinct obligations...and neither group will try to influence the other.
- ❧ Staff members may not break into... homes, or offices.

11 Society

The modern setting of man is an artefact. It is made; it was not given. It is invented, built, and contrived.... It is a product of human projects, even if the projects are made from the givens. Societies consist on the interplay of givens and projects.
— Max Stackhouse, *The Urban Ethos,* 1972

I decided that the right thing to do was to go ahead and pull the building. I ordered the firefighters pulled back from WTC7 and then we pulled it.
— Larry Silverstein, speaking on PBS-TV, re 9/11

11.1 *HOMO SAPIENS'* VALUES

This chapter is largely about the civil society that makes our republic possible. While 'the State' has to do with allotting power and legal authority, the 'society' is much more; it is the people, their livelihoods and relationships, and the traditions that get reproduced over the generations. A *society* also includes, in some intangible way, the pleasures, pains, worries, and dreams of its people.

Because we Americans are civilized, reasonable, and resource-rich, it should be easy for us to use cultural means, when proper government is on holiday, to solve the problems raised in this book. This chapter looks for ways we can use cultural power, rather than strictly legal or political power, to get our nation back on track.

Values guide us. Values are, first of all, biological. For members of a microscopic, mud-dwelling species there are only two values: moisture and warmth. Needless to say, the creature does not require a dedicated apparatus in its 'brain' (it does not even have a brain) to deal with those 'values.' It has inherited an instinct that makes it move away from dry spots into wet spots, and move toward heat.

Homo sapiens, a species that needs dry land, does the opposite: we move away from wet spots. We value warmth, but draw the line at body temperature. Thus, if the ambient temperature approaches that limit (37° Centigrade, 98.6 Fahrenheit) we start to value coolness instead, and look for tree shade. We value many other things too: food, mobility, excitation of the senses, friendship, sex, you name it.

Social values are ones that the group has decided to celebrate and to instill in its members. This often requires holding at bay some behaviors that would likely occur in the absence of such encouragement. Societies, for example, teach children to refrain from lying and stealing. In the green era we teach everyone to recycle.

Traditional values, ones that have existed over a long period of time, usually make good sense. Yet they can differ: one society may value equal opportunity, also known as meritocracy — "Let every individual develop to his best potential." For another society, maintaining the status quo may be what matters most: "Let a young man join only the occupation of his father."

For this book, the concern with values has to do with two current needs — to recognize 'wrong' values so as to be able to weed them out, and to acknowledge that values are important. What has surreptitiously been happening in the schools is that children are being told that values don't matter —or are 'retro.' Since the 1990s, a frequently heard remark in the US (no joke) is:

Grandma, you're out of touch. You don't know *anything!* You're *old.*

To start, we can acknowledge that the species of animal to which we belong has not gotten over its need for the rest of the biosphere. We all breathe air, drink water (half gallon a day — cannot survive more than a few days without it), need protein to work and to grow and even just for the body's ability to repair itself.

There are way too many of us (That's not an insult to anyone) and so there is a coming crunch in the food supply. The time-honored value of working for an honest living is itself skewed by the fact that when there is an army of laborers wanting jobs, employers do not want to give an honest day's pay. We slip into slavery quietly.

Idiotically, we have over-fished the oceans, dumped toxic waste into landfills, paid no attention while virgin forests were cleared, and let the irreplaceable topsoil erode. We are now mixing up species by genetic engineering (ahem, aren't we OK with the species we have?).

In a little-mentioned passage from her posthumously published 1950s essay, "Synergy", the anthropologist Ruth Benedict said that the happiest tribes she studied were ones where doing your selfish thing was geared to helping society. Isn't it stunning that universities don't give courses on, or award prizes for, the creation of 'doable' plans for correlating those two values?

234

11.2 GUIDE TO THIS CHAPTER – *SOCIETY*

Section 11.3 sketches ethical codes of the medical and legal professions. 11.4 discusses media and truth. 11.5 urges a revitalization of the 'citizen swagger.' 11.6 says the mega corporation must go. Section 11.7 calls for art and music. 11.8 is on New Age religions. 11.9 is a reminder that the states contribute variety. 11.10 What To Do? recommends diminution. The appendices to read are F, I, M, U, V, and, if you haven't already braved it, R.

11.3 THE PROFESSIONS' ETHICS

Jane Jacobs is a woman who came from nowhere in the Sixties to make a huge mark on architecture and city planning – simply by pointing out people's need to keep their habitat at human level. She recently wrote that our habits are picked up in childhood mainly by imitation, only rarely by actual instruction. Therefore, she says, we need to work keenly at salvaging the good parts of our culture today.

Dark ages are horrible ordeals….The mass amnesia of survivors becomes permanent. I single out five pillars of our culture that we depend on to stand firm, …they are in process of becoming irrelevant, and so are dangerously close to the brink of lost memory:

[1] Community and family
[2] Higher education
[3] The effective practice of science
[4] Taxes and governmental powers directly in touch with needs and possibilities
[5] **Self-policing by the learned professions**

The five pillars are insidiously decaying. If we pull through we will all deserve posterity's gratitude.

[emphasis added]   ~ Jane Jacobs, *Dark Age Ahead* (2005) p. 24

It is not, repeat *not*, necessary for doctors to give up the pride in their profession that they had as recently as a decade ago. Currently, individual doctors are pressured to sign contracts with health insurance companies, radiology labs, drug firms. **They can say No.**

Doctors could close ranks, and easily appeal to their patients for support in this matter. Consider Dr. Day's insider forecast in 1969, that physicians would become servants without much autonomy. Who actually oversees the medical industry in the US anyway? Largely the Rockefellers designed it, via 'foundations.' Is there any reason at all why this family of oilmen and bankers should dictate the kind of doctor-patient relationship millions of us have?

Ethical doctors could easily put a stop to the medical crimes that are becoming commonplace. The use of diseases for genocide must have been abetted by American doctors. Even if our DoJ is AWOL, our Congress hypnotized, and our judges busy making puerile hand signals, it is still possible for physicians to get their good-for-nothing colleagues struck off the register. Come on, Docs, do it!

Presumably, professions publish their codes of ethics for three reasons. First, they want to assure the public that they recognize certain 'moral hazards.' Hence, the Accountants' Ethics Code assures the clients that yielding their secret bank account numbers to the CPA will not result in the CPA moving to the Bahamas to withdraw all their deposits. For lawyers, a major moral hazard consists of the fact that their interest may conflict with those of the client. In divorce cases, there have been shocking instances of the lawyers on both sides making a deal to stretch out the proceedings, for profit. The ethical code forbids that.

A second reason for codes is solidarity. The codes make dobbing acceptable. (Dobbing: a useful Australian word for tattling-plus-whistleblowing). Each member promises to report breaches. The benefit that accrues to the dobber is that the prestige of her profession is thereby kept intact. Also, the stating of high-minded goals, in the code of ethics, helps to inspire the incoming generation of members to want to be loyal to the profession.

A third reason is that professionals want to police themselves. They prefer answering to peers for breaches of ethics rather than be treated as criminals. The injured party brings her complaint to the licensing board. The offender will be called in to give his side of the story. Such boards often revoke, or temporarily suspend, licenses to practice. Just look up your state board on the Internet; they publish the reprimands with names — disgrace is the punishment. Any citizen can report. A small effort by you may have a very big effect.

Ethics for Lawyers — Houston Bar Association, 1989
I will conduct myself in Court in a professional manner and
demonstrate my respect for the Court and the law.
I will treat opposing counsel, opposing parties, the Court, and
members of the Court staff with courtesy and civility.
I will advise my client of the behavior expected of him or her.
I will be punctual so that preliminary matters may be disposed of in
order to start the trial, hearing, or conference on time...

As for lawyers' licenses, citizens can jump onto the fact that none of our still-living Attorneys General have been disciplined for obstruction of justice. Ashcroft, Gonzalez, Mukasey, Reno, Meese, Wm Barr. Now there's a fertile field! Did you know that President Clinton's license to practice law was suspended for his obstruction of justice in the Paula Jones's case? Strictly a 'political' move, but it shows it can be done. Judges, too, have revocable law licenses....

And wouldn't it be good if academics would start using their well-rested vocal chords to inveigh against the mess that has been made of science? Everyone on campus knows that university research contracts come with stipulations about 'trade secrets' that may prevent revelation of important findings. This is a radical change: older scientists were trained to publicize all their work.

One would not even have to think up new principles – they are already there on the books needing only to be articulated once again. Each academic department could write to the Board of Trustees of its university to outline what their profession is up against. Alumni and students can provide precious solidarity with faculty on this.

11.4 MEDIA AND TRUTH

> This is a critically important issue. National governments have given up huge chunks of sovereignty under NAFTA and GATT and propose to give up even more. While governments and press try desperately to keep the consequences under a veil of secrecy, debate about the balance of benefit, who wins and who loses, is taboo. The Canadian press is so heavily loaded on the neoconservative side that it is almost impossible for dissenting voices to be heard. Neither of the two nationally distributed financial papers, the *Globe and Mail* and the *Financial Post* will print articles critical of the banking system or globalized financial services.
> ~ Paul Hellyer, *Stop Think* (1999) p. 135

Honesty did not precede dishonesty. We were, first, naturally deceptive animals. It is quite an achievement, like a great work of art or architecture, that humans figured out how to make truth-telling a social requirement. So why give centuries of truth-pursuit the flick just because Disney or Fox or *The Chicago Tribune* says so?

Prof Phillips at Sonoma State University suggests we use the word "*media*" in the singular, to reflect the "monolithic top-down power structure of self-interested news giants." Their boards have many interlocks of which a small sample is shown here:

New York Times: Carlyle Group, Eli Lilly, Ford, Johnson & Johnson, Hallmark, Lehman Brothers, Staples, Pepsi [etc.]
Wash. Post: Lockheed Martin, Coca-Cola, J.P. Morgan, Moody's…
News Corp (Fox): British Airways, Rothschild Investments…
GE (NBC): Avon, Bechtel, Chevron/Texaco, Dell, GM, Home Depot, Kellogg, J.P. Morgan, Microsoft, Motorola…
Disney (ABC): Boeing, Northwest Airlines, Estee Lauder, FedEx, Gillette, Halliburton, Kmart, McKesson, Yahoo…
Viacom (CBS): Amex, Consolidated Edison, Oracle…
Gannett: AP, Goldman Sachs, Prudential, Target, Pepsi…
AOL-Time Warner (CNN): Citigroup, Colgate-Palmolive, Hilton

~Peter Phillips, *Big Media Interlocks with Corporate America*
CommonDreams.org June 24, 2005

Wayne Madsen reports that when he and a Congresswoman tried to take out a paid ad in newspapers they were refused!

Think of how many changes in our society came about because the media/Tavistock/US government/weapons manufacturers, etc. exploited 9/11. Is there some reason why we are not punishing the media with a boycott? On the following page is a report that readers may enjoy showing to anyone who says the non-official view of 9/11 is a conspiracy theory. Just ask them if they think the quotes from these scientists could pass the giggle test.

One can see that Tavistockians are addicted to obfuscation and hoaxing. Quite without reference to money or power, it is a high for any human to be so successful at deceiving others. The human instincts for deception and self-deception are superb. However, hoaxing gets in the way of a lot of other important human activities, such as running a republic. So it's time to chop down the tall poppies. Canadian media mogul Conrad Black is in prison for obstruction of justice. Only for destroying documents – but it's a start.

When you get to Congress you can change the law so that the publishing of deliberate hoaxes is punishable by full asset forfeiture. (How about 'corruption of blood,' so one's descendants suffer too!)

As far as mergers are concerned and the top few in media keep on getting fewer – we don't even require new law, just enforcement of the Sherman Antitrust Act. And did you know you can file a "Petition to deny" a TV or radio station's renewal of licence? Write to **fcc.gov** protesting the coverage of 9/11. America is great!

Watch These Afghan Men Gas the Puppies: Check the Sandals!

On the Jim Lehrer News Hour in 2002 I saw a video of what CNN claimed its reporters had 'found' in Afghanistan, purportedly demonstrating Al Qaeda's capacity for chemical warfare. Experiments on puppies were shown, with the narrator using the word 'sandals' to make us perceive that the men are Middle Eastern, even though they are *not shown* in the video.

> "Possibly the scariest and saddest tape…is the one that shows the killing of three dogs. Coalition Intelligence sources who have examined this tape said it appears to be an Al Qaeda experiment with lethal chemicals… They said no intelligence agency is believed to have seen such poison-gas experiments before this tape. The disturbing tape begins with men, some wearing Afghan-style sandals, rushing from a room, shouting to each other to hurry….the men's identity is never revealed."

Naturally, the dog reacted to the gas and perhaps died. Then we heard from four scientists, "The first impression I had is that it is a test…of a very powerful and quick-acting chemical that behaves like a nerve agent…such as Sarin," said **John Gilbert**, a chemical weapons specialist for Science Applications International. **David Kay**, formerly a United Nations weapons inspector in Iraq, said that for him the tapes raised the specter of weapons of mass destruction. "First of all" Kay said, "the emotional response to seeing it is there." CNN also consulted **Jonathan Tucker** from the Monterey Institute:

> He too said he was shocked… "We saw visible fumes…that you wouldn't see from a nerve agent, but it is consistent with production of crude hydrogen cyanide gas," adding that…terrorists would be attracted to it because it is low-tech and safe to use." **Frederick Sidel**, from the US Army's Research Institute of Chemical Defense, said evaluation of the chemical is very difficult… [Sidel also] said "The implication is that Al Qaeda, or another terrorist group could [use it] in an enclosed area, such as a theatre or train."

Your author swallows her pride to say she had no trouble falling for the ruse! This was in the days before she heard of disinformation, and before she had seen on YouTube a video called *Fatty Bin Laden* that shows how ridiculously easy it is to fool an audience. If you watch the Fatty film today you will say "I never fell for that." But almost certainly you did.

– MM

11.5 Doin' the Citizen Swagger

Now to mention a part of our Great Republic that members of today's older generation always took to be the main gig. We believed that we were special because our country was special – and that our country was special because we were special. This all had to do with the Constitution and our 'guaranteed rights.'

For liberals, perhaps our First Amendment right to insult the leaders was the happiest one. For conservatives, Second-Amendment gun rights were especially delightful, although ordering the government to 'stay out of my stuff' under the Fourth Amendment was fun, too. (See Appendix Y, a song).

William Nelson quotes a clergyman in Massachusetts circa 1760. When threatened by the government, he replied swaggeringly:

> Let them come into my field, I will breake theare Heads.
> When it was answered to Him that the General Cort's Committey might Command Assistance, and he would not be abel to do it… his reply was this: I do not fear it, I can have anofe to assist me in that afare; let them Come in to my field if they Dare, I will split theire braines out. ~ William E. Nelson, *Americanization of the Common Law: the Impact of Legal Change on Massachusetts Society* (1975) p.35

The Boomers had plenty of citizen swagger, too. They believed, erroneously, that their swagger brought down the Nixon presidency. What a hoot. Does everyone remember the 'Saturday Night Massacre'?

> In *U.S. v. Nixon,* St. Clair maintained that the president did not have to comply with the special prosecutor's subpoena. Jaworski responded that executive privilege could not be used to shield criminal conduct. [SCOTUS] rejected the claim that the president had the ultimate authority over all executive branch information. Furthermore, the Court reaffirmed the right of the judicial branch to resolve disputes between the political branches ~ Mark Rozell, *Executive Privilege* (1994)

It would be nice if sportsmen, and fans, would start doing the citizen swagger in a manner germane to their sport! Perhaps it will incite them if, once again, they peek at the arrogant predictions of Dr. Day. He said, 40 years ago: "Sports in the US was to be changed, in part as a way of de-emphasizing nationalism. Baseball would be de-emphasized and possibly eliminated because it might be too American."

240

Take Me Out To the Non-Doll Game

As he discussed eliminating [baseball], one's first reaction would be – well, they pay the players poorly ... so they give up **baseball** and go into some other sport or some other activity. But he said that's really not how it works. Actually, the way to break down baseball would be to make the salaries go very high. The idea behind this was that as the salaries got ridiculously high there would be a certain amount of discontent and antagonism as people resented the athletes being paid so much.*****

There was some comment along the same lines about **football**, although I seem to recall he said football would be harder to dismantle because it was so widely played in colleges. Also about the violence in football, it met a psychological need. So football, for that reason, might be left around to meet that vicarious need.*****

The same thing is true of **hockey**. Hockey had more of an international flavor and would be emphasized. There was some foreseeable international competition. **Soccer** was to be the keystone of athletics because it is already a worldwide sport in SouthAmerica, Europe, and parts of Asia. All this would foster competition so that we'd all become citizens of the world to a greater extent than citizens of our own narrow nations. *****

There was some discussion about **hunting**. It requires guns and gun control is a big element in these plans. I don't remember the details much, but the idea is that gun ownership is a privilege. Hunting was an inadequate excuse for owning guns and everybody should be restricted in gun ownership. The few privileged people who should be allowed to hunt could maybe rent or borrow a gun from official quarters rather than own their own. After all, everybody doesn't have a need for a gun, is the way it was put. *****

Very important in sports was sports for **girls**. Athletics would be pushed for girls. This was intended to replace dolls. Baby dolls would still be around, a few of them, but **dolls would not be pushed** because girls should not be thinking about babies and reproduction. Girls should be out on the athletic field just as the boys are. Girls and boys really don't need to be all that different. Just one other thing I recall was that the sports pages would be full of the scores of girls teams just right along there with the boys' teams. And that's recently begun to appear after 20 years in our local papers. So all of this is to change the **role model of what young girls should look to be.*****

~ Dr Dunegan's 1989 Reminiscences of Richard Day's 1969 Speech, posted on Internet by Ms Randy Engel, Director, US Coalition for Life

11.6 THE CORPORATION MONSTER

To form a corporation, a body of people working for some end, is an innocent thing of itself. There are good corporations and bad. But there is also the simple mathematical fact that a corporation can gain enough power to **ruin society's preferred scheme of power distribution.** Today many corporations have all but married one another, creating a force that can dominate just about everything.

The idea that a huge accumulation of power **is evil** was a basic premise for the Framers. They lived in the 1780s and did not foresee the railroads of the next century, but they were aware of potential trouble. Jefferson (who was not a Framer: he was away in France at the time) saw how a 'money power' would take over.

To become 'incorporated,' several individuals form a company and ask one of the states to grant them charter. The charter makes their corporation a 'legal person' that then has the right to do things a person can do, such as own property and borrow money.

Originally, when asking for a charter, the applicants had to show that they were conducting an enterprise of value to society. In exchange for their beneficial efforts, they were given the privilege of limited liability, meaning that if the corporation failed financially, each person could lose, at most, only the amount he had put into it.

Over time, and no doubt with behind-the-scenes persuasion of state legislators by you-know-whom, the rules were softened. Then, thanks to the famous 1886 headnote in the *Santa Clara* case, the corporation-as-person got a ridiculous new interpretation: that corporations could be the beneficiaries of the Bill of Rights.

(In a lawsuit against shoemaker Nike, a plaintiff, Kasky, claimed that Nike published false information about its treatment of employees. He said it should be called 'commercial speech' and not enjoy First-Amendment protection. In other words, Kasky wanted Nike's misrepresentation of facts to be 'actionable.' He subsequently settled with Nike out of court, however, so no ruling was reached.)

A corporation is *not* a human being and does not have the balancing mechanism of the typical human brain, much less does it have sentiment or a conscience. Granted, a corporation may set out to emulate one of those traits and make a real success of it. But the moral hazard lies in the ability of artificial bodies to become Frankensteins, defying their creators.

Also, large corporations have a certain momentum; the momentum can be so awe-inspiring that people think it *must* be followed. Consider the corporations whose purpose is to protect the abstraction known as business (List 11c). There is even an entity called International Chamber of Commerce – rather illogical. These may have came about to suit the purpose of the cabal, but humans generally have a penchant for hypertrophy (overdoing things).

The trick is to remember two things: One: American corporations exist at the mercy of legislatures. Corporations could be outlawed tomorrow. Two: giant business wrecks all non-giant business. (See on Net: David Cushman Coyle, "Who Owns America?" 1928.)

ROCKEFELLER GETS THE CHAIR

Before leaving Beijing I had the chance to meet and talk with Premier Zhao Ziyang, and I liked him immensely.... He was comfortable talking about economic matters and candid about the difficulties that China faced in making its transition to a more market-oriented economy. In talking with him I felt a sense of compatibility I had never experienced with other Chinese leaders. He had Zhou Enlai's urbanity and cosmopolitan interest in the rest of the world. Rong Yiren gave a splendid banquet for Peggy and me... They lived in a beautiful old house ...

and Rong told us about his family's long and interesting history. Later, after we returned to New York, Rong sent me an unusual reclining wooden chair that I had admired in his house. These two gestures of friendship were unique to my experience in China and ones I would have expected from a senior official in the old Imperial China, but not from the representative of a Communist government.

~ David Rockefeller, *Memoirs* (2002)

11.7 ARTISTS AND MUSICIANS, COME IN, PLEASE

By viewing nature, Nature's handmaid, art,
　　Makes mighty things from small beginnings grow.
　　　~ John Dryden, *Annus Mirabilis*

Art matters in every society even though only a small percentage of people have the talent and the drive to express themselves in ways that are universally recognized as artistic. For modern society this includes painting, sculpting, drama, filmmaking, poetry, fiction-writing, and the music of singing, dancing, and instrument-playing.

It is really embarrassing to discover how much of these areas of 'spontaneous, creative' expression have been influenced by World Government. Ch 6.8 claimed that rock music was tasked for social engineering, by Tavistock. Same for 'Hollywood.' Just think how many of our views of 'human nature' are coached by movie writers!

Frances Stonor Saunders, author of *The Cultural Cold War: The CIA and the World of Arts and Letters,* quotes from Mephistopheles in Goethe's *Faust*: "You think you are doing the pushing, But it is you who is being pushed!" She shows that many Anglo writers were involved with the CIA's interest in running a Cold War. Prominence in literary reviews was given to these 'sophisticates.' (Amusingly, one of them, Stuart Hampshire, co-edited a book entitled *The Morality of Scholarship*.) Contemplate how many persons with valuable ideas must have become 'mute Miltons' because of this closed shop.

In symphonic music, too, it seems that the cabal didn't want to just 'let things happen.' In 1952, the Masterpieces of the Twentieth Century festival in Paris was put up by the CIA's 'Congress of Cultural Freedom' (funded by the major foundations, of course).

Sometimes the CIA makes nice music...
The State Department paid for Virgil Thompson's adaptation of Gertrude Stein's *Four Saints in Three Acts*, which starred Leontyne Price. Nabokov later boasted to Arthur Schlesinger. "I started her career..." [The Festival Secretary described] "a strong feeling that the entire cast of *Four Saints* should be American Negro, to counter the 'suppressed race' propaganda and forestall all criticisms to the effect that we had to use foreign negroes because we wouldn't let our own out.'" ~ F.S. Saunders, *Cultural Cold War* (1999) pp. 118-9

Isn't it a relief to see how the cabal members feared the power of real art? They were wise indeed to try to control it, because when you let an artist loose there is no telling what will happen. Dear American filmmakers, songsters, poets, **we need you urgently. Please make something happen!**

It is easy to think of satire about the present situation, but satire does not enrage or stimulate action; it is a safety valve. Chances are that most comedians are 'monitored' because it's important to direct them to certain topics and away from others — as with news anchors.

Is there anything wrong with going heavy? There are two ways even an amateur film maker could 'make a difference.' One would be to present a courtroom scene, with all due solemnity, in which the wheels of justice grind properly. 'Look-alikes' for the main characters would be easy to come by, just hold a look-alike contest.

In 1973 people were glued to their TV sets when Senator Sam Ervin, conducted hearings about 'sins' in Washington. He used big words and acted like a judge. It significantly influenced the citizens' understanding of presidential accountability.

The other way, whether comical or deadpan, is to work out a happy denouement to the present crisis. During the 1990 collapse of Communism in East Europe, one of the few leaders executed was the reputedly cruel Ceausescu of Romania. It was said that he wore a wristwatch with an emergency button on it. If locals got rough with him, he could use it to call the security guards. When he finally did need help, and pressed the button, nobody came! Think: if a fictional scene of such triumph over a despot had been shown in earlier years how it would have fired imaginations in Romania!

11.8 THE VALUE OF WORK

When I lived in the Emirates, from 1988 to 1993, I was delighted to discover, in the writings of the poet Iqbal, that Islam ascribes much value to labor. To think that all we do is mount a Labor Day each year to honor workers! Apart from the family, the workplace is where people have most of their social encounters. Note how on old gravestones the deceased's occupation is his identifier: shoemaker, miner, cook. That's what *community* really is – the totality of 'jobs.'

Recently, researcher Lara Lepionka found that most workers do not realize how important they are to the whole. She interviewed a waitress who, in 37 years, had served nearly a million cups of coffee. Think of how many people's day she made! We need to appreciate everyone's contribution, even if it is on an assembly line. A day will come when the cabal no longer organizes our lives. If we develop, now, a sense that each person has a role to play, the changeover need not bring chaos. Kids should be told that work is honorable!

11.9 THE REALITY OF THE STATES WITHIN THIS NATION

Are you a Texan? A Michigander? A New Hampshirite? The US government is not our only government. Before the US formed, the 13 states each had a complete, sovereign government. In 1787, the delegates at Philadelphia signed up to a relinquishing of only part of the sovereignty of their states, when they handed Congress the 18 powers now listed in the Constitution's Article I, Section 8.

They also agreed that the US Supreme Court could be the final court of appeals for any state case. Furthermore, they agreed to the idea that the states would be prohibited from doing certain things:

Art. I, Sec 10. "No State shall enter into any Treaty, Alliance, or Confederation; grant Letters of Marque and Reprisal; coin Money; emit Bills of Credit; make any Thing but gold and silver Coin a Tender in Payment of Debts; pass any Bill of Attainder, ex post facto Law, or Law impairing the Obligation of Contracts, or grant any Title of Nobility. No State shall, without the Consent of the Congress, lay any Imposts or Duties on Imports or Exports.. [or]…keep Troops, or Ships of War in time of Peace, enter into any Agreement or Compact with another State, or with a foreign Power, or engage in War…

Any power that is not enumerated among Congress's 18 powers belongs to the states. Concerned that someday people might forget this, the states' rights people insisted in 1791 that the Bill of Rights carry this notice, in Amendment X: The powers not delegated to the United States by the Constitution, nor prohibited by it to the states, are reserved to the states respectively, or to the people. Such powers are called 'the reserved powers' or 'residual powers.' They involve education and housing – or no education and no housing, if that is what a state chooses, and the right of a state to collect income tax.

The famous system of checks and balances that the Framers installed in the Constitution includes the fact that the states, being jealous of their privileges, will prevent the feds from encroaching on them. What, technically, is the way in which a state communicates its complaints to the US government? Originally the main way was through the Senate, since each state government decided who would serve as its two US senators, but since passage of 17th Amendment, senators are directly elected by the people. (That amendment happened in 1913. You can bet 'Selwyn' had a hand in organizing it.)

States can create a fuss by any method they like. They rarely do so, and they even more rarely combine to produce a counterweight to the feds. Governors' conferences today tend to rubber-stamp the president's wishes. However, Montana has been holding out against the national ID card. Someone in the New Hampshire House put out a resistance resolution, as displayed in Appendix F. In 1798 the people of Virginia and Kentucky dug their heels in, to insist on a proper balancing of power, and got the Sedition Act repealed.

Probably the greatest power of the states 'against' the power of the federal government is the threat of secession. The document that preceded the Constitution, the Articles of Confederation of

1777, said the new union would be 'perpetual.' One may infer that the Framers' omission of the word *perpetual* was deliberate. Probably they knew states would be less afraid to ratify a Constitution from which they could later opt out. In the 35th year of our Republic one state passed an ordinance saying that a tax-related law created by Congress was unconstitutional, and this caused quite a crisis:

Ordinance of Nullification. The people of the State of South Carolina, in a convention assembled, do declare and ordain... that [those] acts of the Congress of the United States, purporting to be laws for the imposing of duties... are unauthorized by the constitution...
We will not submit to the application of force on the part of the federal government, to reduce this State to obedience, but that we will consider the passage, by Congress, of any act authorizing the employment of military or naval force against the State of South Carolina...hereby declared null and void... and that the people of this State will henceforth hold themselves absolved from all further obligation to maintain or preserve their political connection with the people of the other States; and will forthwith proceed to organize a separate government, and do all other acts...which sovereign and independent States may of right do... [dated 1832]

Please do not construe my exposition of secession to be advocacy of it! Any move in that direction today would only add to the public's insecurity. Rather, the message is that **it is essential to cultivate non-federal sources of authority,** where e'er they be.

11.10 WHAT TO DO? SMALLEN ON DOWN!

This book is in full agreement with Jefferson's discoveries:

Thomas Jefferson to Joseph C. Cabell (in a letter dated 2 Feb. 1816):

I felt the foundations of the government shaken under my feet by the New England townships. **There was not an individual... whose body was not thrown with all its momentum into action.**... As Cato, then, concluded every speech with the words, *"Carthago delenda est,"* so do I every opinion, with the injunction, "divide the counties into wards." **Begin them only for a single purpose; they will soon show for what others** they are the best instruments. God bless you, and all our rulers, and give them the wisdom, as I am sure they have **the will to fortify us against the degeneracy of our government.** [emphasis added]

The US now has a population that is a hundred times what it was at the time of founding in 1776. It would be foolish to say size does not matter. Think of the impression an individual gets as to where she stands vis-à-vis the society's decision makers. In a huge society those people are necessarily far away. She has never interacted with them personally and can hardly assume that they are influenced by her preferences. Size matters heaps, psychologically.

One thing we can do that does not require any legal change, is to put more emphasis on our states, three of which are themselves huge in population; see List 10a. Over the years, state legislatures have shamelessly relinquished some of their powers to the feds.

The Great Depression of 1933, following the Wall Street crash of 1929 (cabal-planned), resulted in FDR's New Deal of the 1930s. People in crisis naturally felt relieved by the passage of the Social Security Act, and other laws that gave Uncle Sam a role in helping citizens directly. But as we saw with education, provision of federal funding is a clever ploy to weaken the states. State legislators feel that if they reject that 'help' they will get mauled by local media.

There is no reason for us to continue on this unconstitutional path. The states should re-assert themselves and we should demand that they do so. Without doubt the great crime of 9/11, as well as the OKC bombing, can be dealt with legally **by local authorities.**

Suggestion: Smallen way down to county and neighborhood level. Here again is an example of the human brain pushing us down the wrong road. It tells us to look for the highest coordinator to solve a problem. We need to erect a sign saying "Wrong way. Go back."

It just is *not true* that 300 million Americans are going to be assisted by, say, a Cabinet member pining for their cause. (As far as I know, no Cabinet member is pining, or has ever pined.) Even if the problem to be solved is a borderless one, such as clean air, or fair wages, the sensible venue for dealing with this is closer to home.

Ch 10's suggestions that you run for office were Congress-oriented. You can do a lot more at county-council level, however. Granted there are infiltrators there too but you can throw your weight around. Why not run for school board? Or, crucially, sheriff.

The suggestion to smallen way down really means as low as you can go. See Jefferson's remark "Begin them only for a single purpose"? If you **invite two friends to your kitchen** to discuss an issue, and make a pact that you will deal with it, **action will follow.**

248

List 11a. Our Grandparents' Low-Technology Skills

How ordinary folks made the best of Earth, pre-1800:

Preying on, or Parasitizing, Animal Species:

spear, sling, ambush, mimicry, smoking-out, herding, grazing, trapping, fish hooks, fish nets, domestication of dairy animals and fowl, shooting, animal husbandry (artificial selection), preserving meat with salt and vacuum jars, clipping wings, provisioning animals with winter fodder.

Influencing Primary Production and Preparing Food:

planting, irrigating, fertilizing, grafting, selecting, rotating crops, terracing, training vines, making scarecrows, plowing, using sugar to preserve fruit, baking, boiling, frying, pickling

Protecting One's Family from the Elements:

glass, fire, thatched roofs, brick walls, stone fences, dikes, igloos, pottery for catching water, tents, fur clothes, weaving with reeds, batting and carding cotton, shearing sheep, tanning hides, burning oil, wood, and coal, tar roofs

Reducing the Work Burden with Non-human Power:

windmills, domestication of oxen and mules, the wheel, the lever, the pulley, the wedge, the mill, the turbine, the drill, the steam engine, steam pump, water wheels, tracks for carts in mines, ropes for hauling stone, work-dogs for herding sheep

Overcoming the Problem of Distance:
timber rafts, dogsleds, axel and wheel, horse and carriage, skates, skis, skin-covered boats, cloth sails, oars, rudder.

SOURCE: George Maxwell, "The Garden Lectures," 1998, based on the five-volume *Oxford History of Technology* (1956). Note: a new book by David Edgerton has an intriguing title: *The Shock of the Old.*

List 11b.   What TV and Magazines Feed Us

TYPICAL WORRISOME NEWS ITEMS OF THE LAST FIFTY YEARS

Fact or Fiction? Any of These May Have Been Scripted:

Cuban Missile Crisis — face-off between JFK and Khrushchev
Core meltdown at Three Mile Island nuclear plant (no follow-up)
Ananda Marga sect bombs the Hilton: Australia's first terrorism
Adolescent in Poland kills his grandmother for her gold teeth
Tylenol capsules sabotaged, 6 fatalities, no arrests, no suspects
Man standing nearby happens to video cops beating Rodney King
After those cops were acquitted, man dragged from truck, killed
Cargo plane [remote controlled] flies into refugees' high-rise
Aum Shinriko sect releases Sarin gas in Tokyo subway, 11 die
Anthrax powder sent to Congress, Capitol Hill closes in response
Sydneysiders boil tap water for 2 weeks in bacteria scare
David Hicks at Gitmo 7 yrs with no hint of help from Oz gov't
Video circulated of beheading of American, Nick Berg, in Iraq
7/7 bombings in London Tube and on bus in Tavistock Square
Man with chainsaw allowed to sashay thru Customs into Maine
Plane explodes over Missouri: 'for insurance money' (45 deaths)
Stuart says pregnant wife murdered in her car by black Bostonian
Baby falls into well in Midland Texas; rescue is televised all day
Cessna lands on White House lawn; pilot deemed head case

These involved well-known persons:

Jane Fonda makes sympathetic visit to enemy in Hanoi as protest
Ted Kennedy nearly drowns at Chappaquiddick, wears neck-brace
Boxer Mike Tyson sued for rape
Canadian athlete Ben Johnson's Olympic medal revoked for drugs
Hanafi Muslims hold hostages, shoot DC City Councilman Barry
Marion Barry, mayor of Wash DC, caught with drugs, in a sting
Actress who plays Lois Lane chastised for opposing Desert Storm
At *The New York Times*, Jason Blair's award rescinded for plagiarism
Michael Jackson pretends to be about to drop baby over balcony
Murdoch editor fired for accepting OJ Simpson's book *If I Did It*
Stingray stabs Steve Irwin in the heart; child inherits his TV role
Rep. Cynthia McKinney almost indicted for shoving a guard
Suspect extradited from Thailand in Jon Benet Ramsey case

List 11c.. Non-State Actors that Make Policy for Nations

These are direct quotes from their official websites:

World Trade Organization – WTO: "[We are] the only global international organization dealing with the rules of trade between nations...WTO agreements [are] signed by the bulk of the world's trading nations....
The goal is to help producers of goods and services, exporters, and importers conduct their business."

Tavistock Institute of Human Relations "formally founded as a registered charity in 1947. In our early work we [tried] to apply psychoanalytic and open systems concepts...
We are particularly known for our capacity to work with issues that are otherwise hidden and sometimes unconscious."*

Council on Foreign Relations – CFR: "Founded in 1921 CFR is dedicated to producing and disseminating ideas so that individuals and corporate members, as well as policymakers, journalists, students, and interested citizens can better under-stand the world and the foreign policy choices facing the US and other governments...."

Business Roundtable: "Business Roundtable is an association of chief executive officers of leading US corporations .... Collectively, they returned more than $98 billion in dividends to shareholders and the economy in 2004....
The Roundtable is committed to advocating public policies that ensure vigorous economic growth, a dynamic global economy, and the well-trained and productive US workforce..."

The Trilateral Commission – TC: "The Trilateral Commission was formed in 1973 by private citizens of Europe, Japan and North America to help think through the common challenges and leadership responsibilities of these democratic industrialized areas in the wider world."

* Well, there you go!

Chapter 12
Instructions To Take Over Government of Spain 1936
- from "Technical Services" [!!] of the Comintern in Paris

Reinforce shock troops in barracks; supply them with pistols. Our groups will break into barracks in uniform, pre-arranged. All commanders shall be eliminated without hesitation. 'Neutrals' will be subjected to severe tests. Vigilance groups outside will enter the barracks on pretense of putting down the rebellion. **The generals have two adjutants and a secretary who must be murdered in their own homes.** When the rebellion breaks out our militant groups wearing uniforms of the Civil Guards shall arrest all heads of all political parties on the pretext of protecting them.

Once in custody they shall be eliminated. Capitalists shall be forced **to hand over the balance of their current accounts at the** banks. In case of concealment they shall be eliminated, including their families without exception. With regard to members of the armed forces who claim to be sympathizers, use the same tactics as in Russia. **First use their services and then eliminate them as enemies.** Militia posted at crossroads must eliminate all defeated troops trying to escape. Liaison shall be by light cars and cyclists who shall be armed with revolvers. **The most intimate details of the lives and characters of all neutrals and sympathizers must be obtained.**

Our militia must be organized to work away from their own homes and locality as experience has shown us that at the last moment, through sentimentalism, men close to their homes have failed to carry out our plan with proper enthusiasm. All owners of gold depots and merchandise shall be regarded as important capitalists. **For using starvation** as a means of reducing opposition quickly, during the first week the supply of food and drink is prohibited. **Infiltrate police and fire departments**; as experience shows that these civic employees tend to remain loyal to their bourgeois bosses. [emphasis added]

Echo de Paris, April 1936,
quoted in Wm. Guy Carr, *Pawns in the Game,* 1970

12 Strategy

No man can serve two masters. – *Matthew* 6: 24

Machiavelli, as usual, has the last word. If you win, he tells us, everyone will judge the means you used to have been appropriate.
– Michael Ledeen, *The War Against the Terror Masters*

12.1 IDENTIFY THE TRAITORS AND PRE-EMPT THEM!

The narrative on the preceding page is relevant to us. It shows that when one group decides to conquer another, any legal protections are a joke. Force wins – especially if it comes as a surprise.

It always involves removal of the group's natural leaders – those to whom the community looks for direction, such as teachers and priests, and activists who have been trying to help. Please don't say "Americans would never do that." We kill activists preemptively right here, and we have famously helped other nations do the same.

Note that surprise is a good tactic, and speed is another. Whenever the biggies decide to go in, it happens in a way that will give you no chance to react smartly in self-defense. Therefore **it is crucial to act pre-emptively**. President Clinton spoke about this:

> Presidential Decision Directive [PDD-39 in The Federal Register] The White House, Washington, June 21, 1995
> Memorandum for the Vice-President [Al Gore], and Cabinet
> Subject: U.S. Policy on Counterterrorism   The... United States regards all such terrorism [the OKC bombing!] **as a criminal act** and will... pursue vigorously efforts to deter and **preempt**, apprehend and prosecute... individuals who perpetrate **or plan to perpetrate such attacks...**   Furthermore, the United States shall seek to identify groups or states that sponsor or support such terrorists and exact a heavy price.... [emphasis added]

For example, now that we have found out that our enemy can do funny things in the sky – such as cause hurricanes or seed the clouds with disease – we must try to block their access to that equipment. PDD-39 says: "deter and preempt, apprehend and prosecute." Like-

253

wise, an authorization for the use of Force, AUMF, was passed by Congress a week after 9/11, saying **force may be used** "to prevent any future acts...."

Luckily, the American Law Institute suggests, in its Model Penal Code, that when we are in great danger of being harmed we may use deadly force and then offer 'justification' as our defense in court:

[C]onduct which would otherwise constitute an offense is justifiable and not criminal when: (a) that conduct is necessary as an emergency measure to avoid an imminent public or private injury, and (b)the threatened injury is of such gravity that according to ordinary standards of intelligence and morality the desirability and urgency of avoiding the injury clearly outweigh [the alternative]. – Tentative Draft 11, sec 3, American Law Institute

That doesn't say the laws against violence have been lifted. It says sometimes you must break the law and face trial later, hoping a jury of peers will acquit, because you have presented a good defense.

But first there is the basic problem: how to say out loud that any 'prestigious' person is really a traitor. Henry Kissinger wants arresting for levying war against the US via AIDS. Hitchens (2002) says HK has received summonses from 3 nations. McCain and Lieberman, I claim, are traitors for trying to remove our basic protection of habeas corpus. (Granted that takes a broader reading of 'three-three.')

It would be a mistake to start offering excuses for the traitors in advance. Some of them, perhaps HK and GB, were victims of cruelty as children; Skolnick's Chief Judge showed what judges may be up against. Don't wory, justice can be done. The priority is to reorient our thinking so we see how they've injured us. And don't be reluctant to go for small fry. Anything that will help call attention to treason will awaken people to the danger we're in, and to our power.

12.2 GUIDE TO THIS CHAPTER – *STRATEGY*

12.3 shows you how to award a medal 'within budget.' 12.4 states the legal way to stamp out FBI 'rogues.' 12.5 says churches provide troops for the good fight. 12.6 tells what happens in a panic. 12.7 invites your rage. 12.8 introduces Truth Commissions. 12.9 says Sue the so-and-so's. 12.10, the What To Do section, entitled "Go Retro," suggests that you get verbal with friends. The most obvious thing we are doing wrong is keeping quiet. Talking will save us! Appendices for this chapter are C, I, M and Q. Q is the Constitution. Why not reduce the print size and carry it in your wallet?

Suggestion: Use the Freedom of Information Act. A healthy way to feel the old feelings of being the boss in this beautiful nation is simply to exercise a right. Why not email the feds for info? (States have FOI Acts, too.) Ask for an item that has a naughty aspect to it, so you will experience the arrogance of the Citizen-in-Charge. They must reply in 20 days. I once got an answer back in an hour. It is simple to sue an agency that refuses; the legislation provides for that:

Freedom of Information Act As Amended [5 USC 552]
...(ii) fees shall be limited to reasonable standard charges for document duplication ... (iii) **Documents shall be furnished without any charge** or at a charge **if** disclosure of the information is in the public interest because it is likely to contribute significantly to public **understanding** of the operations or activities of the government... (B) On complaint, the district court ...has jurisdiction to enjoin the agency from withholding [or] order the production of any agency records **improperly** withheld from the complainant. In such a case the court may examine the contents of such agency records *in camera* to determine whether such records or any part shall be withheld.

Try this: write to the US State Department and ask if anything was ever found to counteract the testimony by Polish Communist defector Michael Goleniewski that Henry Kissinger was a general in the KGB. Then when Foggy Bottom refuses to produce, slap down your $350 at federal district court and proceed as in iii (B) above.

12.3 EMBRACE THE POSITIVE! AWARD A MEDAL!

Do you wish to be acknowledged for your contribution to the nation? Of course, and others do, too. You can surprise them with a medal, in the form of an electronic photo of a medal that they can print out – like a certificate. For example:

The 'Rescuing America medal'
is hereby awarded by Mary Maxwell to
F. William Engdahl
for his tireless and creative efforts to make people
aware of the effect on farmers of patenting
of life-forms (seeds).

Any person you feel grateful to, for helping America, can 'qualify.' Perhaps you'd rather craft a trophy? Go for it!

255

A Pause for A Visual Review of This Book's Major Claims. This book claims that a cabal runs us. It meets in clubs such as the Bilderdergers, Trilateral Council, and Skull and Bones. For a quick 'visual' review of that claim, re-read the lists, such as 6b, Foundations; 3c, the P2 Masonic Lodge; and 3b, the stunning list of CFR members at the top of our government in the last 63 years.

A related claim of this book is that government leaders are selected by the cabal and controlled by compromise or fear. Evidence of *that* claim can be seen in List 8a, on assassinations; 2a on IMF; 9b on naughty Congress, 10c's wistful look at amendments (that should never have been needed), and 2b on how 'the Hill' makes law.

As for the way in which we make *war*, please look at lists 4c, and 5c, showing how the Iran-Contra men got promoted, 2c, on weather warfare, and 8c, for the favored use of airport terrorism.

Perhaps we also need to expand the definition of war to include the 'strategy of tension' as used by NATO's Gladio (recall the supermarket massacres in Brabant?). Their method of waging war on us also includes direct injury to minds as seen in 1c and 7c, fiddling with culture by changing school curricula as in 6a, or by sponsoring serial killers as in 7a. Note: It is admitted on the record that since 1914, militaries attempt to break an enemy nation's will or morale.

12.4 ARREST ROGUE FBI PERSONNEL!

Now here is a statement that all good, patriotic, dedicated FBI men are probably longing to hear: Arrest bad FBI men and women.

Dear Reader, if you are one of those Johnny-Come-Lately's, like myself, who start reading a book from the end backwards: *Welcome.* Let me tell you the real action was in Parts One and Three – and no, the words "Arrest the FBI" do not trip easily off my tongue. We have been slogging through the Constitution and trying to disabuse ourselves of the notion that any person with a badge or a title is our friend and salvation – or has 'immunity,' or is guaranteed protection.

At present there are dozens of federal agencies that have thousands of armed personnel, for example: FBI, DEA, and FEMA. Of course there are also local and state police, and those absolutely not-mentioned members of foreign armies stationed in 46 states (see Appendix Z) under auspices of a NATO 'partnership' program.

Weapons on the shelf today include the pain truck, white phosphorus (possibly that one eliminates the stink of putrefaction, which would surely be an issue), and miniscule UAV's – un-manned aerial vehicles that may have your coordinates on them even as we speak!

It may be unfair to pick on the FBI since the real directors of the cabal are much higher up, but we go with the targets we have. A priority could be the arrest or detaining for questioning, or detaining as a material witness, of Robert Mueller, the current head of FBI, **who was appointed five days before September 11, 2001**. Herewith an Open Letter to Eric Holder:

July 20, 2010
Dear United States Attorney General Eric Holder
Greetings and Happy New Decade!

I write to ask if you would please consider making this new decade one to rejoice about. As a US citizen I believe that America's Attorney General is just the person who could take away our dread and give us our country back.

I have recently finished writing a book entitled *Prosecution for Treason*. Its final chapter contains a section entitled "Arrest Bad FBI Men." A certain logic emerged from the earlier part of the book, namely, that the key to the unlawfulness of our government today is your department, the Department of Justice.

I am not here to complain; I want to show you what a simple *fiat* from your office could do, to make the world go right. President George Washington appointed the first Attorney General in 1789 for the purpose of giving legal counsel to the new US government. He did not limit the duties in a way that would prevent the AG from giving counsel to the nation.

I understand that the Solicitor General, under your supervision, is the lawyer for the government as such. Hence when a US vice-president, Dick Cheney, was the defendant in a civil action in 2004, our SG (Ted Olson) pleaded the VP's case before the Supreme Court, and won. The plaintiff was a public interest group, seeking to make the VP reveal what had taken place at an 'advisory' meeting on Energy Policy. To me in the audience it seemed as though we could, at least theoretically, have seen the AG act for the plaintiff.

No, I don't suggest that we start doing this; I am merely trying to sort out where the loyalties of an American Attorney General are supposed to lie. The organizational chart of the DoJ indicates that several offices exist precisely so the US can sue, or prosecute, *on behalf of* the nation. Your predecessors historically enforced the Sherman Antitrust Act and the Civil Rights Act in that way. That is, they spoke for the nation or for individual citizens.

So all it would take is a shift in weight. Your job would *not* be to protect the president from criminal charges — as Alberto Gonzales did, unabashedly, regarding wiretaps and torture. You would be our lawyer. Anyway, we pay your salary and we sure do need a lawyer!

Sir, if you will grant me an interview, I can get to DC in 72 hours or less. I want to persuade you that our Constitution is extremely strong, unbelievably strong, and that 'the criminals' do know that, and thus they *will not mess with you* if you take up the good cause. Here is an example of what you could do for us, and history would thank you: You could interrogate General Tommy Franks about his knowledge of a terrorist act. In December 2003 Franks said, in an interview with a magazine called *Cigar Aficionado,*

> A terrorist, massive, casualty-producing event [will occur] somewhere in the Western world — it may be in the US — that causes our population to question our own Constitution and to begin to militarize our country in order to avoid a repeat of another mass, casualty-producing event.

This does not sit well with me (and of course I don't agree that people will drop the Constitution. All the letting-go of it since 1995 has been against our will). Please also interrogate FBI Director Robert Mueller, since you are his direct supervisor, and multi-billionaire Warren Buffett.

Buffett must be a clairvoyant, like Franks, because he scared us all with his remark that 9/11 was 'nuttin' compared to what will happen next. It is undisputed that on 9/11 Buffett was hosting a lunch at Offutt AF Base (**didn't know civilians could do that!**), the very base to which Bush flew. Buffet admits that one of *his* planes was near 'Flight 93' when it 'crashed,' so please get an explanation.

The Internet also informs us that Rep Rush Holt, on March 2, 2007, sent this request to Justice Committee members Waxman and Conyers:

> The Department of Justice and FBI have openly asserted their belief that Congress should be kept in the dark on this vital national security issue [anthrax]. Mr. Chairman, I ask for your

258

help in determining why we have been unable to bring the perpetrators of this heinous act to justice.

While I personally believe there is less to this 'heinous act' than meets the eye, I certainly balk at the DoJ's claim to have a right to conceal reports. By the way, I find it appalling that the FBI's website refers to "Amerithrax." At one point, that website went so far as to dress up that full-screen-size word, Amerithrax, with stars, stripes and other national symbols. It was soooo Tavistock.

Also, Mr. Holder, if I may respectfully inquire, doesn't it get your goat – since you are African-American – that the FBI has had a traditional role in belittling, demoralizing, harassing, and committing out-and-out violence on 'Blacks'? What about this statement from Morton Halperin in *The Lawless State* (1976) p. 80:

[In 1963] the FBI held a conference at the beginning of December to plan its campaign to destroy King and the civil rights movement. At that all-day meeting FBI officials ...agreed to use "all available investigative techniques" to develop information for use "to discredit" King. Proposals discussed included using ministers, "disgruntled" acquaintances, "aggressive" newsmen, "colored" agents, ... and "placing a good looking female plant in King's office" to develop discrediting information and to take action that would lead to his disgrace.

What is this about a Constitutional government *smearing* people? Speaking of smearing, Prof. Anita Hill told an interviewer that after the Clarence Thomas confirmation hearings, the FBI harassed her parents. As you know, David Brock – who contributed to the smearing of Anita – expressed his remorse in *Blinded by the Right* (2002). He said the comments were baseless. Just imagine *going after her Mom and Dad!* The mind boggles. I think I'll make a FOIA request to see how much it cost taxpayers to hurt the Hills.

Mr. Attorney General, what to do about Kenneth Trentadue's torturers? I doubt if they should be blamed – they were after all simply "following orders." But who did the instructing? Brother Jesse said it was an FBI job, and the family received compensation based on that. If I go to jail for jaywalking will I be tortured? This has all gone too far, and – no joke – I know how to stop it.

First, please accept that the FBI has, on occasion, admitted to, and proffered a 'justification' for its crimes: For example:

A federal judge Thursday ordered the government to pay more than $101 million in the case of four men who spent decades in prison for a 1965 murder they didn't commit after the FBI withheld evidence of their innocence. *The FBI encouraged perjury*, helped frame the four men and withheld *for more than three decades* information that could have cleared them, U.S. District Judge Nancy Gertner said in issuing her ruling Thursday. Four men convicted on Barboza's lies were treated as "*acceptable* collateral damage" because the FBI's priority at the time was taking down the Mafia, their attorneys said. [emphasis added] – Associated Press, Boston.

I am trying to fit that into any theory of law I've ever heard. Allow me to provide one more example. This is from Rodney Stich, a former inspector in the Federal Aviation Authority, published in his book *Defrauding America*, which is available free, online:

Novinger said to me that she discovered during an FBI investigation that Vice President George Bush and two of his sons were using drugs and prostitutes in a Florida hotel while Bush was vice president. She said that when she reported her findings to her FBI supervisors they warned her not to reveal what she had discovered. Novinger had been requested to infiltrate drug trafficking operations in South America and the US. She was pressured to quit her FBI position; her husband was beaten to death; and four hours after she appeared on a July 1993 talk show describing her findings (after she was warned not to appear), her father mysteriously died.

When we read whistleblower books, like Stich's we get conditioned to the idea that the government 'has to' deal with persons like Novinger in such a fashion. After all, the government can't let her talk freely about bad government – politicians might get prosecuted. So I have been trying for a while to find the answer to this dilemma. And, by golly I have found it. I have figured out how the matter should have been handled, and I honestly believe it will surprise you.

It is simply this: The DoJ should have arrested Vice President Bush. (That would not, of course, remove him from office. Politically it would be up to Congress to decide whether to impeach or not.) Ah, but I hear you say that the AG is only a department head, and the ultimate boss was President Reagan and that he would have prevented the AG from acting. Wrong! and that's my big contribution here. Even strictly 'politically,' Reagan would *not* have been able to prevail over an AG in such an instance. Think about it and you will agree!

What I am saying, Sir, is: *Know your strength.* We will support you. As they say in the mid-West, "We've got your back."

I realize there's many a thug out there pushing presidents, Congresspersons, and judges around – *they* will order you to desist. There again, not a problem! Just refuse them and they're licked. That *really is how it works.* Human nature has not changed. The legitimate authority, who today is Eric Holder, can do wonders.

If I may be excused for mentioning this, Sir, I know you have the same background as Chertoff, Giuliani, and Deval Patrick, namely you were an attorney in the Criminal Division of the DoJ. That does not 'look good on your resumé' as my Mother used to say. In Al Martin's book *The Conspirators*, published long before you got the top job, Martin says of Eric Holder "I've got a file six inches thick on him." Attorney General, that's OK by me. We can still do business.

So just call me if you want help. And remember, we are 300 million strong (give or take a mil). We believe in law, therefore the present lawlessness is a historic deviation. It is the product of some very sick minds -- and it mainly belonged to a generation of planners who have been pushing up daisies for a long time. You are young and still can enjoy God's good earth. Trust me: our nation *does not have a problem!*

All can yet be well.

Yours respectfully,

Mary Maxwell, Ph.D. (and soon to be LL.B.)
dual citizen of US and Australia,
Marblehead, Massachusetts

12.5 BEG CO-RELIGIONISTS!

Citizens, if you've been going to church, synagogue, or mosque all these years you have potential teammates for the good fight, who already profess beliefs in integrity, responsibility, generosity, etc. Your clergypersons are *not* likely to join the team. After all, what have they ever said in the years since the Twin Towers 'fell down?'

A word to Catholics: What a national treasure you (we) are in the US. And just think – you are already in parishes! You even have a meeting room available, 'for a small donation,' in the church hall. Our religious hierarchy (ahem, did Jesus ever call for a hierarchy?) has contributed substantially to some of the evils mentioned in this book. Never you mind that; we can start from innocence, forthwith.

How about we do something to assist our ancestral religion, Judaism. American Jews are under pressure today even beyond the pressure that all Americans are under. A tour of the Internet reveals that some websites, such as Rense.com, are full of condemnation of Jews for being the force behind the Illuminati, the force behind pornography, the force behind just about everything.

Have you seen Philip Roth's novel *The Plot against America* about persecution of Jews by the US government? It seems to me that, just as every African-American has cause to worry (based on historical and contemporary persecution by the US government), so does every Jewish American have cause to think pogroms may lurk.

Here's an idea. A group from a Catholic parish can buddy-up with congregants from a synagogue nearby. 'Bob' can buddy up with 'Eli' and simply be there for him. Why is it helpful for Eli to have Catholic Bob on tap? Because a coalition of Jews expressing their innocence of evil looks like a coalition of any group expressing innocence – not very persuasive. Let Bob speak on Eli's behalf. Please eyeball this for a moment:

Jack Ruby, in prison, wrote to his brother: "You must believe what I've been telling you for the past two and a half years. If you only would have believed me all along you would have found some way to check out what I said. You would have saved Israel, but now they are doomed, because they think the U.S. are for them, but they are wrong because [LBJ] wants to see them [the Jews] slaughtered and tortured."
~ W. Bowart, *Operation Mind Control* (1978) p. 199   *Note:* Ruby begged Earl Warren to let him travel from prison to DC to testify that "a whole **new form of government** is going to **take over our country**... I wish LBJ [hadn't] relinquished certain powers to certain people."

12.6 OUT-TAVISTOCK TAVISTOCK: REHEARSE THE PANIC!

Put yourself in the cabal's place. They are planning something huge for America. They can't possibly be sure it will work, but they can at least apply the 'foolproof' technique of the past, namely, to turn off everyone's rational mental processes by causing a panic.

In *Death in Washington* (1980), Donald Freed reports on the 1973 Kissinger-enabled coup in Chile. The need to get **the soldiers** on the right side, before Pinochet came to power, called for a big psy-op. This took the form of a man's body being found quartered, i.e., mutilated – with the implication that the same could happen to the soldiers. Freed even hints that the plane-crash in the Andes, which resulted in cannibalism among the stranded survivors, was somehow connected with this psy-op. (I'd like to run a *find-the-psy-op* contest!)

Once an individual gets into a panic, no amount of soothing advice can help, **because the part of his brain that is attending to the crisis is in the primitive part**. The only advice that can be suggested here is that neighbors get together well before the 'event' and go through some sort of play-acting. Rehearse what it will feel like to hear over the TV that martial law is declared and that everyone must stand outside his house with his i.d. card.

---

800 years of this stuff. When a person has undergone a severe emotional experience – as, for example, in fear – it is common knowledge that [he/she] is then more receptive to new patterns of thought and behavior. Back in the twelfth century whenever the Mongols wished to invade a new territory, they invariably preceded their invasion with a campaign of terror. During this preliminary campaign, inhabitants were reduced to a state of fear and rendered immobile. The Mongols would then take walled city after walled city **without any organized opposition from the citizens**.   [emphasis added] ~ Paul Verdier, *Brainwashing and the Cults* (1977) p. 109

The real benefit of doing a tryout with neighbors is the chance to think "What is this all about?" In Australia, people are saying that the terrorist act at Pt. Arthur, Tasmania in 1996 was intended to trigger the government's buyback of guns owned by citizens. The massacre took place only weeks after John Howard became prime minister; his announcement of the buyback followed so swiftly that it had to have been planned. (Note to Aussies: Carl Wernerhoff, an insider, has put on the Net a report about Bryant that I think is absolutely spot on.)

12.7 RAGE, RAGE!

This chapter on Strategy is the last of Part Four "Hurry! It's Easier If You Act Now." To encourage you to act now, here are a few snippets that are meant to drive you into a rage. After all, fury is a useful motivating force.

To start with, consider the affrontery of DHS veritably announcing its plans to give us more disasters. As Professor Michel Chossudovsky says on his website globalresearch.ca, these 'scenarios' are the very ones FEMA is equipped to produce:

> Yahoo News: An upcoming Homeland Security Department report outlines…hypothetical scenarios…to spur state and local preparedness – against security risks – including nerve gas, anthrax, pneumonic plague, and truck bomb [and] infecting cattle with foot and mouth disease in several places, resulting in hundreds of millions of dollars in losses… The report also includes scenarios of natural disasters to hit cities, including the 7.2 magnitude earthquake and a Category 5 hurricane.
> ~ Lara Jakes Jordan, AP, *Security Report Outlines Terror Scenarios*

Next, why don't we hear firefighters screaming about the WTC 'explosions' on 9/11? Could it be that hush money was handed out? The following is from a book by the man who was allowed to distribute the funds to survivors of the deceased:

> *(Note: the average payment was* **$1.8 million** *per family!!)*
> The American character includes an overwhelming generosity. ….
> The 9/11 fund was America onstage for all the world to see….
> I witnessed the reaction firsthand, everyday, when meeting with undocumented worker families in Manhattan and foreign claimants in London. There response was the same. "America is giving me $2 million… What's the catch? Will I be deported? … This must be a trick!" [There] were no tricks…. The nation would take no quarter in pursuing the terrorists in Afghanistan…. [It] would also undertake an equally determined effort to … comfort the grieving.
> ~ Kenneth Feinberg, *What Is Life Worth?* (2005) pp. 190-191

How about being enraged by words that were published in 1905: The following is a distillation of Appendix X, which, in turn, is a distillation of the infamous protocols. Someone carried out all the threats raised here – except the last two – and what an attitude!

> They all die as from a normal kind of illness/ We have already wiped out every kind of rule except for our own..../ Capital must be free to establish a **monopoly of industry**/ The intensification of armaments, the increase of police forces, are all essential/ We shall erase from the memory of men all facts of previous centuries/ Who are desirous of writing against us, they will not find any person eager to print their productions...   [Remember, this is from 1905!!]
> **It is indispensable** to trouble people's relations with their governments so as **to utterly exhaust humanity** with dissension ... even by the use of torture starvation, **inoculation of disease**./
> To sum up our system of keeping the governments in Europe in check ... we shall respond **with the guns of America or China** or Japan/ Who will ever suspect then that all these peoples were stage-managed?/ We will come into our kingdom **with coups d'état prepared everywhere for one and the same day**/ With this purpose we shall **slay without mercy**. ~ 1905 (See Appendix X)

And get a load of our new defenders of law, Chertoff and Rumsfeld:

> Marty Bhamonde was the only FEMA employee in New Orleans from Aug 27 to Aug 30... For the next two days he was the only FEMA employee at the Superdome (p. 46). ...Michael Chertoff told the media that FEMA's response was slow because "our constitutional system really places the primary authority in each state with the governor" (p. 43). Donald Rumsfeld was reluctant to offer humanitarian military assistance. He used Posse Comitatus [as the excuse] for not acting. (p. 40)
> More than 80% of the first $1.5 billion in post-Katrina contracts was issued without bids (pp. 76-79). **There were numerous instances of law enforcement from other jurisdictions forcing victims trying to walk out of the city to turn back** to the [centers which lacked] food, water, medical supplies (p. 15). [emphasis added]
> ~ Walter Brasch, *Unacceptable: The Federal Response to Katrina* (2005)

Now to autism, which, if it was intentionally spread, must stand out as a great evil. Temple Grandin, author of *Animals in Translation,* says that her autism made her live in a state of **dread**, until age 34 when she got medicine. The dread was caused by her inability to connect the past with the present and thus to know what was likely to happen next. Consider this remark about the CDC, that is, the Centers for Disease Control, which is now a federal agency within the (non-constitutional) Department of Health and Human Services but which originated as a spin-off from the Rockefeller Foundation:

From "Deadly Immunity," by Robert F. Kennedy, Jr. at salon.com:
The CDC [Center for Disease Control] placed politics over science. The agency turned its database on childhood vaccines – which had been developed largely at taxpayer expense – over to a private agency, America's Health Insurance Plans, **ensuring that it could not be used for additional research.**
According to transcripts of the meeting, the committee's chief staffer, Kathleen Stratton, predicted that the IOM would conclude that the evidence was "inadequate to accept or reject a causal relation" between thimerosal and autism. **That, she added, was the result "Walt wants"**– a reference to Dr. Walter Orenstein, director of the National Immunization Program for the CDC. The IOM declared the case closed and – in a startling position for a scientific body – recommended that no further research be conducted. (July 23, 2005) [Now why would Walt want something like that?]

I mentioned in Ch 2.9 that my late dear spouse was onto the fact that autism was not a 'disease' but he would never have been able to think through – as I, post 9/11, have been able to do – the possibility that a great and gratuitous malice was involved. I also think the 1954 polio epidemic was 'that way,' but I have zero proof.

Finally here's an enraging quote you could carry in your wallet. Then, when you are accused of being a conspiracy theorist, moonbat, grassy knoller, or tin-foil hat wearer, you can whip it out and ask your interlocutor to **explain how** Udall could have thought this up:

Former cabinet member Stewart Udall, *Myths of August* (1994) p. 169:
I've known people who've acquired [security clearances] and I have a pretty good sense of what the effects of receiving the clearances are... First you will feel like a fool for having studied, written and talked about these subjects... for years without having known of the existence of all of this **inside information**... Then... you will forget there ever was a time you didn't have it, and you'll be aware only of the fact that you have it now and the others don't... **and that all other people are fools.** Over a longer period of time, it will become very hard for you to learn from anybody who doesn't have these clearances... You'll become incapable of learning from most people in the world, no matter how much experience and knowledge they may have. *[emphasis added]*

12.8 OFFER AN OUT: TRUTH COMMISSIONS!

Only presidents and governors have the power to give an *official* pardon, but every citizen can offer personal forgiveness or make a gesture of understanding. We are *all* to blame for the current condition of our nation, are we not? And most of those who have harmed us probably got roped into it rather than sought it. **They may want out.** Let's not miss any opportunity to shorten the list of 'wanteds.'

'Transitional justice' has been called on, since 1990, in various countries that were climbing out of horrible conditions. El Salvador, South Africa and South Korea have had Truth Commissions. People who participated in death squads were asked to come forward and give details. Usually there is a deal made by which the person who furnishes genuine information gets a form of amnesty.

You would not be breaking the law or usurping office by hosting a panel to conduct interviews, so long as you don't try to promise immunity from prosecution. If you advertise merely your willingness to listen to anyone's 'truth report,' that may do the trick. For now I suggest that persons with a story to tell, ring a convent doorbell and confide it to a nun. Seriously, nuns are trustworthy and sympathetic.

Whoops, I have just read that Senator Patrick Leahy, giving a lecture at Georgetown U, has proposed an official Truth and Reconciliation Commission, a TRC. No way! With the current state of our courts and DoJ, that would be a trick, like a Constitutional Convention. This is all the more reason for citizens to grab the initiative.

'Pragmatics' must be catered for. In the years that led up to the 1990 vote in South Africa, the stickiest issue was the pensions of police who would be laid off for their treatment of non-whites. Likewise today many Americans stand to suffer if the necessary move against the cabal takes place. If some extraordinary amnesty is the practical way to go, I, for one, would support it. Sure, revenge is an important human endeavor, but so is getting us out of this crisis.

If you yourself are one of the cabal's criminals, please think of what you can do to crawl out of your situation. We realize it is not easy, but it must be done. Perhaps you have been only a low-level participant, e.g., accepting grants for publishing misleading works. Will the public be angry with you for confessing? Unlikely. (See the dedication page of this book!) Will your handlers car-bomb you, or give your family horrible diseases? Maybe, but they may do that anyway. If the hold they have over you is blackmail, please consider frustrating that set-up by admitting your 'sin' openly!

12.9 PROSECUTE! COMPLAIN! SUE!

This penultimate section underscores the book's title. Ch 7 showed that our judiciary is corrupt. We need to correct that and how better to do so than by shepherding some prosecutions successfully through the courts? As Ch 1.5 acknowledged, the Department of Justice puts up an initial barrier by declining to prosecute governmental folk – so the matter never even reaches the judicial branch. (In some of the states, state attorney generals do likewise.) But we can't let it rest there. That situation is poisoning the country. The DoJ is saying, in effect, "Criminal government is hunky-dory."

A second issue was identified in Ch 7.9 as control from the top. That control is seen in such nasty things as gagging, plea bargaining, SLAPP suits, and other tricks that thwart justice. Control from the top tells us that a judge is not independent – she is 'taking directions.' Those directions may seem, to her, to come from the Supreme Court, but the Supreme Court itself takes directions! Hence, it falls to the citizen to see that rule of law gets restored. This will entail **making a stink** about every obstacle 'they' put in the way.

It will be easy to do this. All you need is confidence in the Constitution. (Also, please read your state's constitution; there are bound to be some pleasant surprises there for you.) If crime is happening, it is society's right and/or duty to stop it. You can try to prosecute a case yourself. Recall that two centuries ago prosecutions were typically brought that way. Today Kentucky allows citizens to prosecute (as do Canada's western provinces). Check your state.

At the very least, any citizen can file a complaint – sometimes this is called 'laying an information.' Ch 7.6 outlined the procedure, in Boston, for going to the police station first, and then carrying an 'incident report' to the courthouse. (See the last page of my recap.)

A possible way to get around the barriers is the RICO Act. It allows persons to bring a civil action, i.e., a suit for damages. You need to show that the 'defendants' caused you to suffer **an economic loss.** You must file before the statute of limitations runs out. On this, federal-court RICO cases will honor the pertinent state statute. For instance, Georgia has a a one-year statute of limitations.

Please know that there are risks and that you should seek legal advice. For a worst-case-scenario, look at what happened to lawyer Daniel Sheehan when he filed a RICO suit on behalf of the Christic Institute. He apparently had the goods about CIA drug-smuggling. (*Mother Jones* Feb 1988 edition says he had depositions from Ted

Shackley and other spooks). Judge James King, ordered the plaintiff to pay nearly one million dollars for bringing a 'frivolous' lawsuit.

I suspect that order was *ultra vires,* and that 'the bench' would not be so punitive today. In the 1980s people did not know the extent of CIA and Army involvement in drug-running and illegal arms deals, but we do now! The racketeering charges Sheehan outlined involved Iran-Contra players Hakim, North, Secord, and Singlaub.

I imagine you could file a civil claim for damages against former President Bush, Sr. in his personal capacity, not as president, *if you have suffered the effects of illegal drug distribution* in the US (and who hasn't?). Look up the hearings that Rep Maxine Waters conducted on this, plus the Iran-Contra hearings. Oliver North got immunity for his testimony about arms but he was never asked about drugs, so presumably **he has no immunity on that subject.**

Another trick that gets played on the public: your case can be dismissed without a hearing, if filed on matters for which you lack 'standing.' In the eyes of the Framers (based on law at that time) it must have seemed natural that any citizen could take to court a matter of government wrongdoing. The standing trick needs to be laughed out of court. We've got a lot of laughing to do in that area.

Your court activity can be based on whatever you care about. I personally think the managers of local news stations that broadcast the 'puppy' gassing (Ch 11.4) can be charged with treason. **Let them say they thought it was OK to tell US audiences that Afghanis are mixing chemicals to poison us.** As soon as you try to frame the charges, you'll see how treasonous it all is. Don't be confused by the First Amendment's protection of press freedom; just say "Amendments can't be intended to protect those who use chicanery, lies, and perjury to push a society into war – *that would be absurd!*"

Remember that you can also seek a court declaration:

> 28 USC 2201 (a): 'In a case of actual controversy within its jurisdiction … any court of the United States, upon the filing* of an appropriate pleading, may declare the rights and other legal relations of any interested party seeking such declaration.' [* the fee is $350 in 2010]

"Dear Court, What are my rights to damages for emotional distress caused by Tom Ridge's baselessly changing amber to orange alerts? He already admitted that he did so – while head of *Homeland Security!* Have I a right to compensation? Can he be prosecuted? If reporters knew it was all for fear-mongering, can I sue them too? Thanks."

We can hold mock trials of **deceased traitors.** In the US, when a person dies, he loses the right to defend himself against slander, libel, and false accusations. For that reason one should be hesitant to 'try' the dead. Yet we need to do it. Ch 7.10 spoke of ways to prosecute the crime of menticide. One of the now-deceased perpetrators was Dr. Sidney Gottlieb. Dr. Martin Orne helped suppress the stories of the mind-control survivors. Why should Americans be deprived of seeing all the evidence laid out as a court would do?

It is easier, both financially and emotionally, to talk about the crimes of the dead than those of the living. Ch 3 stated that one of the traitors in the Cold War was Henry Dixon White. We can at least study whether and how his actions **deviated from the stated policies of the day** (of the State Department, in White's case). We would want to ask: If he gave the maps of US cities to the Soviets, where was the authority for that? Why was it done?

Anton Chaitkin has done a masterful job in his book *Treason in America* (1994) in which he indicates treachery on the part of Teddy Roosevelt (US president 1901-13). Chaitkin did not call him a traitor as such. I agree with the wisdom of not attacking any of our presidents. Yet Chaitkin did bare his teeth when discussing Harriman. (Harriman had done an injury to Chaitkin's Dad.) Also, he found out much about a Swiss family that harmed our country generation after generation. Very few Americans have heard of this.

Universities could offer Ph.D.'s to scholars who produce 'antique-white papers' on the drug-trade's history (see Trocki 1999). Veterans groups could conduct some sort of trial of war profiteers, using Smedley Butler's information as their take-off point. Polish Americans can look into the 60-year US coverup of the Katyn massacre. The 2010 plane crash killing the Polish leadership (*en route* to a memorial service for Katyn!) looks awfully like 'the original.' Did we play a part? Remember, the US denied strenuously that the USSR was the perpetrator of the 1940 Katyn massacre. *Cui bono?*

Oh, I looked up "suspicious deaths" on the Internet and found "The South Korean Center for Suspicious Deaths." Gee, if they can have a center, can't we muster one, too? Would you run it for us?

It may sound like I have a mad taste for accusations. Actually I don't! All of the above is unpleasant and wants forgetting. Still, if we don't snoop around past injuries we won't find out who means to destroy us now. You say no one? *Bewdy!* But just in case, I've put a page on **getting an arrest warrant** in the Recapitulation chapter.

A Pause To Stop WWIII. My old friend 'P' grew up outside the US, and he threw down a gauntlet to me after reading my manuscript. He thinks my observations of America are *insufficiently* sociobiological. He smirks at how I was propagandized to believe nonsense about 'the weak restraining the strong' via law.

Dear Reader, whom are you going to believe – me, or him? I think you should believe him. I talk about the beauty of the law but, as P has reminded me, members of the ruling class merely break or ignore the law, and **never face punitive measures.** He claims that Americans take their ideology so seriously they can't see this. Hmm.

Well, there is only one way to fight 'genes' and that is with genes. Darwinian natural selection has provided us with selfish instincts aplenty. Altruism itself boils down to selfishness – for one's family (kin altruism) or for one's chance to get the advantage of cooperation (reciprocal altruism). What about the instinct to kill the enemy? Granted, that is provided for, through our 'gift' of xenophobia, as well as by the human ability to enjoy killing in battle.

Is there anything to counteract P's cynical *weltanschaaung?* There had better be, as World War III seems to be getting close! Are we so genetically determined that we can't get past our 'past'? Max Stackhouse notes that the modern city may be a triumph of reason – its skyscrapers and communication media were developed out of rational processes, yet "The triumph of these forms of reason does not provide the purposes and ends of action" (*Urban Ethos,* 1972: 2). Now recall from Ch 6.10 Crawford's concept of ancestralization. He says our genetic proclivities are all we've got, *if* society's thought-up arrangements are in collapse. Stackhouse says "There are no obvious cues to action. A society can become organized chaos, as portrayed in the novels of Kafka" (p. 2). That is happening in Haiti and Sudan today and will presumably happen in our country when war begins.

This is a nationalist book, my celebration of the American tribe. Just as it is about to be published, however, I have 'P' mocking me. "Americans are no better at dealing with their outrageous ruling class than other nations." Will you pick up the gauntlet with me?

So far we're not impressive. Heck, we don't even stand up to our politicians. What could swing the difference now is our discovering that we have been deceived massively, and accepting the truth that we are in extreme trouble. Parents who want their children to survive can articulate that as the 'end' that cues action. Maternal **protectiveness** seems to me to be the sociobiological element here.

12.10 WHAT TO DO? GO RETRO!

Dear Reader, thanks for getting this far. At the end, i.e., now, I do not want to disappoint you. I am worried that I *am* going to do that, as my advice for fighting our enemy does not say "Stock up on food and learn ham radio for contacting relatives." Much less does it say "Join a militia and buy some surface-to-air missiles." I do realize we may have to resort to the violent option, but that will be a mess.

My advice to Americans is this: Go retro. Gather our country back. Let's see the beautiful US governed as a republic, not from the recesses of intelligence/security agencies or boardrooms of corporations. We *are* smarter than the current rulers. They are very twisted.

To readers who are waiting for me to come to the point, I must say *I already came to the point.* This whole book is about pre-empting the coming attack by using law, and by using our sensibility, including loyalty to 'the flag.' If there is a class of Americans whose loyalty lies elsewhere, we don't have to tolerate **their treasonous behavior. When you put up with it you, too, hurt our society, our tribe.**

Please know that some of your friends will not be able to handle this and may get hostile; there is plenty of 'denial' out there and it cannot be overcome by rational persuasion, so don't even try. But if the scared ones **notice a lot of people taking an interest,** their subconscious will tell them "Yep, it's OK to think about this now."

Don't forget things covered earlier such as the four deaths surrounding the OKC affair, the murder of West Pointer Ted Wustinghus, the lady in the purple hat who heard the levees explode. There's nothing to prevent you getting on your high horse about that is there? Anything to prevent your wearing a teeshirt or at least a button that says "I'm against treason"? Be brave: ask your college to provide a lecture on terminator seeds, or on weather control. You know that those professors are aware of the facts. You are paying their salaries. I'll bet they **wish you would ask such questions**!

Do you realize that it's also OK to talk about kindness, understanding, and love? Do you know that it is not unmanly to oppose war? Men, why don't you protect your mother, wife, and daughters from having their picture taken nude at airports – as is now the case.

To make a long story short, **attaining normalcy is the goal and is also the weapon.** Of what does the gap between our current life and normalcy consist? It consists primarily of OUR SILENCE. We need TO TALK.

Take up cudgels or take up megaphones. Your choice.

List 12a.   Make Them Answer These Questions

1. Do biowar experts know the cure for AIDS, ebola, & cancer?

2. Which US Supreme Court judges belong to secret societies?

3. What did NYFD and Mayor know prior to 8 a.m. on 9-11?

4. What happened to TWA Flight 800, KAL 007, PanAm 103?

5. Was North Vietnam's Ho Chi Minh always a Western agent?

6. Did Waco occur because a sleeper cell mistakenly woke up?

7. Is Jim Colliers' allegation about the 1988 NH primary true?

8. Why did McCloy release Nazi war criminal Krupp from jail?

9. Did Admiral J Boorda attempt to arrest Pres Clinton? Why?

10. Only French troops were spared Gulf War Syndrome. Why?

11. Does science know how to tap free electromagnetic energy?

12. Which Secret Service men saw Brady get shot with Reagan?

13. Who bombed the US army mess hall in Mosul, Iraq in 2005?

14. Who owns and operates HAARP? Do they do earthquakes?

15. Who decided DNC would mainly fund pro-war candidates?

16. What is the facility at Lourdes, Cuba for? Is it NATO-run ?

17. Was Kissinger a KGB officer, as Charlotte Iserbyt was told?

18. Did Tavistock train Hitler in 1912, as Greg Hallett claims?

19. Most important: **How can we de-program our soldiers?**

*(Also see, on the Net, 9/11 Family Steering Committee's Unanswered Questions
— a veritable Who's Who of persons we need to speak to.)*

List 12b.   Tips for Recognizing Panic-Makers

Luckily, we can prepare for the coming crisis, because the design team is so predictable. For example:

They cut the electricity and stop collecting the garbage 🗑

They publish 'news' that mutilated bodies were found. ✂

They warn you to be ready to choose sides. ☑

Then they predict that, no, there will be no trouble. ✋

Their goon squads light a few fires, smash a few cars. ☛

They intimidate your pharmacists, school principals, etc.. 🖨

All communication is forbidden except theirs. ✎

Some of your neighbors seem to be unaccounted for. ❓

Goods are cleared from the shops by panic buying. ⊗

One ethnic minority or occupational group is declared ☒
an enemy and you are asked to make reports on them.

No one is allowed out; there are house searches, beatings. ⊘

A rumor is spread that outside help is on the way… ☎

Note: All of the above is done to weaken and confuse you.

The best way to deal with this, of course, is to recognize it early and oppose those who are doing it. What prevents you, right now, from seeing all the pieces of **police state** falling into place – even including **secret prisons**? Are you afraid to see it because there does not seem to be any way out? Don't be so sure! The miscreants may be demented but they do realize they are **vulnerable to arrest.** They are worried! So what are good cops waiting for? **Act now while the weather 'holds out.'** As I write (August 2010): floods in Pakistan, bushfires near Moscow, volcano ash in Iceland, earthquake in Vanuatu, heat-wave in India. And NATO is planning *nuclear* war.
      You are your clan's leader. It has fallen to you by default.

List 12c.   Herculean Effort Required of Heroes?

Much of what prevents us from taking action against outrages probably boils down to habits that are innate or were instilled in childhood, and that actually do require the strength of Hercules to overcome.

1. Ego-Preserving Habits
- fear of not being believed, of looking like a fool
- reluctance to state a truth because it's unpopular
- tendency to magnifying voices of one's critics

2. Habits of Calculating the Future with Hope:
- trusting that a problem will simply get resolved
- tending to let bad things ride for just a little longer
- rejecting any assessment that the situation is dire

3. Habits of Courteous Social Relations:
- the difficulty of saying to someone "You are lying."
- the taboo on criticizing members of one's own club
- waiting for properly credentialed person to do the job

4. Habits That Assure Steadiness and Predictability:
- over-cautiousness about the method of proceeding
- need to be absolutely sure of the facts when deciding
- sticking to a plan after it can be seen to be a failure

5. Habits of Trust in One's Group and One's Leader:
- faith that an institution does what it claims to do
- absolute blindness to the sins of one's nation
- reacting to 'disloyalty' if group criticized from within

6. General Habits That Are Doing Us In:
- ability to ignore even a huge elephant in the room
- attributing prestige and importance to 'secret' things
- preferring death to the discomfort of embarrassment!

Heroes: Now re-read that list asserting the opposite behavior.

END OF PART FOUR (*"HURRY, ACT NOW"*) – A CHRONOLOGY

1792 Congress's pay amendment proposed; it passes 200 yrs later

1966 US's Freedom of Information Act; many nations then copy it

1987 Rodney Stich imprisoned & impoverished for whistle blowing

1988 Equal Rights Amendment not ratified as of 7- year deadline

1988 Collier brothers crack mystery of TV's predictions of votes

1990 Sherman Skolnik uses a cable channel; defies media blackout

1992 Act demands release of JFK assassination info, is disobeyed

1992 First Lady B. Bush writes jaw-dropping memoir about Robin

1995 US joins WTO without benefit of Senate ratifying any treaty

1998 Raye Allan (Russbacher) opens important rumormillnews.com

2002 Lovely TN garden memorialises the deceased of MK-Ultra

2004 US Army kills Pat Tillman as later documented by his mother

2005 Plane-spotters record CIA taking people to rendition sites

2005 Johnson's RICO alleges Dyncorp's sale of Kosovo women

2005 Dr Cantwell promotes forbidden subject: bacteria in cancer

2005 Tennessee medical board hears complaints re Sen. Wm Frist

2005 Several city councils resolve not to implement Patriot Act

2006 Pilots' Association gathers signatures indicating 9/11 a hoax

2006 Speaker Pelosi takes her very likely presidency off the table

2006 Vermonter runs for Congress promising to arrest Pres Bush

2007 Bilderberger,' 'Trilateral,' 'left gatekeeper' are familiar terms

2008 Electoral College declines to show interest in Obama's birth

2009 Desperate, Engstahl markets *Seeds of Destruction* creatively

2010 EU folk quickly speculate head-on train crash was deliberate

2010 McCain and Lieberman openly propose a *coup d'état* – 'by law'

2010 Spill. Oil pouring into Atlantic; supervision is 'privatized'

ΨΨΨΨ

Rough Chronology: Half-a-Millenium of Globalizing Efforts

QE runs effective spy system in Europe, penetrates guilds, clergy
Royalty gives charters for corporate finance of explorations, trade
British East Indies Company imitates Dutch, makes huge fortune
Holland defeats Catholic Spain's Armada, 1588, forms a republic
Mayflower, ship of 'religious refugees,' pauses in Holland in 1620
Cromwell takes over England after Charles I's beheading in 1649
Science flourishes; fire and bubonic plague hit London mid 1660s
Dutch William and Scot Mary become British monarchs in 1688
(At this time there is no nation called Germany, Italy, or America)
Weishaupt in Bavaria founds the Illuminati (of ancient pedigree?)
Elector of Bavaria blows whistle, but monarchs don't hear, 1782
1776 our independence; 1789 French revolution, Jacobin Terror
For US to keep control of money requires War of 1812 vs. British
Napoleon's wars spread republic ideas to Europe, South America
1819 Bolivar helps liberate 5 South American nations from Spain
Bostonian Albert Pike carries secret plans to Arkansas, N. Mexico
Rothschild makes huge loan to Brits re 1849 Ireland potato blight
Bankers squeeze Lincoln; Russia helps him in Civil War, 1863-65
World Revolution idea, 1870s, in political and social communes
Bismarck invents welfare state to keep population 'on side,' 1870
Cecil Rhodes captures much of S Africa; war against Boers 1902
1904, bankers pay Japan to invade Russia to weaken rule of Tsar
Wall St organizes Panic of 1907 to soften Americans up for Fed
Great War starts in 1914; 'Spanish flu' finishes off more millions
Warburgs pay Lenin/Trotsky to create Russian Revolution, 1917
1919 Peace Conference crushes Germans to help rise of Nazis
Wall St crashes to make Depression and big government control
Mussolini programmed, as is Hitler? Churchill? Franco? Teddy R?
1944 Nazis start migrating to S America and store weapons there
Fake Cold War with 'Soviets' plants seeds for WorldWar III
US and NATO bases multiply for the coming world dictatorship
Fantastically successful, hidden dumbing-down of children occurs
Pentagon privatized; army mind-controlled; SOGs do their thing
Incredible but true: France, Italy, and UK lose their sovereignty
Conditioning by media makes Yanks forget how to gather & talk
Parties let candidates feign ignorance of North American Union
US citizens surrender their dignity, without a fight, 'because of 9/11'

RECAP OF SECTION HEADINGS OF CHS 1-12 (except the 'guides')

1. Treason	2. An IMF Package	3. Nation To Stay
Grand Juries	Hurricane Katrina	Cold War/Commies
Oaths of Office	The Emergencies Acts	European Union
Dept of Justice	Exec. Order: Not Law	'NAU Is for Trade'
Oklahoma Bomb	Weather Warfare	Mixed Militaries
Rule of Law	What's an Emergency?	NATO, Gladio, P2
Mind Control	FEMA, COG, Rex-84	Open Conspiracy
Ethnic Persecution	AIDS-Autism-Vaccine	The CFR
Use Citizen's Arrest!	Denounce Nullables!	Pin Down the Past!

4. Love	5. Masons/The Order	6. Menticide Is Crime
Avarice & Predation	Military of the US	Celebs and Robotoids
Attachment, Ideals	Machiavelli Not Apt	All-New Personality
Genocide and War	Mars Is Not Venus	What Schools Do
Love of Life	Morrison and Lopez	Dr Day's Report
Devil-Worship	'Manchurian' Delta's	Treetops Propaganda
Leadership	Mutiny/COMU	Sex/Music/LSD
Deceitfulness	Mafias Are Predicted	Tavistock and Islam
Work with Nature!	Men, Defend Us!	Praise Reasoning!

7. Ubi Societas...	8. President's Job	9. Congress Is Tops
No Way, Mr Padilla	Assassinations/Coups	Legislative Hopper
Law Showcase	Putting JFK to Rest	Overseeing Gov't
Fake Cases Galore	Controlled Substances	Guarding the Purse
Perfect Justice	Are Coverts 'Legal?'	'Federal' Reserve
Skolnick, Our Rabbi	Roads to White House	Treason on the Hill
Judicial Conference	President Immune?	Those Dogs of War
Control from Top	Mad Privatization	Martial Law
Prosecute Menticide!	Detect Impostors!	Protect Congress!

10. Your First Week	11. H. sapiens' Values	12. Pre-empt Them!
A Cheap Campaign	Professions' Ethics	Award a Medal
The Maternal Brain	Media and Truth	Arrest Rogue FBI!
Conservative/Left	The Citizen Swagger	Beg Co-religionists!
Party Grip	Corporation Monster	Rehearse the Panic!
Votescam Software	Artists, Musicians	Rage, Rage!
Electoral College	The Value of Work	Truth Commission?
Amending? Beware	States in the Nation	Prosecute! Complain!
Start Ombudizing!	Smallen On Down!	Go Retro!

Recapitulation

The frightening thing, he reflected for the ten thousandth time …was that it might all be true. If the Party could thrust its hand into the past and say of this or that event, it never happened – that, surely, was more terrifying than mere torture and death?
– George Orwell, *Nineteen Eighty-Four*

TAILOR: (inspecting the torn trousers): Euripides?
CUSTOMER: (after nodding his head): Eumenides?
TAILOR (handing back the trousers): Euripides, *Eu*menides.

The ten pages here, labeled A through K, recap material covered in this book on the following themes:

A. miscellaneous federal legislation

B. court cases, especially Supreme Court, both civil and criminal

C. rules for decoding disinformation, per suggestion of U. Eco

D. citizens who were very likely murdered for trying to help us

E. clever means of upsetting Framer's balance in the parchment

F. helpful ways to employ constitutional, federal, and state law

G. five types of evidence used to buttress arguments in this book

H. conspiracies that look like reality to this author as of mid-2010

I. philosophy-of-law on which this book is premised

J. emergency measures

K. ways to get an arrest warrant going

It is hoped that you by now feel familiar with the following concepts: The Great Republic, House rules, fast-track, the punishment for genocide, common law, injunctive relief, false-flag, antitrust, mind enhancement, psy-ops, imposture, the purse, HAARP, pre-emption, jury nullification, conspiracist, counter-mutiny. List of section headings on opposite page serves as reminder of 108 other topics.

A. Miscellaneous Federal Laws (with informal comment):

Judiciary Act, 1789: sets up federal court, 'material witness'
Logan Act, 1799: citizen may not negotiate with foreign gov't
Posse Comitatus Act, 1878: soldiers mustn't be law enforcers
Sherman Antitrust Act, 1890: government can veto mergers
Trading with Enemy Act, 1917: basis for ban on trade w/Cuba
Neutrality Acts, 1930s: Americans can't fight in others' wars!
Rules Enabling Act, 1934: rules of federal court procedure
National Security Act, 1947: permits CIA-type agencies
Freedom of Information Act, 1966: truly a child of the Sixties
Omnibus Crime Control Act, 1968: forbids interstate trade in
   handguns (to help end assassinations such as RFK, MLK!)
Privacy Act, 1974: entitles you to see and correct your FBI file
Victim of Crimes Act, 1984: amended in 2001 to set aside $50
   million to compensate 9/11 victims of hijacking, etc
Genocide Convention Implementation Act, 1987: treaty=law
Stafford Disaster Relief Act, 1988: president may fund states
War Crimes Act, 1991: incorporates 'Geneva's' into US law;
North Am. Free Trade Agreement, 1994: softens borders of US
No Child Left Behind Act, 2001: mental health 'teen screen'
Patriot Act, 2001: attempts to squelch American liberties
Help America Vote Act, 2002: funds states to replace 'chads'
Homeland Security Act, 2002: vaccinations can be forced
National Intel. Reform Act, 2004: 'To safeguard [?[objectivity'
(New NI Director Lt Clapper is from Nat'l Geospatial Agency)
Real ID Act, 2005: harmonization of drivers' licenses, etc.
USA Patriot… Reauthorization Act, 2006: the sun did not set
(in Oz, a 2005 law forbids 'urging disaffection toward Australia')
Pets Evacuation Act, 2006: response to Hurricane Katrina

Bills Pending (HR= House; S= Senate) as of June, 2010:
H.R.875 Food Safety Modernization Act: organic farmers must
   have expensive machines to clean seeds or could be arrested
S.1959 Homegrown Terrorism Act: to control Internet speech
H.R.1913 Local Law Enforcement Hate Crimes Act: US may
   punish any crime motivated by prejudice.
S.3081 Enemy Belligerent Interrogation & Detention Act. omg!

Note: all pending federal legislation is easily trackable on Thomas.loc.gov

B. Court Cases Referred to in the Text (all are on Internet):
Disposition of case, as shown here, is informal only!

Civil Actions:
Anant Kumar Tripati v County. pending: vital fraud-upon-court action!
Bissonette v Haig, 1985: Wounded Knee: search by military is unlawful
Campbell v Clinton, 2000: Congressmen protest Kosovo air strike
Ex parte Milligan: no martial law during Civil War; court did function
Gore v Bush, 2000: Florida recount, decided on 'equal protection'
Hamdi v Rumsfeld, 2004: Scalia dissented in favor of habeas corpus
Harbury v Deutch, 2000: Court ruled that CIA deliberately misled her
Hollander v McCain and RNC, 2008: re candidate 'not natural born'
Jones v Clinton, 1998: sexual harassment, president found not immune
Kasky v Nike (settled): Can commercial speech enjoy 1st amendment?
Kelo v City of New London, 2005: eminent domain OK for developer
Korematsu v US: no right of Japanese Americans to travel during war
Maxwell v Bush, 2006: asks injunction against bombing of Iran/Syria
Martin v Mott, 1816 : NY militia; this case billed as 'inherent powers'
Marbury v Madison, 1802: Constitution controls which laws are OK
McGrain v Daugherty, 1927: Congress can demand Executive's info
Nation Magazine v US DOD, 1991: opposed 'news pool' in Gulf War
Rodriguez v Bush, 2004: 9/11 RICO case; Diebold was a defendant!
Stone and Melanson v FBI, 1987: FOI release of RFK assassin. papers
US v Reynolds, 1953: State secrets must not be revealed in lawsuit!
Vietnam Veterans of America v CIA, 2009: medical experiments unfair
Wyatt v Cole, 1992: Malicious prosecutor must pay
Yates v Aiken, 1988: judge mis-instructed jury about burden of proof
Youngstown Sheet & Tube v Sawyer, 1951: Truman can't seize steel mills

Criminal or Contempt Cases – Government Is Prosecutor:
California v Cohen 1971: obscenity on jacket: 1st Amendment rights
Nebraska v Owen, 1989: child-abuse witness gets 20 years for perjury
State of Georgia v Troy Davis, 1989: his parents forbidden to attend trial
US v Armstrong, 1966: plaintiff must prove government in the wrong
US v Helms, 1977: perjury by CIA: felony reduced to misdemeanor
US v Lake Resources, 1989: Hakim's theft of government property
US v Lopez, 1995: Thomas' opinion: US has no federal police power
US v Lopez-Lima, 1990: He hijacked plane to Cuba for CIA in 1964
US v McVeigh, 1998: Convicted. Bomb in OKC killed 168 persons
US v Nixon, 1974: Nixon required to surrender White House tapes
US v One Eldorado Cadillac Sedan, 1977: asset forfeiture, car is guilty!
US v Stewart, 2007: lawyer helped her client, a convicted terrorist
R (the Crown) v Martin Bryant, 1996: Australia's fake spree-killer case

C. Rules for Decoding :Lies, Silence, and Disinformation:
as suggested by Umberto Eco in *Faith in Fakes*, 1986

1. The Yeakey rule. Police hurriedly call a death a 'suicide'
 = (decoded): "He was murdered by government hitmen." <u>12</u>

2. The pretend-emergency rule. They say "Emergency! Epidemic!"
 = "We are passing a law to ensure your blind obedience." <u>34</u>

3. The Romney rule. Politician alleges ignorance of, say, NAU.
 = "I am perfectly aware of it but must keep it secret." <u>55</u>

4. The genocide-resources rule. Odd disease/storm kills thousands.
 = "We need to remove excess people in areas with resources." <u>85</u>

5. The McChrystal rule. Soldier's family is told it was 'friendly fire.'
 = "Look, you dopes, we can't admit half of what we do." <u>104</u>

6. The magazine cover rule. Person or event appears in all media.
 = "World Gov't needs to distract you today, or teach you." <u>121</u>

7. The Conyers rule. Litigant's case is denied; he never follows up.
 = "I sue so citizens will think the right thing is being done." <u>150</u>

8. The Jodie Foster rule. Major assassin acted for a corny reason.
 = "Marksmen did the job, as usual, Secret Service assisted." <u>169</u>

9. The GAO rule. "Honesty is assured; we have a mechanism."
 = "We know you idiots will be lulled if we but give it a name."<u>194</u>

10.The We Have Only One Party rule. "Give Democrats money."
 = "All the money you send us will be used against you." <u>220</u>

Note the patterns:
Rules 1, 3, 4, 5, and 8 are all for cover-up, to evade blame. (Importantly these indicate 'guilty knowledge' of the crime committed!)
Rules 2, 6, and 10 are meant to distract you from noticing what is currently happening (e.g., Congress passing unacceptable laws, 'Selwyn' running both parties). Rules 7 and 9 are lullabies.

D. Killed for Trying To Help Us? (a very abbreviated 'D' List)
CITIZENS:

Author James Banfield published Bush's AWOL record in Texas
Author Jim Keith revealed NATO state partners are on US soil
Author Iris Chang was making discoveries re Japan and China
Aaron Russo made film *Freedom to Fascism,* challenging IRS 'law'
Antony Sutton researched Skull & Bones and US funding of USSR
Sherman Skolnick said Corporate Sole in Chicago owns Catholic $
Journalist Gary Webb told how CIA sold drugs via gangs in US
Danny Casalaro sleuthed Promis software and Octopus drug cartel
Jim Collier showed how media and LWV control the 'vote-count'
Tim Russert was preparing to grill VP Cheney on *Meet the Press*
Ms Beverly Eckert kept hammering away at 9/11 nonsense
Gary Caradori fought against child abusers in Omaha, Nebraska
Ted Strecker noticed AIDS spread in an actuarially unpredicted way
Paul Wilcher found DoJ selling Promis software to foreign agencies

OFFICIALS:

General Patton saw how US was aiding Soviet Union ridiculously
Navy Capt. Gunther Russbacher explained consensual Clear Eyes
Air Force Col Ted Wustinghus 'audited' Carlyle transactions in Iraq
Footballer Pat Tillman was having doubts about Afghanistan war
Judge Roland Barnes made witty remarks about judicial goings-on
Pvt. Alyssa Peterson in Iraq criticized US's interrogation practice
DEA Supervisor David Wilhelm knew Atlanta Customs dirt, 2005
Officer Terrance Yeakey told us of explosives inside OKC Bldg
Defense Secy. Jas. Forrestal wrote diary about WW II's big treason
Sen. Joe McCarthy saw George Marshall aid Communism in China
Rep. Larry McDonald (He is still alive if KAL 007 crash was fake!)
Rep. Julian Dixon knew too much about the CIA drug importation
Sen. Mo Udall was potential presidential candidate, hence a 'threat'
Rep. Hale Boggs doubted Warren Commission re JFK assassination
Rep. McFadden opposed Federal Reserve, 1930s, was shot at twice

---

The US also dispatches entertainers who have loyal fans, such as
  John Lennon and Bob Marley (and John Denver? Gilda Radner?)
US kills the loved ones of outspoken persons, such as both siblings
  of Rep. Kucinich , and Darlene Novinger's spouse and father
US culls independent thinkers (C. Sagan? E. Said, J.Shklar?, M.Scott
  Peck? M. Harrington?) and local folks who show strong character.

(Note: I believe all our First Ladies and judges are continually at risk.)

E. How Framer's Balance of Powers Can Be Subverted

After 1880:

Santa Clara 'headnote' of 1886 underpins corporations' civil rights
States hand to two Parties the right to choose electoral college
Bill carries a rider for 'Bureau of Investigation' – it becomes FBI
Temperance amendments assist in corrupting police and judges
British W Stephenson sits in Rockefeller Bldg, NY, runs our OSS
In 1913 Congress betrays US by putting purse in foreign hands
In the New Deal of 1930s, FDR builds huge federal bureaucracy
SCOTUS pretends FDR court-packing threat makes them 'defer'
FDR false-flags Pearl Harbor, then asks Congress to declare war
Richard Gehlen recruits hundreds of Nazis for new CIA, 1946
Nat'l Security Act OK's unspecified 'other functions' for coverts
Slew of Executive Orders fails to worry Congress in 'Cold War'
Undeclared Korean Conflict cast as UN blue helmet job, not war

After 1950:

Senate, home of some CFR men, always confirms Cabinet CFR's
Not a peep heard in 1950s when isolationist senators die young
No peep either when JFK's Dad buys 1960 Illinois vote for him
Warren Court makes law by new liberal interpretation of rights
Goldwater in 1964 is last true conservative presidential candidate
In 1972 Congress OK's Fast Track, thus NAFTA won't be treaty
War Powers Act gives president initiatives belonging to Congress
1976 Nat'l Emergency Act: Congress agrees to stay mum 6 mos.
Carter signs EO 12148 purporting to legitimize shadowy FEMA
Congress gives role of writing the budget to executive OMB
Reagan loses all interest in controlling the nation's debt after '81
Wars in Grenada, Nicaragua, Panama, not declared by Congress
Ollie North disobeys Boland amendment; weak hearings follow

After 1990:

Congress relaxed about US troops for NATO action in Kosovo
McKinney asks about missing $3 tril, her colleagues blush for her
Anthrax shuts down Supreme Court; 'Patriot' Act passes easily
No effective opposition to Votescam, despite Collier's revelations
Halliburton moves to Dubai, continues to get no-bid contracts
Bush assumes he can get away with merging Canada, Mexico, US
SCOTUS refuses to hear cases challenging Obama's eligibility

Students: find relevant section of Constitution for each subversion shown.

F. Five Types of 'Evidence' Presented in This Book

Type I. **Admissions of Guilt.** See the Table of 40 Gov't Documents at the front of this book. For example, for evidence of mind control there was a "Memo from Technical Services" that damningly laid out some projects that the CIA would *only have been involved in* if they were working to control people's minds. The chapter on Menticide referred to other admissions, such as the Church Committee revelations re LSD. Ch 1 quoted Dr Gottlieb's request that hypnosis be controllable by a signal.

Type II. **Revelations by Insiders.** I stated that I take Orwell to have been an insider and I also showed my faith in Gunther Russbacher, as a CIA man. (Both assumptions are disputable). Orwell told us that Big Brother put history down the Memory Hole as a major means of mind control. From Russbacher we got a description of how new personalities are made.

Type III. **Allegations by Victims and Observers.** For mind control, see my paraphrases of five women who were victims of mind control (List 7c), and similarly, the testimony of Chris DeNicola (frontispiece of Ch 6). 'Observations' include the report about Luis Castillo that Walter Bowart got from a doctor who examined Castillo. In the education aspect of mind control we had Eakman's revelation about the Midnight Artists question on a high school test, and Iserbyt's reporting of Nelson's discovery that mathematics were to be mis-taught.

Type IV. **Analyses or Theorizing.** Once a certain amount of data becomes public, folks analyze it, or form theories to explain it – even if they do so only privately. I myself analyzed the trend in songs 'from the days of Hubba Hubba' (list 6b). Alex Carey pointed out that intellectuals were coming under control (Pres Eisenhower said so, too), from which he theorized that there was organized propaganda at 'treetops' level.

Type V. **Deductions That Can Be Made from Types I– IV.** One need only ask "Is it not logical, and reliable, to deduce that the US participates in a malevolent program of mind control based on the above separate facts (e.g., that a panel of educators decided to mis-teach math; that a member of a well-documented group of nuclear radiation experimentees states that she was 'worked on' mentally, too; and that a declassified CIA memo shows an interest in developing drugs that would cause a person to be 'discredited')"?

G. Good Ways To Use State, Federal, and Constitutional Law:
American law is wonderfully complete, reflects high principles, and has provisions to *make the law work even where that is conspired against!*:

The Congress's right to expel any member by 2/3 vote
States' right to ask Congress to **impeach a federal judge**
People's right to amend the Constitution if 3/4 states wish
Judge's right to issue bench warrant; citizens' right to arrest
Availability, in some states, of **prosecution by aggrieved party**
Usability of Civil **RICO** against racketeering activity by gov't
Ability to sue for injunctions, declaratory judgments, damages
Equity precedents for making fraudsters **disgorge** ill-gotten gain
The supremacy of the Constitution and Amendments over statute
Congress's right to repeal any law (and duty to repeal bad law?)
Ability to call officials to account for malfeasance or **treason**
Handy criminal charges of misprision and obstruction of justice
Ability to make doctors, **including coroners,** lose their licenses
Right of all to report bad lawyers (including judges) to state board
Legislatures' right to compel testimony, cite for contempt, arrest
The Senate's option to not confirm federal judicial nominee
Citizen's ability to become county sheriff by running for election
Congress's option to change the number of SCOTUS Justices [!]
Legislators' **immunity from libel** when speaking from the floor
Obligation of (high-paid) Inspectors General to report corruption
Ability of states to control, or end, any corporation via its charter
Legal right of any shareholder to speak **at company's meeting**
Nuremberg Principles that make heads of state prosecutable
Ditto for non-exemption of persons '**only obeying orders**'
Charge of assault for medical experiments done without consent
Tort law, to sue for invasion of privacy (e.g., invading the brain)
The independence of **every judge**, and her large discretion
People's rights to use jury nullification and to form grand juries
President's incapacity to make law, even by 'Executive Order'
Impossibility of US merging with other nations or militaries
Civil rights laws that punish wrongs done **under color of law**
Judge's right to stop abuse-of-process by prosecutors or plaintiffs
Provision that a ruling won't hold, if fraud was **upon-the-court.**
FCC revocability/non-renewal of any radio or TV station licence

Important! Pick three that you can use and discuss them with friends now!

286

H. Conspiracy Theories That I Find Persuasive, in Mid-2010:

Chem and bio experiments on soldiers, prisoners, mental patients
   Note: President Bill Clinton issued a formal apology for the 1930s medical
   experiments on African-American men at Tuskegee. Any act of levying war
   on the citizens shows a treasonous government. Consider that in some of these:

Torture of kids (repeat: torture of kids) for CIA (Nazi) MK-Ultra
Use of *agents provocateurs* to make political protests turn physical
Invention of AIDS, SARS, W. Nile virus, Alzheimer's, perhaps MS
Programming the brains of Delta Forces, SEAL's, without consent
Suppressing info about cancer cure and free electromagnetic energy
Exploding the levees in New Orleans to flood poor districts
OKC and '93 bombing of basement of WTC to set stage for 9/11
Assassinating JFK, RFK, MLK; disabling Gov Wallace, Jim Brady
Murdering Malcolm X in front of his daughters and pregnant wife
'Manchurian' serial killers, produced to make us fear our neighbors
Making hurricanes, blizzards, droughts, floods, quakes, volcanoes
Subjecting US soldiers overseas to DU and malicious anthrax shots
Demolishing Twin Towers, leaving hazardous air for New Yorkers
Selectively arresting African-Americans to defame them *en masse*
Imprisoning Middle Easterners in US to imply danger to society
Frightening people about 'imminent' nuclear attack in Cold War
Teaching kids to depend on Big Brother -- and to scorn parents
Stirring social conflict by manipulation of race and ethnic relations
Setting up the Jews to take the rap for war, pornography, capitalism
Psy-ops in media intended to deprive people of their reasoning
Importing, distributing cocaine and heroin to poor and to the elite
Providing musical beat calculated to make youth more suggestible
Building a culture with symbols of death, artificiality of relationships
Offering plea bargains so maximum number of men get jailed
Promoting promiscuity and divorce to destabilize the family
Policy of unemployment and deliberate de-industrializing of the US
Urging the use of 'plastic,' at high interest rate, to put all in debt
Teaching kids to read poorly by using 'whole language' not phonics
Making forest fires in California, Australia, Indonesia & elsewhere
Planning to close down Internet sites that tell us about these things
Producing TV shows that make men, especially Dads, look stupid

Conspiracy Theories That Fail To Interest Me: Mayan calendar, visitors from other planets, end times, Morgellons disease, mind-reading, UFO's, moon landings (i.e., non-landings), global warming.

I. The 'Philosophy of Law' on Which This Book Is Premised.

The *Homo sapiens* **raw material.** All mammals (which is the class of vertebrates to which we belong) are selfish. Male mammals are competitive in order to form hierarchies. Female mammals give milk; this assures the primary social bond. Humans cooperate well in society up to the tribal level. If we hadn't developed law, raw competition would be the norm among members of society, except that families would protect their own 'genes,' and persons who need each other for large projects (getting resources) would cooperate.

Pre-historic law: *lex talionis.* Since everyone will try to get the best deal for himself, it pays to have rules of restraint imposed on all individuals by society. People seem to have an innate sense of reciprocity, so it is predictable that punishment for bad behavior would take the form of "an eye for an eye, a tooth for a tooth." 'Authority' may be vested in a village chief or an institution such as the Oracle.

Pre-modern English law as seen in Magna Carta. King John did not have enough power to lord it over the nation; a band of strong men (barons) forced him to 'earn' his privileges by guaranteeing a society that didn't reward oppressors. This meant that standard tricks, such as false witness, were to be thwarted by law. "All fines made unjustly shall be entirely remitted." My goodness!

The Parchment, 1787. The 55 delegates in Philadelphia had been raised with that British expectation of rights and freedoms. They put the same clever restraints on an elected government as the barons put on the monarch. They foresaw that politicians would develop means of feathering their own nests while in parliament. I believe they thought of everything we require for establishing justice.

Contemporary American Law. The Patriot Act is a nice kettle of fish, isn't it? How did it happen? I was trained (pre-2005) to think 'social forces' had caused things to go a bit bad — I did not realize that it was the usual mammalian stuff. Having been converted by revisionist history, conspiracy theory, and the Internet, I find myself back to evolutionary theory. Spotted hyena, fur seal, *homo sapiens,* etc. Mammals are: (Repeat the first paragraph of this page). Someone got in there and so cleverly tried to take away all we have (culture, religion, trust, family ties, patriotism, rights) so they could rule the globe. I truly think they're geniuses for reducing us to idiocy. Bravo!

That said, enough is enough. We need to help them get out of their bind, and get ourselves out of our crisis of selfishness. "Every man for himself" is a recipe for auto-genocide. We can do better.

J. Emergency Measures

Recap of the What-To-Do's: Use Citizens' Arrest, Denounce Nullables, Pin Down the Past, Work with Nature, Men Defend Us, Praise Reasoning, Prosecute Menticide, Detect Impostors, Protect Congress, Start Ombudizing, Smallen Down, Go Retro.

Recap of Suggestions: Start Your Own Grand Jury (such as a 'Clarendon Assize'), Bluff (by inviting police to your meeting,) Stop Believing Globalization is Inevitable, Have a Moratorium on Breeding, Do Not Ancestralize, Get with the Law, Be Skeptical about 'Findings. Breathe New Life into the Concept of *Hostis Humani Generis,* Stop Saying 'Congress Is Run by the Jews', Start a Counter-Mutiny Club, Go Now to the Person You Would Go to in a Crisis, Have a Maternal Draw, Use Freedom of Information Act, Beg Co-Religionists, Arrest Rogue FBI, Rehearse the Panic, Rage, Rage!, Identify the Traitors and Pre-empt Them, Ask How To Deprogram Our Soldiers, Run for Congress, Be a hero, please!

Recap of How Individuals Can Enforce the Law: Recall that talking to friends is a way of turning the present situation around, as it leads to empowerment and to bringing moral pressure on the baddies. Don't forget Ch 5.10's discussion of the concept of outlawry and *"Caput gerat lupinum"* – wearing the head of a wolf, as a last resort for dealing with sociopaths.

For that matter, recall the maxim *Necessitas non habet legem:* when it comes down to survival, obeying the law is secondary. Two legal writings were quoted in that regard: Schmallager's textbook on the individual's right of self-defense (It exists in common law throughout the 50 states), and The American Law Institute's (draft version) proposal that a reasonable decision to pre-empt can be pleaded later as a defense in court.

Don't forget your ability to be a *pro se* litigant in federal district court for $350 (*gratis* for paupers!) and to bring a civil RICO case to reveal patterns of criminal government behavior. And while it's hard to make judges accountable, most of them hold law licences; you can complain to that licencing board. Remember that your state legislature has investigatory powers at which you can give testimony.

If you really have faith in law **you will win.** Really, how could you lose?

(And now would Monsieur P please see my pièce de résistance *on next page*

K. Procuring an Official Arrest Warrant *(This bit is not 'recap'; it's new)*

Why not avoid the hazards of citizens' arrest by getting a state authority to write an arrest warrant? (Once a warrant exists, both police and citizens are allowed to can catch the person.) I earnestly suggest that you practice writing up a warrant. You could then respectfully submit to a magistrate or judge who may well feel obliged to sign it!

Or you could send your "draft-of-a-warrant" to members and leaders of your state legislature: they have power (as a body, not individually) to issue arrest warrants. If your state has grand juries you can mail it to the foreman, "receipt return requested."

You must submit a supporting **affidavit** (a sworn statement that carries a penalty for perjury if you lie) with *facts* that show a felony was committed, and on what basis you accuse someone of it.

Reuters. yahoo news *July 13, 2010:* The International Criminal Court issued an **arrest warrant** on Monday for Sudan's President Omar Hassan al-Bashir for orchestrating genocide in the Darfur region, where as many as 300,000 people have died since 2003.... "**There are reasonable grounds** to believe him responsible for three counts of genocide ...." the ICC appeals judges said. The ICC warrant was the first issued against a sitting head of state by the court....

Bashir remains at large as the ICC has no police force....

The 'accused' is protected by the 4th Amendment against arbitrary seizure by government. Hence the magistrate must document *'probable cause'* before she will sign an arrest warrant. Also, the warrant is required to identify, as much as possible, who is to be arrested (since the magistrate will be signing a demand that the person be arrested and be brought to the nearest available judge).

Perhaps you could withhold the name, offering to furnish it as soon as the authority has had a look at the nature of the crime. ("John Doe" is used for temporary privacy in some court work.) Note: if you *publish* accusations, you may be sued for libel, or see a backlash.

You need to gather evidence that can meet an *objective* standard of probable cause. It is not your duty to prove a case or convict anyone; you are only bringing the crime to the court's attention. All the better if you do this as *a group* (of neighbors, of law professors, whatever), each of whom signs the cover letter and an affidavit.

Mao Zedong said, in his *Little Red Book,* "A revolution is not a dinner party." Well, treason is not shoplifting — y'know what I'm sayin'? Treason is lethal and must be stopped. If friends laugh at you, just whack 'em with the parchment. Just fly the flag. Just *do* it.

WELCOME TO THE **APPENDICES**!

26 OF THEM, FOR YOUR READING ENJOYMENT

(Single-page documents appear in black borders)

* as author of these six items, I hereby permit anyone to copy freely. All others are in the public domain except, perhaps, R.

APPENDIX A
First Clear Ruling against Today's Police State

United States District Court for Eastern Michigan
Case No. 06-CV-10204

AMERICAN CIVIL LIBERTIES UNION [ET AL], Plaintiffs,
v.
NATIONAL SECURITY AGENCY / CENTRAL SECURITY SERVICE; and LIEUTENANT GENERAL KEITH B. ALEXANDER, in his official capacity as Director of the National Security Agency and Chief of the Central Security Service, Defendants.

MEMORANDUM OF OPINION

1 This is a challenge to the legality of a secret program (hereinafter "TSP") undisputedly inaugurated by the National Security Agency (hereinafter "NSA") at least by 2002 and continuing today, which intercepts without benefit of warrant or other judicial approval, prior or subsequent, the international telephone and Internet communications of numerous persons ... in this country.

...Congress then, in 1968, enacted Title III of the Omnibus Crime Control and Safe Streets Act... governing all wire and electronic interceptions in the fight against certain listed major crimes. The Statute defined an "aggrieved person," and gave such person standing to challenge any interception allegedly made without a judicial order supported by probable cause,... In 1972 the court decided U.S. v. U.S. District Court... (the Keith case) ... [That] for lawful electronic surveillance even in domestic security matters, the Fourth Amendment requires a prior warrant.

".... In Entick v. Carrington... decided in 1765, one finds a striking parallel to the executive warrants utilized here.... Entick, a critic of the Crown, was the victim of one such general search during which his seditious publications were impounded. **He brought a successful damage action for trespass** against the messengers.... In a related and similar proceeding, Huckle v. Money... the same judge who presided over Entick's appeal held for another victim of the same despotic practice, saying '(t)o **enter a man's house** by virtue of a nameless warrant, in order to procure evidence, **is worse than the Spanish Inquisition . . .**'"

292

The Fourth Amendment, accordingly, was adopted to assure that Executive abuses of the power to search would not continue in our new nation.

...Karo is consistent with Katz where Justice Stewart held that: "Over and again this Court has emphasized that the mandate of the (Fourth) Amendment requires adherence to judicial processes,' and that **searches conducted outside the judicial process, without prior approval by judge or magistrate, are per se unreasonable** under the Fourth Amendment – subject only to a few specifically established and well-delineated exceptions...."

Justice Powell's opinion in the Keith case also stated that: **"The Fourth Amendment does not contemplate the executive officers of Government as neutral and disinterested magistrates....** The historical judgment, which the Fourth Amendment accepts, is that unreviewed executive discretion may yield too readily to pressures to obtain incriminating evidence and overlook potential invasions of privacy and protected speech....

In the framework of our Constitution, the President's power to see that the laws are faithfully executed refutes the idea that he is to be a lawmaker.
These secret authorization orders must, like the executive order in that case, fall. **They violate the Separation of Powers ordained by the very Constitution of which this President is a creature.**

VIII. The Authorization for Use of Military Force
After the terrorist attack on this Country of September 11, 2001, the Congress jointly enacted the Authorization for Use of Military Force (hereinafter "AUMF") which states: That the President is authorized to use all necessary and appropriate force against those nations, organizations, or persons he determines planned, authorized, committed, or aided the terrorist attacks that occurred on September 11, 2001, or harbored such organizations or persons, in order to prevent any future acts of international terrorism against the United States by such nations, organizations or persons.

The Government argues here that **it was given authority by that resolution to conduct the TSP** in violation of ...FISA ....

[Quoting Justice Sandra Day O'Connor] However, she continued, **indefinite detention for purposes of interrogation was certainly not authorized** and it raised the question of what process is constitutionally due to a citizen who disputes the enemy combatant status assigned him. Hamdi, 542 U.S. at 521, 524.... Accordingly, her holding was that the Bill of Rights of the United States Constitution must be applied despite authority granted by the AUMF.

She [Justice O'Connor] stated that: "It is during our most challenging and uncertain moments that our Nation's commitment to due process is most severely tested; and it is in those times that we must preserve our commitment at home to the principles for which we fight abroad.

* * * *

Any process in which the Executive's factual assertions go wholly unchallenged or are simply presumed correct without any opportunity for the alleged combatant to demonstrate otherwise falls constitutionally short...."

...**Defendants have violated the Constitutional rights of their citizens** including the First Amendment, Fourth Amendment, and **the Separation of Powers doctrine.**

The Permanent Injunction of the TSP requested by Plaintiffs is granted inasmuch as each of the factors required to be met to sustain such an injunction have undisputedly been met. The **irreparable injury necessary to warrant injunctive relief is clear,** as the First and Fourth Amendment rights of Plaintiffs are violated by the TSP. See Dombrowski v. Pfister, 380 U.S. 479 (1965). The irreparable injury conversely sustained by Defendants under this injunction may be rectified by compliance with our Constitution and/or statutory law, as amended if necessary. Plaintiffs have prevailed, and **the public interest is clear, in this matter. It is the upholding of our Constitution.** [emphasis added]

IT IS SO ORDERED.

Date: August 17, 2006   s/**Anna Diggs Taylor**
Detroit, Michigan   ANNA DIGGS TAYLOR
     UNITED STATES DISTRICT JUDGE.

APPENDIX B   Freedom of Speech, US Supreme Court
COHEN v. CALIFORNIA, decided June 7, 1971

... Appellant was convicted of violating that part of California Penal Code Sec. 415 which prohibits "maliciously and willfully disturb[ing] the peace or quiet of any neighborhood or person...by...offensive conduct," for wearing a jacket bearing the words "Fuck The Draft" in a corridor of the Los Angeles Courthouse. The Court of Appeal held that "offensive conduct" means "behavior which has a tendency to provoke others to acts of violence or to in turn disturb the peace," and affirmed the conviction. [This conviction was then overturned by the Supreme Court]

... MR. JUSTICE HARLAN delivered the opinion of the Court.

This case may seem at first blush too inconsequential to find its way into our books, but the issue it presents is of no small constitutional significance.

... "The defendant did not engage in, nor threaten to engage in, nor did anyone as the result of his conduct in fact commit or threaten to commit any act of violence....

... Additionally, we cannot overlook the fact, because it is well illustrated by the episode involved here, that much linguistic expression serves a dual communicative function: it conveys not only ideas capable of relatively precise, detached explication, but otherwise inexpressible emotions as well. In fact, words are often chosen as much for their emotive as their cognitive force. We cannot sanction the view that the Constitution, which solicitous of the cognitive content of individual speech, has little or no regard for that emotive function which, practically speaking, may often be the more important element of the overall message sought to be communicated.

Indeed, as Mr. Justice Frankfurter has said, "one of the prerogatives of American citizenship is the right to criticize public men and measures – and that means not only informed and responsible criticism but the freedom to speak foolishly and without moderation" *Baumgartner v. United States* (1944)....

[emphasis added]

Note: this case is about dissent, not obscenity. Regarding dissent this case was modified by the 2007 SCOTUS ruling in the Bong Hits 4 Jesus case. (Yet the Online Protection Act was ruled unconstitutional on 1st amendment grounds.) Regarding obscenity, many states prohibit it in public and that includes on buses. I suspect Cohen's case and Bong Hits were both set-ups, to enable policy. – MM

APPENDIX C RICO Complaint in Civil Action Filed in 10/04 Dismissed by US District Court for Southern New York

PHILIP J. BERG, ESQ., attorney for WILLIAM RODRIGUEZ, PLAINTIFF

-against-

George Herbert Walker Bush, George Walker Bush, John "Jeb" Bush, Neil Mallon Bush, Marvin Bush, Richard Cheney, Donald H. Rumsfeld, Dov Zakheim, Colin Powell, Richard Armitage, Condoleezza Rice, John Ashcroft, Robert S. Mueller III, David Frasca, George Tenet, Porter Goss, Norman Y. Mineta... The Republican National Committee, Inc., Alan Greenspan... Halliburton Company, Kellogg Brown & Root Services, The Project for the New American Century, Inc., Election Systems & Software, Diebold Voting Systems, Inc....[and several others], DEFENDANTS

... III. Facts on which claims for relief are predicated:

A. The WTC Twin Towers, as well as WTC building #7, were destroyed by controlled demolition, as clearly proven by the laws of physics; this demolition could only have been an 'inside job.'
B. FEMA, which removed the evidence before it could be independently examined, maintains a black-op shadow government designed to replace the elected government of the United States.
C. Defendants deliberately concealed the fact that they had ample warnings of terrorist attacks and failed to act on them, a war on terrorism being necessary to justify their political agenda.
D. Defendants conspired to and did allow the attacks to happen by delaying military interception of the hijacked planes....
E. The enterprise has engaged in a conspiracy to commit election fraud.
F. Enterprise's Florida recount riot: additional predicate acts under RICO.
G. Additional allegations as to individual defendants, predicate acts of racketeering committed by them, and their roles in the RICO enterprise.

The foregoing facts support claims against the defendants for multiple acts of conspiracy, racketeering, domestic terrorism and other crimes.

Note: I suspect this case of being a set-up for the reason I gave about Watada's case in Ch 5.8. Also note: One man, Judge Alvin Hellerstein controls all federal '9/11' lawsuits. – MM

APPENDIX D Law Maxims, General Principles of Law

Selected from the *Law Dictionary*, 1888
(Wesley Gilmer's 1986 revision of Wm. Cochran Cox's 1976 edition)
English version (Latin version provided below)

1. **Acting and consenting parties are liable to the same punishment**.
2. The niceties of the law are not the law.
3. It is the duty of a good judge to enlarge his jurisdiction, i.e., to amplify the remedies of the law.
4. A good judge decides according to equity and right, and prefers equity to strict law.
5. A judicial writ does not fail through defect of form.
6. A custom founded on a certain and reasonable ground supersedes the common law.
7. Crime vitiates all that springs from it.
8. He who has authority to do the more important ought not to be prohibited from doing that which is less important.
9. Gross negligence is held equivalent to intentional wrong.
10. Let the punishment be proportionate to the crime.
11. **False in one thing, false in all**.
12. He who flees judgment confesses his guilt.
13. Let justice be done, though the heavens should fall.
14. It is the same thing to say nothing as it is not to say enough.
15. Impossibility is an excuse at law.
16. **Impunity always invites to worse faults**.
17. In contracts, matters of custom and general usage are implied.
18. We should judge by the laws, not precedents.
19. These are the precepts of the law: to live honorably, to hurt nobody, to render to everyone his due.
20. **Necessity has no law**.
21. Law will more readily tolerate a private loss than a public evil.
22. The law provides for the future, the judge for the past.
23. Law is the dictate of reason.
24. Law is a rule of right.
25. The law pays regard to equity.
26. The law will always furnish a remedy.
27. The law regards the course of nature.
28. The law assists minors.

29. The law speaks to all in the same way
30. Long sufferance is construed as consent.
31. An evil custom should be abolished.
32. Wretched is the slavery where the law is changeable or uncertain.
33. Nature aspires to perfection; so does the law.
34. Where there is a similar reasoning, the law is the same.
35. Public necessity is stronger than private.
36. **Nothing is so opposed to consent as force and fear**.
37. Too much subtlety in law is reprehensible.
38. By too much altercation truth is lost.
39. They are not considered to consent who act under a mistake.
40. He who cannot be known from himself may be known from his associates.
41. By no contract can one effect that a fraud shall be maintained.
42. Odious and dishonest things are not to be presumed in law.
43. Every ratification has a retrospective effect.
44. He who acts through another acts by or for himself.
45. He who does not disapprove approves.
46. **He who spares the guilty punishes the innocent**.
47. Let him be deceived who wishes to be deceived.
48. That which is invalid in its commencement gains no strength by lapse of time.
49. What is done contrary to law is considered as not done.
50. That which necessity compels she excuses.
51. The law does not require what is vain and useless.
52. The reason of the law is the life of the law.
53. **The safety of the community is the highest law**.
54. Where there are many counselors there is safety.
55. To write is to act.
56. Suppression of the truth is [equivalent to] false representation.

Note: Maxims do not actually have numbers. The ones shown above were arbitrarily assigned for this book, to assist the match-up of Latin and English. There are hundreds of maxims; these are but a sample. Not all are of Roman origin: Latin was the language of the courts of England until 1666!

Student Assignment: Write an essay on 'Necessitas non habet legem.'

The Same 56 Maxims, in Latin

1. Agentes et consentientes pari poena plectentur. *2. Apices juris non sunt jura. 3. Boni judicis est ampliare jurisdictionem 4. Bonus judex secundem quequum et bonum judicat, et aequitatem stricto juri praefert. 5. Breve judiciale non cadit pro defectu formae. 6. Consuetudo ex certa causa rationabili usitata privat communem legem. 7. Crimen omnia ex se nata vitiat. 8. Cui licet quod majus non debet quod minus est non licere. 9. Culpa lato dolo aequiparatur. 10. Culpae poena par esto.*

11. Falsus in uno, falsus in omnibus. *12. Fatetur facinus qui judicium fugit. 13. Fiat justitia, ruat coelum. 14. Idem est nihil dicere et insufficienter dicere. 15. Impotentia exusat legem.*

16. Impunitas semper ad deteriora invitat. *17. In contractibus tacite insunt quae sunt moris et consuetudinis. 18. Judicandum est legibus, non exemplis. 19. Juris praecepta sunt haec, honeste vivere, alterum non laedere, suum cuique tribuere.*

20. Necessitas non habet legem. *21. Lex citius tolerare vult privatum damnum quam publicum malum. 22. Lex de futuro, judex de praeterito. 23. Lex est dictamen rationis. 24. Lex est norma recti. 25. Lex respicit aequitatem. 26. Lex semper dabit remedium. 27. Lex spectat naturae ordinem. 28. Lex succurrit minoribus. 29. Lex uno ore omnes alloquitur. 30. Longa patientia trahitur ad consensum. 31. Malus usus est abolendus. 32. Misera est servitus ubi jus est vagum aut incertum.*

33. Natura appetit perfectum, ita et lex. 34. Ubi eadem ratio, ibi eadem lex. 35. Necessitas publica major est quam privata.

36. Nil consensui tam contrarium est quam vis atque metus. *37. Nimia subtilitas in jure reprobatur. 38. Nimium altercando veritas amittitur. 39. Non videntur qui errant consentire. 40. Noscitur ex sociis, qui non cognoscitur, ex se. 41. Nulla pactione effici potest ut dolus praestetur. 42. Odiosa et in honesta non sunt in lege praesumenda. 43. Omnis ratihabitio retrotrahitur et mandato priori aequiparatur. 44. Qui facit per alium facit per se. 45. Qui non improbat approbat.*

46. Qui parcit nocentibus, innocentes punit. *47. Qui vult decipi decipiatur. 48. Quod ab initio valet, in tractu temporis non convalescet. 49. Quod contra legem fit, pro infecto habetur. 50. Quod necessitas cogit, excusat. 51. Quod vanum et inutile est, lex non requirit. 52. Ratio legis est anima legis.*

53. Salus populi est lex suprema. *54. Salus ubi multi consiliarii. 55. Scribere est agere. 56. Suppressio veri, expressio falsi.*

APPENDIX E   **Example of Congress's Oversight over DoJ**

Dear [FBI] Director Mueller: January 9, 2003

I am writing to express my concern and inquire about an award you recently gave to Marion "Spike" Bowman for "meritorious service." Mr. Bowman, as deputy general counsel who is in charge of the FBI's National Security Law Unit, has much authority....

The case of Zaracarias Moussaoui, who has been charged in
connection with the terrorist attacks of September 11, 2001, is a prime example of the FBI's problems with FISA warrants.
The 26-page Electronic Communication from the Minneapolis Division contained information that a reasonable person would have concluded is sufficient to obtain a FISA warrant. The application should have gone forward to the Justice Dept and the FISA court. ...

In light of the consequences of the decision not to even attempt to seek the FISA warrant, and Mr. Bowman's concurrence with that, it is shocking then that you gave Mr. Bowman the award known as the "Presidential Rank of Meritorious Service."

.... This also fits with a disturbing pattern of rewarding wrongdoing or mistakes by top officials at the FBI. . ..To my knowledge, agents who were investigating leads on the hijacking plot prior to September 11, 2001, have neither been thanked nor awarded. ... Please answer the following questions.
How and why was Mr. Bowman selected for this award?
Was this award given by your sole discretion as director, or
were others involved in nominating or selecting Mr. Bowman?
If others were involved, please identify them and include their reasons for thinking Mr. Bowman should be rewarded...

Please provide any and all documents relating to the decision to grant Mr. Bowman this award.

I would appreciate a full response in writing by January 27.

Sincerely,
Charles E. Grassley
Ranking Member, Subcommittee on Crime and Drugs

HCR 6 – AS INTRODUCED, 2009 House Concurrent Resolution
A resolution affirming States' rights based on Jeffersonian principles

SPONSORS: Rep. Itse, Rock 9;   Rep. Ingbretson, Graf 5;
Rep. Comerford, Rock 9;   Sen. Denley, Dist 3
COMMITTEE: State-Federal Relations and Veterans Affairs

Whereas the Constitution of the State of New Hampshire, Part 1, Article 7 declares that the people of this State have the sole and exclusive right of governing themselves as a free, sovereign, and independent State; and do, and forever hereafter shall, exercise and enjoy every power, jurisdiction, and right, pertaining thereto, which is not, or may not hereafter be, by them expressly delegated to the United States of America in congress assembled; and …now, therefore, be it Resolved by the House of Representatives, the Senate concurring:

That the several States composing the United States of America, **are not united on the principle of unlimited submission to their General Government;** but that, by a compact under the style and title of a Constitution for the United States, and of amendments thereto, they constituted a General Government for special purposes, – delegated to that government certain definite powers, reserving, each State to itself, the residuary mass of right to their own self-government; **and that whensoever the General Government assumes undelegated powers, its acts are unauthoritative, void, and of no force**; that to this compact each State acceded as a State, and is an integral party, its co-States forming, as to itself, the other party:

that the government created by this compact was not made the exclusive or final judge of the extent of the powers delegated to itself; since that would have made its discretion, and not the Constitution, the measure of its powers; but that, as in all other cases of compact among powers having no common judge, **each party has an equal right to judge for itself, as well of infractions as of the mode and measure of redress; and**

That the Constitution of the United States, having delegated to Congress a power to punish treason, counterfeiting…, piracies, and felonies committed on the high seas, and offences against the law of nations, slavery, **and no other crimes whatsoever**; and it being true as a general principle, and one of the amendments to the Constitution having also declared, that "the powers not delegated to the United States by the Constitution, nor prohibited by it to the States, are reserved to the States respectively, or to the people," **therefore all acts of Congress which assume to create, define, or punish crimes, other than those so enumerated in the Constitution are altogether void, and of no force;**

... And that in addition to this general principle and express declaration, another and more special provision has been made by one of the amendments to the Constitution, which expressly declares, that "Congress shall make no law respecting an establishment of religion, or prohibiting the free exercise thereof, or abridging the freedom of speech or of the press:" thereby guarding in the same sentence, and under the same words, the freedom of religion, of speech, and of the press: **That, therefore, all acts of Congress of the United States which do abridge the freedom of religion, freedom of speech, freedom of the press, are not law, but are altogether void, and of no force; and**

That the construction applied by the General Government (as is evidenced by sundry of their proceedings) to those parts of the Constitution of the United States which delegate to Congress a power "to lay and collect taxes, duties, imports, and excises, to pay the debts, and provide for the common defense and general welfare of the United States," and "to make all laws which shall be necessary and proper for carrying into execution the powers vested by the Constitution in the government of the United States, or in any department or officer thereof,"

goes to the destruction of all limits prescribed to their power by the Constitution: that words meant by the instrument to be subsidiary only to the execution of limited powers, ought not to be so construed as themselves to give unlimited powers **that the proceedings of the General Government under color of these articles,** will be a fit and necessary subject of revisal and correction; and; **and that therefore this State is determined... to submit to undelegated, and consequently unlimited powers in no man, or body of men on earth:** that in cases of an abuse of the delegated powers, the members of the General Government, being chosen by the people, a change by the people would be the constitutional remedy; **but, where powers are assumed which have not been delegated, a nullification of the act is the rightful remedy: that every State has a natural right in cases not within the compact, (casus non foederis), to nullify of their own authority all assumptions of power by others within their limits:** that without this right, they would be under the dominion, absolute and unlimited, of whosoever might exercise this right of judgment for them:

that if the acts before specified should stand, these conclusions would flow from them: that it would be **a dangerous delusion were a confidence in the men of our choice to silence our fears for the safety of our rights:** that confidence is everywhere the parent of despotism – free government is founded in jealousy, and not in confidence; it is jealousy and not confidence which prescribes limited constitutions, to bind down those whom we are obliged to trust with power:

that our Constitution has accordingly fixed the limits to which, and no further, our confidence may go. In questions of power, then, let no more be heard of confidence in man, but bind him down from mischief by the chains of the Constitution.

…. Acts which would cause such a nullification include, but are not limited to: I. Establishing martial law or a state of emergency within one of the States comprising the United States of America without the consent of the legislature of that State.

II. Requiring involuntary servitude, or governmental service other than a draft during a declared war, …

IV. Surrendering any power delegated or not delegated to any corporation or foreign government.

V. Any act regarding religion; further limitations on freedom of political speech; or further limitations on freedom of the press.

VI. Further infringements on the right to keep and bear arms;….

Note: Much of the foregoing is a direct quote from Jefferson's "Resolutions Relative to the Alien and Sedition Acts" of Nov. 1798.

APPENDIX G
Articles of Impeachment of US President, 1991
Introduced in the US House by Rep Henry Gonzalez

ARTICLE I

In the conduct of the office of President of the United States, George Herbert Walker Bush, in violation of his constitutional oath faithfully to execute the office of President and, to the best of his ability, preserve, protect, and defend the Constitution, and in violation of his constitutional duty to take care that the laws be faithfully executed, has violated the equal protection clause of the Constitution. US soldiers in the Middle East are overwhelmingly poor white, black, and Mexican-American, and their military service is based on the coercion of a system that has denied viable economic opportunities to these classes of citizens. Under the Constitution, all classes of citizens are guaranteed equal protection, and calling on the poor and minorities to fight a war for oil to preserve the lifestyles of the wealthy is a denial of the rights of these soldiers.

ARTICLE III

[He]…has prepared, planned, and conspired to engage in a massive war against Iraq employing methods of mass destruction that will result in the killing of tens of thousands of civilians, many of whom will be children. This planning includes the placement and potential use of nuclear weapons,…

… From August, 1990, through January, 1991, the President embarked on a course of action that systematically eliminated every option for peaceful resolution of the Persian Gulf crisis. Once the President approached Congress for a declaration of war, 500,000 American soldiers' lives were in jeopardy — rendering any substantive debate by Congress meaningless. The President has not received a declaration of war by Congress, and in contravention of the written word, the spirit, and the intent of the US Constitution has declared that he will go to war regardless of the views of Congress and the American people. In failing to seek a declaration of war, …George Herbert Walker Bush has acted in a manner contrary to his trust as President and subversive of constitutional government, to the great prejudice of the cause of law and justice and to the manifest injury of the people of the United States.…

Wherefore George Herbert Walker Bush, by such conduct, warrants impeachment and trial, and removal from office. …

APPENDIX H   What Kind of Presidency Do We Want?

Madison's Notes from the Constitutional Convention, 1787

M^r. SHERMAN said he considered the Executive magistracy as nothing more than an institution for carrying the will of the Legislature into effect, that the person or persons ought to be appointed by and accountable to the Legislature only, which was the depositary of the supreme will of the Society.

M^r. GERRY favored the policy of annexing a Council to the Executive in order to give weight & inspire confidence.

 M^r. RANDOLPH strenuously opposed a unity in the Executive magistracy. He regarded it as the foetus of monarchy. We had he said no motive to be governed by the British Governmt. as our prototype. He did not mean however to throw censure on that Excellent fabric. If we were in a situation to copy it he did not know that he should be opposed to it; but the fixt genius of the people of America required a different form of Government. He could not see why the great requisites for the Executive department, vigor, despatch & responsibility could not be found in three men, as well as in one man.

…M^r. PINKNEY moves for seven years.

M^r. SHERMAN was for three years, and agst. the doctrine of rotation as throwing out of office the men best qualifyed to execute its duties.

M^r. MASON was for seven years at least, and for prohibiting a reeligibility as the best expedient both for preventing the effect of a false complaisance on the side of the Legislature towards unfit characters; and a temptation on the side of the Executive to intrigue with the Legislature for a re-appointment.

M^r. BEDFORD was strongly opposed to so long a term as seven years. He was for a triennial election, and for an ineligibility after… nine years.

On the question for seven years, Massts .dividd…
N. J. Cont. no. N. Y. ay.
Pena. ay. Del. ay. Virga. ay. N. C. no. S. C. no. Geor. No.

APPENDIX I   *The Secret North American Union*

Statement by Ministers Responsibility [sic] for the Security and Prosperity Partnership of North America   February 23, 2007

Ottawa - The Leaders of Canada, Mexico and the United States launched the Security and Prosperity Partnership of North America (SPP) to increase security, prosperity, and improve the quality of life for the citizens of each sovereign nation.
    Last March in Cancun, Leaders reaffirmed their commitment to the SPP and identified five priorities:
1) Strengthening Competitiveness through creation of a private sector-led North American Competitiveness Council (NACC), and enhancing regulatory cooperation;
2) Emergency Management;
3) Avian and Pandemic Influenza;
4) Energy Security; and 5) Smart, Secure Borders.

We met today to review progress since the Leaders' meeting in Cancun and are pleased to report that progress has been achieved in a number of areas.

- We directed the members of the Coordinating Body to finalize the North American Plan on Avian and Pandemic Influenza by June '07…

- We established a senior level coordinating body to prioritize and oversee emergency management activities in the following areas:
1) emergency response; 2) critical infrastructure protection;
3) border resumption in the event of an emergency; and
4) border incident management…

- We took note of the progress achieved by Energy Ministers in implementing priorities identified by Leaders in the areas of innovation, energy efficiency and technology development, and energy market facilitation, and look forward to further progress in advance of the Leaders' meeting…

APPENDIX J   'Russian' Mind Control

MEMORANDUM FOR: The Honorable J. Edgar Hoover, Director, FBI

The attached study on brainwashing was prepared by my staff. It represents the thinking of leading psychologists, based in turn on interviews with many individuals who have had personal experience with Communist brainwashing, and on extensive research and testing.

(signed) Allen W. Dulles [CIA Director]   April 25, 1956

Brainwashing, as a technique, has been used for centuries and is no mystery to psychologists. In this sense, brainwashing means involuntary re-education of basic beliefs and values. All people are being re-educated continually. New information changes one's beliefs. The experience of the brainwashed individual differs in that the inconsistent information is forced upon the individual under controlled conditions after the possibility of critical judgment has been removed by a variety of methods.

PRINCIPLES OF ...HUMAN REACTION TO CONTROL

There are progressive steps in exercising control over an individual and changing his behaviour: 1. Making the individual aware of control is the first stage in changing his behaviour. [A child sees that he is helpless against a strong parent who can control him completely.] So, a controlled adult comes to recognize the overwhelming powers of the state and the impersonal, "incarcerative" machinery in which he is enmeshed.

2. Realization of his complete dependence upon the controlling system is a major factor. He is forced to accept that the only food, tobacco, praise, and social contact he will get will come from the very interrogator who exercises control over him.

3. The awareness of control and recognition of dependence results in causing internal conflict and breakdown of previous patterns of behaviour. Since the brainwasher-interrogators aim to have the individuals undergo profound emotional change, they force their victims to seek out painfully what is desired by the controlling individual. During this period the victim is likely to have a mental breakdown [with] delusions and hallucinations.

4. Discovery that there is an acceptable solution to his problem is the first stage of reducing the individual's conflict. [It gives great] feeling of relief that the horror of internal conflict would cease and that perhaps they would not, after all, be driven insane. It is at this point that they are prepared to make major changes in their value-system. This is an automatic rather than voluntary choice. They have lost their ability to be critical.

5. Reintegration   (SECTION DELETED BY CIA) His new value-system, his manner of perceiving, organizing, and giving meaning to events, is virtually independent of his former value system. He is no longer capable of thinking or speaking in concepts other than those he has adopted. He tends to identify by expressing thanks to his captors for helping him see the light. Brainwashing can be achieved without using

illegal means.

b. Elicitation for the purpose of brainwashing consists of questioning, argument, indoctrination, threats, cajolery, praise, hostility, and a variety of other pressures. The aim of this interrogation is to hasten the breakdown of the individual's value system and to encourage the substitution of a different value-system. The procurement of protected information is secondary and is used as a device to increase pressure upon the individual.

a. The first type is one in which the victim has a passive role in the pain inflicted on him (e.g., beatings). Threats of torture were found more effective, as fear of pain causes greater conflict within the individual than does pain itself.

b. The second type of torture is represented by requiring the individual to stand in one spot for several hours or assume some other pain-inducing position. Such a requirement often engenders in the individual a determination to "stick it out." This internal act of resistance provide a feeling of moral superiority at first. As time passes and his pain mounts, however, the individual becomes aware that it is his own original determination to resist that is causing the continuance of pain. A conflict develops within the individual between his moral determination and his desire to collapse and discontinue the pain. It is this extra internal conflict, in addition to the conflict over whether or not to give in to the demands made of him, that tends to make this method of torture more effective in the breakdown of the individual personality.

3. Reaction varies with the conditions of the isolation cell. Some sources have indicated a strong reaction to filth and vermin. The predominant cause of breakdown in such situations is a lack of sensory stimulation (i.e., grayness of walls, lack of sound, absence of social contact, etc.). Experimental subjects exposed to this condition have reported vivid hallucinations and overwhelming fears of losing their sanity.

4. Another wrinkle in communication control is the informer system. The recruitment of informers in POW camps discouraged communication between inmates.

5. Induction of Fatigue. This is a well-known device for breaking will power and critical powers of judgment. Deprivation of sleep results in more intense psychological debilitation.... "Conveyor belt" interrogation that lasts 50-60 hours will make almost any individual compromise, but there is danger that this will kill the victim. It is safer to conduct interrogations of 8-10 hours at night while forcing the prisoner to remain awake during the day. Additional interruptions in the remaining 2-3 hours of allotted sleep quickly reduce the most resilient individual. Fatigue, in addition to reducing the will to resist, also produces irritation and fear that arise from increased "slips of the tongue."

6. No food and little or no water is permitted the individual for several days prior to interrogation. When the prisoner first complains of

this to the interrogator, the latter expresses surprise at such inhumane treatment. He makes a demand of the prisoner. If the latter complies, he receives a good meal. If he does not, he gets a diet of unappetizing food containing limited vitamins, minerals, and calories.

7. Criticism and Self-Criticism. These are mechanisms of communist thought control. In brainwashing, after a sufficient sense of guilt has been created in the individual, sharing and self-criticism permit relief. The price paid for this relief, however, is loss of individuality and increased dependency.... 10 d. Prisoners are often humiliated by refusing them the use of toilet facilities during interrogation until they soil themselves. Often prisoners were not permitted to bathe for weeks until they felt contemptable. A feeling of helplessness in the face of the impersonal machinery of control is carefully engendered within the prisoner. The individual who receives the preliminary treatment described above not only begins to feel like an "animal" but also feels that nothing can be done about it.

The first steps in "depersonalization" of the prisoner have begun. He has no idea what to expect. Ample opportunity is allotted for him to ruminate upon all the unpleasant or painful things that could happen to him. He approaches the main interrogator with mixed feelings of relief and fright. The prisoner is rarely prepared for the fact that the interrogators are usually friendly and considerate at first. The first occasion he balks at satisfying the interrogator, however, he is in for another surprise. The formerly reasonable interrogator unexpectedly turns into a furious maniac. These surprising changes create doubt in the prisoner as to his very ability to perceive another person's motivations correctly. The prisoner may begin to channel so much energy into trying to predict the behaviour of the interrogator that he loses track of what is happening inside himself.

The prisoner finds himself in a constant state of anxiety which prevents him from relaxing even when he is permitted to sleep. Short periods of isolation now bring on visual and auditory hallucinations. The prisoner seriously begins to doubts his own memory. The prisoner must undergo additional internal conflict when strong feelings of guilt are aroused within him. As any clinical psychologist is aware, it is not at all difficult to create such feelings. He cannot think constructively. If he is to maintain any semblance of psychological integrity, he must bring to an end this state of interminable internal conflict. He signifies a willingness to write a confession.

The interrogator questions every sentence of the confession. He begins to edit it with the prisoner. The prisoner is forced to argue against every change. This is the essence of brainwashing. Every time that he gives in on a point to the interrogator, he must re-write his whole confession. Still the interrogator is not satisfied. In a desperate attempt to maintain some semblance of integrity and to avoid further brainwashing, the prisoner must begin to argue that what he has already confessed to is true.

APPENDIX K

Sen. Jesse Helms' Warning against the New World Order, in a Speech to the Senate, December 15, 1987

This campaign against the American people – against traditional American culture and values - is systematic psychological warfare. It is orchestrated by a vast array of interests comprising not only the Eastern establishment but also the radical left. Among this group we find the Department of State, the Department of Commerce, the money center banks and multinational corporations, the media, the educational establishment, the entertainment industry, and the large tax-exempt foundations.

Mr. President, a careful examination of what is happening behind the scenes reveals that all of these interests are working in concert with the masters of the Kremlin in order to create what some refer to as a New World Order. Private organizations such as the Council on Foreign Relations, the Royal Institute of International Affairs, the Trilateral Commission, the Dartmouth Conference, the Aspen Institute for Humanistic Studies, the Atlantic Institute, and the Bilderberger Group serve to disseminate and to coordinate the plans for this so-called New World Order in powerful business, financial, academic, and official circles. . . .

The psychological campaign that I am describing, as I have said, is the work of groups within the Eastern establishment, that amorphous amalgam of wealth and social connections whose power resides in its control over our financial system and over a large portion of our industrial sector. The principal instrument of this control over the American economy and money is the Federal Reserve System. The policies of the Industrial sectors, primarily the multinational corporations, are influenced by the money center banks through debt financing and through the large blocks of stock controlled by the trust departments of the money center banks.

Anyone familiar with American history, and particularly American economic history, cannot fail to notice the control over the Dept of State and the Central Intelligence Agency which Wall Street seems to exercise.... The influence of establishment insiders over our foreign policy has become a fact of life in our time. This pervasive influence runs contrary to the real long-term national security of our Nation. It is an influence which, if unchecked, could ultimately subvert our constitutional order.

The viewpoint of the establishment today is called globalism. Not so long ago, this viewpoint was called the "one-world" view by its critics. The phrase is no longer fashionable among sophisticates; yet, the phrase "one-world" is still apt because nothing has changed in the minds and actions of those promoting policies consistent with its fundamental tenets.

Mr. President, in the globalist point of view, nation-states and national boundaries do not count for anything. Political philosophies and political principles seem to become simply relative. Indeed, even constitutions are irrelevant to the exercise of power. Liberty and tyranny are viewed as neither necessarily good nor evil, and certainly not a component of policy.

In this point of view, the activities of international financial and industrial forces should be oriented to bringing this one-world design – with a convergence of the Soviet and American systems as its centerpiece - into being. . . . All that matters to this club is the maximization of profits resulting from the practice of what can be described as finance capitalism, a system which rests upon the twin pillars of debt and monopoly. This isn't real capitalism. It is the road to economic concentration and to political slavery.

Note: an Internet search for 'Jesse Helms' brings up, foremost, that he sponsored a 'racist' campaign commercial. But if you find it on YouTube you will see that it's not the least bit racist! A good guess is that Helms was smeared for his opposition to World Government. As whistleblowers might put it, "You're nobody till somebody smears you." Your author expects to make her debut in this area soon.

APPENDIX L   "Warning of America's Communism"
Read into the Congressional Record – January 10, 1963
    by Rep A. S. HERLONG, JR.

CURRENT COMMUNIST GOALS [abridged list]:

...4. Permit free trade between all nations regardless of Communist affiliation and regardless of whether or not items could be used for war.

5.   Extension of long-term loans to Russia and Soviet satellites.

7.   Grant recognition of Red China. Admission of Red China to the U.N.

8.   Set up East and West Germany as separate states in spite of Khrushchev's promise in 1955 to settle the German question by free elections under supervision of the U.N.

11. Promote the U.N. as the only hope for mankind.   If its charter is rewritten, demand that it be set up as a one-world government with its own independent armed forces. ...

13. Do away with all loyalty oaths.

14. Continue giving Russia access to the U.S. Patent Office.

15. Capture one or both of the political parties in the U.S.

17. Get control of the schools. Use them as transmission belts for socialism and current Communist propaganda.   Soften the curriculum.   Get control of teachers' associations.   Put the party line in textbooks.

18. Gain control of all student newspapers. [Ahem, ahem.]

20. Infiltrate the press. Get control of book-review assignments, editorial writing, policymaking positions.

21. Gain control of key positions in radio, TV, motion pictures.

22. Continue discrediting American culture by degrading all forms of artistic expression.   An American Communist cell was told to "eliminate all good sculpture from parks and buildings, substitute shapeless, awkward and meaningless forms."

23. Control art critics and directors of art museums. "Our plan is to promote ugliness, repulsive, meaningless art."

25. Break down cultural standards of morality by promoting pornography and obscenity in books, magazines, motion pictures, radio, and TV.

27. Infiltrate the churches and replace revealed religion with "social" religion...

28. Eliminate prayer or any phase of religious expression in the schools on the ground that it violates the principle of "separation of church and state."

29. Discredit the American Constitution by calling it inadequate, old-fashioned, out of step with modern needs, a hindrance to cooperation between nations on a worldwide basis.

30. Discredit the American Founding Fathers. Present them as selfish aristocrats who had no concern for the "common man."

31. Belittle all forms of American culture and discourage the teaching of American history ...

32. Support any socialist movement to give centralized control over any part of the culture – education, social agencies, welfare programs, mental health clinics, etc.

37. Infiltrate and gain control of big business.

39. Dominate the psychiatric profession and use mental health laws as a means of gaining coercive control over those who oppose Communist goals.

40. Discredit the family as an institution. Encourage promiscuity and easy divorce.

41. Emphasize the need to raise children away from the negative influence of parents....

43. Overthrow all colonial governments before native populations are ready for self-government.

44. Internationalize the Panama Canal.

~ This list was composed by Patricia Nordman of De Land, FL.

APPENDIX M   The 'Torture Memo,' signed by Jay Bybee
[To] Alberto R. Gonzales, Counsel to the President (2002)

You have asked for our Office's views regarding the standards of conduct under the Convention Against Torture and Other Cruel, Inhuman or Degrading Treatment or Punishment as Implemented by Sections 2340-2340A of title 18 of the United States Code. As we understand it, this question has arisen in the context of the conduct of interrogations outside of the United States.... In Part I, we examine the criminal statute's text and history. We conclude that for an act to constitute torture as defined in Section 2340, it must inflict pain that is difficult to endure. **Physical pain amounting to torture must be equivalent in intensity to the pain accompanying serious physical injury, such as organ failure, impairment of bodily function, or even death.**

For purely mental pain or suffering to amount to torture under Section 2340, it must result in significant psychological harm of significant duration, e.g., from one of the predicate acts listed in the statute... The legislative history simply reveals that Congress intended for the statute's definition to track the Convention's definition of torture and the reservations, understandings, and declarations that the United States submitted with its ratification.

... In Part IV, we examine international decisions regarding the use of sensory deprivation techniques. These cases make clear that while many of these techniques may amount to cruel, inhuman or degrading treatment, they do not produce pain or suffering of the necessary intensity to meet the definition of torture. From these decisions, **we conclude that there is a wide range of such techniques that will not rise to the level of torture....** We find **that in the circumstances of the current war against al Qaeda and its allies, prosecution** under Section 2340A may be barred because enforcement of the statute would represent **unconstitutional infringement of the President's authority to conduct war.** In Part VI, we discuss defenses to an allegation that an interrogation method might violate the statute. We conclude that, under the current circumstances, **necessity or self-defense may justify interrogation methods that might violate Section 2340A**
[Emphasis added]

APPENDIX N

SECRET AND STRICTLY PERSONAL – UK EYES ONLY [PART OF THE DOWNING ST MEMO OF JULY 23, 2002 BY BRITISH OFFICER MATHEW RYCROFT]

C reported on his recent talks in Washington. Military action was now seen as inevitable. Bush wanted to remove Saddam through military action, justified by the conjunction of terrorism and WMD, but the intelligence and facts were being fixed around the policy... There was little discussion in Washington of the aftermath after military action...

The Defense Secretary said that the US had already begun "spikes of activity" to put pressure on the regime.

No decisions had been taken, but he thought the most likely timing in US minds for military action to begin was January, with the timeline beginning 30 days before the US Congressional elections.

It seemed clear that Bush had made up his mind* to take military action, even if the timing was not yet decided.

But the case was thin. Saddam was not threatening his neighbors, and his WMD capability was less than that of Libya, North Korea or Iran...

The Attorney-General said that the desire for regime change was not a legal base for military action....

The Prime Minister said that it would make a big difference politically and legally if Saddam refused to allow in the UN inspectors....

Note: This was leaked to London's Sunday Times in 2003 but not 'picked up' by American mainstream press until 2004. In 2005, Rep. John Conyers held hearings on it.

(Probably this memo is a hoax, as it would not be at Bush's level that a war would be arranged, and if genuine it is not to be expected that *The Times* would print it.)

APPENDIX O
1948 Convention on the Prevention and Punishment of the Crime of Genocide [ratified 1981 by US Senate]

Article I The Contracting Parties confirm that genocide, whether committed in time of peace or in time of war, is a crime under international law, which they undertake to prevent and to punish.

Article II In the present Convention, genocide means any of the following acts committed with intent to destroy, in whole or in part, a national, ethnical, racial or religious group, as such:

(a) Killing members of the group;

(b) Causing serious bodily or mental harm to members of the group;

(c) Deliberately inflicting on the group conditions of life to bring about its physical destruction in whole or in part;

(d) Imposing measures intended to prevent births within the group;

(e) Forcibly transferring children of the group to another group.

Article III The following acts shall be punishable:

(a) Genocide;

(b) Conspiracy to commit genocide;

(c) Direct and public incitement to commit genocide;

(d) Attempt to commit genocide;

(e) Complicity in genocide.

Article IV Persons committing genocide or any of the other acts enumerated in Article III shall be punished, whether they are ... public officials or private individuals...

Note: After almost four decades, this became domestic law, signed by President Ronald Reagan in 1987. The requirement is that the genocide was carried out in whole or in part in the US or that the offender be a national of the US or be found present in the US. You will find it at 18 USC 1091.

APPENDIX P   *During World War II, more than 100,000 persons of Japanese descent, including US citizens, were forcibly removed from their homes in the states on the West coast. Their property was later seized. Who could guess that from the benign-sounding text of this executive order? Beware sneakiness!*

Executive Order 9066 – Permitting Martial Law

Whereas, the successful prosecution of the war requires every possible protection against espionage and against sabotage to national-defense material…

Now therefore, by virtue of the authority vested in me as President of the United States, and Commander in Chief of the Army and Navy, I hereby authorize and direct the Secretary of War, and the Military Commanders whom he may from time to time designate, whenever he or any designated Commander deems such action to be necessary or desirable, to prescribe military areas in such places and of such extent as he or the appropriate Military Commander may determine…

The Secretary of War is hereby authorized to provide for residents of any such area who are excluded there from, such transportation, food, shelter, and other accommodations as may be necessary…

I hereby further authorize and direct the Secretary of War and the said Military Commanders to take such other steps as [they] may deem advisable to enforce compliance …including the use of Federal troops …with authority to accept assistance of state and local agencies. I hereby further authorize and direct all Executive Departments, independent establishments and other Federal Agencies, to assist the Secretary of War or the said Military Commanders in carrying out this Executive Order, including the furnishing of medical aid, hospitalization, food, clothing, …and other supplies, equipment, utilities, facilities and services.

This order shall not be construed as… modifying the duty and responsibility of the Federal Bureau of Investigation, with respect to the investigations of alleged acts of sabotage …

Signed, Franklin D. Roosevelt, The White House, February 19, 1942

APPENDIX Q

Note: Underlined passages were discussed within the text of this book. Italicized passages are ones that have become obsolete over time or by amendment. The latter will say, e.g., "[See Am 14]" meaning that you must go to that Amendment for update. Our original Constitution never gets reworded when amended. Spelling, capitalization here as in original.

CONSTITUTION FOR THE UNITED STATES

We the People of the United States, in Order to form a more perfect Union, establish Justice, insure domestic Tranquility, provide for the common defence, promote the general Welfare, and secure the Blessings of Liberty to ourselves and our Posterity, do ordain and establish this Constitution for the United States of America.

Article I.

Section. 1. All legislative Powers herein granted shall be vested in a Congress of the United States, which shall consist of a Senate and House of Representatives.

Section. 2. The House of Representatives shall be composed of Members chosen every second Year by the People of the several States, sand the Electors in each State shall have the Qualifications requisite for Electors of the most numerous Branch of the State Legislature. No Person shall be a Representative who shall not have attained to the age of twenty five Years, and been seven Years a Citizen of the United States, and who shall not, when elected, be an Inhabitant of that State in which he shall be chosen. Representatives *and direct Taxes* [See Am 16] shall be apportioned among the several States *which may be included this Union,* according to their respective Numbers, *which shall be determined by adding to the whole Number of free Persons, including those bound to Service for a Term of Years, and excluding Indians not taxed, three fifths of all other Persons.* [See Am 14]The actual Enumeration shall be made within three Years after the first Meeting of the Congress of the United States, and within every subsequent Term of ten Years, in such Manner as they shall by Law direct. The Number of Representatives shall not exceed one for every thirty Thousand, but each State shall have at Least one Representative; *and until such enumeration shall be made, the State of New Hampshire shall be entitled to chuse three, Massachusetts eight, Rhode-Island and Providence Plantations one, Connecticut five, New-York six, New Jersey four, Pennsylvania eight, Delaware one, Maryland six, Virginia ten, North Carolina five, South Carolina five, and Georgia three.*[obs] When vacancies happen in the Representation from any State, the Executive Authority thereof shall issue Writs of Election to fill such Vacancies. The House of Representatives shall chuse their Speaker and other Officers; and shall have the sole Power of Impeachment.

Section. 3. The Senate of the United States shall be composed of two Senators from each State, *chosen by the Legislature thereof,* [See Am 17] for six Years; and each Senator shall have one Vote. Immediately after they shall be assembled in Consequence of the first Election, they shall be divided as equally as may be into three Classes. The Seats of the Senators of the first Class shall be vacated at the Expiration of the second Year, of the second Class at the Expiration of the fourth Year, and of the third Class at the Expiration of the sixth Year, so that one third may be chosen every second Year; *and if Vacancies happen by Resignation, or otherwise, during the Recess of the Legislature of any State, the Executive thereof may make temporary Appointments until the next Meeting of the Legislature, which shall then fill such Vacancies.* [See Am 17] No Person shall be a Senator who shall not have attained to the Age of <u>thirty</u> Years, and been nine Years a Citizen of the United States, and who shall not, when elected, be an Inhabitant of that State for which he shall be chosen. The Vice President of the United States shall be President of the Senate but shall have no Vote, unless they be equally divided. The Senate shall chuse their other Officers, and also a President pro tempore, in the Absence of the Vice President, or when he shall exercise the Office of President of the United States. The Senate shall have the sole Power to try all Impeachments. <u>When sitting for that Purpose, they shall be on Oath or Affirmation. When the President of the United States is tried the Chief Justice shall preside: And no Person shall be convicted without the Concurrence of two thirds of the Members present.</u> Judgment in Cases of Impeachment shall not extend further than to removal from Office, and disqualification to hold and enjoy any Office of honor, Trust or Profit under the United States: but the Party convicted shall nevertheless be liable and subject to Indictment, Trial, Judgment and Punishment, according to Law.

Section. 4. <u>The Times, Places and Manner of holding Elections for Senators and Representatives, shall be prescribed in each State by the Legislature thereof; but the Congress may at any time by Law make or alter such Regulations</u>, except as to the Places of chusing Senators. The Congress shall assemble at least once in every Year, and such Meeting shall be *on the first Monday in December*, [See Am 20] unless they shall by Law appoint a different Day.

Section. 5. <u>Each House shall be the Judge of the Elections, Returns and Qualifications of its own Members, and a Majority of each shall constitute a Quorum to do Business;</u> but a smaller Number may adjourn from day to day, and may be authorized to compel the Attendance of absent Members, in such Manner, and under such Penalties as each House may provide. Each House may determine the Rules of its Proceedings, punish its Members for disorderly Behaviour, and, with the Concurrence of two thirds, expel a Member. Each House shall keep a Journal of its Proceedings, and from time to time publish the same, excepting such Parts as may in their Judgment require Secrecy; and the Yeas and Nays of the Members of either House on any question shall, at the Desire of one fifth of those Present, be entered on the Journal. Neither House, during the Session of Congress, shall, without the Consent of the other, adjourn for more than three days, nor to any other Place than that in which the two Houses shall be sitting.

Section. 6. The Senators and Representatives shall receive a Compensation for their Services, to be ascertained by Law, and paid out of the Treasury of the United States. They shall in all Cases, except Treason, Felony and Breach of the Peace, be privileged from Arrest during their Attendance at the Session of their respective Houses, and in going to and returning from the same; and for any Speech or Debate in either House, they shall not be questioned in any other Place. No Senator or Representative shall, during the Time for which he was elected, be appointed to any civil Office under the Authority of the United States, which shall have been created, or the Emoluments whereof shall have been increased during such time; and no Person holding any Office under the United States, shall be a Member of either House during his Continuance in Office.

Section. 7. All Bills for raising Revenue shall originate in the House of Representatives; but the Senate may propose or concur with amendments as on other Bills. Every Bill which shall have passed the House of Representatives and the Senate, shall, before it become a law, be presented to the President of the United States: If he approve he shall sign it, but if not he shall return it, with his Objections to that House in which it shall have originated, who shall enter the Objections at large on their Journal, and proceed to reconsider it. If after such Reconsideration two thirds of that House shall agree to pass the Bill, it shall be sent, together with the Objections, to the other House, by which it shall likewise be reconsidered, and if approved by two thirds of that House, it shall become a Law. But in all such Cases the Votes of both Houses shall be determined by Yeas and Nays, and the Names of the Persons voting for and against the Bill shall be entered on the Journal of each House respectively. If any Bill shall not be returned by the President within ten Days (Sundays excepted) after it shall have been presented to him, the Same shall be a Law, in like Manner as if he had signed it, unless the Congress by their Adjournment prevent its Return, in which Case it shall not be a Law. Every Order, Resolution, or Vote to which the Concurrence of the Senate and House of Representatives may be necessary (except on a question of Adjournment) shall be presented to the President of the United States; and before the Same shall take Effect, shall be approved by him, or being disapproved by him, shall be repassed by two thirds of the Senate and House of Representatives, according to the Rules and Limitations prescribed in the Case of a Bill.

Section. 8. <u>The Congress shall have Power</u> [1] <u>To lay and collect Taxes, Duties, Imposts and Excises, to pay the Debts and provide for the common Defence and general Welfare of the United States</u>; but all Duties, Imposts and Excises shall be uniform throughout the United States; [2] <u>To borrow Money on the credit of the United States</u>; [3] <u>To regulate Commerce with foreign Nations, and among the several States, and with the Indian Tribes</u>; [4] <u>To establish an uniform Rule of Naturalization, and uniform Laws on the subject of Bankruptcies throughout the United States</u>; [5] <u>To coin Money, regulate the Value thereof, and of foreign Coin,</u> and fix the Standard of Weights and Measures; [6] To provide for the Punishment of <u>counterfeiting</u> the Securities and current Coin of the United States; [7] To establish Post Offices and post Roads; [8] To promote the Progress of Science and useful Arts, by securing for limited Times to Authors and Inventors the exclusive Right to their respective Writings and Discoveries; [9] <u>To constitute Tribunals inferior to the supreme Court</u>; [10] To define and punish <u>Piracies</u> and Felonies committed on the high <u>Seas</u>, and Offences against the <u>Law of Nations</u>; [11] <u>To declare War, grant Letters of Marque and Reprisal, and make Rules concerning Captures on Land and Water</u>; [12] <u>To raise and support Armies, but no Appropriation of Money to that Use shall be for a longer Term than two Years</u>; [13] <u>To provide and maintain a Navy</u>; [14] <u>To make Rules for the Government and Regulation of the land and naval Forces</u>; [15] <u>To provide for calling forth the Militia to execute the Laws of the Union, suppress Insurrections and repel Invasions</u>; [16] To provide for organizing, arming, and disciplining, the Militia, and for governing such Part of them as may be employed in the Service of the United States, reserving to the States respectively, the Appointment of the Officers, and the Authority of training the Militia according to the discipline prescribed by Congress; [17] To exercise exclusive Legislation in all Cases whatsoever, over such District (not exceeding ten Miles square) as may, by Cession of Particular States, and the Acceptance of Congress, become the Seat of the Government of the United States, and to exercise like Authority over all Places purchased by the Consent of the Legislature of the State in which the Same shall be, for the Erection of Forts, Magazines, Arsenals, dock-Yards and other needful Buildings;— And [18] To make all Laws which shall be necessary and proper for carrying into Execution the foregoing Powers and all other Powers vested by this Constitution in the Government of the United States, or in any Department or Officer thereof.

Section. 9. *The Migration or Importation of such Persons as any of the States now existing shall think proper to admit, shall not be prohibited by the Congress prior to the Year one thousand eight hundred and eight, but a Tax or duty may be imposed on such Importation, not exceeding ten dollars for each Person* [obs].The Privilege of the Writ of Habeas Corpus shall not be suspended, unless when in Cases or Rebellion or Invasion the public Safety may require it. No Bill of Attainder or ex post facto Law shall be passed. *No Capitation, or other direct, Tax shall be laid, unless in Proportion to the Census of Enumeration herein before directed to be taken.* [See Am 16] No Tax or Duty shall be laid on Articles exported from any State. No Preference shall be given by any Regulation of Commerce or Revenue to the Ports of one State over those of another: nor shall Vessels bound to, or from, one State, be obliged to enter, clear or pay Duties in another. No Money shall be drawn from the Treasury, but in Consequence of Appropriations made by Law; and a regular Statement and Account of the Receipts and Expenditures of all public Money shall be published from time to time. No Title of Nobility shall be granted by the United States: And no Person holding any Office of Profit or Trust under them, shall, without the Consent of the Congress, accept of any present, Emolument, Office, or Title, of any kind whatever, from any King, Prince or foreign State.

Section. 10. No State shall enter into any Treaty, Alliance, or Confederation; grant Letters of Marque and Reprisal; coin Money; emit Bills of Credit; make any Thing but gold and silver Coin a Tender in Payment of Debts; pass any Bill of Attainder, ex post facto Law, or Law impairing the Obligation of Contracts, or grant any Title of Nobility. No State shall, without the Consent of the Congress, lay any Imposts or Duties on Imports or Exports, except what may be absolutely necessary for executing it's inspection Laws: and the net Produce of all Duties and Imposts, laid by any State on Imports or Exports, shall be for the Use of the Treasury of the United States; and all such Laws shall be subject to the Revision and Controul of the Congress. No State shall, without the Consent of Congress, lay any Duty of Tonnage, keep Troops, or Ships of War in time of Peace, enter into any Agreement or Compact with another State, or with a foreign Power, or engage in War, unless actually invaded, or in such imminent Danger as will not admit of delay.

Article II

Section. 1. The executive Power shall be vested in a President of the United States of America. He shall hold his Office during the Term of four Years, and, together with the Vice President, chosen for the same Term, be elected, as follows: Each State shall appoint, in such Manner as the Legislature thereof may direct, a Number of Electors, equal to the whole Number of Senators and Representatives to which the State may be entitled in the Congress: but no Senator or Representative, or Person holding an Office of Trust or Profit under the United States, shall be appointed an Elector. *The Electors shall meet in their respective States, and vote by Ballot for two Persons, of whom one at least shall not be an Inhabitant of the same State with themselves. And they shall make a List of all the Persons voted for, and of the Number of Votes for each; which List they shall sign and certify, and transmit sealed to the Seat of the Government of the United States, directed to the President of the Senate. The President of the Senate shall, in the Presence of the Senate and House of Representatives, open all the Certificates, and the Votes shall then be counted. The Person having the greatest Number of Votes shall be the President, if such Number be a Majority of the whole Number of Electors appointed; and if there be more than one who have such Majority, and have an equal Number of Votes, then the House of Representatives shall immediately chuse by Ballot one of them for President; and if no Person have a Majority, then from the five highest on the List the said House shall in like Manner chuse the President. But in chusing the President, the Votes shall be taken by States, the Representatives from each State having one Vote; a quorum for this Purpose shall consist of a Member or Members from two thirds of the States, and a Majority of all the States shall be necessary to a Choice. In every Case, after the Choice of the President, the Person having the greatest Number of Votes of the Electors shall be the Vice President. But if there should remain two or more who have equal Votes, the Senate shall chuse from them by Ballot the Vice President.* [See Am 12] The Congress may determine the Time of chusing the Electors, and the Day on which they shall give their Votes; which Day shall be the same throughout the United States. No Person except a natural born Citizen, *or a Citizen of the United States, at the time of the Adoption of this Constitution,* [obs] shall be eligible to the Office of President; neither shall any person be eligible to that Office who shall not have attained to the Age of thirty five Years, and been fourteen Years a Resident within the United States. *In Case of the Removal of the President from Office, or of his Death, Resignation, or Inability to discharge the Powers and Duties of the said Office, the Same shall devolve on the Vice President, and the Congress may by Law jprovide for the Case of Removal, Death, Resignation or Inability, both of the President and Vice President, declaring what Officer shall then act as President, and such Officer shall act accordingly, until the Disability be removed, or a President shall be elected.* [See Am 25] The President shall, at stated Times, receive for his Services, a Compensation, which shall neither be encreased nor diminished during the Period for which he shall have been elected, and he shall not receive within that Period any other Emolument from the United States, or any of them. Before he enter on the Execution of his Office, he shall take the following Oath or Affirmation:—"I do solemnly swear (or affirm) that I will faithfully execute the Office of President of the United States, and will to the best of my Ability, preserve, protect and defend the Constitution of the United States."

Section. 2. The President shall be Commander in Chief of the Army and Navy of the United States, and of the Militia of the several States, when called into the actual Service of the United States; he may require the Opinion, in writing, of the principal Officer in each of the executive Departments, upon any Subject relating to the Duties of their respective Offices, and he shall have Power to Grant Reprieves and Pardons for Offences against the United States, except in Cases of Impeachment. He shall have Power, by and with the Advice and Consent of the Senate, to make Treaties, provided two thirds of the Senators present concur; and he shall nominate, and by and with the Advice and Consent of the Senate, shall appoint Ambassadors, other public Ministers and Consuls, Judges of the Supreme Court, and all other Officers of the United States, whose Appointments are not herein otherwise provided for, and which shall be established by Law: but the Congress may by Law vest the Appointment of such inferior Officers, as they think proper, in the President alone, in the Courts of Law, or in the Heads of Departments. The President shall have Power to fill up all Vacancies that may happen during the Recess of the Senate, by granting Commissions which shall expire at the End of their next Session.

Section. 3. He shall from time to time give to the Congress Information on the State of the Union, and recommend to their Consideration such Measures as he shall judge necessary and expedient; he may, on extraordinary Occasions, convene both Houses, or either of them, and in Case of Disagreement between them, with Respect to the Time of Adjournment, he may adjourn them to such Time as he shall think proper; he shall receive Ambassadors and other public Ministers; he shall take Care that the Laws be faithfully executed, and shall Commission all the Officers of the United States.

Section. 4. The President, Vice President and all Civil Officers of the United States, shall be removed from Office on Impeachment for and Conviction of, Treason, Bribery, or other high Crimes and Misdemeanors.

Article III

Section. 1. The judicial Power of the United States, shall be vested in one supreme Court, and in such inferior Courts as the Congress may from time to time ordain and establish. The Judges, both of the supreme and inferior Courts, shall hold their Offices during good Behaviour, and shall, at stated Times, receive for their Services, a Compensation, which shall not be diminished during their Continuance in Office.

Section. 2. The judicial Power shall extend to all Cases, in Law and Equity, arising under this Constitution, the Laws of the United States, and Treaties made, or which shall be made, under their Authority;—to all Cases affecting Ambassadors, other public ministers and Consuls;—to all Cases of admiralty and maritime Jurisdiction;—to Controversies to which the United States shall be a Party;—to Controversies between two or more States;—*between a State and Citizens of another State;* [See Am 11]—between Citizens of different States;—between Citizens of the same State claiming Lands under Grants of different States, *and between a State, or the Citizens thereof, and foreign States, Citizens or Subjects.* [See Am 11] In all Cases affecting Ambassadors, other public Ministers and Consuls, and those in which a State shall be Party, the supreme Court shall have original Jurisdiction. In all the other Cases before mentioned, the supreme Court shall have appellate Jurisdiction, both as to Law and Fact, with such Exceptions, and under such Regulations as the Congress shall make. The Trial of all Crimes, except in Cases of Impeachment, shall be by Jury; and such Trial shall be held in the State where the said Crimes shall have been committed; but when not committed within any State, the Trial shall be at such Place or Places as the Congress may by Law have directed.

Section. 3. Treason against the United States, shall consist only in levying War against them, or in adhering to their Enemies, giving them Aid and Comfort. No Person shall be convicted of Treason unless on the Testimony of two Witnesses to the same overt Act, or on Confession in open Court. The Congress shall have Power to declare the Punishment of Treason, but no Attainder of Treason shall work Corruption of Blood, or Forfeiture except during the Life of the Person attainted.

Article IV.

Section. 1. Full Faith and Credit shall be given in each State to the public Acts, Records, and judicial Proceedings of every other State. And the Congress may by general Laws prescribe the Manner in which such Acts, Records and Proceedings shall be proved, and the Effect thereof.

Section. 2. The Citizens of each State shall be entitled to all Privileges and Immunities of Citizens in the several States. A Person charged in any State with Treason, Felony, or other Crime, who shall flee from Justice, and be found in another State, shall on Demand of the executive Authority of the State from which he fled, be delivered up, to be removed to the State having Jurisdiction of the Crime. *No Person held to Service or Labour in one State, under the Laws thereof, escaping into another, shall, in Consequence of any Law or Regulation therein, be discharged from such Service or Labour, but shall be delivered up on Claim of the Party to whom such Service or Labour may be due.* [See Am 13]

Section. 3. New States may be admitted by the Congress into this Union; but no new State shall be formed or erected within the Jurisdiction of any other State; nor any State be formed by the Junction of two or more States, or Parts of States, without the Consent of the Legislatures of the States concerned as well as of the Congress. The Congress shall have Power to dispose of and make all needful Rules and Regulations respecting the Territory or other Property belonging to the United States; and nothing in this Constitution shall be so construed as to Prejudice any Claims of the United States, or of any particular State. Section. 4. The United States shall guarantee to every State in this Union a Republican Form of Government, and shall protect each of them against Invasion; and on Application of the Legislature, or of the Executive (when the Legislature cannot be convened) against domestic Violence.

Article V.

The Congress, whenever two thirds of both Houses shall deem it necessary, shall propose Amendments to this Constitution, or, on the Application of the Legislatures of two thirds of the several States, shall call a Convention for proposing Amendments, which, in either Case, shall be valid to all Intents and Purposes, as Part of this Constitution, when ratified by the Legislatures of three fourths of the several States, or by Conventions in three fourths thereof, as the one or the other Mode of Ratification may be proposed by the Congress; Provided that *no Amendment which may be made prior to the Year One thousand eight hundred and eight shall in any Manner affect the first and fourth Clauses in the Ninth Section of the first Article; and that* [obs] no State, without its Consent, shall be deprived of its equal Suffrage in the Senate.

326

Article VI.

All Debts contracted and Engagements entered into, before the Adoption of this Constitution, shall be as valid against the United States under this Constitution, as under the Confederation. This Constitution, and the Laws of the United States which shall be made in Pursuance thereof; _and all Treaties made,_ or which shall be made, under the Authority of the United States, <u>shall be the supreme Law of the Land; and the Judges in every State shall be bound thereby,</u> any Thing in the Constitution or Laws of any state to the Contrary notwithstanding. The Senators and Representatives before mentioned, and <u>the Members of the several State Legislatures, and all executive and judicial Officers, both of the United States and of the several States, shall be bound by Oath or Affirmation, to support this Constitution;</u> but no religious Test shall ever be required as a Qualification to any Office or public Trust under the United States.

Article VII.

The Ratification of the Conventions of nine States, shall be sufficient for the Establishment of this Constitution between the States so ratifying the same. Done in Convention by the Unanimous Consent of the States present on the Seventeenth Day of September in the Year of Our Lord one thousand seven hundred and Eighty seven and of the Independence of the United States of America the Twelfth

In Witness thereof We have hereunto subscribed our names

G. Washington-Presidt. and deputy from Virginia
New Hampshire: John Langdon, Nicholas Gilman
Massachusetts: Nathaniel Gorham, Rufus King
Connecticut: Wm: Saml. Johnson, Roger Sherman
New York: Alexander Hamilton
New Jersey: Wil: Livingston, David Brearly, Wm. Paterson, Jona: Dayton
Pennsylvania: B. Franklin, Thomas Mifflin, Robt. Morris, Geo. Clymer, Thos FitzSimons, Jared Ingersoll, James Wilson, Gouv Morris
Delaware: Geo: Read, Gunning Bedford jun, John Dickinson, Richard Bassett, Jaco: Broom
Maryland: James McHenry, Dan of St Thos. Jenifer, Danl Carroll
Virginia: John Blair--, James Madison Jr.
North Carolina: Wm. Blount, Richd. Dobbs Spaight, Hu Williamson
South Carolina: J. Rutledge, Charles Cotesworth Pinckney, Charles Pinckney, Pierce Butler
Georgia: William Few, Abr Baldwin

[All underlining, italicization, and clause numbers added. See also Ap T.]

APPENDIX R – EXERCISING THE FIRST AMENDMENT

Quotes from Kay Griggs: "They get rid of the good guys. The Marine Corps are the assassins for the Mob. The military is run by the Mob. The military IS the Mob. **They nurture–they cultivate– the sons of prominent families. They're called "rising stars." They rope them in. Then they "turn" them. What my husband does for a living is train mercenaries – young boys from countries like Romania, Dominican Republic, Haiti.** They're training them to be murderers, … They psychologically profile them. The profile is similar to my husband's…McVeigh's, and others who were all part of this program. Jeffrey Dahmer was part of this program. They're all Army. They were all picked out because they were perverted or twisted. [The military profiles for] strong mother, weak father, no father, poor. Because these guys are looking for security, so they will stay in the military and do anything for that security. (Disk 1). **When you work in the White House, you work under the Army.** The Marines have no overlord, as such. They can float….. (Disk 2) St. Elizabeth's [and] Eastern State Hospital has Army intelligence…. **People who have decided to tell the truth, who are trying to get things straightened out.** If they upset somebody in high command …they all of a sudden move from being a person to being a target. Therefore, the enemy. (Disk 3) **This CIA thing, from my experience, is bogus. Every person I've known who was in the CIA was in military intelligence first.** [My husband is] a Marine Corps high-level intelligence officer, but he's under all these Army people. (Disk 3) My husband, being Chief of Staff, told his men it was like this: It's the Marine Corps first – the Brotherhood, the Cherry Marines, the bonding that goes on. The Marine Corps comes before God…[Their god is] the Brotherhood. **It's very German, it has Masonic leanings. They're all Masons. This Brotherhood – Opus Dei – they're the Mob. The Marine Corps are the hit men.** They're mercenaries. They'll switch hats. … The Marine Corps is just a smoke-and-mirrors thing. [At my husband's] level, he said we've never been an enemy to the Soviet Union. They work with these Communists… **The judges now in the courts are all military officers** following chain-of-command orders. They're not independent judges." (Disk 4)

[emphasis added] ~ *from Interviews with Pastor Rick Strawcutter, disks available at website* kaygriggstalks.com

Paid Smearing of Kay Griggs? (These are from freerepublic.com.)

~ Kay Griggs **may have a few threads of truth** to her yarn. However, since she defends an ex-President that has no sexual morals, her entire story of accusations can easily be discredited. [!!!]

~ I have Faith, as our motto is "Always Faithful" that such accusations of "cherry Marines" won't go very far. I don't doubt the character of those **my father and I had the honor of serving**.

~ Did General Krulak keep in the company of trained killers? Yes, he told me and a whole battalion of Marines of his combat experience while visiting Okinawa. Did Krulak support or allow sexual misconduct? Hardly. **His visit to Okinawa was to bring justice** to 3 rapists who terrorized a young Okinawan girl.

~ While President Clinton got a pass for his immorality (for much more than a few indiscretions), the US Military towed [sic] the line.

So why does Kay Griggs find the relished companionship that enjoys her embellished stories? This hatred stems from a perverted **minority that's been excluded from the privilege** to serve. **A wicked person can only view the rest of the world as wicked as that individual is evil**. Maybe Kay Griggs sincerely believes her husband's stories. Maybe [they are] **her own fabrication**.

~ I pray for Kay's tortured soul (she will get a Mass Card from me).

~ When the US Military went all-volunteer, the massive increase in moral character ushered forth **unprecedented professionalism** and productivity. The decisive battle results of the First Persian Gulf War proved **the new American Military's effectiveness**.

~ Yet of all the sexual misconduct that she aggressively accuses, Kay protects Clinton from the same bad behavior./ Military members will come under extreme scrutiny not because Kay Griggs and her crowd have a genuine love of discipline and responsibility for those in power, but because **that crowd wants power for themselves**.

~ To: **Aluminum Foil Deflector Beanie**, The full-court press is on to discredit our military, our progress in Iraq and **our President**. It's quite amazing (and disgusting) to watch./ **I'm not a psychologist, but I worry for this Kay Griggs.**

~ I hope someone she names in one of her hair-brained accusations **sues the crap out of her**. She might be a bit looney tunes.

~ **A shriveled up old lady** who dreams of herself as some kind of Helen of Troy waiting for a huge phallus to run her through?

Note: Bolded items are proven methods of accessing your emotions – while the target is being smeared. It is useful to memorize them to enable decoding.

APPENDIX S   **Amendments 1-10 – 'The Bill of Rights'**

I. Congress shall make no law respecting an establishment of religion, or prohibiting the free exercise thereof; or abridging the freedom of speech, or of the press; or the right of the people peaceably to assemble, and to petition the government for a redress of grievances.

II. A well regulated militia, being necessary to the security of a free state, the right of the people to keep and bear arms, shall not be infringed.

III. No soldier shall, in time of peace be quartered in any house, without the consent of the owner, nor in time of war, but in a manner to be prescribed by law.

IV. The right of the people to be secure in their persons, houses, papers, and effects, against unreasonable searches and seizures, shall not be violated, and no warrants shall issue, but upon probable cause, supported by oath or affirmation, and particularly describing the place to be searched, and the persons or things to be seized.

V. No person shall be held to answer for a capital, or otherwise infamous crime, unless on a presentment or indictment of a grand jury, except in cases arising in the land or naval forces, or in the militia, when in actual service in time of war or public danger; nor shall any person be subject for the same offense to be twice put in jeopardy of life or limb; nor shall be compelled in any criminal case to be a witness against himself, nor be deprived of life, liberty, or property, without due process of law; nor shall private property be taken for public use, without just compensation.

VI. In all criminal prosecutions, the accused shall enjoy the right to a speedy and public trial, by an impartial jury of the state and district wherein the crime shall have been committed, which district shall have been previously ascertained by law, and to be informed of the nature and cause of the accusation; to be confronted with the witnesses against him; to have compulsory process for obtaining witnesses in his favor, and to have the assistance of counsel for his defense.

VII. In suits at common law, where the value in controversy shall exceed twenty dollars, the right of trial by jury shall be preserved, and no fact tried by a jury, shall be otherwise reexamined in any court of the United States, than according to the rules of the common law.

VIII. Excessive bail shall not be required, nor excessive fines imposed, nor cruel and unusual punishments inflicted.

IX. The enumeration in the Constitution, of certain rights, shall not be construed to deny or disparage others retained by the people.

X. The powers not delegated to the United States by the Constitution, nor prohibited by it to the states, are reserved to the states respectively, or to the people.

[Ratified by eleven states as of 1791]

APPENDIX T   Constitutional Amendments XI – XXVII

Note: To save space I will insert Symbol ❏ to replace the recurring phrase "Congress shall have the power to enforce this article by appropriate legislation."]

XI (1795) The Judicial power of the United States shall not be construed to extend to any suit in law or equity, commenced or prosecuted against one of the United States by Citizens of another State, or by Citizens or Subjects of any Foreign State.

XII (1804) The Electors shall meet in their respective states and vote by ballot for President and Vice-President, one of whom, at least, shall not be an inhabitant of the same state with themselves; they shall name in their ballots the person voted for as President, and in distinct ballots the person voted for as Vice-President, and they shall make distinct lists of all persons voted for as President, and of all persons voted for as Vice-President, and of the number of votes for each, which lists they shall sign and certify, and transmit sealed to the seat of the government of the United States, directed to the President of the Senate; -- the President of the Senate shall, in the presence of the Senate and House of Representatives, open all the certificates and the votes shall then be counted; -- The person having the greatest number of votes for President, shall be the President, if such number be a majority of the whole number of Electors appointed; and if no person have such majority, then from the persons having the highest numbers not exceeding three on the list of those voted for as President, the House of Representatives shall choose immediately, by ballot, the President. But in choosing the President, the votes shall be taken by states, the representation from each state having one vote; a quorum for this purpose shall consist of a member or members from two-thirds of the states, and a majority of all the states shall be necessary to a choice. *And if the House of Representatives shall not choose a President whenever the right of choice shall devolve upon them, before the fourth day of March next following, then the Vice-President shall act as President, as in case of the death or other constitutional disability of the President. [Italicized part superseded by XX, 3]* The person having the greatest number of votes as Vice-President, shall be the Vice-President, if such number be a majority of the whole number of Electors appointed, and if no person have a majority, then from the two highest numbers on the list, the Senate shall choose the Vice-President; a quorum for the purpose shall consist of two-thirds of the whole number of Senators, and a majority of the whole number shall be necessary to a choice. But no person constitutionally ineligible to the office of President shall be eligible to that of Vice-President.

XIII (1865) Section 1.❏ Neither slavery nor involuntary servitude, except as a punishment for crime whereof the party shall have been duly convicted, shall exist within the United States, or any place subject to their jurisdiction. Section 2. ❏

XIV (1868) Section 1. ❏ All persons born or naturalized in the United States, and subject to the jurisdiction thereof, are citizens of the United States and of the State wherein they reside. No State shall make or enforce any law which shall abridge the privileges or immunities of citizens of the United States; nor shall any State deprive any person of life, liberty, or property, without due process of law; nor deny to any person within its jurisdiction the equal protection of the laws.

Section 2.   Representatives shall be apportioned among the several States according to their respective numbers, counting the whole number of persons in each State, excluding Indians not taxed. But when the right to vote at any election for the choice of electors for President and Vice-President of the United States, Representatives in Congress, the Executive and Judicial officers of a State, or the members of the Legislature thereof, is denied to any of the male inhabitants of such State, being twenty-one years of age, and citizens of the United States, or in any way abridged, except for participation in rebellion, or other crime, the basis of representation therein shall be reduced in the proportion which the number of such male citizens shall bear to the whole number of male citizens twenty-one years of age in such State.

Section 3.❏ No person shall be a Senator or Representative in Congress, or elector of President and Vice-President, or hold any office, civil or military, under the United States, or under any State, who, having previously taken an oath, as a member of Congress, or as an officer of the United States, or as a member of any State legislature, or as an executive or judicial officer of any State, to support the Constitution of the United States, shall have engaged in insurrection or rebellion against the same, or given aid or comfort to the enemies thereof. But Congress may by a vote of two-thirds of each House, remove such disability.

Section 4. ❏ The validity of the public debt of the United States, authorized by law, including debts incurred for payment of pensions and bounties for services in suppressing insurrection or rebellion, shall not be questioned. But neither the United States nor any State shall assume or pay any debt or obligation incurred in aid of insurrection or rebellion against the United States, or any claim for the loss or emancipation of any slave; but all such debts, obligations and claims shall be held illegal and void.

Section 5. ❏ The Congress shall have the power to enforce, by appropriate legislation, the provisions of this article.

XV (1870) Section 1. The right of citizens of the United States to vote shall not be denied or abridged by the United States or by any State on account of race, color, or previous condition of servitude. Section 2. ❏

XVI (1913) The Congress shall have power to lay and collect taxes on incomes, from whatever source derived, without apportionment among the several States, and without regard to any census or enumeration.

XVII (1913) The Senate of the United States shall be composed of two Senators from each State, elected by the people thereof, for six years; and each Senator shall have one vote. The electors in each State shall have the qualifications requisite for electors of the most numerous branch of the State legislatures. When vacancies happen in the representation of any State in the Senate, the executive authority of such State shall issue writs of election to fill such vacancies: Provided, That the legislature of any State may empower the executive thereof to make temporary appointments until the people fill the vacancies by election as the legislature may direct. This amendment shall not be so construed as to affect the election or term of any Senator chosen before it becomes valid as part of the Constitution.

XVIII (1919) Section 1. ❏ After one year from the ratification of this article the manufacture, sale, or transportation of intoxicating liquors within, the importation thereof into, or the exportation thereof from the United States and all territory subject to the jurisdiction thereof for beverage purposes is hereby prohibited. Section 2. ❏ The Congress and the several States shall have concurrent power to enforce this article by appropriate legislation. Section 3. ❏ This article shall be inoperative unless it shall have been ratified as an amendment to the Constitution by the legislatures of the several States, as provided in the Constitution, within seven years from the date of the submission hereof to the States by the Congress.

XIX (1920).The right of citizens of the United States to vote shall not be denied or abridged by the United States or by any State on account of sex. ❏.

XX (1933) Section 1. ❏ The terms of the President and the Vice

President shall end at noon on the 20th day of January, and the terms of Senators and Representatives at noon on the 3d day of January, of the years in which such terms would have ended if this article had not been ratified; and the terms of their successors shall then begin.

Section 2. ❏ The Congress shall assemble at least once in every year, and such meeting shall begin at noon on the 3d day of January, unless they shall by law appoint a different day.   Section 3. ❏ If, at the time fixed for the beginning of the term of the President, the President elect shall have died, the Vice President elect shall become President. If a President shall not have been chosen before the time fixed for the beginning of his term, or if the President elect shall have failed to qualify, then the Vice President elect shall act as President until a President shall have qualified; and the Congress may by law provide for the case wherein neither a President elect nor a Vice President shall have qualified, declaring who shall then act as President, or the manner in which one who is to act shall be selected, and such person shall act accordingly until a President or Vice President shall have qualified.

Section 4. ❏ The Congress may by law provide for the case of the death of any of the persons from whom the House of Representatives may choose a President whenever the right of choice shall have devolved upon them, and for the case of the death of any of the persons from whom the Senate may choose a Vice President whenever the right of choice shall have devolved upon them.   Section 5. ❏ Sections 1 and 2 shall take effect on the 15th day of October following the ratification of this article.   Section 6. ❏ This article shall be inoperative unless it shall have been ratified as an amendment to the Constitution by the legislatures of three-fourths of the several States within seven years from the date of its submission.

XXI (1933) Section 1. ❏ The eighteenth article of amendment to the Constitution of the United States is hereby repealed.   Section 2. ❏ The transportation or importation into any State, Territory, or Possession of the United States for delivery or use therein of intoxicating liquors, in violation of the laws thereof, is hereby prohibited.

Section 3. This article shall be inoperative unless it shall have been ratified as an amendment to the Constitution by conventions in the several States, as provided in the Constitution, within seven years from the date of the submission hereof to the States by the Congress.

XXII (1951) Section 1. No person shall be elected to the office of the President more than twice, and no person who has held the office of President, or acted as President, for more than two years of a term to which some other person was elected President shall be elected to the office of President more than once. But this Article shall not apply to any person holding the office of President when this Article was proposed by Congress, and shall not prevent any person who may be holding the office of President, or acting as President, during the term within which this Article becomes operative from holding the office of President or acting as President during the remainder of such term.

Section 2. This article shall be inoperative unless it shall have been ratified as an amendment to the Constitution by the legislatures of three-fourths of the several States within seven years from the date of its submission to the States by the Congress.

XXIII (1961) Section 1. ❑ The District constituting the seat of Govern- ment of the United States shall appoint in such manner as Congress may direct   A number of electors of President and Vice President equal to the whole number of Senators and Representatives in Congress to which the District would be entitled if it were a State, but in no event more than the least populous State; they shall be in addition to those appointed by the States, but they shall be considered, for the purposes of the election of President and Vice President, to be electors appointed by a State; and they shall meet in the District and perform such duties as provided by the twelfth article of amendment. Sec. 2 ❑

XXIV (1964) Section 1. ❑ The right of citizens of the United States to vote in any primary or other election for President or Vice President, for electors for President or Vice President, or for Senator or Repre- sentative in Congress, shall not be denied or abridged by the United States or any State by reason of failure to pay poll tax or other tax. Section 2. ❑

XXV (1967) Section 1.   In case of the removal of the President from office or of his death or resignation, the Vice President shall become President.   Section 2. ❑ Whenever there is a vacancy in the office of the Vice President, the President shall nominate a Vice President who shall take office upon confirmation by a majority vote of both Houses of Congress.   Section 3. ❑ Whenever the President transmits to the President pro tempore of the Senate and the Speaker of the House of Representatives his written declaration that he is unable to discharge the powers and duties of his office, and until he transmits to them a written declaration to the contrary, such powers and duties shall be discharged by the Vice President as Acting President.   Section 4. ❑

Whenever the Vice President and a majority of either the principal officers of the executive departments or of such other body as Congress may by law provide, transmit to the President pro tempore of the Senate and the Speaker of the House of Representatives their written declaration that the President is unable to discharge the powers and duties of his office, the Vice President shall immediately assume the powers and duties of the office as Acting President.

Thereafter, when the President transmits to the President pro tempore of the Senate and the Speaker of the House of Representatives his written declaration that no inability exists, he shall resume the powers and duties of his office unless the Vice President and a majority of either the principal officers of the executive department or of such other body as Congress may by law provide, transmit within four days to the President pro tempore of the Senate and the Speaker of the House of Representatives their written declaration that the President is unable to discharge the powers and duties of his office. Thereupon Congress shall decide the issue, assembling within forty-eight hours for that purpose if not in session. If the Congress, within twenty-one days after receipt of the latter written declaration, or, if Congress is not in session, within twenty-one days after Congress is required to assemble, determines by two-thirds vote of both Houses that the President is unable to discharge the powers and duties of his office, the Vice President shall continue to discharge the same as Acting President; otherwise, the President shall resume the powers and duties of his office.

XXVI (1971) Section 1. The right of citizens of the United States, who are eighteen years of age or older, to vote shall not be denied or abridged by the United States or by any State on account of age.
Section 2. ❑

XXVII (1992) No law, varying the compensation for the services of the Senators and Representatives, shall take effect, until an election of representatives shall have intervened.

Note on the alleged 'Titles Of Nobility Amendment'. A group calling itself TONA is trying to prove that a 13th amendment was ratified in 1812 and became part of the Constitution. TONA's sleuth work on this is interesting.

APPENDIX U
Circumstantial Evidence of Inside Job on 9/11

Jan.   CFR's Hart and Rudman draft a 'Homeland Security bill.'

April   Pentagon comptroller quits while $2 trillion missing; he goes to work for specialists in remote-controlled flight!

May   Vice Pres Cheney takes control of future war exercises! He also establishes new chain of command for Air Force stand-downs, with himself as decision maker.

June   An exercise, Vigilant Guardian, is arranged for Sept. 11th.

July   James Hatfield publishes in *onlinejournal.org* that the European intelligence hints of coming attack on US are of US origin, distributed via back channels!

          US warns Taliban to allow pipeline or we will attack Afghanistan in October (says Niaz Niak later on BBC).

          Twin towers leased by Port Authority of NY/NJ to Frank Lowy of Australia and Larry Silverstein, specifying huge compensation if two separate attacks occur!

Aug.   Bush makes Gen. R. Myers head of Joint Chiefs of Staff.

Sept.   Gov. Jeb Bush declares emergency in Florida on 9/6; FEMA ship docks at NY pier to prepare 'exercise,' 9/8.

          Three NY skyscrapers razed by high-tech controlled demolition but no criminal investigation allowed by any authority!

Oct.   We round up Muslims in US and carpet-bomb Afghanis. Sen. Leahy allegedly receives anthrax; FBI won't help; Congress passes Patriot Act without even reading it!

Nov.   Negroponte lies to UN: "clear and compelling information that [Al Qaeda] had a central role in the attacks."

APPENDIX V

Impeaching Judges or Other Officials
Q & A   by Mary Maxwell

1.   Q: How long does it take to impeach someone?

A: Theoretically it could be done in a day. In the morning a member of the House of Representatives could propose Articles of Impeachment and the House could then vote to impeach (i.e., send the case to trial.) In the afternoon the Senate could conduct the trial.

2.   Q: Why is it so simple?

A: Because ejecting a person from high office is political, not judicial. The only punishment to be meted out is removal from office, not fines or imprisonment.

3.   Q: Doesn't the Senate have to provide such things as reasonable time of the defense to prepare its case, and a close scrutinizing of evidence?

A: Not absolutely. The Senate is procedurally bound only by the rules it makes for itself, per Art. I, Sec 5 of the Constitution. Even if the Senate today has a rule on the books calling for, say, twenty days of preparation, it can vote to change that.

4.   Q: Is there any good argument against impeaching a vice president based on the notion that the person of greater authority – the president – should take responsibility for whatever happens in his administration?

A: No, in fact if both are under suspicion it would be quite proper to deal with the lesser office first.

5.   Q: What is an impeachable offence?

A: Any misdemeanor would qualify. Article II, section 4 says <u>The President, Vice President, and all civil Officers of the United States, shall be removed from Office on impeachment for, the Conviction of, Treason, Bribery, or other high Crimes and Misdemeanors.</u> Future President Gerald Ford correctly said in 1970, "An impeachable offence is whatever the majority of the House of Representatives consider it to be at any given moment in its history."

6.   Q: Doesn't the accused have rights? Where are the wheels of justice here?

A: Justice does not come into it. Think of it this way: If a Congresswoman has done a fabulous job for two years, but fails to win reelection, does she have any redress? Of course not. She holds office at the pleasure of the voters, and they indicate that pleasure every two years. A president takes office at the pleasure of the voters, but he holds onto the office at the pleasure of Congress.

7.   Q: When a Congressperson brings forth Articles of Impeachment, does it get handled expeditiously?

A: As soon as it is put in the House legislative hopper, all other business should be postponed and a debate of the matter must be conducted, but committees can stymie this.

8.   Q: What does an impeachment trial look like?

A: It is held in the Senate Chamber and looks like a normal Senate session, except that all Senators are sworn in as jurors (and there may be a table for exhibits). Art. I, Sec 3 says <u>When sitting for that Purpose, they shall be on Oath or Affirmation.</u> The man of the hour may attend or send someone to represent him. He can plead guilty or refute the charges. Per Senate Rules, each Senator must stand at her place and pronounce her judgment as 'guilty' or 'not guilty.'

The Constitution requires, at Art. I, Sec 3, that <u>The Chief Justice shall preside: and no Person shall be convicted without the Concurrence of two thirds of the Members present.</u>

9.   Q: Is it easy to eject someone with whom the people are dissatisfied?

A: Yes, it's a snap. It takes only one House member to propose impeachment. Then, 219 out of the 435 members must agree, if all are present and voting (fewer, if some are absent from the House or abstain from voting). So your question boils down to: Are there 219 House members willing to vote to impeach? The answer is "Yes, if they feel that it is in their interest" – whatever way they may calculate that interest. Part of their calculation may be to look ahead and see if 67 Senators would be willing to convict.

10. Q: The number sixty-seven seems very high. Would it ever be possible to get that many votes?

A: It is possible to get the full 100 Senate votes if all you are asking about is 'possibility.' In reality, during President Andrew Johnson's impeachment trial in 1867, only a single vote in the Senate spared him from conviction. (Since there were fewer states then, the two-thirds majority was smaller than 67.) At President Bill Clinton's trial, the vote on one of the two Articles of impeachment was 55-45. On the other, it was 50-50.

11. Q: Could the president offer a pardon to thwart the process of impeachment?

A: No. The Constitution, in Art. II, Sec 2, puts only one restriction on the president's power to pardon, namely it cannot be used in cases of impeachment.

12. Q: Strategically, from the viewpoint of an official, what would be the best move for her to make if there were rumors that she was about to be impeached?

A: She can correct the offending behavior if it be correctable. Otherwise she should resign.

13. Q: Doesn't that defeat the intention of the Framers?

A: Of course not. The Framers have no particular wish to see an official impeached. The whole point is that the very threat of it should work wonders.

14. Q: How many judges have been impeached in American history?

A: So far eight. The first, in 1804, was a Judge of a District Court of New Hampshire. One of the charges against him was "disregard for the terms of applicable Federal Statutes."

Note: This Q & A was published in 2005 at globalresearch.ca and onlinejournal.com. Publishers' permission to reprint is gratefully acknowledged.

APPENDIX W (Exhibit 1 in civil action F1-06-CV- 348)
Supreme Court Declines To Hear War-Powers Cases
All were dismissed at District Level or at Circuit Court of Appeals
on jurisdictional grounds of: Standing (Plaintiff not the right party
to file), Ripeness (hasn't reached impasse), Mootness (issue is
dead), or 'the Political Question' (Leave it to the elected branches).

Year Decided	Grounds	Court	Plaintiff	Defendant
VIETNAM				
1967	Pol. Question	DC Cir	Luftig	McNamara
1969	Standing	10th Cir	Velvel	Nixon
1971	Pol. Question	1st Cir	Massachusetts	Laird
1971	Pol. Question	2nd Cir	Orlando	Laird
1972	Standing	9th Cir	Mottola	Nixon
1972	Pol. Question	9th Cir	Sarnoff	Connally
1973	Pol. Question	2nd Cir	Dacosta	Laird
1973	Standing	DC Cir	Mitchell	Laird
CAMBODIA				
1973	Pol. Question	2nd Cir	Holtzmann	Schlesinger
1973	Pol. Question	MA Dist	Drinan	Nixon
EL SALVADOR				
1983	Pol. Question	DC Cir	Crockett	Reagan
NICARAGUA				
1985	Pol. Question	DC Cir	Sanchez-Espinoza	Reagan
GRENADA				
1985	Mootness	DC Cir	Conyers	Reagan
PERSIAN GULF				
1988	Pol. Question	DC Cir	Lowry	Reagan
1990	Ripeness	DC Dist	Dellums	Bush
IRAQ				
2003	Standing	10th Cir	Curtis	Bush
2003	Standing	DC Cir	Mahorner	Bush
2003	Ripeness	1st Cir	Doe	Bush
2003	Pol. Question	8th Cir	O'Connor	Bush
KOSOVO				
2006	Pol. Question	DC Cir	Campbell	Clinton
IRAN/SYRIA				
2007	Pol. Question	NH Dist	Maxwell	Bush

APPENDIX X "My Protocols" Mary Maxwell September, 2009

The item from which the 12 excerpts below were chosen by yours truly was published in a Russian newspaper in 1905. It was attributed at that time to "the elders of Zion," however the Zionists disclaimed authorship. I have often thought that the tone of voice is wrong for it to be the work of the persons who actually carried out the plot which it describes. More likely it was produced by someone wanting to put Jews in a bad light (which is something the ADL has always done with great finesse, in my opinion). Anyway, since nobody wants to own the protocols, I claim them as mine. No copyright applies. Even Disney's doesn't last 106 years. [All emphasis added; numbering is arbitrary.]

1. In these [Masonic] lodges we shall find our principal intelligence office and means of influence.... Among the members of these lodges will be almost all the agents of international and national police since their service to us is irreplaceable. [They keep from view] our activities and provide pretexts for discontents *[e.g., 'Atlanta child murders']* We execute Masons in such wise that none save the brotherhood can ever have a suspicion of it. **They all die as from a normal kind of illness.**
2. The people, under our guidance, have eliminated the aristocracy, who were their one and only defense and foster mother.... Masonry blindly serves as a screen for us. We appear on the scene as alleged saviors – Socialists, Anarchists, Communists, to whom we always give support in accordance with alleged brotherly rule (of the solidarity of all humanity) of our social masonry. De facto **we have already wiped out every kind of rule except for our own**.... Nowadays, if any States raise a protest against us it is only proforma, and by our direction. *[Iran]*
3. **Capital must be free to establish a monopoly** of industry and trade .... This freedom *[as in 'a free hand']* will give political force to those engaged in industry, and that will help to oppress the people.... **The intensification of armaments, the increase of police forces – are all essential** for the completion of the aforementioned plans.
4. All organs of the press are bound together by professional secrecy ....**We shall erase from the memory of men all facts of previous centuries**.... Through the Press we have gained the power to influence while remaining ourselves in the shade.... And if there should be any found **who are desirous of writing against us, they will not find any person eager to print their productions**.... Trial shots... fired by us in the third rank of our press, will be energetically refuted by us in our semi-official organs. *[Note: I could paper the wall of my dining room with letters of rejection I have received from book publishers over the years. – MM]*

5. [Our other secret of success is] to multiply to such an extent national failings, habits, passions, conditions of civil life, that it will be impossible for anyone to know where he is in the resulting chaos... **There is nothing more dangerous than personal initiative** *[See 'D' list in Recap]:* if it has genius behind it, such initiative can do more than can be done by millions of people **among whom we have sown discord.**

6. In all ages [people] have **accepted words for deeds.** They rarely pause to note, in the public arena, whether promises are followed by performance. **Therefore we shall establish show institutions.** *[!!]*

7. Our directorate will have knowledge of all the secrets of the social structure...with the whole underside of human nature, with all its sensitive chords on which they will have to play. **Persons [who disobey] our instructions, must face criminal charges** or disappear.

8. We shall arrange elections in favor of such presidents as have in their past some dark, undiscovered stain. **We** shall invest the president with the right of declaring a state of war. *[See Maxwell v Bush.]* **No one outside ourselves will any longer direct the force of legislation.** *[despite Congress pay: $174K.]* We shall instigate officials near the president to evade his dispositions by taking measures of their own. **He will further annul [laws] when we indicate to him to do so.**

9. It is indispensable to trouble people's relations with their governments so as to utterly exhaust humanity with dissension ...even by the use of torture, **starvation, inoculation of diseases,** so that [they have no option but] to take refuge in our complete sovereignty in money and in all else. *[IMF calling]* How clear is the undeveloped power of thought of the purely brute brains of the [masses] as expressed in the fact that they have been borrowing from us with payment of interest.

10. Thanks to the Press *[NYT et al]* we have got the gold in our hands. We have had to gather it out of the **oceans of blood and tears**.... To sum up our system of keeping the governments in Europe in check . . . **we shall respond with the guns of America [!!] or China or Japan.**

11. **Who will ever suspect** then that all these peoples were **stage-managed** by us according to a political plan which no one has so much as guessed at in the course of many centuries? *[Note: It infuriates me that my dear parents had to go to their graves without finding out any of this. – MM]*

12. When we at last definitely come into our kingdom [it will be] by the aid of **coups d'état prepared everywhere for one and the same day**.... With this purpose **we shall slay without mercy** all who take up arms to oppose our coming into our kingdom. *[C'mon, dear Readers, admit that you'd never imagined anything so clever as a universal takeover. – MM]*

Note: Try comparing this Ap (1905) with Ap K (1987) and Ap Z (2009).

APPENDIX Y   RIGHTS TO LOVE, FOREVER
                                    - by Mary Maxwell

On the 1st day of Christmas my true love sent to me
(sol sol sol, do do do ti, do re mi fa re mi),
a par-tri-idge in a pear tree   *(fa sol la fa mi do re do)*.
IN THE FI-IRST AMENDMENT THE FRAMERS GAVE TO ME
THE RIGHT TO-O SPE-EAK FREE-LY.

On the 2nd day of Christmas my true love sent to me, 2 turtle doves
(sol re mi fa, mi) and a partridge in a pear tree.
IN THE SEC-OND AMENDMENT THE FRAMERS GAVE TO ME
A CANNISTER OF MACE, AND THE RIGHT TO SPEAK FREELY.

On the 3rd day of Christmas my true love sent to me, 3 French hens,
2 turtle doves, and a partridge in a pear tree
(sol re mi fa, sol re mj fa, mi fa sol, la fa mi do re do).
IN THE THI-IRD AMENDMENT
THE FRAMERS GAVE TO ME NO DUTY TO BILLET, A CANNISTER
OF MACE, AND THE RIGHT TO SPEAK FREELY.

On the 4th day of Christmas my true love sent to me, 4 calling birds,
3 French hens, etc *(sol fa mi re do, mi sol do, re do ti la sol)*.
IN THE FO-OURTH AMENDMENT THE FRAMERS GAVE TO ME
"STAY OUT OF MY STUFF," NO DUTY TO BILLET, A CANNISTER
OF MACE, AND THE RIGHT TO SPEAK FREELY.

On the 5th day of Christmas my true love sent to me, 5 **go-old** rings *(sol la
fi sol)*, fo-our calling birds *(sol fa mi re do, mi sol do, re do ti la sol)*.
IN THE FI-IFTH AMEND MENT THE FRAMERS GAVE TO ME "I'LL
NEV-ER SING," "STAY OUT OF MY STUFF,"etc.

On the 10th day of Christmas my true love sent to me, 10 lords a-
leaping, 9 ladies dancing, 8 maids a-milking, 7 swans a-swimming,
6 geese a-laying *(sol re mi fa re, etc)* 5 **go-old** rings, etc.
IN THE TE-ENTH AMENDMENT THE FRAMERS GAVE TO
ME: ALL RESIDUAL POWERS, RIGHTS BEYOND THOSE
LISTED, NO CRUEL OR UNUSUAL, "I'll SUE THE
BASTARDS," HEAPS OF DUE PROCESS, "I'LL **NEV-ER**
SING," "STAY OUT OF MY STUFF," NO DUTY TO
BILLET, A CANNISTER OF MACE, AND THE **RIGHT TO-O
SPE-EAK FREE-LY**!

[Your lyricist hereby permits copying and performing ad lib.]

APPENDIX Z   Location of Foreign Troops in US Today
-- allegedly for training

by the Authority of **State Partnerships Program (of the
National Guard Bureau)** in connection with NATO

↑ Alaska/Mongolia
↙ Hawaii/Guam, Philippines

Eight states, shown as X's, were not participating as of 2007 :
ID, IO, ME, NM, OR, RI, SC, SD. But by 2010, new partners were
added: CA/Nigeria – NM/Costa Rica – FL/Virgin Islands –
SD/Surinam – ME/Montenegro – HI/Indonesia.

*(This map was compiled from information on website of Michigan
government, April 2008, by Mary Maxwell.
She hereby permits anyone to copy it.)*

CREDITS

Did you think I would forget the most important person to credit? Have *you* forgotten the one who has been working for years to save our country? I am referring to the reader. Ahem, ahem. *Cough, cough.* You.

The fact that you picked up this book, *Prosecution for Treason,* indicates that you are more than likely an activist of one sort or another. The time has come to take a bow. It has been the work of individuals — most of them isolated, I'll bet — that finally added up to our present situation of knowledge and confidence.

We can rejoice and be glad! This was pointed out to me by Kathleen Sullivan, MSW, a survivor of brutal mind-control, who recently formed a Truth and Reconciliation Coalition to deal with the subject of 'extreme abuse.' She reckons her group had to pass through many stages of fear and depression before the members could see their way to doing something positive for others.

They have persuaded me that the tide is turning and I humbly wish to share that thought with you. Moreover, there is no telling what is next on the menu! Just imagine all the goodwill that has been maneuvered into inaction for so long. Once it is allowed to come out, is there anything it won't be able to attain?

In any case, on behalf of the nation, I thank you for hoisting placards about 9/11, or blogging to warn people about mandatory flu shots, ... or... or... all those other things. Especially thanks for realizing that Congress's passing of unconstitutional laws means the worst.

I congratulate you for putting up with many a frustration and lost ground. Not to mention the loss of one's time! I console you for having to have friends doubt your mental health, and for your guilty feelings over upsetting the family with 'realistic' news. I'm sorry that you had to forego promotions at work for being a non-team-player.

If you are one of the physical victims, I hug you — and I join with others in apologizing for not being alert soon enough to prevent what happened to you.

And now I dare to smile, at your smile of satisfaction over the fact that it none of it was for naught.

Mary Maxwell   August 6, 2010
Email address: Mary.Maxwell@alumni.Adelaide.edu.au

Author's Parents: Patricia and John Whalen, Alabama, 1943

About the Author

Mary was born into the Whalen family in 1947 and was happy to be
schooled by Boston's nuns. In the 1970s she worked in a NY Social
Security office (which later moved into the Twin Towers!). Mary is
the widow of a wonderful Australian, George Maxwell. For the last
30 years she has lived mainly in Oz, but also in Germany and the
United Arab Emirates. Inspired by EO Wilson, she published three
books on sociobiology. In 2010 she is helping to establish a
US Truth and Reconciliation Coalition. Her Ph.D. is in Politics.
She likes to give public lectures and sing in a chorus.

Bibliographical Essay

How wonderful it was to discover persons who worked night and day for decades to uncover facts that we all would have learned except for suppression by the media. For starters there are Rodney Stich, Eustace Mullins, and Antony Sutton. Another two lads are British: Admiral Barry Domville and A. Ramsey, a member of the House of Commons, both of whom were imprisoned by their own government during World War II because they knew of the fakery involved (the mind-boggling fakery).

I am beholden to the Internet for making me aware of such persons. Also I obtained many of the books, pre-loved, from alibris.com. Most of them are not in big bookstores or in most libraries. How's that for disgraceful? But in big libraries you can find old gems that were not popularized much, such as the ones by Lane, Kubek, Jordan, and McCarthy. Was I ever humbled to learn that the bad rap Sen Joe McCarthy got was unfair. He wasn't paranoid about Communists in the State Department. They ran the place *openly!*

I realize I have a lot of 'splainin' to do to show why my sometimes extreme-sounding statements should be given credence. But I myself can never be certain that the sources I used are truly reliable. I went through about a thousand books and chose the 250 here because they seemed insightful. In a few cases I at first tossed a book aside, such as the ones by Jim Keith and John C. Coleman, as I found in them some statement that I doubted, yet brought them back on board later when other readings clued me in.

I did list two samples of blatant, hilarious disinfo — J. Tucker's book on terrorism, and James Clarke's on presidential assassinations. You simply could not be fooled reading them. There is also another kind of misinfo, one that is very helpful, as when an author appears to be a loner (like me) but must surely have a pipeline to major insiders. The books below by Livingstone, McGowan, and Eppersson appear to be that type, and, fascinatingly, the ones by Canning.

There is one type of 'controlled press' that really irks me: the stuff that either tells the sad facts of this world, or intellectualizes about Orwellianism, without bothering to say what can be done. One should assume that they are 'atmosphere setters' – paid.

Can't explain why I find the MK-Ultra survivors sincere – not to mention inspiring! I gladly take the risk of trusting Brice Taylor.

As for the Freemasonry books, Masons should take a look at them. I agree with John Robinson (not to be confused with John

Robison, an Illuminati whistleblower in 1798) that Freemasons seem to be a continuation of the Templars. Frankly I went light on that club out of fear of litigation. Some mind-control victims, such as Neil Brick and Kathleen Sullivan, have been threatened with suit for alleging that their ritual abuse took place in Masonic halls. If Masons did sue Sullivan, couldn't she ask in court how libel laws can protect secret societies? If a club refuses to say what it does, isn't the public entitled to entertain suspicions?

Books that I tagged 'B' for biology' and 'L' for law are clean. Ah, remember when you could assume that all science publications were clean? That was because each writer really did police himself lest he lose his career. Oh, there is only one listed book I did not read, Vladimir Binhi's *Magnetobiology*. I tried but it was over my head. I included it to indicate that there really is a scientific field covering such 'science fiction' things as ELF waves and weather modification. Becker's book on electric medicine is readable and full of hope.

Fact is, the reader nowadays has to read several books on a topic in order to come to a judgment of the accuracy of any of them. Has my book given off trustworthy vibes? If yes, that doesn't mean that the truth can be found here. How would laypersons like me and thee know who really thought up 9/11, or AIDS? It is a guess.

I steered clear of the subject of the holocaust, as one Australian, Fred Toben, is now doing time in a labor camp for his publications, as is Ernst Zundel, an American/Canadian extradited to Germany against the laws of US and Canada. It is my impression that Zundel was jailed in order to provoke Germans and also in order to harm ordinary Jewish folks. WW II was deliberately mis-taught to us.

After finishing my manuscript I came into possession of *OP.JB* by the British spy, Christopher Creighton. To me it seems plausible. It will break the hearts of those who fought for either side (the sides being not 'Allies and Axis,' but, really, 'people and cabal'). I note that he, Creighton, resents having been tricked into it by Desmond Morton. Greg Hallett's stunning book calls Morton, i.e., MI6, *"higher than the Crown."* Hmm. An immensity in those four words?

Let me now give credit to my thesaurus. No, it is not an electronic one, or even a bound-book thesaurus. It is my sister, Anne. Whenever I need a word (or a line from a poem) I call her, any hour of the day or night. She never lets me down. Thanks, Sis! Finally, I salute a bunch of beautiful people who 'took dictation' and typed for me: M, L, A, J, B, E, and, in Germany, S.

BIBLIOGRAPHY -- Lightly Annotated

Key
__ Underlined name: That book formed my thoughts for this book. __ Underlined date: That book contains things that shocked me. Shaded title: so-called revisionist history (to undo our mis-learning) L, B   L= a good book about law   B= book relies on biology ⊛❀ Bouquets go to ten books that are intellectually thrilling. To learn of the **existence** of similar books, visit the Library of Congress catalogue at loc.gov. Jot down the book's LoC number, then use that to browse all related books online. Miracles, eh? Then go to worldcat.org to see which libraries near you have the book.

Adams, S. *The Legalized Crime of Banking and A Constitutional Remedy.* Hawthorne, CA: Omni, 1976. Small-town court case; good. L

Agnew, Spiro T. *Go Quietly…or Else: His Own Story of the Events Leading to His Resignation.* NYC: Morrow, 1980. Says Haig was the boss.

Alexander, R. *Biology of Moral Systems.* Hawthorne, NY: Aldine, 1987. B

Allen, Gary. *Kissinger: The Secret Side.* NYC: '76 Press. 1976. Thank Gary.

Amen, Daniel. *Making a Good Brain Great.* NYC: Three Rivers, 2005. B

American Law Institute. *Restatement of Law.* St. Paul, MN: ALI, 1990. L

Antelman, Rabbi Marvin. *To Eliminate the Opiate.* Self-published, Israel, Vol. I, 2004, Vol. II, 2002. Hits nail on head, blames Frankism.

App, Austin. *Morgenthau Era Letters,* Philadelphia: Boniface, 1966. Fine.

Bacu, D. *Anti-Humans: "Re-Education" in Romanian Prisons.* Englewood, CO: Soldiers of Cross, 1971. They killed inmates via a flood!

Bacque, James. *Other Losses: An Investigation into the Mass Deaths of German Prisoners at the Hands of the French and Americans after World War II.* Toronto: General Paperbacks 1989. So revealing, so sad.

Barlow, Maude and Tony Clarke. *Blue Gold: Stop the Corporate Theft of the World's Water.* NYC: New Press, 2002. (website: canadians.org)

Barnes, Harry Elmer. "Blasting the Historical Blackout; A Review of A.J.P. Taylor's *The Origins of the Second World War* (1960)." Undated. He says British Foreign Secretary Lord Halifax, "was mainly responsible for the outbreak of war in September 1939" There is meticulous scholarship here, as in days of old. Hooray!

Barnett, Thomas. *The Pentagon's New Map.* NYC: Putnam, 2004. Help!

Barone, M., and G. Ujifusa with R. Cohen. *Almanac of American Politics.*

Wash., DC: National Journal, 1998. Handy for candidates.

Bassiouni, M. Cherif. *Citizen's Arrest.* Springfield, IL: Thomas, 1977. Gives info about each state but is out of date. Cost $99 used! L

Batista, Paul A. and Mark S. Rhodes. *Civil Rico Practice Manual.* NYC: Wiley, 1992. Provides a template for you to use in RICO. L

Becker, Robert O. and Gary Selden. *The Body Electric: Electromagnetism and the Foundation of Life.* NYC: Morrow, 1985. Uplifting! B

Bellant, R. *Old Nazis, the New Right and the Reagan Administration.* Cambridge, MA: Political Research Associates, 1989. Such intrigue.

Ben-Menashe, Ari. *Profits of War: Inside Secret U.S.-Israeli Arms Network.* NYC: Sheridan Sq, 1992. Kiss, tell. He authored JoeVialls.com?

Berman, Harold. *Law and Revolution: the Formation of the Western Legal. Tradition.* Cambridge, MA: Harvard U. Press, 1983. Cool. L

Binhi, Vladimir. *Magnetobiology.* San Diego CA: Academic, 2002. Heavy.

Black, Donald W., *Bad Boys, Bad Men; Confronting Anti-Social Personality Disorder.* NYC: Oxford U. Press, 1999. Not really their fault.

Booker, Christopher and Richard North. *Great Deception: The Secret History of European Union.* London: Continuum, 2003. Whither EU?

Bowart, Walter. *Operation Mind Control.* NYC: Dell, 1978. Inside dirt. B

Brasch, Walter M. *Unacceptable: The Federal Response to Hurricane Katrina.* Charleston, SC: BookSurge, 2005. See Congress's report instead.

Brewton, Pete. *The Mafia, CIA, George Bush,* NYC: Shapolsky, 1992. Yes.

Brock, D. *Blinded by the Right.* NYC: Crown, 2002 Vindicates Anita Hill.

Bryant, Nick. The *Franklin Scandal: A Story of Powerbrokers, Child Abuse & Betrayal.* Walterville, OR: TrineDay, 2009. Honors Alisha Owen.

Buckley, William.M., Jr. and L.B. Bozell. *McCarthy and His Enemies: The Record and Its Meaning.* Chicago: Regnery, 1954. The truth.

Bugliosi, Vincent. *The Betrayal of America.* (Supreme Court halted the FL recount.) NYC: Nation. Books, 2001. Full of false fiestiness? L

Burghardt, Tom, ed. *Police State America: U.S. Military "Civil Disturbance" Planning.* Montreal: Arm the Spirit/Solidarity, 2002. Tragic.

Burnham, Terry, and Jay Phelan. *Mean Genes.* NYC: Simon & Schuster, 2000. How to modify addictions like gambling. You'll like it. B

Bush, Barbara. "Robin" in *Barbara Bush: A Memoir.* NYC: Scribner,1994 1953 leukemia death of child: I believe Mom is crying to us.

Butler, Gen. Smedley. *War Is a Racket.* Los Angeles: Feral House, 2003.

Call, Max. *Hand of Death: The Henry Lee Lucas Story.* Lafayette, LA: Prescott, 1985. Lucas reports a Florida death cult; cops won't listen!

Canning, John, ed. *100 Great Modern Lives.* NYC: Beekman, 1972. Seems to me to be a quiet revelation of whodunnit in the past.

Canning, John, ed. *Great Disasters.* NYC; Gallery Books, 1976. Ditto. Surely Boston's Coconut Grove 1942 fire was not planned?

Cantwell, Alan, M.D. *Four Women Against Cancer: Bacteria, Cancer, and the Origin of Life.* Los Angeles: Aries Rising Press, 2005. Please see his Internet articles for the real scoop on cancer. It's very hopeful. B

Capell, Frank A. *Henry Kissinger: Soviet Agent.* Zarephath, NJ: The Herald of Freedom, 1974. I find Capell persuasive on this.

Carey, Alex. *Taking the Risk Out of Democracy: Propaganda in the US and Australia.* Sydney: U. of NSW Press, 1995. Coins term *treetops*.

Carr, Wm. *Pawns In The Game.* St. George. Glendale, CA. 1970. Vital.

Carrington, Andrew H. *The Synagogue of Satan.* Austin: RiverCrest, 2007. Says '91 US massacre on Basra Rd celebrated feast of Purim.

Chaitkin, A. *Treason in America: From Aaron Burr to Averell Harriman.* Wash., DC: Executive Intelligence Review, 1998. Don't miss.

Cheney, Margaret. *Tesla: Man Out of Time.* NYC: Dorset, 1989. Fun.

Cheney, Richard and Lynne Cheney. *Kings of the Hill.* NYC: Simon & Schuster, 1996. Excellent anecdotal history of Capitol Hill.

Churchill, W. and Jim Vander Wall. *Cointelpro Papers: FBI's Secret Wars against Dissent in the US.* Boston: South End Press, 1990. FBI jobs.

Chennault, C. *Way of a Fighter.* NYC: Putnam, 1949. We hurt China bad.

Clarke, James. *American Assassins: The Darker Side of Politics.* Princeton, NJ: Princeton U. Press, 1982. The Jodie Foster rule writ large.

Clough, Bryan. *State Secrets: The Kent-Wolkoff Affair.* E Sussex: Hideaway, 2005. Kent got punished for telling us FDR's shenanigans.

Cole, David. *Enemy Aliens,* NYC: New Press, 2003. Immigrants. Fine L

Coleman, John C. *Conspirators' Hierarchy: Story of the Committee of 300.* Carson City, NV: America West, 1992. Exposes Tavistock.

Colby, Gerard. *DuPont: Behind the Nylon Curtain.* Englewood Cliffs, NJ: Prentice-Hall, 1974. Makes you sorry chemistry was invented.

Collier, Christopher and James Lincoln Collier. *Decision in Philadelphia: Constitutional Convention of 1787.* NYC: Ballantine, 1986. Warm.

Collier, James M. and Kenneth Collier. *Votescam: The Stealing of America.* NYC: Victoria House, 1992. TKO! His web: constitution.org.

Compton, P. *The Broken Cross: The Hidden Hand in the Vatican.* Veritas. Western Australia: Cranbrook, 1990. Seems reasonable.

Conrad, C. *Jury Nullification.* Durham: Carolina Academic Press, 1998.

Congressional Research Service. *Weather Modification.* 2004. 100% awful.

Constantine, Alex. *Psychic Dictatorship in the U.S.A.* Los Angeles: Feral House, 1995. Plenty of info on McMartin pedophilia.

Cookridge, E. *Gehlen: Spy of the Century.* NYC: Random, 1971. Showy.

Copeland, Miles. *Without Cloak or Dagger.* NY: Simon & Schuster, 1974.

Cornell U. *Constitution, annotated.* law.cornell.edu/ancon. Gorgeous.

Cornwell, John. *Hitler's Pope.* NYC: Penguin, 2003. Yes, Pacelli, as Nuncio in Germany, could have stopped Nazism from the pulpit.

Crawford, C. "Environmental Adaptations, Then and Now," in Crawford and D. Krebs, eds, *Handbook of Evolutionary Psychology*. Mahwah, NJ: Erlbaum, 2001. EvPsy is sociobiology, sort of.

Creighton, C. *OP.JB*. London: Simon & Schuster, 1996. Real MI6 data.

Cumbey, C. *Hidden Dangers of the Rainbow: New Age Movement and the Coming Barbarism*. Shreveport LA: Huntington, 1983. Don't miss.

Davis, Jayna. *Third Terrorist*. Nashville: WND, 2004. Perfect re OKC.

Davis, Patti. *The Way I See It*. NYC: Putnam 1992. Helpful, touching. Says Dad (Ronald Reagan) had anti-Communist monologue on tap and even used it with his kids. I assume he was fully programmed.

DeCamp, John W. *The Franklin Cover-up: Child Abuse, Satanism, Murder*. Lincoln, NE: AWT, 1996. See David Shurter's Omaha videos.

DePoncins, Leon. *Freemasonry & Judaism*. Brooklyn: A & B, 1994. Old.

Dieckmann, Ed, Jr. *Beyond Jonestown: 'Sensitivity Training'* Newport Beach, CA: Noontide, 1981. Beware 'change agents' and groupthink. Fab.

Dion, Robt. *Crimes of the Secret Police*. Montreal: Black Rose, 1982. Clear.

Dillon, Emile J. *The Inside Story of the [1919] Peace Conference*. NYC: Biblio Bazaar, 2006. Can't get more inside than this. He went as linguist.

Doidge, N. *The Brain That Changes Itself*. NYC: Penguin, 2007 Fab! B

Domville, Barry. *From Admiral to Cabin Boy*. Sons Of Liberty. Metairie, LA. 1981. Navy men will value this superior critique of WWII.

Draffan, George. *Elite Consensus*. NYC: Apex Press, 2003. WTO and other entities that make decisions affecting us all. Awesome.

Dubber, Markus Dirk. *The Police Power*. NYC: Columbia U., 2005. OK.

Dubos, Rene. *Celebrations of Life*. NYC: McGraw-Hill, 1981. ✿❀ B

Dugatkin, Lee. *Cheating Monkeys and Citizen Bees: The Nature of Cooperation in Animals and Humans*. NYC: Free Press, 1999. Enjoyable. B

Dycus, Stephen, Arthur L. Berney, William C. Banks, and Peter Raven-Hansen. *National Security Law*. NYC: Aspen, 2002. Super. L

Eakman, B.K. *Cloning of the American Mind:* Lafayette, LA: Huntington, 1998. Specific strategic tips for your PTA to use against tricksters.

Eco, Umberto. *Faith in Fakes*. London: Secker Warburg, 1986. Great.

Emmons, Freda. *Flame of Healing; A Daily Journey of Healing from Abuse and Trauma*. Tate Publishing, 2006. Helps victim write journal.

Endicott, S. and E. Hagerman. *The United States and Biological Warfare*. Bloomington: U. Indiana, 1998. See sunshine-project.org. Fine.

Engdahl, F. William. *Seeds of Destruction: The Hidden Agenda of Genetic Manipulation*. Canada: Global Research, 2007. Urgent. Buy this.

Engel, Randy. *Sex Education: The Final Plague*. Rockford, IL: Tan, 1993.

Enloe, Cynthia. *Does Khaki Become You? Militarization of Women's Lives*. London: Pandora Press, 1988. Rape is epidemic in our co-ed army.

Epperson, A. Ralph. *The Unseen Hand: An Introduction to the Conspiratorial*

View of History. Tucson, AZ: Publius, <u>1985</u>. Many secrets out.

Estulin, Daniel. *The True Story of the Bilderberg Group*, 2nd ed. Walterville, OR: TrineDay, 2009. The photos of these bozos tell it all.

Estulin, Daniel. *Shadow Masters: How governments and intelligence agencies are working with internat'l drug dealers and terrorists for mutual profit.* Trine Day, 2010. Author has addressed European Parliament, will travel.

<u>Evans-Pritchard</u>, Ambrose. *The Secret Life of Bill Clinton: The Unreported Stories.* Wash., DC: Regnery, <u>1997</u>. Drugs, Mena,Vince Foster.

<u>Fagan</u>, Myron C. *How Our Patriots Die Mysteriously*, October-November, <u>1971</u> News-Bulletin, No. 158. We should have listened to him.

Feinman, Jay M. *Un-Making Law: The Conservative Campaign To Roll Back Common Law.* Boston: Beacon, 2004 He also wrote Law 101. L

Fisher, Helen. *The First Sex: The Natural Talents of Woman and How They Are Changing the World.* NYC: Ballantine, 1999. You go, girl! B

Fisher, Louis. *American Constitutional Law: Vol 1, Separated Powers and Federalism.* Durham, NC: Carolina Academic, 1995. Lovely. L

Flynn, John. *Truth About Pearl Harbor.* Metairie, LA. Sons of Liberty, 1981. He wrote it in 1944 when it was plain for anyone to see.

<u>Freed</u>, Donald with Fred Landis. *Death in Washington: The Murder of Orlando Letelier.* Westport, CT: Lawrence Hill, <u>1980</u>. Detailed.

<u>Ganser</u>, Daniele. *NATO's Secret Armies: Operation Gladio and Terrorism in Western Europe.* London: Frank Cass, <u>2005</u>. A major scoop.

Garrison, Jim. *On the Trail of the Assassins.* NYC: Warner, <u>1988</u>. As DA of New Orleans he almost solved 'Dallas.' Very motivational book.

<u>Gatto</u>, John Taylor. *The Underground History of American Education.* Oxford, NY: Oxford Village Press, <u>2006</u>. Weep for our kids!

Geoghegan, T. *See You in Court.* NYC: New Press, <u>2007.</u> ✿❀ Spiffy. L

Gibney, Alex and Eugene Jarecki. *The Trials of Henry Kissinger (DVD)* Jigsaw Productions, 2002. "I tremble for my country…"

Ginsberg, Benjamin. *The Fatal Embrace: Jews and the State.* Chicago: U. of Chicago Press, 1993. Says better for Israel not to be a state.

Goldsmith, Jack. *The Terror Presidency.* NYC: Norton, 2007. Lousy book.

Goldstein, Norm, ed. *Associated Press Style Book.* Cambridge, MA: Perseus, 2002. Nifty, e.g.: "round up (v.) roundup (n.)" TGFE!

<u>Goni</u>, U. *The Real Odessa: Peron's Argentina.* Loudon, NY: Granta, 2002.

Goodman, Walter. *All Honorable Men: Corruption and Compromise in American Life.* Boston: Little, Brown, 1963. Ahead of his time!

<u>Gould</u>, Jay M. and Benjamin A. Goldman, *Deadly Deceit: Low-Level Radiation.* NYC: Four Walls, <u>1991</u>. What fools we idiots be!

Graetz, H. *History of the Jews*, Vol V Philadelphia: The Jewish Publication Society of America, 1895. Analytical and very informative.

Grandin, Temple. *Animals in Translation.* Orlando: Harcourt, 2005

Autistic lady shows us how animal mind works. Fascinating. B

Griffin, David Ray. *9/11 Contradictions*. Northampton, MA: Olive
Branch, 2007. Shows how Rumsfeld kept changing his story. Tops.

Griffin, G. Edward. *Creature from Jekyll Island* (Federal Reserve). Appleton WI: American Opinion, 1994. Griffin devotes his life to us.

Halperin, Morton, Jerry J. Berman, Robert L. Borosage, and Christine
Marwick. *The Lawless State*. NYC: Penguin, 1976. Helpful. L

Hallett, Greg and the Spymaster. *Hitler Was a British Agent*. Auckland,
NZ: FNZ Inc., 2006. I'm prejudiced toward accepting this shocker.

Who's Paranoid?   The British Government was an exceptionally
diligent government. [Its] diplomatic system, whatever the political and
moral merits of particular decisions, seemed then to be a system of
wonderful elegance and efficiency, operated by people of exceptional
qualities of mind and character.

The reality, I came to understand, was quite other than the
appearance. British diplomacy had for centuries played a leading part in
making a world-system whose peculiar rationality could also be seen as
a form of madness. Politicians and diplomats were privileged
inhabitants of a world of unreality, and unreality which was life-
threatening on a grand scale, a world which nevertheless seemed to its
inhabitants, in characteristic paranoid fashion, to be perfectly real and
natural and inevitable and right

~ Preface to *Eunomia* (1990) by Philip Allott, British diplomat

---

Haslam, E. *Dr Mary's Monkey*. Walterville, OR: TrineDay, 2007. Bewdy.

Handberg, R. *Savage Justice*. NYC: Harper, 1993. Novel: pedophile judge.

Hastings, Anne S. *From Generation to Generation: Understanding Sexual
Attraction to Children*. Tiburon, CA: 1994. Great. She gives real help!

Hellyer, Paul. *STOP THINK*. Toronto: Chimo Media, 1999. Readable.

Helms, Harry. *Inside the Shadow Government: National Emergencies and the
Cult of Secrecy*. Los Angeles: Feral House, 2003. Informative. L

Hepburn James. *Farewell America: The Plot To Kill JFK*. Roseville, CA:
Penmarin, 2002. Explains how Dallas police did the coverup.

Hersha, Cheryl and Lynn Hersha with Dale Griffis and Ted Schwarz.
Secret Weapons. Far Hills, NJ: New Horizon, 2001. Strong.

Higham, Jim. *Errol Flynn: the Untold Story*. NYC: Doubleday, 1980. Says
Eleanor Roosevelt protected Nazi spy from prosecution!

Hinsley, F.H. *Sovereignty*. 2nd ed. Cambridge: CU Press, 1986. Crisp.

Hitchens, Christopher. *The Trial of Henry Kissinger*. London: Verso, 2002.

Hoffman, David. *The Oklahoma City Bombing and the Politics of Terror*.
Venice, CA: Feral House, 1998. Major, in-depth coverage.

Hoffman, Michael A. II. *Secret Societies and Psychological Warfare.* Coeur d'Alene, ID: Independent History and Research, 1989. Deep!

Hoffman, Paul. *Lions of the Eighties: The Inside Story of the Powerhouse Law Firms.* NYC: Doubleday, 1982. The scales fell from my eyes.

Hopsicker, Daniel. *Barry and 'the boys:' The CIA, the Mob and America's Secret History.* Venice, FL 2001. His web: madcowprod.com.

Horowitz, Leonard. *Emerging Viruses: AIDS, Ebola – Natural, Accidental, or Intentional?* Tetrahedron.com 1996. Boggles the mind. B

Horowitz, L. *Death in the Air.* Idaho. 2001. Chemtrails. Over my head.

House Select Committee. *The Final Assassinations Report:* London: Bantam, 1978. They concluded JFK's was probably a conspiracy(!)

Hrdy, Sarah Blaffer. *Mother Nature: A History of Mothers, Infants, and Natural Selection.* NYC: Pantheon, 1999. Good for mothers! B

Hunt, Linda. *Secret Agenda: The United States Government, Nazi Scientists, Project Paperclip, 1945 to 1990.* NYC: St. Martin's, 1991. Serious.

Hyde, Rep. Henry. *Forfeiting Our Property Rights.* Wash., DC: Cato, 1995. Police could seize property legally even before the Patriot Act.

Iserbyt, Charlotte. *The Deliberate Dumbing Down of America.* Ravenna, OH Conscience Press, 1999. Her column: newswithviews.com.

Jacobs, Jane. *Dark Age Ahead.* NYC: Random, 2004. Written when Jacobs, the famous town planner, was 91, and it shows! ✿❀

Jennings, Eugene E. *An Anatomy of Leadership.* NYC: McGraw-Hill, 1960. Leaders emerge naturally and this book helps 'em. B

Johnson, Alison. *Gulf War Syndrome.* Brunswick, ME: MCS Info Exchange, 2001. Devastation. Her left hook is inspiring. B

Johnson, Chalmers. *The Sorrows of Empire: Militarism, Secrecy, and the End of the Republic.* NYC: Henry Holt, 2004. Laments 800 US bases.

Jordan, George Racey with Richard Stokes. *From Major Jordan's Diaries.* Belmont, MA: Western Islands, 1952. Re Lend-lease. Spot on.

Juhasz, Antonia. *The Bush Agenda.* NYC: Harper Collins, 2006. Private auction of Iraqi assets held in US before invasion. Dear God.

Keith, Jim. *Black Helicopters over America.* IllumiNet, 1995. *Vale,* Jim.

Keith, Jim. *Mass Control: Engineering Human Consciousness.* Kempton, IL: Adventures Unlimited, 1999. Mind control of us all. Good.

Keith, Jim. *Secret and Suppressed.* San Fran: Feral House, 1993. Important.

Kelly, John F. and Phillip K. Wearne. *Tainting Evidence: Inside the Scandals at the FBI Crime Lab.* NYC: Free Press, 1998. Makes its point.

Kelly, Rev. Clarence. *Conspiracy against God and Man:.* Belmont, MA: Western Islands, 1974. Responsibly documents Illuminist plot.

Kittichaisaree, K. *International Criminal Law.* Oxford: OUP, 2001. An excellent introduction on law of war and politics of treaties. L

Kjos, B. *Brave New Schools.* Eugene, OR: Harvest, 1995. Offers solution.

Koh, Harold Hongju. *The National Security Constitution: Sharing Power After the Iran-Contra Affair.* New Haven: Yale UP, 1990. Clear. L

Korten, David C. *When Corporations Rule the World.* West Hartford & San Francisco: Berrett-Koehler & Kumarian, 1995. Not obsoleted.

Kronenwetter, Michael. *The FBI and Law Enforcement Agencies of the U.S.* Springfield, NJ: Enslow, 1997. Junior level, uncritical but good.

Kubek, Anthony. *How the Far East Was Lost: American Policy and the Creation of Comunist China.* Chicago: Regnery, 1963. Superb!

Kurland, Philip and Ralph Lerner, eds. *The Founders' Constitution, Vols 1- 4,* Indianapolis: Liberty Fund, 1982. Online, free. Delightful. L

Lane, Arthur B. *I Saw Poland Betrayed.* Belmont, MA: 1965. Crikey!

Livingstone, David. *Terrorism and the Illumnati.* Charleston SC: Booksurge, 2007. Quite surprising. Three thousand years history!

Lockhart, William., Yale Kamisar, Jesse. Choper, Steven. Shiffrin and Richard. Fallon, Jr. *Constitutional Law: Cases-Comments-Questions.* 8th ed. St. Paul, MN: West Pub. 1996. Garage sale gold. L

Lowenstein, Roger. *Buffett: Making of a Capitalist.* NYC: Random, 1995.

Madsen, Wayne. *Overthrow a Fascist Regime on $15 a Day.* Walterville, OR: TrineDay, 2008. His daily reports: waynemadsenreport.com.

Magid, Ken, Dr. and Carole McKelvey. *High Risk: Children without a Conscience.* Golden, CO: Bantam, 1989. Assist babies now!

Malbin, Michael. *Unelected Representatives* (Hill staff) NYC: Basic, 1979.

Maltz, Earl. *The Chief Justiceship of Warren Burger: 1969-1986.* S. Carolina: U of S. Carolina Press, 2000. Good overview of reasonings. L

Mangold, Tom and Jeff Goldberg. *Plague Wars.* NYC: St. Martin's, 1999.

Marcus, M. *Origins of the Federal Judiciary.* NYC: Oxford U. Press, 1992. More fun than a barrel of monkeys for those who love law. L

Martin, Al. *The Conspirators: Secrets of an Iran-Contra Insider.* Pray, MN: Nat'l Liberty Press, 2001. Web: almartinraw.com He admits to being a fraudster for CIA, and they continually harass him.

Maxwell, Mary, ed. (18 authors)*The Sociobiological Imagination.* Albany S SUNY Press, 1991. To get the hang of evolutionary theory. B

Maxwell, Mary. *"A Reflection on Human Responsibility."* *Ethics & International Affairs.* NYC: Carnegie Council, 1998. 179-193.

Maxwell, Mary. *Morality among Nations.* Albany: State U of NY Press, 1991. Sincere, but at that time she did not know the score. B

Mayer, Kenneth R. *With the Stroke of A Pen: Executive Orders and Presidential Power.* Princeton, NJ: PUP 2001. Neat, but too timid. L

Mazur, Allan. *Biosociology of Dominance and Deference.* NYC: Rowman and Littlefield, 2005. We choose our male politicians by jaw size! B

McCarthy, Sen. Joseph. *America's Retreat from Victory.* Milwaukee, WI: Senator Jos. McCarthy Education Foundation, 1979. Amazing.

McGowan, David. *Programmed To Kill: The Politics of Serial Murder.* iUniverse.com, 2004. Many cases, including Dutroux. Wow.

McKenney, Tom C. *Please Tell Me… Questions People Ask About Freemasonry -- And The Answers.* Lafayette, LA: Huntington House, 1994. Calm. How many good investigators we have today!

McManus, John. *Changing Commands: The Betrayal of America's Military.* Appleton, WI: The John Birch Society, 1995. Terrible truth.

Meagher, Sylvia. *Accessories after the Fact.* NYC: Bobbs-Merrill, 1967. To get in on JFK assassination research you need only this. Flawless.

Meiers, Michael. *Was Jonestown a CIA Medical Experiment?* Lewiston, NY Edwin Mellen Press, 1988. Author makes huge claim of Yes.

Melanson, Phillip. *Secrecy Wars: National Security, Privacy, and the Public's Right To Know.* Wash., D.C.: Brassey's, 2001. A good FBI bloke?

Melville, Cecil. *The Russian Face of Germany,* 1938. Krupp evaded Versailles by making weapons 'behind the Urals.' And why not.

Moreno, Jonathan D. *Mind Wars: Brain Research and National Defense.* NYC: Dana, 2006. Deliberately mocks MK-Ultra victims. Shame.

Moynahan, Brian. *The Faith: A History of Christianity.* London: Pimlico, 2003. Fascinating tales of how so many sects got formed.

Moore, Kathleen Dean. *Pardons.* NYC: Oxford U, 1989. Quiet but OK.

Moore, R. and D. *School Can Wait.* Washougal, WA: Hewitt. 1982. Yes.

Morrison, Reg. *The Spirit in the Gene.* Ithaca, NY: Cornell, 1999. ✺ ✤ B

Mullins, Eustace. *Rape of Justice: America's Tribunals Exposed.* Staunton, VA: Legal Studies Group, 1989. Hard to believe, but… L

Mullins, Eustace. *The Secrets of the Federal Reserve.* 1985. Essential.

Mullins, Eustace. *World Order: A Study in the Hegemony of Parasitism.* 1985 Staunton, VA: Ezra Pound Institute of Civilization. First, best.

Nader, Ralph and Lori Wallach. "GATT, NAFTA, and the Subversion of the Democratic Process." See: thirdworldtraveler.org. Fine.

Nelson, William E. *Americanization of the Common Law… 1760-1830.* Cambridge, MA: Harvard, 1975. Re New England. L ✺ ✤

Noakes, J. and G. Pridham. *Nazism.* UK: Exeter U, 1995. Documents!

Noblitt, Randy and Pamela, eds. *Ritual Abuse in the 21st Century.* Bandon, OR: Reed. 2008. Fotheringham priceless on creation of multiples.

O'Brien, Cathy with Mark Phillips. *TranceFormation of America.* Las Vegas Reality Marketing, 1995. (*Caveat:* I am not sure she wrote this.)

Oksana, Chrystine. *Safe Passage to Healing: Guide For Survivors of Ritual Abuse.* iUniverse, 2001. Well-reputed book among survivors.

Orwell, George. *1984.* NYC: New American Library, 1949. Unerring.

Palmer, Jack A. and Palmer, Linda K. *Evolutionary Psychology: Ultimate Origins of Human Behavior.* Boston: Allyn and Bacon, 2002. B

Paris, E. *The Secret History of the Jesuits.* Ontario, CA: Chick. 1975. Fair.

Parry, R. *Fooling America*. NYC: Morrow, 1992. (Consortiumnews.com)

Payson, Seth. *Proof of the Illuminati*, 1802. InvisibleCollegePress.com.
Pastor in Rindge NH, watching Illuminati destroy Christianity.

Pinay, M. *Plot against the Church*. Palmdale, CA: Christian Book, 2000.
Stunner! Every Catholic and Jew must read this immediately.

Piper, Michael Collins. *Final Judgment: JFK Assassination Conspiracy*.
Wash., DC: The Center of Historical Review, 1998. Packed!

Pool, James. *Hilter and His Secret Partners*. NYC: Pocket Books, 1997.

Potter, J. and F. Bost. *Fatal Justice*: *Reinvestigating the MacDonald Murders*.
NYC: Norton, 1995. Unscrupulous prosecutions get tedious! L

Quigley, Carroll. *Tragedy and Hope*. NYC: Macmillan, 1965. Famous.

Radosh, R. *Prophets on the Right:* NYC: Free Life Additions, 1978. Tops.

Ramsey, Capt. A. *The Nameless War.* [1952], Reprinted by Boring, OR
CPA Books, 2008. The correct name for pointless WWII. True.

Ridley, Matt. *The Agile Gene: How Nature Turns On Nurture.* Toronto:
Harper, 2003. You can't afford not to learn some genetics today.. B

Robinson, John J. *Born in Blood: The Lost Secrets of Freemasonry.* London:
M. Evans, 1989. Templars went underground but reemerged.

Robson, William. *Civilisation and the Growth of Law.* London: Macmillan,
1935. Simply delicious. (Many books of the 1920s are fab too.) L

Ross, Robert G. *The Elite Don't Dare Let Us Tell the People.* US: Ross
International Enterprises. (www.4rie.com), 2001. re CFR's.

Ross, Si. *The Wallace Contract.* Jed Morse, 1974. Brilliant re Nixon.

Rozell, Max. *Executive Privilege.* Baltimore: JHU, 1993. Nixon tapes.

Rubin, Alfred. *Ethics and Authority in International Law.* Cambridge, CU
Press, 1997. ✹❀ "Internat'l law not possible." I'm with Rubin. L

Russbacher, Gunther. "Gunther's Story" in Rayelan Alan, *The Obergon
Chronicles.* PO Box 1994, Freedom CA 95019. Rayelan rocks.

Rutz, Carol. *A Nation Betrayed: The Chilling True Story of Secret Cold War
Experiments.* Grass Lake, MI: Fidelity, 2001. She used Freedom of
Info law to verify her suspicions. Life-changing for me.

Sacks, Lord Rabbi J. *The Politics of Hope.* London: Random, 1997. Nice.

Samaha, Joel. *Criminal Law.* St. Paul, MN: West Pub. 1993. Readable. L

Saunders, Frances Stonor. *The Cultural Cold War: The CIA and the World
of Arts and Letters.* NYC: New York Press, 1999. Backstage...

Saussy, F. *Rulers of Evil.* NYC: HarperCollins 1999. Jesuits. Implausible.

Schmalleger, Frank. *Criminal Justice.* New Jersey: Prentice Hall, 2001. L

Schor, Juliet. *Born To Buy.* NYC: Scribner, 2004. Teen gullibility. Sharp!

Schor, J. *Overspent American.* NYC: Basic, 1998 "Culture alterable." ✹❀

Seldes, George. *Sawdust Caesar: Untold History of Mussolini and Fascism.*
NYC: Grosset & Dunlap, 1935. Seldes was there in the '20s.

Seldes, George. *Tell the Truth and Run.* NYC: Greenberg: 1954. Witty.

Seroussi, Karyn. *Unraveling The Mystery of Autism and Pervasive Development Disorder.* NYC: Simon & Schuster, 2000. By a keen parent.

Shawcross, William. *Murdoch.* London: Chatto, 1992. re Rupe. Bewdy!

Shearman, D. & Gary Sauer-Thompson. *Green or Gone: Health, ecology, plagues, greed and our future.* Kent Town, South Australia: Wakefield Press, 1997. We destroy virgin land at our peril. A must read. B

Shepherd, J.E.C. *The Babington Plot.* Toronto: Wittenburg, 1987. Jesuits.

Shklar, Judith. *Ordinary Vices.* Cambridge, MA: Belknap/HUP, 1984. ❁ ❀ You can never go wrong reading Shklar. Try her *Legalism.*

Shorrock, Tim. *Spies for Hire.* NYC: Simon & Schuster, 2008. Realistic.

Simpson, Christopher. *Science of Coercion: Communication Research & Psychological Warfare 1945-1960.* NYC: Oxford U., 1994. Surprising.

Simpson, Christopher. *Blowback.* NYC: Weidenfield & Nicolson, 1988.

Simpson, Cornell, *The Death of James Forrestal.* Belmont, MA: West'n Is., 1966. Damn! We knew so much then, but it got suppressed!

Singer, P.W. *Corporate Warriors.* Ithaca, NY: Cornell U., 2003. Loaded!

Skolnik, Sherman. *Ahead of the Parade: A Who's Who of Treason.* Tempe, AZ: Dandelion, 2003. Dirty, funny, inspiring, worrying, right.

Skolnick, Sherman. *Overthrow of The American Republic.* Tempe, AZ: Dandeion, 2006. Every Seppo should read this now. *Vive Skolnik!*

Skousen, W. Cleon. *The Naked Capitalist: A Review of Dr. Carroll Quigley's Tragedy and Hope.* Salt Lake City: Deseret News, 1970. Easy, good.

Smith, Jerry E. *Weather Warfare.* Kempton, IL: Adventures Unltd. 2009. See jerryesmith.com. Exposed HAARP, got pancreatic cancer.

Somoza, A. *Nicaragua Betrayed.* Belmont, MA: W'n Islands, 1980. Ouch.

Spotts, Greg. *CAFTA and Free Trade: What Every American Should Know.* NYC: Disinformation Co, 2005. Ignore name of publisher!

Sprague, Richard E. *The Taking of America: 1,2,3.* NYC: Rush Harp, 1979. Congress on 4 assassinations. Sprague proves "Media did it."

Stich, Rodney. *Defrauding America.* Alamo, CA: Western Diablo, 1998. He's been a Fed Aviation Agency investigator. Path-breaking.

Stich, Rodney. *Congress and Other U.S. Cesspools.* Silverpeak Enterprises, Inc. Alamo, CA. 2008. He uses official records to teach us.

Stinnett, Robert. *Day of Deceit.* NYC: Simon & Schuster, 2000. Infamy.

Sturdza, Michel. *Betrayal by Rulers.* Belmont, MA: Western Islands, 1976. Sturdza was a prince of Romania. He said in 1976: "When the US has progressed to the point reached by Romania in 1948, there will be no place on earth to which Americans can flee, and there will be no one to hear their screams." Something to think about, eh?

Sullivan, Kathleen. *Unshackled.* Tempe, AZ: Dandelion, 2001. Best!

Sutton, A. *America's Secret Establishment.* Walterville, OR: TrineDay, 2002.

Sutton, A. *National Suicide: Military Aid to the Soviet Union.* New Rochelle,

NY: Arlington House, 1973. Cold war a joke: he persuades me.

Tamari, Meier. *The Challenge of Wealth.* Chatham NJ: Aronson, 1990.
My second favorite book. Google for 'Maxwell, Katrina, Hertz.' L

Taylor, Brice. *Thanks for the Memories.* Landrum, SC: 1995. Magnificent!
But mega-sex in this book takes away from the really sexy stuff.

Thomas, Gordon. *Secrets and Lies.* They're smearing him; he must be ok.

Thomas, Kenn, ed. *NASA, Nazis & JFK: The Torbitt Document & JFK Assassination.* Kempton, IL: Adventures Unlimited, 1996. Yes.

Tomes, LTC J. *Servicemember's Legal Guide,* PA: Stackpole, 2001. Helpful.

Trocki, C. *Opium, Empire, and Global Political Economy.* NYC: Routledge, 1999. "It enslaved millions and enriched only a few." S'truth!

Tucker, J, ed. *Toxic Terror.* Cambridge, MA: MIT, 2000. Gas that puppy.

Udall, Stewart L. *The Myths of August.* NYC: Pantheon, 1994. Re Navajo suing, in vain, re nuclear testing. Udall is now blind. A real man..

Uttley, Sandra. *Dunblane Unburied.* 2006. You recall the 16 first-graders slain in 1996? Uttley went behind the scenes to find the truth.

van den Berghe, Pierre. *The Ethnic Phenomenon.* NYC: Elsevier, 1981. B Bio-anthropology. ✿❀ Anything Pierre writes is worth a look.

Verdier, Paul. *Brainwashing and the Cults: An Exposé on Capturing the Human Mind.* North Hollywood CA, Wilshire, 1977. Jackpot!

Wakefield, Andrew, *Callous Disregard.* NYC: Skyhorse, 2010, autism B Perfect comeback after losing British med license. Pity the GMC.

Webster, Nesta. *World Revolution: The Plot Against Civilization.* Palmdale, CA: Omni, 1994 [1922] It's hard to fault her sources, her logic.

Weeramantry, C.G. *Justice without Frontiers: Furthering Human Rights. Vol.1.* The Hague: Kluwer Law Internat'l, 1997. ✿❀ Wide. L

Weisberg, Harold. *Whitewhash II.* NYC: Dell, 1966. Blames FBI for JFK.

Wells, H.G. *The War in the Air.* Lincoln: U. Nebraska Press 2007 [1908] The minute air travel was invented Wells wrote of war being aerial. Couldn't go near London, he says, for the stink of dead bodies.

Wilson, Edward O. *Biophilia* Cambridge, MA. Harvard U Press, 1984. Disclosure: Ed has been a mentor to me. This is his poetry. B

Wormser, Rene. *Foundations.* NYC: Devin-Adair, 1958. Fool me once…

Wrangham, R. and Peterson, Dale. *Demonic Males: Apes and the Origins of Human Violence.* Boston: Houghton Mifflin, 1996. We genocide.

Wylie, J. *Jesuits: Moral Maxims and Plot against Kings.* Reprint 2009. True?

Zerubavel, Eviatar. *The Elephant in the Room: Silence and Denial in Everyday Life.* NYC: Oxford U., 2006. And he never mentions 9/11?

Note: Worldcat.org shows that only one library, Citadel Military College, SC, has Brice Taylor's book (two copies; one checked out). You can request it locally via Interlibrary Loan. I will give Australia a copy.

Webography

Frequently visited websites: juscogens.org; globalresearch.ca; rense.com waynemadsenreport.com; commondreams.org; rigorousintuition. ca. I have only just discovered henrymakow.ca and historycommons. org. Wheat amongst the chaff at rumormillnews.com helped me immensely.

Once a week I get hot-potato free emails from legitgov.org, where I learned that NI Director Dennis Blair informed Congress that he is authorized to assassinate US citizens overseas but would not do so "merely because they used freedom of speech." Whew! What a relief.

UnitedStatesTRC.com has links to great sites about mind control and truth-getting. Charles Gittings, who now has lung cancer, runs pegc.us to get war crimes prosecuted. Go Gittings!

Then there is the wonderful website **youtube.com**. It provides video clips of 2-5-minute duration of many of the 20th and 21st century moments discussed in this book, such as Jim Garrison re JFK; Peter Jennings re Bin Laden; Kay Griggs re the Marines; the Strecker memo; Norman Dodd re Foundations, David Shurter re Omaha, and Dean Loren on microbiologists. Or cheer up with dear Elvis or Mao Asada.

My own 2008 efforts at 'acting' can be found on youtube.com. Y'all are invited to film yourself and submit it as a riposte to someone else's work. If no takers, come to my account, but only as a last resort, please. Any oldies out there who are (understandably) resisting the computer? I recommend you just bite the bullet and learn to watch YouTube. Note: the people of the People's Republic of China are not allowed to watch YouTube, and it's on the cards that we, too, will soon be forbidden. You don't believe that? If they have the gall to blast New York skyscrapers in broad daylight, what don't they have the gall to do?

INDEX

Chart of headings at beginning
of Recap can serve as an
additional locator, as can the
Table of Gov't documents
provided at front of book.